Cocker Spaniel
in the
Federal Courts

edited by

JOSHUA WARREN

DEDICATION

In memory of
Lacey
beloved cocker spaniel
(1993-2009)

TABLE OF CONTENTS

ACKNOWLEDGMENT

This book would not be possible without the continuing support of **my family and all our wonderful dogs.**

CHRONOLOGICAL
TABLE OF AUTHORITY

EDITOR'S NOTE

The following are nearly full federal court opinions with minimal editing. Where excerpts have been removed the symbol #***# has been added. All other marks are from the original opinion text. As best as possible, footnotes retain their numbering but original page numbers have been removed. In each case the phrase "cocker spaniel" has been bolded and made larger for easier visibility. An index of select terms of interest is also provided at the end of this book.

FOREWARD

The idea of studying law by searching for a single term would usually be considered poor legal research. Cocker spaniels are a phrase but this raw search view of law will not yield any kind of complete picture of law related to cocker spaniels. The law deals with abstract concepts of responsibilities and liabilities, causation and consideration. Learning the law for a type of object requires more than merely the history of legal interactions regarding that object.

Nevertheless because of computer search technology it is now relatively easy to search for words and read the cases. This is both entertaining and informative for those with interest in law and cocker spaniels. These real case decisions should be read primarily for entertainment but also to increase the readers' vocabulary of legal procedure for general understanding of American jurisprudence.

INTRODUCTION TO STRUCTURE
of the U.S. FEDERAL COURTS

U.S. SUPREME COURT

U.S. COURT OF APPEALS
12 Circuit Courts of Appeals
1 U.S. Court of Appeals for the Federal Circuit

U.S. DISTRICT COURTS
94 Judicial Districts
U.S Bankruptcy Courts

U.S. COURT OF INTERNATIONAL TRADE
U.S. COURT OF FEDERAL CLAIMS

OTHER FEDERAL COURTS
Military Courts (Trial and Appellate)
Court of Veteran's Appeals
U.S. Tax Court
Federal administrative agencies and boards

for much more information about the structure and jurisdiction of the US Courts see their website at UScourts.gov
http://www.uscourts.gov/EducationalResources/FederalCourtBasics.aspx

INTRODUCTION TO READING COURT OPINIONS FOR FUN (and learning)

THE ONLY RULE is PATIENCE

If you are reading this then, you already know how to read. Go somewhere with appropriate lighting and a comfortable chair and read patiently. Mark unusual words and move on, and later use a legal dictionary and internet search engines to amplify your understanding. With patience you will learn to read more.

As you begin to read a case, notice the year and notice what branch of the federal court is writing the opinion. Identify the parties, what they are seeking, what prior legal actions have occurred. Or just jump right to any paragraph you want and start reading.

This book is designed to read cases. There is no over-reaching legal thesis and the cases are not individually summarized. These real cases are simply arranged with hopes of sparking interest in reading law. The goal is merely to enjoy the reading.

Reading law will improve your ability to read law.

As you read you may consider yourself as a law clerk and try to summarize the arguments and holdings of each opinion. This is good practice and any attempt to write (and re-write) a case summary will promote your thinking. But if you prefer, just sit under a tree and enjoy the writings of the U.S. Federal Courts.

These are all serious legal texts each with a serious legal purpose but they are also appreciable as the high art of American legal civilization. This collection is gathered with the hope of finding entertainment in these works of jurisprudential art.

INTRODUCTION TO COCKER SPANIEL IN THE FEDERAL COURTS

Cocker Spaniels are a unique breed of dog. According to the American Kennel Club website for the cocker spaniel, they are "a merry, well-balanced dog that is capable of considerable speed and great endurance." The AKC site also mentions that the breed was "in the US since the 1880s" and that in "the 14th Century there is mention of the Spanyell". Read more at: http://www.akc.org/breeds/cocker_spaniel/index.cfm

In the federal courts the breed name is strongly connected to copyright and patent litigation since 1950, but also to the 4th amendment, to breed-specific legislation against pit bulls and to a sort of blind follower-like ignorance. In this set of 35 court decisions there are both literal references to cocker spaniel dogs in the facts of the case and also metaphoric references to cocker spaniels as unreasonable middle managers.

A brief description of the 7 sections of this book:

Chapter 1) In this section is a sequence of three cases that provide a good introduction to the structure of the American appellate process. The cases are about copyright law in the 1950s but remain applicable to current debates in the field. The Woolworth retail chain tried to flood the market with imitation art (cocker spaniel statues) and was held liable.

Chapter 2) The Woolworth cases from the first section are cited substantially throughout federal case law. In the second section are those cases where the usage of "cocker spaniel" describes the holding from Woolworth. These cases reflect a range of products involved in both patent and copyright litigation.

Chapter 3) Cocker spaniel statues (similar to those in Woolworth) appear in tax import cases. These cases present an interesting question of whether mass reproductions are art under the tax code. (They are.)

Chapter 4) Statues of cocker spaniels were also made as toy banks. Again these items qualify as art despite alternative utility.

Chapter 5) Business ventures involving cocker spaniels including grooming and breeding.

Chapter 6) Actual dogs involved in the case facts. This section includes 4th amendment searches justified by the presence of dogs, injured dogs and other real cocker spaniel dogs in case facts.

Chapter 7) Metaphoric usages of "cocker spaniel" in Federal Courts
This section includes a juror's reference to theory of relativity in inability to convince others and Warren Buffett's reference to middle management.

Overall, cocker spaniels appear as a character in American culture with a role in American law.

1
THE WOOLWORTH CASES

This three opinion series is important for understanding vicarious infringement and statutory damages under the copyright act. The three opinions demonstrate the traditional appellate sequence (District Court, Court of Appeals, Supreme Court) and culminate in a still controversial Supreme Court decision. Justice Black's dissent resonates with current arguments about internet copyrights.

Presented in this section: the district court opinion, the appellate court affirmation, and the Supreme Court opinion (majority opinion by Justice Jackson, affirming, followed by dissent from Justice Black).

Contemporary Arts, Inc. v. F. W. Woolworth Co.,
   93 F. Supp. 739 (1950)
F. W. Woolworth Co. v. Contemporary Arts, Inc.,
   193 F.2d 162 (1951)
F. W. Woolworth Co. v. Contemporary Arts, Inc.,
   344 U.S. 228 (1952)

CONTEMPORARY ARTS, Inc.
v.
F.W. WOOLWORTH CO.

Civ. No. 8771

UNITED STATES DISTRICT COURT
FOR THE DISTRICT OF MASSACHUSETTS

93 F. Supp. 739

August 11, 1950

Cedric W. Porter and Dike, Calver & Porter, all of Boston, Mass., for plaintiff.

Clarence A. Barnes, Douglas Smerdon, Boston, Mass., for defendant.

Judge McCarthy

OPINION

This is an action for infringement of copyright under the Copyright Laws of the United States, Title 17 U.S.C.A. § 1 et seq., brought by Contemporary Arts, Inc., a Massachusetts corporation, having a principal place of business at 31 Stanhope Street, Boston, Massachusetts, against the defendant F. W. Woolworth Company, a corporation of Pennsylvania, having numerous retail stores throughout the United States and in the District of Massachusetts.

The copyrighted work is an original sculpture and work of art entitled 'Cocker spaniel in Show Position', designed in 1942 by Elizabeth Philbrick (now Mrs. Glenn G. Hall) of Dedham, Massachusetts, under the professional name of 'Jan Allan', and on which Registration of Copyright was duly granted by the Register of Copyrights Class G Pub. No. 39960, with a publication date of March 26, 1942 (Plf's Exh. 3).

Miss Philbrick duly assigned her copyright to the plaintiff by an assignment dated June 15, 1943 (Plf's Exh. 4).

Sculptured models embodying the plaintiff's copyrighted work, which the plaintiff sells commercially, are a red plaster model which sells at retail for $ 4 (Plf's Exh. 5), a red porcelain model selling at retail for $ 9 (Plf's Exh. 6) and a black and white porcelain model selling for $ 15 (Plf's Exh. 7).

The infringement charged is the sale of ceramic models of a **cocker spaniel** in show position by the defendant F.W. Woolworth Company in its retail stores. One of such ceramic models was bought at the Woolworth Store in New York City at Fifth Avenue and 39th Street by Fred Press, the plaintiff company's chief designer and production man, on May 5, 1949, for $ 1.19. The model itself is plaintiff's Exhibit 1 and the sales slip showing the purchase is plaintiff's Exhibit 2. A second such Woolworth model is marked defendant's Exhibit A.

It appeared at the trial that the defendant F.W. Woolworth Company bought 127 dozen of the alleged infringing ceramic models from the Sabin Manufacturing Company of McKeesport, Pennsylvania, which were delivered to the Woolworth Company in March, April and May, 1949. The Sabin Manufacturing Company, jobber and dealer in such articles, is a partnership (one of the partners being Sam Sabin).

The alleged infringing models were manufactured by the Lepere Pottery Company, of Zanesville, Ohio, which sold them to the Sabin Manufacturing Company. The Lepere Pottery Company is apparently a partnership owned and operated by Otto and Paul Herold.

It is the plaintiff's contention that the ceramic models sold by the Woolworth Company (Plf's Exh. 1 and Deft's Exh. A) were directly copied from one of the plaintiff's plaster models, such as Plaintiff's Exhibit 5, which the plaintiff has been selling on the open market through dealers, pet shops, gift shops and the like continuously since 1942.

All of the plaintiff's copyrighted models bear a copyright notice, the plaster models such as plaintiff's Exhibit 5 having a 'C' in a circle impressed on the left hind foot and the name 'Jan Allan', and the porcelain models (plaintiff's Exhibits 6 and 7) carrying the copyright notice on a small printed label attached to the model.

The business of the plaintiff Contemporary Arts, Inc. is the designing, manufacture and sale of small sculptured figurines and statuettes, principally dancing and national figures and objects, and dogs and other animals. The plaintiff designs, manufactures and sells some 250 different pieces of sculpture currently, all of which are originals designed by the plaintiff's own sculptors, and 100 of them are dog models. All of the plaintiff's designs are original and exclusive with plaintiff and all are copyrighted.

Its principal designers are Elizabeth Philbrick, whose professional name is 'Jan Allan', Elizabeth Dyer and Fred Press. Miss Philbrick has designed most of their dog models, as well as the '**Cocker spaniel** in Show

Position', and the plaintiff's catalog (plaintiff's Exhibit 10) states 'The Jan Allan dog collection is the most complete in this country'. The '**Cocker spaniel** in Show Position' as sculptured by Jan Allan is original and the copyright in it is valid. The sculpture of an animal is copyrightable subject matter under the copyright laws. 17 U.S.C.A. § 5. It is not the subject but the treatment thereof that is protected by the statute. Stephens v. Howells Sales Co., D.C., 16 F.2d 805.

In designing dog sculptures the plaintiff makes every effort to make the dog model authentic, realistic and true to type. Prize-winning dogs, their anatomy, physical structure and features are carefully studied, dog experts and judges are consulted for criticism of the first soft clay model, and again on the completion of the final commercial models in both plaster and porcelain. Great care is similarly taken in the manufacturing process to have the models accurate, authentic and of the highest quality. The reason for this research and careful workmanship is that the bulk of the plaintiff's sales of its dog models is made to dog owners and dog fanciers, who demand authentic types.

The research, original design and careful workmanship of the plaintiff in creating and producing its sculptures necessarily requires that plaintiff's statuettes be sold at higher prices than similar statuettes in both plaster or porcelain made by competitors can command.

The plaintiff makes and sells its designs in both plaster and porcelain. Some understanding of the steps involved in the manufacture of both plaster and porcelain models is necessary for appraising the defendant's defense of non-infringement or non-copying of the plaintiff's copyrighted dog. In making plaster models, after the preliminary research as to the physical structure and features of prize-winning dogs, a soft clay or plasterlene model is first designed which, when it has received the approval of the dog experts, is then transferred into durable plaster. For this purpose a mold is first made from the soft clay model and in so doing the soft clay model is necessarily destroyed. The cavity in the mold is then filled with plaster and this plaster model becomes the master copy. In making this hard plaster model and master copy, the mold is chipped away and destroyed. The hard master mold is then used for making flexible rubber molds, used in commercial manufacture of the plaster models. After a plaster model is pulled out of its rubber mold, it is cleaned; the mold seams are smoothed off; the model is dried in a hot room, colored, and the dog's features carefully painted on by hand. The model is then glazed, i.e. coated with a fine powdered glass which is then baked at a high temperature which fuses the glass onto the model.

In producing a model in ceramic or porcelain, changes and additional steps in the manufacturing process are required. Ceramic is a generic term for describing articles made of clay, which are then fired or baked (such as earthenware, pottery and porcelain). The quality and temperature of the firing depends on the grade or kind of clay used. Starting with the same plaster master-copy used in making the plaster models, the plaster master-copy must be altered to fit the demands of ceramic. In ceramics a hard plaster mold which will not pull away or around an undercut is employed. Thus, the plaster master-copy has to be altered to make it possible to pull away the various sections of the hard mold. For this purpose all undercuttings are filled in or eliminated. The hard plaster model is then made (in sections) over the plaster master-model and the model is removed. From then on it is merely a question of pouring the ceramic clay into the hard plaster mold. The ceramic clay (which is different from the plaster used in making the plaster model) is caused to settle in the mold and a large part of the moisture in the clay is absorbed into the plaster. The sections of the mold are then removed; the model is covered with a filler of glaze (powdered glass) and placed in a kiln to bake at a very high temperature. The plaintiff's porcelain models are baked at 2300 degrees F. Hand decoration is applied around the eyes, nose and muzzle of the dog in the form of fine particles of ground glass and the model is then fired a second time to fuse the decoration into the first glaze. Before firing, the ceramic clay dog is the same size as its plaster master model, the degree of shrinkage depending on the fineness of the clay used and the temperature used in firing the clay. In ceramics it is impossible to obtain the same detail as in plaster, because the glazing cannot be accurately controlled and while in molten condition will frequently run in an unpredictable manner. A large number of second, third and fourth quality pieces are obtained in making ceramic and particularly porcelain models.

I find from comparing plaintiff's plaster model (plaintiff's Exhibit 5) with the Woolworth ceramic model (plaintiff's Exhibit 1 and defendant's Exhibit A) that the Lepere Pottery Company has directly copied the plaintiff's plaster model (plaintiff's Exhibit 5) by using one of them as its own master model from which it made its own molds used in making its ceramic models sold by the Woolworth Company (plaintiff's Exhibit 1 and defendant's Exhibit A). The hair conformations and arrangements which appear on the plaintiff's copyrighted plaster model (plaintiff's Exhibit 5) appear in substantial identity on the Woolworth ceramic models (plaintiff's Exhibit 1 and defendant's Exhibit A); these are features which no two sculptors doing original and independent work could probably make identical through coincidence.

There are some differences between the plaintiff's plaster model (plaintiff's Exhibit 5) and the Woolworth ceramic model (plaintiff's Exhibit 1 and defendant's Exhibit A). But, of course, it is not necessary that a copy be a 'Chinese copy' in order to find infringement. Pellegrini v. Allegrini,

D.C., 2 F.2d 610; Fleischer Studios v. Ralph A. Freundlich, Inc., D.C., 5 F.Supp. 808, 18 C.J.S., Copyright and Literary Property, § 94, p. 215. The most striking difference is that, where the plaintiff's plaster model is substantially smooth-surfaced, particularly on the neck and back, the Lepere Pottery Company has scratched or cut irregular grooves into the surface of its model to indicate hairlines. If these grooves or incisions were filled in the respective dog models would be identical in appearance. The Woolworth ceramic dog is likewise smaller in size than plaintiff's plaster model (plaintiff's Exhibit 5), but this is due to its being cast in ceramic clay, which shrinks during firing. The plaintiff's porcelain models (plaintiff's Exhibits 6 and 7) are likewise even smaller than the Woolworth ceramic model (plaintiff's Exhibit 1 and defendant's Exhibit A), due to the finer quality of porcelain and the higher firing temperature used. Other slight differences appear where the undercuttings have been filled in, particularly at the neck, and the vertical line of the legs and feet have been straightened, again to eliminate undercuttings. But these changes to eliminate undercuttings are required to be done to prepare a plaster model for casting in ceramic clay, as pointed out above in which a hard mold is used, and the mold cannot be stretched or pulled around the undercuttings, as is possible with the flexible rubber molds used in making plaster models.

Since the Lepere Pottery Company has directly copied one of plaintiff's plaster models such as plaintiff's Exhibit 5, by using it as its own model, the changes caused by adding the hairline markings and filling in undercuttings to prepare its model for ceramic casting do not avoid infringement of plaintiff's copyright. It is still an infringement if it appears that the copyrighted work has been copied, although altered or paraphrased.

A comparison of plaintiff's plaster model (plaintiff's Exhibit 5) with the grey plaster model (defendant's Exhibit 7) produced by defendant's witness Harry Moyer is informative. This grey plaster model has the hairlines cut into it and the undercuttings have been filled in and eliminated, as in defendant's ceramic models (plaintiff's Exhibit 1 and defendant's Exhibit A) to permit casting in ceramic. But otherwise the grey plaster model is identical in measurement, in the three dimensions of length, width, and height, of head, body, legs and tail and in the hair conformations and arrangements, with plaintiff's plaster model (plaintiff's Exhibit 5). This was demonstrated by the sculptress Miss Philbrick when she applied a pair of calipers to the two models respectively, making repeated measurements and comparisons at a great number of points. Such identity in measurement, shape and hair conformation to the minutest detail hardly could be the result of coincidence and precludes the contention that the Lepere Pottery Company did original and independent work. The similarities being so striking, access may be inferred. Arnstein v. Porter, 2 Cir., 154 F.2d 464.

The court in a copyright case must determine whether or not the fact of infringement is proven, and the opinion of experts, although helpful, may not be substituted for the court's judgment. Encyclopedia Britannica Co. v. American Newspaper Association, C.C.N.J., 130 F. 460; West Publishing Co. v. Edward Thompson Co., C.C.N.Y., 169 F. 833; Allegrini v. DeAngelis, D.C., 59 F.Supp. 248. 'The existence of such infringement is dependent upon the question whether the ordinary reasonable person would fail to differentiate between the two works or would consider them dissimilar by reasonable observation. Hein v. Harris, C.C.N.Y., 175 F. 875.' Allegrini v. DeAngelis, supra, 59 F.Supp. at page 251. The test is that of 'the library rather than that of the dissecting room'. (Eisman v. Samuel Goldwyn, Inc., D.C., 23 F.Supp. 519, 520); for that reason I am convinced that, while the defendant's expert dog-breeder and fancier may be able to distinguish between the dogs for technical reasons, the average reasonable observer would not. The question of artistic merit or value has no bearing upon the rights of the parties. Pellegrini v. Allegrini, supra.

The only defense to this evidence of direct copying of plaintiff's copyrighted plaster model by Lepere Pottery Company is the testimony of one Harry Moyer, employed by the Lepere Pottery Company, who stated that he himself created the identical design embodied in Miss Philbrick's copyrighted design in suit, in 1938, four years earlier than Miss Philbrick. He testified that the grey plaster model (defendant's Exhibit F) was 'exact like' his own prior design; that the grey plaster model (defendant's Exhibit F) which is marked on the bottom 'A.M. Co. 1938' is 'an exact dog of the one which I made for Burley Pottery in 1938' from an English **cocker spaniel** which had been given to him; that he had found the grey plaster model in a cabinet at the Lepere Pottery Company in the early part of 1950; that it was in the cabinet of the Lepere Pottery Company when he went there in 1945; that his own **cocker spaniel** model, of which the grey plaster model (defendant's Exhibit F) is an exact likeness, was made and sold commercially by the Burley Pottery Company in 1938, when he was working for Burley, and again by Lepere Pottery since 1945; that he had never asked nor was paid anything for this design, either by the Burley Pottery or Lepere Pottery. Moyer further admitted that he had no sculpturing experience, was not a dog expert, knew nothing about **cocker spaniels**, that his own dog was an English **cocker spaniel**, which was 'very heavy coated', and which was never trimmed for showing purposes. But, as Miss Philbrick testified, her own copyrighted **cocker spaniel** was a composite or 'ideal **cocker spaniel**', in which she sought to embody all the good points and features desired by **cocker spaniel** judges and experts in the American **Cocker spaniel** in 1942.

Her own **cocker spaniel** model is shown in show position and has been trimmed for showing. I find it difficult to believe that Moyer could have created by his own original independent work, and as a pure coincidence, an English **cocker spaniel** model, identical in its minutest details of hair configurations and dimensions (except for the added hairline carvings and filling in of undercuttings mentioned above with plaintiff's copyrighted model of the 'Ideal American **Cocker spaniel** of 1942', which had been trimmed for showing.

Moyer was entirely at a loss to account for or to explain the notation 'A.M. Co. 1938' which appears on the grey plaster model (defendant's Exhibit F), and that fact is wholly without probative significance to indicate that the grey plaster model (defendant's Exhibit F) was made in 1938. It could readily be scratched on the model at any time by any one desiring to do so. Mr. Press showed how this could be done by scratching similar markings on his own plaster model (plaintiff's Exhibit 11) in the presence of the Court during trial.

The Moyer testimony further conflicts with the previous statements as to the origin of the infringing Woolworth model (plaintiff's Exhibit 1 and defendant's Exhibit A), which appear in the letter of Sabin Manufacturing Company to the Woolworth Company dated October 31, 1949 (plaintiff's Exhibit 15) which stated:

'In regard to your recent letter, I am sorry this was not answered sooner, but I have checked quite thoroughly into the matter. We have purchased these molds from a pottery who has been making this dog since 1936.

'Please be advised that he states this was copied from a glass dog made in England. However, he is trying to find the original of this dog and up to the present writing, we have been unable to secure this sample. However, we would like to know when this copyright was put into effect.'

No evidence was produced supporting the statements made in this letter. This earlier statement conflicts with Moyer's testimony produced at the trial.

The account given by the witness was uncorroborated. Viewing it as a whole, I am unable to give credence to his testimony.

I find that the plaintiff's copyright has been infringed by the defendant's sale of ceramic models copied from the plaintiff's sculpture.

The plaintiff offered testimony that the sale of its plaster and porcelain models of its '**Cocker spaniel** in Show Position', embodying the copyright in suit, and selling at $ 4, $ 9 and $ 15 respectively, was harmed by the sale of the 'Woolworth dog' in the defendant's stores for $ 1.19. The plaintiff has had to design a new model of a **cocker spaniel** in show position, which has been done by Mr. Press, and which model is plaintiff's Exhibit 12, to replace Miss Philbrick's model. It is natural for dealers to think that the plaintiff is making and selling a cheaper reproduction of inferior quality through the Woolworth Company at a much lower price, and to refuse to do business with the plaintiff. It is difficult, if not impossible, for the plaintiff to prove its actual damages and defendant's profits, with the certainty required by the law for recovery of actual damages and profits.

The evidence shows that the defendant has bought 127 dozen or a total of 1524 of the infringing **cocker spaniel** ceramic models from the Lepere Pottery Company. The Copyright Act, Title 17 U.S.C.A. 101, permits the Court 'in lieu of actual damages and profits' to award 'such damages as to the court shall appear to be just, and in assessing such damages the court may, in its discretion' allow a sum not exceeding $ 5,000, nor less than $ 250, which shall not be regarded as a penalty, at the rate of $ 10 in the case of a painting, statue, sculpture, for every infringing copy made or sold by or found in the possession of the infringer, his agents or employees. The number of 1,524 copies of the infringing **cocker spaniel** shown to have been sold by the Lepere Pottery Company to the defendant Woolworth Company is obviously more than the number required to justify the Court in awarding the maximum statutory damages of $ 5,000, at the rate of $ 10 per infringing copy.

Pursuant to § 101 of the Copyright Act, and 'in lieu of actual damages and profits' the Court in its discretion awards the plaintiff statutory damages in the amount of $ 5,000, at the rate of $ 10 per infringing copy for the first 500 infringing copies.

In the light of the testimony at the trial I do not find it necessary to issue an injunction restraining the defendant from any further sales of this sculptured object.

Judgment may be entered for the plaintiff in conformity with this memorandum.

F.W. WOOLWORTH CO.

v.

CONTEMPORARY ARTS, Inc.

No. 4584

UNITED STATES COURT OF APPEALS
FIRST CIRCUIT

193 F.2d 162

December 26, 1951

Judge Woodbury

OPINION

This is an appeal from a judgment for the plaintiff in a suit for infringement of copyright.

In 1942 Elizabeth Philbrick, now Mrs. Glenn C. Hall, using the professional name of 'Jan Allen,' applied for and received a certificate of copyright registration for a sculptured work of art entitled 'Cocker-spaniel in show position.' The certificate gives the date of publication as March 26, 1942; the date when copies were received as March 28, 1942, and the Entry as Class G pub. No. 39960. In June 1943 'Jan Allen' assigned all her right, title and interest in the copyright to the plaintiff-appellee, Contemporary Arts, Inc., a Massachusetts corporation engaged in the business of manufacturing and selling small sculptured figurines of various kinds and also statuettes of many different breeds of dogs which are said to be highly authentic even to the minutest detail. Among the items in the second category it manufactured and sold, from 1942 (when it had commissioned 'Jan Allen' to do her work) until the date of the alleged infringement complained of herein, three models said to embody the copyrighted work, all reproductions of which bore notice of copyright in the statutory form. One of the embodiments relied upon is a buff colored plaster model about nine inches long by seven inches high which sold at retail for $ 4.00; another is a slightly smaller (about eight by six inch) red porcelain model which sold at retail for.$ 9.00, and the third is a hand painted black and

28

white porcelain model which retailed for $ 15.00.[1]

The infringement charged was the sale at retail for $ 1.19 by F.W. Woolworth Co., a Pennsylvania corporation operating a nation-wide chain of stores, of ceramic models of a **cocker spaniel** said to be essentially the same as the copyrighted work. It appears and is not disputed that the Woolworth Co. bought 127 dozen of the accused statuettes from the Sabin Manufacturing Company, a partnership of McKeesport, Pennsylvania, in March, April and May, 1949, for $ .60 apiece, and that Sabin in turn had purchased the statuettes from the manufacturer, Lepere Pottery Co., another partnership, of Zanesville, Ohio. At the outset of the trial counsel for the defendant informed the court that Sabin was openly assisting the defense since he had the real financial interest therein because of an indemnification agreement with the Woolworth Co., and that the latter, although recognizing its primary liability, if there was any, was 'here simply to watch the proceedings.'

The principal issue at the trial, which was hotly contested, was that of infringement. And this issue the court below resolved against the defendant. After detailed consideration it reached the ultimate conclusion that 'the plaintiff's copyright has been infringed by the defendant's sale of ceramic models copied from the plaintiff's sculpture.' Then, regarding an injunction as unnecessary under the circumstances, the court awarded the plaintiff $ 5,000 statutory damages in lieu of actual damages and profits, a $ 2,000 attorney's fee, and costs.

The appellant's first contention is that Contemporary Arts has wholly failed to establish any basis for a claim of copyright infringement by failing to show which, if indeed any one, of the three models it manufactured and sold was a copy of the model upon which the copyright certificate was issued. The argument is that since the three models differ from one another, only one at the most could possibly be the copyrighted dog, and the plaintiff has failed to prove which one this was. We regard this contention as without merit for the reason that it rests upon a misconception of the nature of the protection afforded a work of art by copyright.

It is the well established rule that a copyright on a work of art does not protect a subject, but only the treatment of a subject. Stephens v. Howells Sales Co., Inc., D.C. 1926, 16 F.2d 805, 808. The proposition was elaborated by Mr. Justice Holmes in Bleistein v. Donaldson Lithographing Co., 1903, 188 U.S. 239, 249, 250, 23 S.Ct. 298, 299, 47 L.Ed. 460, wherein with respect to cromolithographs of a circus scene prepared for advertising

---

[1] Contemporary Arts, Inc., apparently also manufactured and sold a black porcelain model.

purposes he said: 'But even if they had been drawn from the life, that fact would not deprive them of protection. The opposite proposition would mean that a portrait by Velasquez or Whistler was common property because others might try their hand on the same face. Others are free to copy the original. They are not free to copy the copy. Blunt v. Patten, (3 Fed.Cas.No. 1,580) 2 Paine 397, 400. See Kelly v. Morris, L.R. 1 Eq. 697; Morris v. Wright, L.R. 5 Ch. 279. The copy is the personal reaction of an individual upon nature. Personality always contains something unique. It expresses its singularity even in handwriting, and a very modest grade of art has in it something irreducible, which is one man's alone. That something he may copyright * * * .' Here the 'something irreducible' which was 'Jan Allen's' alone was certainly not a matter of subject, nor was it a matter of size or material, nor even of color, for it is well known that **cocker spaniels** are typically of several colors. Her 'something irreducible' was shape. This does not mean stance, for show position in a dog is a standardized, stylized position which anyone is free to reproduce. It means the proportion, form, contour, configuration, and conformation, perhaps the latter in details too subtle for appreciation by anyone but a fancier, of the dog represented by the sculptured work of art. And in these respects the plaintiff's three models are exactly alike except for the elimination in the two higher priced models of undercuts, so called, which was required by the mechanical technique of casting in porcelain and other ceramic clays from a plaster master model.

It appears from the undisputed testimony and the findings of the court in accordance therewith that the first step in the manufacture of statuettes such as those with which we are here concerned is to fashion a soft plasticene model, and the second is to make a plaster mold from the soft model. In removing the mold the original model is necessarily destroyed. The cavity of the plaster mold is then filled with a durable plaster, and after this hardens the plaster mold is chipped away, and in its turn destroyed, so that the hard plaster model becomes the master copy from which rubber production molds are made. These rubber molds are used in the production of the plaster copies, but they cannot be used to produce ceramic copies. The reason for this is that ceramic copies must be cast from plaster molds, and this requires some modification of the master copy because plaster molds, unlike flexible rubber molds, cannot be pulled away from undercuts. To meet the demands of production in ceramic, therefore, undercuts in the master copy are filled in and eliminated, but in doing so every effort is made to retain the original conception of the artist insofar as possible. Both plaster and porcelain copies are dried and sprayed with paint after the casting process, and the porcelain copies are given a glaze finish which is baked on at a high temperature with the result that more shrinkage occurs in them than in the plaster models. The quality of the ceramic used also seems to bear some relation to the degree of shrinkage.

It is evident from the foregoing that the elimination of undercuts from the plaintiff's two porcelain models, and also their smaller size, are merely factors of the mechanical process of reproduction in ceramics which have no appreciable significance upon the artistic conception of the work. We therefore regard the differences between the plaintiff's plaster and its ceramic reproductions in size, and in the elimination in the latter of undercuts, as inconsequential so far as the coverage of the copyright is concerned.

Thus when counsel for the plaintiff early in the trial offered sample of the three above mentioned Contemporary Arts models of **cocker spaniels** in show position, as, he said, 'embodying the copyrights in suit,' and the samples were marked as exhibits without any objection, all concerned in the trial were entirely correct in regarding, as they did from then on, the differences between the samples as without bearing on proof of copyright. Furthermore the statement made by counsel in offering the samples as exhibits, which was corroborated later by testimony, to the effect that the samples embodied the copyrighted dog is enough to establish the plaintiff's prima facie case for there is no evidence whatever, and we certainly are not going to assume without proof, that the plaintiff fraudulently substituted for its copyrighted dog other spurious ones, and fraudulently placed notices of copyright thereon. Gerlach-Barklow Co. v. Morris & Bendien, Inc., 2 Cir., 1927, 23 F.2d 159, 162.

From the foregoing discussion it is also clearly evident that from our allowing the plaintiff's three models of **cocker spaniels** in show position, diverse as to color, size and materials, and in inconsequentially minor ways as to shape, to stand as embodiments of the plaintiff's copyright, we are not in effect holding that the plaintiff 'has a monopoly in the subject of a cocker-spaniel in show position in a sculpture or statuette,' as the defendant contends. We conclude, therefore that the plaintiff has adequately established its copyright.

The findings of the court below on the issue of infringement are fully supported by the evidence. There is ample evidence in the record that the plaintiff's dog and the Woolworth one embody the identical intellectual or artistic conception of a dog of the breed involved in show attitude. Moreover, this evidence is strongly supported by visual comparison. It is true that a dog with short hair on the head, neck and upper two thirds of the body is represented in the plaintiff's statuettes, whereas the dog in the Woolworth model is represented as having long hair on the body and neck. This difference, however, is unimportant, for on ample evidence the court below found that the representation of long hair on the Woolworth model could readily have been accomplished, and was in fact accomplished, by etching in wavy lines on a plaster master model made from one of the plaintiff's plaster statuettes. What is highly, if not conclusively, significant of copying is the fact that the plaintiff's and the defendant's statuettes are identical in proportion, and so far as we can see with inexpert eyes in conformation,[2] and furthermore the configuration of the curls and folds of the long hair represented on the under body and the represented on the legs of the plaintiff's statuette are shown as asymmetrical, and the defendant's statuette shows the identical lack of symmetry in these respects. Thus there is ample evidence that one model was copies from the other. There also being ample evidence that 'Jan Allen' did the original work, in that drawing upon her own intimate knowledge of dogs and after research and consultation with experts, she fashioned a plasticene model of the dog she had in mind from which the plaster master model of the Contemporary Arts dogs was made, if follows that the ultimate finding by the court below of infringement by the defendant by copying the plaintiff's statuette cannot be successfully assailed.

Other matters, however, remain for consideration and the first of these is whether the court below erred in excluding certain testimony offered by the defendant-appellant in surrebuttal. To understand this question it is necessary to state the defendant's case in some detail.

The defendant's primary defense was that the ceramic statuette of a dog which it had sold was not copied, directly or indirectly, from the plaintiff's copyrighted work of art, but was reproduced from a statuette independently sculptured by a craftsman named Moyer, using his own pet spaniel of English type as the model, in 1938 when he was working for a pottery company in Zanesville, Ohio, which later burned and went out of business. In support of this defense Moyer took the stand and testified to his making a model of a **cocker spaniel** under the circumstances outlined above, and then produced a grey plaster statuette which he identified as his, or a replica of his, which he said he found in 1945 or 1950, (his testimony as to the date was vague) with a set of dies and molds from which to make it, in the storeroom of the Lepere Company, for which he went to work after the pottery company for which he worked when he made the model closed its doors. He did not know definitely how, or under what circumstances, the statuette, molds and dies came into Lepere's possession, but he said the Woolworth dog was made from this model, as seems evident from

---

[2] The plaintiff's expert witness and the defendant's expert disagree on this, but visual inspection leads us to agree with the court below that the plaintiff's expert was correct. At any rate, we cannot say that the court below was 'clearly erroneous' in accepting the testimony of the plaintiff's expert on this point.

inspection. Etched on the bottom of the model appears the legend 'AMCO 1938' the presence of which, however, neither Moyer nor any other witness was able to explain.

To refute Moyer's testimony, which the court below found vague and 'difficult to believe' and said it could not 'give credence to,' the plaintiff in rebuttal called its general manager back to the stand who said that he could not tell the age of Moyer's model by inspection of the plaster of which it was made, but that the wavy lines on it to represent long body hair and the legend 'AMCO 1938' could readily at any time have been scratched on a wet plaster model made from the plaintiff's plaster statuette, and that the appearance of age exhibited by Moyer's model could have been achieved by washing it when it was dusty and dirty, which Moyer said he had done when he found his model in order to clean it. Then, to rebut this testimony, the defendant in rejoinder offered an expert witness to testify that he could tell the age of plaster by inspection, and that Moyer's model was as old, or approximately as old, as the date which it bore. The court rejected this proffered testimony on the ground that it should have been offered as part of the defendant's case in chief and came too late in surrebuttal.

The permissible range of testimony offered in rejoinder, or surrebuttal, as it is sometimes called, is to a large extent discretionary with the trial court. Ordinarily at that late stage in a trial only evidence to explain away new facts brought forward by the proponent in rebuttal, or evidence to impeach witnesses who testified in rebuttal, is properly admissible. Otherwise orderly presentation, and hence clarity, would bow to the convenience, or even whim, of counsel, and afterthoughts, with consequent confusion, would be encouraged at the expense of thorough preparation by counsel in advance of trial.

The surrebuttal testimony offered by the defendant and refused admission by the court does not fall squarely into either one of the two classes of evidence ordinarily admissible in rejoinder enumerated above. The age of Moyer's model was in issue from the beginning for it was offered as the master copy from which the Woolworth dog was made, which indeed it appears to be, and as antedated the copyrighted work of 'Jan Allen.' Thus the defendant should . have anticipated that the plaintiff would offer evidence in rebuttal to show that Moyer's model was not as old as the date on it would seem to indicate by putting on a witness to testify that the date, like the wavy hair lines, could readily at any time after casting have been inscribed on a moistened plaster copy of the plaintiff's plaster model.

If the defendant had wished to buttress Moyer's testimony as to the age of his plaster model by the testimony of its expert, it could certainly have done so as part of its defense in chief. Having chosen instead to wait until surrebuttal to offer its evidence, it gambled on a favorable discretionary ruling by the court, and having lost, it can hardly be heard to complain. Nor does the testimony offered by the defendant in surrebuttal tend to impeach the plaintiff's rebuttal witness for the latter did not say that no one could tell the age of plaster by inspection but only that he was unable to do so.

The next matter for consideration is the appellant's contention that the court below erred in awarding the plaintiff-appellee statutory damages in the amount of $ 5,000 and a $ 2,000 attorney's fee. We dispose of the matter of the attorneys' fee with the bare comment that the court below in making its award committed no error of discretion that we can see. The substance of the appellant's argument on statutory damages can be briefly stated. It says that by affirmatively establishing without objection by the plaintiff a gross profit of $ .59 per dog, (it ignored possible deductions for dogs not sold, selling costs, etc. which it did not bother to show) it absolutely precluded any assessment of statutory damages under the 'in lieu' clause of Sec. 25(b) of the Copyright Act of 1909, 35 Stat. 1081, as amended by the Act of 1912, 37 Stat. 489 and enacted into law by the Act of 1947, 61 Stat. 661, 17 U.S.C. § 101(b), quoted in material part in the margin,[3] leaving as the only alternative an award of profits computed by multiplying the gross profit on each dog by the number of dogs involved, or $ 899.16.

The argument is fundamentally fallacious for the reason that it rests upon the not uncommon confusion of profits with damages, both of which are recoverable in copyright cases, but which are nevertheless distinct items of recovery and are awarded on quite different principles. Damages are awarded to a copyright proprietor on the conventional legal principle of affording compensation in money for the harm inflicted upon him by the wrongful act of the infringer, whereas an infringer's profits from his wrongful act are awarded to the copyright proprietor, not to inflict punishment on the infringer, but as appropriate equitable relief incident to a decree of injunction in order to prevent the infringer's unjust enrichment. Sheldon v. Metro-Goldwyn Pictures Corp., 1940, 309 U.S. 390, 399, 60 S.cT. 681, 84 L.Ed. 825; Sammons v. Colonial Press, 1 Cir., 1942, 126 F.2d 341, 344, 345 and cases cited.

---

[3] 'If any person shall infringe the copyright * * * such person shall be liable: * * * . To pay to the copyright proprietor such damages as the copyright proprietor may have suffered due to the infringement, as well as all the profits which the infringer shall have made from such infringement * * * or in lieu of actual damages and profits, such damages as to the court shall appear to be just (within a minimum limit of $ 250 and a maximum limit of $ 5,000), and shall not be regarded as a penalty.'

It is true that there is language in the cases relied upon by the appellant,[4] which taken out of context, seems to lend support to its argument that proof of actual profits precludes the assessment of statutory damages under the 'in lieu' clause. The language of this court in Sammons v. Colonial Press, 1 Cir., 126 F.2d 341, 350 is typical, wherein, with citation of cases, this court said: 'No evidence of actual damages having been given, if Colonial Press made no profits for which it is accountable the assessment by the district court under Sec. 25(b) of statutory damages against Colonial in the minimum amount of $ 250 cannot be reviewed upon appeal. * * * However, if the district court finds after further hearing upon remand that Colonial Press made profits for which it must account, the amount of such; profits will be the measure of recovery, and it will no longer be permissible to decree statutory damages 'in lieu of actual damages and profits."

It is of primary significance to note, however, that in the Sammons case, as well as in the cases cited therein and in those upon which the appellant relies, it is made clearly to appear that there was no issue on the plaintiff's damages, the only recovery sought, or the only recovery available on the evidence, being the infringer's profits. Since there was no question of damages in those cases, the language used therein is entirely accurate, for when no damages are recoverable to permit a recovery under the 'in lieu' clause of profits in excess of the amount of the actual profits clearly established by the evidence would be to use the 'in lieu' clause for the imposition of a penalty which the statute categorically forbids.[5] In the case at bar, however, the plaintiff in its complaint specifically demanded, in addition to an injunction, attorney's fees and costs, both damages and profits in such amount 'as to the court shall appear proper within the

---

[4] Principally Davilla v. Brunswick-Balke Collender Co., 2 Cir., 1939, 94 F.2d 567; Sammons v. Colonial Press, 1 Cir., 1943, 126 F.2d 341; Washingtonian Pub. Co. v. Pearson, 1944, 78 U.S.App.D.C. 287, 140 F.2d 465; Malsed v. Marshall Field & Co., D.C.Wash.1951, 96 F.Supp. 372.

[5] Furthermore, in the Sammons case, supra, the plaintiff took an appeal on the ground that it was error to give judgment merely for the minimum statutory damages of $ 250 when, as plaintiff contended, the evidence showed that the infringer had made actual profits considerably in excess of that sum. This raised an accounting problem as to the allocation of overhead, and we sent the case back to the district court for further determination as to the amount of profit, if any, made by the infringer. Of course, if it should be established with legal certainty that the amount of the infringer's profits, properly computed, exceeded the sum of $ 250, plaintiff was entitled to judgment for the larger sum, as we instructed the district court in our opinion.

provisions of the copyright statutes, but not less than two hundred and fifty dollars.' That is to say, it asked for an assessment of both damages and profits by the court under the 'in lieu' clause of Sec. 25(b) of the Copyright Act of 1909, supra. It maintained this position throughout the trial, insisting that it had suffered damage and that the defendant had made profits, although it made no effort to prove the actual dollars and cents amount of either, and the court below on adequate evidence categorically found both that the plaintiff had suffered damage from the infringement and also that the defendant had made a profit therefrom, but that it was difficult if not impossible for the plaintiff to prove the actual amount of either its damage or of the defendant's profits with the certainty required by law. Thus the case at bar differs radically from those upon which the appellant relies in that here we have a live issue of damages. In this situation it would be illogical to take the language of the cases cited out of context, and use it to support the proposition that proof of actual profits precludes any assessment of damages under the 'in lieu' clause whenever an actual profit in some amount has been shown, for recovery under the clause is for both 'damages and profits' and those are separate and distinct items of recovery. Moreover to hold that a defendant by proving its profits, which might have been small or even non-existent, could prevent a plaintiff from recovering any damages whatever under the 'in lieu' clause, even though he might show that his damage was heavy although incalculable with legal certainty, would serve to defeat the purpose of the clause which is to permit recovery of more than a merely nominal sum when, as is not uncommon in these cases, it is difficult or impossible for a plaintiff to prove the actual amount of either damages or profits with the certainty required by law. Douglas v. Cunningham, 1935, 294 U.S. 207, 55 S.Ct. 365, 79 L.Ed. 862.

It is true that the defendant by showing its gross profits, which the plaintiff does not dispute and with which the defendant appears to be content, has made clearly erroneous the district court's finding that profits cannot be determined with legal certainty. Thus any assessment of profits under the 'in lieu' clause is precluded. However, deducting profits, which must be taken as $ 899.16, from the gross award of $ 5,000, leaves $ 4,100 and odd cents attributable to damages. Since this is not an irrational amount to award as damages, and the gross award is within the statutory limits, the assessment is not to be disturbed on appeal. Douglas v. Cunningham, supra.

The final contention of the appellant for our consideration is that it did not receive a fair and impartial trial in the court below, and for that reason the case should be remanded for a new trial before another judge. In support of this contention the appellant points to several instances in the record of irrelevant and prejudicial comments and remarks by counsel for the plaintiff, and also to instances of like remarks by Judge McCarthy who presided at the trial.

It seems to us that appellant is somewhat hypercritical in its objection to certain remarks by plaintiff's counsel, prompted perhaps by excess of zeal in a hotly contested trial, particularly in view of the fact that the trial was not before a jury, and that usually, when plaintiff's counsel made comments to which opposing counsel took exception, the court remarked that it would not heed any prejudicial matter thus interjected.

As to the criticisms of the trial judge, we are bound to say that certain of his remarks in the course of the proceeding were both unseemly and uncalled for. It is the duty of the trial judge not only to afford the parties a fair trial, but also to conduct the proceedings with such poise and dignity and evident impartiality that, so far as is reasonably possible, the parties may leave his courtroom with a feeling that they have been given a fair trial. But after careful consideration of the record as a whole we have concluded that the particular remarks of the judge which would better have been left unsaid, and are better not quoted, do not rise to the seriousness of reversible error. Having regard for the convincing nature of the plaintiff's proof, and the unconvincing nature of that of the defendant, we do not feel that the decision reached by the court below can be attributed to bias and prejudice. That is to say, we feel that the defendant really had a fair and impartial trial.

The judgment of the District Court is affirmed, with the addition of an attorney's fee of $ 500 to counsel for the plaintiff-appellee for services on this appeal.

F. W. WOOLWORTH CO.
v.
CONTEMPORARY ARTS, INC.

No. 42

SUPREME COURT
OF THE UNITED STATES

344 U.S. 228
73 S. Ct. 222

November 17, 1952, Argued
December 22, 1952, Decided

Kenneth W. Greenawalt argued the cause for petitioner. With him on the brief were Martin A. Schenck and John H. Barber.

Cedric W. Porter argued the cause for respondent. With him on the brief was Harry F. R. Dolan.

Justices of the Supreme Court:
Vinson, Black, Reed, Frankfurter, Douglas, Jackson, Burton, Clark, Minton

OPINION

MR. JUSTICE JACKSON delivered the opinion of the Court.

Respondent brought this action under the Copyright Act to recover for infringement of copyright on a work of art entitled "**Cocker spaniel** in Show Position." The District Court found the copyright, of which respondent was assignee, valid and infringed and awarded statutory damages of $ 5,000, with a $ 2,000 attorney's fee. The Court of Appeals affirmed.[1] 1 We granted certiorari, [2] limiting the issues to the measure of the recovery, as to which conflict appears among lower courts.[3]

Respondent made small sculptures and figurines, among which were statues of the **cocker spaniel**, and marketed them chiefly through gift and art shops. Petitioner, from a different source, bought 127 dozen **cocker spaniel** statuettes and distributed them through thirty-four Woolworth stores. Unbeknown to Woolworth, these dogs had been copied from respondent's and by marketing them it became an infringer.

By the Act an infringer becomes liable --

"To pay to the copyright proprietor such damages as the copyright proprietor may have suffered due to the infringement, as well as all the profits which the infringer shall have made from such infringement, and in proving profits the plaintiff shall be required to prove sales only, and the defendant shall be required to prove every element of cost which he claims, or in lieu of actual damages and profits, such damages as to the court shall appear to be just, and in assessing such damages the court may, in its discretion, allow the amounts as hereinafter stated . . . and such damages shall in no other case exceed the sum of $ 5,000 nor be less than the sum of $ 250, and shall not be regarded as a penalty. . . ." 17 U. S. C. § 101 (b).

Profits made by the petitioner from the infringement were sufficiently proved to enable assessment of that element of liability. Petitioner itself showed, without contradiction, that the 127 dozen dogs were bought at 60 cents apiece and sold for $ 1.19 each, yielding a gross profit of $ 899.16. The infringer did not assume the burden, which the statute casts upon it, of proving any other costs that might be deductible, so the gross figure is left to stand as the profit factor of the infringer's total liability.

As to the other ingredient in computing liability, damages suffered by the copyright proprietor, the record is inadequate to establish an actually sustained amount. Enough appears to indicate that real and substantial injury was inflicted. Respondent had gross annual income of about $ 35,000

---

[1] 193 F.2d 162.

[2] 343 U.S. 963.

[3] F. W. Woolworth Co. v. Contemporary Arts, 193 F.2d 162, 167-169; Sammons v. Colonial Press, 126 F.2d 341, 350; Davilla v. Brunswick-Balke Collender Co., 94 F.2d 567; Malsed v. Marshall Field & Co., 96 F.Supp. 372, 376-377

and engaged only eight employees, indicating its small production. Its statuettes were of three media and prices: red plaster retailed at $ 4, red porcelain at $ 9, while a black and white porcelain brought $ 15. There was evidence that the cheaper infringing statuette was inferior in quality. Respondent proved loss of some customers and offered, but was not allowed, to show complaints from sales outlets about the Woolworth competition, decline in respondent's sales, and eventual abandonment of the line with an unsalable stock on hand. The trial judge excluded or struck most of this testimony on the ground that authority to allow statutory damages rendered proof of actual damage unnecessary. It might have been better practice to have received the evidence, even if it fell short of establishing the measure of liability; for when recovery may be awarded without any proof of injury, it cannot hurt and may aid the exercise of discretion to hear any evidence on the subject that has probative value. However, petitioner cannot complain of this exclusion, which was in response to its objections. At length, the court said: "If you establish this was an infringement of copyright, it is inescapably clear there is enough evidence in this case upon which to predicate damage up to $ 5000. I don't think Mr. Barnes [counsel for defendant] disagrees with that, do you?" Mr. Barnes: "No, your Honor."

The court, having found infringement, accordingly allowed recovery of "statutory damages in the amount of Five Thousand Dollars ($ 5,000.) as provided by the Copyright Laws of the United States," with an injunction and attorney's fee.

Petitioner's contention here is that the statute was misapplied because its own gross profit of $ 899.16 supplied an actual figure which became the exclusive measure of its liability. It argues that an infringing defendant, by coming forward with an undisputed admission of its own profit from the infringement, can tie the hands of the court and limit recovery to that amount. We cannot agree.

In Douglas v. Cunningham, 294 U.S. 207, 209, we said:

"The phraseology of the section was adopted to avoid the strictness of construction incident to a law imposing penalties, and to give the owner of a copyright some recompense for injury done him, in a case where the rules of law render difficult or impossible proof of damages or discovery of profits."

To fulfill that purpose, the statute has been interpreted to vest in the trial court broad discretion to determine whether it is more just to allow a recovery based on calculation of actual damages and profits, as found from evidence, or one based on a necessarily somewhat arbitrary estimate within the limits permitted by the Act.

"In other words, the court's conception of what is just in the particular case, considering the nature of the copyright, the circumstances of the infringement and the like, is made the measure of the damages to be paid, but with the express qualification that in every case the assessment must be within the prescribed limitations, that is to say, neither more than the maximum nor less than the minimum. Within these limitations the court's discretion and sense of justice are controlling, but it has no discretion when proceeding under this provision to go outside of them." L. A. Westermann Co. v. Dispatch Printing Co., 249 U.S. 100, 106-107.

Few bodies of law would be more difficult to reduce to a short and simple formula than that which determines the measure of damage recoverable for actionable wrongs. The necessary flexibility to do justice in the variety of situations which copyright cases present can be achieved only by exercise of the wide judicial discretion within limited amounts conferred by this statute. It is plain that the court's choice between a computed measure of damage and that imputed by statute cannot be controlled by the infringer's admission of his profits which might be greatly exceeded by the damage inflicted. Indeed sales at a small margin might cause more damage to the copyright proprietor than sales of the infringing article at a higher price.

Whether discretionary resort to estimation of statutory damages is just should be determined by taking into account both components and the difficulties in the way of proof of either. In this case the profits realized were established by uncontradicted evidence, but the court was within the bounds of its discretion in concluding that the amount of damages suffered was not computable from the testimony. Lack of adequate proof on either element would warrant resort to the statute in the discretion of the court, subject always to the statutory limitations.

The case before us illustrates what capricious results would follow from the practice for which petitioner contends. It has admitted gross profits, which make no deduction for sales costs, overheads or taxes and, hence, may appear substantial on this particular record. But gross profits is not what a copyright owner is entitled to recover, but only such profits as remain after the defendant reduces them, as it may, by proof of allowable elements of cost. If we sustain petitioner's contention that profits may be the sole measure of liability as matter of law, such profits could be diminished even to the vanishing point.

Net profits realized by a far-flung distributing enterprise like Woolworth's upon sales of a given item in a few of its many stores can be calculated only by a process of allocating overheads, sales expenses, taxes, and a host of items. A plaintiff in the position of the present one could hardly verify or contest such apportionments unless it should audit the whole Woolworth business.

Moreover, a rule of liability which merely takes away the profits from an infringement would offer little discouragement to infringers. It would fall short of an effective sanction for enforcement of the copyright policy. The statutory rule, formulated after long experience, not merely compels restitution of profit and reparation for injury but also is designed to discourage wrongful conduct. The discretion of the court is wide enough to permit a resort to statutory damages for such purposes. Even for uninjurious and unprofitable invasions of copyright the court may, if it deems it just, impose a liability within statutory limits to sanction and vindicate the statutory policy.

Petitioner cites Sheldon v. Metro-Goldwyn Pictures Corp., 309 U.S. 390, 399, where this Court said that the "in lieu" clause "is not applicable here, as the profits have been proved and the only question is as to their apportionment," a statement on which petitioner leans almost its whole weight. There net profits from exhibition of an infringing picture were found to be $ 587,604.37. The copyright owner could show no such value to himself of his copyright; indeed, he had negotiated its sale at $ 30,000. The Court of Appeals cut the award of these actual profits to one-fifth thereof, upon the ground that success of the picture had been largely due to factors not contributed by the infringement. The propriety of this reduction was the sole issue before this Court. Petitioner copyright owner asserted that in such circumstances the "in lieu" clause "is not involved here." This Court agreed that under those facts resort to the statute was not appropriate. That case did not present the question now here. Nor does anything in Jewell-LaSalle Realty Co. v. Buck, 283 U.S. 202, in the light of its facts, support petitioner. It holds use of the "in lieu" clause permissible, "there being no proof of actual damages," but it does not hold that partial or unacceptable proof on that subject will preclude resort to the "in lieu" clause.

We think that the statute empowers the trial court in its sound exercise of judicial discretion to determine whether on all the facts a recovery upon proven profits and damages or one estimated within the statutory limits is more just. We find no abuse of that discretion.

The judgment below is

Affirmed.

DISSENT

MR. JUSTICE BLACK,
with whom MR. JUSTICE FRANKFURTER concurs, dissenting.

The earthenware dogs found to infringe respondent's copyright were bought by F. W. Woolworth Company in good faith at a total cost of $ 914.40. Woolworth's total profit from the sale of the dogs was $ 899.16. The Court now holds that Woolworth must pay the dogs' copyright owner $ 5,000. This award is said to be allowed by § 101 (b) of the Copyright Act, 17 U. S. C. § 101. We do not think that section authorizes any such manifestly unjust exaction. This Court pointed out in Sheldon v. Metro-Goldwyn Pictures Corp., 309 U.S. 390, 400-401, that § 101, like an analogous patent law section, was not intended to award a copyright owner both damages and profits, but only "one or the other, whichever was the greater." Under this rule, profits only should be awarded to respondent in this case.

Reliance for awarding $ 5,000 against Woolworth is naturally placed on that provision of § 101 (b) which provides for damages not in excess of $ 5,000 "in lieu of actual damages and profits." But this Court has said that the purpose of this section was to recompense for injury done "where the rules of law render difficult or impossible proof of damages or discovery of profits." Douglas v. Cunningham, 294 U.S. 207, 209. Here proof of profits was neither difficult nor impossible. And in the carefully considered case of Sheldon v. Metro-Goldwyn Pictures Corp., supra, at 399, Mr. Chief Justice Hughes speaking for the Court declared, ". . . the 'in lieu' clause is not applicable here, as the profits have been proved . . . ." See also to the same effect Davilla v. Brunswick-Balke Collender Co., 94 F.2d 567; Sammons v. Colonial Press, 126 F.2d 341. We would adhere to this view and limit this recovery to profits made by Woolworth. This Court should heed the admonition given in the Sheldon case to remember that the object of § 101 (b) is not to inflict punishment but to award an injured copyright owner that which in fairness is his "and nothing beyond this." Sheldon v. Metro-Goldwyn Pictures Corp., supra, at 399.

The following circumstances bear on the question of unfairness of the amount of damages awarded. Petitioner contended in the Court of Appeals that the district judge did not give it a fair and impartial trial. "In support of this contention," the Court of Appeals said, "the appellant points to several instances in the record of irrelevant and prejudicial comments and remarks" made by the trial judge. Considering the judge's remarks as "both unseemly and uncalled for," the Court of Appeals said:

"But after careful consideration of the record as a whole we have concluded that the particular remarks of the judge which would better have been left unsaid, and are better not quoted, do not rise to the seriousness of reversible error. Having regard for the convincing nature of the plaintiff's proof, and the unconvincing nature of that of the defendant, we do not feel that the decision reached by the court below can be attributed to bias and prejudice. That is to say, we feel that the defendant really had a fair and impartial trial." 193 F.2d 162, 169.

We accept the Court of Appeals' appraisal of the consequences of the judge's remarks on the factual issue of copyright infringement. But here the trial judge gave judgment for statutory damages in an amount that smacks of punitive qualities. And this Court has held that the amount of such damages is committed to the unreviewable discretion of a trial judge. Douglas v. Cunningham, 294 U.S. 207, 210. In view of the remarks of the trial judge directed against the Woolworth Company, we think it had a just right to complain that the amount of damages imposed ought not to stand.

We would reverse and remand this case for a new trial by another judge.

2
IMPLICATIONS OF WOOLWORTH

The Woolworth case is cited in hundreds of federal opinions for the applications of statutory damages and vicarious liability for copyright infringement. In nine of these cases the court cites Woolworth along with specific reference to the cocker spaniel. These cases reveal the cocker spaniel as protector of copyrights in aesthetic property but lesso in patent law, where analysis is based on utility. Cocker spaniels are a form of nature but individual aesthetic expressions acquire strong copyright protection.

Columbus Plastic Prods. v. Rona Plastic Corp., 111 F. Supp. 623 (1953)
Harms, Inc. v. F. W. Woolworth Co., 163 F. Supp. 484 (1958)
Prestige Floral v. Cal. Artificial Flower Co., 201 F. Supp. 287 (1962)
Blazon, Inc. v. De Luxe Game Corp., 268 F. Supp. 416 (1965)
Davis v. E. I. DuPont de Nemours & Co., 249 F. Supp. 329 (1966)
Gardenia Flowers, Inc. v. Joseph Markovits, Inc., 280 F. Supp. 776 (1968)
Rogers v. Koons, 777 F. Supp. 1 (1991)
King Records, Inc. v. Bennett, 438 F. Supp. 2d 812 (2006)
Stockart.Com, LLC v. Caraustar Custom Packaging Group, Inc,
240 F.R.D. 195 (2006)

COLUMBUS PLASTIC PRODUCTS Inc.

v.

RONA PLASTIC CORP. et al.

UNITED STATES DISTRICT COURT
FOR THE SOUTHERN DISTRICT OF NEW YORK

111 F. Supp. 623

April 22, 1953

Burke & Burke, New York City (McDowell & Rambo and James M. Hengst, Columbus, Ohio of counsel), for plaintiff.

H. C. Biefman, New York City, for defendants.

Judge Murphy

OPINION

This is an action for unfair competition and infringement of design and mechanical patents arising out of defendants' alleged manufacture, sale and use of plastic kitchen canister sets virtually identical with plaintiff's prior product. The original complaint, grounded only on unfair competition, was filed March 15, 1951 and demanded temporary and permanent injunctions, accounting, punitive damages, destruction of defendants' molds, costs and attorneys' fees. The answer denied the unlawfulness of defendants' conduct and a cross-claim was made for libel and slander arising out of a circular letter by plaintiff warning customers of defendants' product as well as for punitive damages under the Sherman Act and attorneys' fees. A supplemental complaint filed April 12, 1951 alleged infringement of a design patent issued to plaintiff on March 20, 1951. On June 8, 1951, this court per Leibell, J. granted a temporary injunction (Civ. No. 65-18,[1] filed May 29, 1951) but refused on October 10, 1951 to allow contempt based upon alleged infringement of a second set of canisters manufactured and

---

[1] No opinion for publication.

sold by defendants. After issuance to plaintiff of a mechanical patent on November 20, 1951, a second supplemental complaint was filed December 7, 1951 alleging its infringement. The issues before this court after trial without jury accordingly are: whether the temporary injunction relating to defendants' first allegedly infringing product should be made permanent; whether a permanent injunction should issue with respect to defendants' second product; defendants' cross-claim; and other remedies demanded by both parties.

The court makes the following

Findings of Fact.

1. The plaintiff is a corporation organized under the laws of the State of Ohio, and defendant, Rona Plastic Corporation, is a New York corporation, with a place of doing business within this judicial district. Defendants, Louis Stahl, Yale J. Halperin, and Solomon Jack Stahl, are citizens of the State of New York and residents within this judicial district. The matter in controversy exceeds, exclusive of interest and costs, the sum of $ 3,000.

2. Plaintiff is manufacturer of a set of four plastic kitchen canisters, rectangular in shape, with flat sides having rounded edges and tapering inward slightly from top to base. The color of the flat lid which has a round knob contrasts with the rest of the canister. The vertical legend 'Flour', 'Sugar', 'Coffee' and 'Tea', respectively, indicates the use for each canister which diminishes in size in that order. The canisters are made so that each smaller one may be 'nested' or telescoped within a larger one.

3. Plaintiff's canisters were designed by an engineer employed by them since 1040. A design patent was issued to plaintiff (No. 162,579) on March 20, 1951 upon application of the designer made March 10, 1950, and a mechanical patent (No. 2,575,770) was issued November 20, 1951.

4. These canisters bear the name 'Lustro-Ware' molded on the bottom.

5. Plaintiff's canisters were first displayed and sold to wholesalers and retailers in January, 1950. Between January, 1950 and February 28, 1951, plaintiff's sales of these canisters totalled $ 2,159,439. Plaintiff expended less than $ 26,000 in advertising these canisters during this period.

6. During this period canister sets by at least two manufacturers similar in appearance to plaintiff's were on the market.

7. During this period public acceptance of plaintiff's canisters was due to their usefulness and attractive appearance without regard to their source of manufacture.

8. In January, 1951, defendant Rona Plastic Corporation with which the individual defendants are associated, commenced manufacture and sale of sets of canisters virtually identical in contour, size and detail to those of

plaintiff. The only difference between the two sets are the mark on the bottom and a stripped border on top of the lid of defendant Rona's set. These differences would not be distinguishable to the ordinary purchaser.

9. Some time in 1951, defendant Rona manufactured and sold a second set of canisters identical in all respects to its first set except that the knob on the lid was now rectangular in shape and on each side and corresponding portion of the lid, two sets of three decorative panels were embossed. As in the case of its first set, these differences would not be distinguishable to the ordinary purchaser. A design patent (No. 165,403) was procured by defendant Stahl for this set on December 11, 1951 upon application filed July 6, 1951.

10. In the four months following March 1, 1951, plaintiff's sales of its canisters decreased $ 538,685.86, as compared with the four previous months. Plaintiff's sales continued to fall off in succeeding months.

Discussion.

The issues in a case such as this have been thus stated by Frank, C. J., in Briddell, Inc. v. Alglobe Trading Corp., 2 Cir., 194 F.2d 416, 418:

'The fact that the design of an article is strikingly novel and beautiful, and the fact that its first producer has spent large sums in advertising which has made the article popular with consumers, give the first producer no rights against others who subsequently imitate it and (taking advantage of the consumer-popularity of the article, due to the first producer's advertising) sell it competitively- unless the first producer has a monopoly based upon (1) a patent on the design or (2) a so-called secondary meaning. Absent (1) and (2), the first producer has no legal complaint because the imitators have been enriched by his efforts, have enjoyed what is known as a 'free ride."

I

We consider first the matter of secondary meaning.

The nature of the remedy sought- permanent injunction for unfair competition- should be appraised at the outset. When a product of plaintiff's ingenuity, investment, time and effort has been lavishly imitated by defendant, several remedies under varying circumstances may be available. A design copyright might be obtained if the product could qualify under the copyright statute as, perhaps, 'a work of art.' 17 U.S.C.A. § 5(h, g); Bleistein v. Donaldson Lithographing Co., 188 U.S. 239, 23 S.Ct. 298, 47 L.Ed. 460; King Features Syndicate v. Fleischer, 2 Cir., 299 F. 533. To a large extent this would depend upon its non-utilitarian aspects. Cf. Stein v. Expert Lamp Co., 7 Cir., 188 F.2d 611, certiorari denied, 342 U.S. 829, 72 S.Ct. 53, not stem merely from similarity or even identity of questioned product with that 96 L.Ed. 627; Jack Adelman, Inc. v. Sonners & Gordon,

Inc., D.C.S.D.N.Y., 112 F.Supp. 187. Under somewhat stringent requirements of inventiveness in this circuit, 'any new, original and ornamental design for an article of manufacture', 35 U.S.C.A. § 171, might be protected by design patent. Cf. Briddell, Inc., v. Alglobe Trading Corp., supra, 194 F.2d 416, 419 note 3 (cases collected). But these remedies grant a monopoly of sharply limited duration, and then only upon the basis of a legislative appraisal of the conflicting interests involved which is specifically authorized by the Constitution. Art. I, Sec. 8. What is sought here is a monopoly eternal in duration and grounded only upon judicial appraisal of conflicting interests, without possibly any legislative resolution of them. Cf. Lanham Act, 15 U.S.C.A. § 1126(h, i); Dad's Root Beer Co. v. Doc's Beverages, 2 Cir., 193 F.2d 77, 79-82.

It is not surprising that protection so considerable requires surmounting several serious hurdles. Conceding the copying, identical appearance and competitive sale in the same market of defendant's product with plaintiff's, plaintiff must establish that (3 Restatement, Torts (1938) Sec. 741):

'(b) the copied or imitated feature has acquired generally in the market a special significance identifying the other's good, and

'(i) the copy or imitation is likely to cause prospective purchasers to regard his goods as those of the other, and

'(ii) the copied or imitated feature is non-functional, or, if it is functional, he does not take reasonable steps to inform prospective purchasers that the goods which he markets are not those of the other.'

The evidence is undisputed that plaintiff's canisters were put into commercial production in the latter part of 1949 and sold about January 1, 1950. Defendants entered the market with their copy in January, 1951. This latter date fixes the time at which plaintiff's product must have acquired the special significance requisite for its protection.

Although plaintiff had been in business since 1938, had used the trade name 'Lustro-Ware' in connection with its 115 products and had realized sales in excess of $ 6 million in 1951, its sales of the canisters in question from January, 1950 to the end of February, 1951 amounted to slightly more than one-third of this figure. Although plaintiff had spent about $ 100,000 in advertising all of its products in 1951 only slightly more than one-quarter of this sum was expended on its canisters. During 1950 at least two manufacturers had rectangular plastic canisters on the market, one of these as early as 1948.

To establish the existence of secondary meaning during this period, plaintiff called three housewives as witnesses. One, Mrs. Atlas, testified that defendants' canister sets were purchased without knowing of its manufacturer at the time. She 'wanted a cookie jar to match it', saw 'an ad in the paper about (plaintiff), about plastics', and 'thought maybe if I wrote to the firm I would know of the place where I could buy it.' She did not learn who manufactured her set until a lawyer for the plaintiff telephoned her. At the time of acquisition she neither cared who the manufacturer was nor had ever heard of plaintiff or defendants.

Similar testimony was given by Mrs. Hughes. She too had purchased defendants' product and had written to plaintiff after seeing one of its advertisements because it 'might know where I could purchase one of the lids' which had been lost. At the time of acquisition she also neither cared who manufactured the product nor had ever heard of plaintiff or defendant. 'I think,' she testified, 'the first time I saw a set was the first time I bought one.'

Mrs. Bird, after seeing an advertisement, wrote to two or three manufacturers, including plaintiff, and apparently received no replies. She recalled plaintiff only because one of its attorneys later telephoned her. As a Christmas present, she received defendants' set. Like the others, she neither know nor cared who was the manufacturer.

The test of secondary meaning is of course likelihood of confusion' and not actual confusion. But the confusion does not stem merely from similarity or even identity of the questioned product with that of the first come; it must be a confusion of manufacture and relate to that which attaches to the personality of the manufacturer. The first maker of plastic canisters in this appealing style may have created public desire for one of two things: (1) plastic canisters made by him alone, above all other plastic canister makers; or (2) plastic canisters in a particular form regardless of who makes them. The sweeping monopoly granted by the law of unfair competition extends only to the first of these conditions. At most the testimony of these witnesses tends to establish only the second. In the oft-quoted words of Learned Hand, C. J., in Crescent Tool co. v. Kilborn & Bishop Co., 2 Cir., 247 F. 299, 300:

'(I)t is an absolute condition to any relief whatever that the plaintiff in such cases show that the appearance of his wares has in fact come to mean that some particular person- the plaintiff may not be individually known- makes them, and that the public cares who does make them, and not merely for their appearance and structure.'

One wholesale distributor and a salesman for plaintiff manufacturer's personal representative testified that they knew of palming off by distributors of defendants' wares for those of plaintiff. Such behavior is tortious and actionable. But the wholesale distributor- the plaintiff's witness and current jobber- named himself as the deceiver. The salesman- obviously interested in the outcome- knew of instances perpetrated by distributors in his presence. If such deception occurred, these distributors- including plaintiff's witness- may be enjoined, provided they are made parties in a proceeding. These witnesses are far from establishing the probability of confusion requisite for the perpetual decree sought against the manufacturing defendants.

A number of witnesses employed by plaintiff testified concerning the popularity, eye-appeal and 'on the spot' acceptance of plaintiff's product. This was attributed by many of them to its so-called nonfunctional features. No fewer than nine of these were ascribed to the plastic container with rectangular sides tapering slightly inward from top to base; 'flat surface square or cubical body'; 'downwardly and inwardly tapering form'; 'molded plastic composition'; 'uniform coloration'; 'rounded edges and corners at top, bottom and sides'; 'vertical lettering on the front flat surface of the body'; 'flat-top lids of colors contrasting with colors of body'; 'wide diametered hollow knobs'; and 'rounded corner edges.'

It must be seriously doubted whether these are all 'nonfunctional' characteristics. The line between what is superfluously decorative and what is usefully decorous must necessarily be shadowy for an attractive container. 'When goods are bought largely for their aesthetic value, their features may be functional because they definitely contribute to that value and thus aid in the performance of an object for which the goods are intended. Thus, the shape of a bottle or other container may be functional though a different bottle or container may hold the goods equally well.' Restatement, Torts (1938) Sec. 742, Comment a. Functional or not, these features have not been established by a preponderance of evidence as associating in the minds of its purchasers, plaintiff's product with plaintiff as its source. Accordingly the application for injunction based upon of damages only), 344 U.S. 228, 73 S.Ct. 222. On the other hand, the figure

II.

A more limited monopoly is claimed by plaintiff by dint of a design patent (No. 162579) issued March 20, 1951 and a mechanical one (No. 2,575,770) granted November 20, 1951.

With respect to these, the recently enacted patent statute apparently applies. Section 4(a) of the Act July 19, 1952, c. 950, 66 Stat. 815, 35 U.S.C.A. preceding section 1, provides in part: 'This Act shall take effect on January 1, 1952 * * * It shall apply to unexpired patents granted prior to such date except as otherwise provided.' The test for design patents remains substantially the same: 'Whoever invents any new, original and ornamental design for an article of manufacture * * *,' together with a statement assimilating requirements of patents for technological advances, 'The provisions of this title relating to patents for inventions shall apply to patents for designs * * *.' 35 U.S.C.A. § 171.

It is not clear that the ornamental nature of plaintiff's design possesses enough merit to meet the standards of novelty and originality. In A. C. Gilbert 476. 'Simple variants upon old themes, such as capable designers can turn out observed:

'If the design goes no farther than to embody an obvious neatness and

'more is required for a valid design patent than that the design be new and pleasing

than has generally been the case, this is not in itself enough. The shape of a tin can might be thought to reach this degree of attractiveness, yet it would

skill of the ordinary designer.' Neufeld-Furst & Co., Inc. v. Jay-Day

of design patents is difficult, for there are no standards. Yet we are obliged to determine, as best we may, whether the design in question is original and aesthetic and involved a step beyond the prior art requiring what it termed 'inventive genius."

In passing the contrast should be noted between the standards of artistic merit requisite for copyright and design patent. A plastic statuette of a typical **cocker spaniel** in ordinary pose known as 'show position' has been upheld as valid for copyright. Contemporary Arts, Inc. v. F. W. Woolworth Co., D.C. Mass., 93 F.Supp. 739, affirmed 1 Cir., 193 F.2d 162, affirmed (certiorari on issue of damages only), 344 U.S. 228, 73 S.Ct.222. On the other hand, the figure of a girl posed naturally as an ash tray ornamentation, has been held invalid as a patent design. Frankart, Inc. v. Apt Novelty Co., D.C.S.D.N.Y., 57 F.2d 757.

 The question then of 'inventive genius' becomes paramount. Evidence of prior art shows rectangular canisters with rounded corners, tapered sides and flat lid. Round, wide-diametered knobs are even more archaic. Plaintiff's step forward then consists of little more than the combination of the knob with the canister. As Judge McGohey observed in Grinoch v. Tuxton Cravats, Inc., D.C.S.D.N.Y., 101 F.Supp. 391, 392:

'Mere regrouping of elements old in the field will not suffice unless it rises 'above the commonplace' or demonstrates 'originality which is born of the inventive faculty".

An 'unstartling regrouping of old elements,' Knickerbocker Plastic Co. v. Allied Molding Corp., 2 Cir., 184 F.2d 652, 654, is far from demonstrating 'the same exceptional talent that is required for a mechanical patent.' Nat Lewis Urses, Inc. v. Carole Bags, Inc., 2 Cir., 83 F.2d 475, 476. 'Simple variants upon old themes, such as capable designers can turn out almost by permutation of old elements', are not proper subjects for patent protection. White v. Leanore Frocks, Inc., 2 Cir., 120 F.2d 113, 114. Indeed 'mor: is required for a valid design patent than that the design be new and pleasing enough to catch the trade; it must be the product of 'invention,' by which is meant that conception of the design must demand some exceptional talent beyond the skill of the ordinary designer.' Neufeld-Furst & Co., i Nc. v. Jay-Day Frocks, Inc., 2 Cir., 112 F.2d 715, 716.

 The presumption of patentability sometimes said to arise from the issue of a patent, cf. Mumm v. Jacob E. Decker & Sons, 301 U.S. 168, 57 S.Ct. 675, 81 L.Ed. 983, must in this case be viewed in the light of the grant of design patent to defendant Stahl for its second canister set which is quite indistinguishable from plaintiff's in appearance.

Accordingly, this design patent must be held invalid.

Under design patent the appearance of the article rather than its mechanical function receives protection, even where the design contributes to the performance of the mechanical function. See Gorham Mfg. Co. v. White, 14 Wall. 511, 524-525, 20 L.Ed. 731; In re La Montagne, 47 F.2d 975, 18 C.C.P.A., Patents, 1147. If the visual and mechanical aspects are inseparable, only one type of protection, either design or mechanical patent, is available. In re Barber, 81 F.2d 231, 23 C.C.P.A., Patents, 834.

Plaintiff's mechanical patent is based on the 'nesting' or telescoping aspect of its product by which packing and shipping are facilitated by having the larger canisters contain the smaller ones. The existence of prior art involving this 'nesting' principle involving canisters as well as lids in such a manner as to prevent lateral displacement, has been established. Accordingly, the mechanical patent of plaintiff must be held invalid.

No evidence has been adduced by defendants in support of their cross-claim for damages in libel and under the Sherman Act, 15 U.S.C.A. §§ 1-7, 15 note, and accordingly, it must be dismissed.

Conclusions of Law.

1. This court has jurisdiction of the parties and the subject matter.
2. Plaintiff's design patent (No. 162,579) is invalid.
3. Plaintiff's mechanical patent (No. 2,575,770) is invalid.
4. Plaintiff's application for injunction based upon defendants' unfair competition is denied.
5. Plaintiff's application for injunction based upon defendants' infringement of its design and mechanical patents is denied.
6. Defendants' cross-claim for damages is dismissed.

HARMS, INC.,

a corporation, et al., Plaintiffs,

v.

F. W. WOOLWORTH CO.,

a corporation, et al., Defendants.

M. WITMARK & SONS et al.,

Plaintiffs,

v.

MAY COMPANY,

a corporation, Defendants

Nos. 47-58, 255-57

UNITED STATES DISTRICT COURT FOR THE SOUTHERN DISTRICT OF CALIFORNIA, CENTRAL DIVISION

163 F. Supp. 484

July 16, 1958

Fink, Levinthal & Lavery, Los Angeles, Cal., by Arthur S. Katz, Los Angeles, Cal., for plaintiff.

Glickfeld & Goldstein, by Irving B. Glickfeld, Los Angeles, Cal., for defendant.

Judge Yankwich

OPINION

The various motions of the parties, heretofore heard, argued and submitted, are now decided as follows:

(1) The defendants' motion filed March 10, 1958, to dismiss the

Complaint in case No. 47-58-Y under Rule 12(b)(6), Federal Rules of Civil Procedure, 28 U.S.C.A. for failure to state a claim is hereby denied.

(2) The motions of all the defendants filed on June 23, 1958, to dismiss the complaints in the above two cases, since consolidated, under Rule 12(b)(6) for failure to state a claim are denied.

(3) The motions of the defendants to require the plaintiff to separately state the claims under Rule 10(b), Federal Rules of Civil Procedure, and for a more definite statement under Rule 12(e), Federal Rules of Civil Procedure, are denied.

(4) The motions of the defendants to strike certain portions of the complaints under Rule 12(f), Federal Rules of Civil Procedure, are denied.

(5) The motion of the plaintiff filed May 26, 1958, for a partial summary judgment under Rule 56(a) and (c), Federal Rules of Civil Procedure, is granted only insofar as it relates to the subject of liability only. The Court deems it inappropriate at this time to segregate other facts which may be left open for determination, as requested in said motion, under Rule 56(d), Federal Rules of Civil Procedure.

Formal findings granting such partial summary judgment to be prepared by counsel for the plaintiff under Local Rule 3(d)(2), West's Ann.Cal.Code.

The defendants are granted thirty days in which to file responsive pleadings to the issues raised by the Complaints other than liability.

Comment

The Complaints are in the usual form. They sufficiently apprise the defendants of the claim against them (Rule 8, Federal Rules of Civil Procedure; Fed.Rules Civ.Proc. Official Form 17, 28 U.S.C.A.; see, Sidebotham v. Robison, 9 Cir., 1955, 216 F.2d 816, 830-831). As the Complaints in both cases are against so-called 'seller defendants', they are in a better position than plaintiff to know in greater detail what, if any, of the musical compositions they have sold.

As to the main issue, liability, the Court adheres to the position stated in the prior opinion in Harms, Inc., v. Tops Music Enterprises, D.C.Cal., 1958, 160 F.Sipp. 77. The Court is of the view that Shapiro, Bernstein & Co. v. Goody, 2 Cir., 1957, 248 F.2d 260, correctly expresses the law that persons who sell and distribute records of pirated songs are liable in an independent action under the Copyright Law. The Court chooses to follow that decision rather than the decision on that point in the District Court in the same case. Miller v. Goody, D.C.N.Y.1956, 139 F.Supp. 176. The decision of the Court of Appeals has, at least, the implicit approval of the Supreme Court which, on March 3, 1958, denied certiorari. See, Goody v. Shapiro, Bernstein & Co., Inc., 1958, 355 U.S. 592, 78 S.Ct. 536, 2 L.Ed.2d 529. The argument presented at the hearing that by allowing suit to be brought against manufacturers, the owners of the copyright may be allowed to recover more than the minimum royalty under 17 U.S.C.A. § 101(b) or, even more than the profit that the dealers made, was answered by the Supreme Court in an identical case involving one of the defendants in this case.

In F. W. Woolworth Co. v. Contemporary Arts, 1952, 344 U.S. 228, 73 S.Ct. 222, 97 L.Ed. 276, an award of damages in the amount of $ 5,000 for infringement of copyright on a work of art entitled 'Cocker-Spaniel in Show Position' and statutory attorney's fees of $ 2,000 were granted. Woolworth had purchased the statuettes from another source than the respondent who was the assignee of the copyright. Disposing of the question of liability, the Court said:

'Unbeknown to Woolworth, these dogs had been copied from respondent's and by marketing them it became an infringer.' 344 U.S. at page 229, 73 S.Ct. at page 223. (Emphasis added.)

To the contention that the 'seller' was being held to a measure of liability which greatly exceeded the gross profits which were alleged to have been only $ 899.16, the Court made this answer:

'Moreover, a rule of liability which merely takes away the profits from an infringement would offer little discouragement to infringers. It would fall short of an effective sanction for enforcement of the copyright policy. The statutory rule, formulated after long experience, not merely compels restitution of profit and reparation for injury, but also is designed to discourage wrongful conduct. The discretion of the court is wide enough to permit a resort to statutory damages for such purposes. Even for uninjurious and unprofitable invasions of copyright the court may, if it deems it just, impose a liability within statutory limits to sanction and vindicate the statutory policy. * * * We think that the statute empowers the trial court in its sound exercise of judicial discretion to determine whether on all the facts a recovery upon proven profits and damages or one estimated within the statutory limits is more just. We find no abuse of that discretion.' 344 U.S. at pages 233-234, 73 S.Ct. at page 225.

This decision quite clearly, considering infringement by a seller to be a tort, gives to the copyright owner, under statutory mandate, a measure of damages greater than the mere licensing fee to which the proprietor of the copyright would have been entitled, had a license been sought. This and later cases decided both under the old and the new statutes recognize a discretion in the courts to determine damages within the maximum and minimum statutory limits, as the Court's sense of justice may determine. (See, L. A. Westermann Co. v. Dispatch Printing Co. 249 U.S. 100, 106-109, 39 S.Ct. 194, 63 L.Ed. 499; Markham v. A. E. Borden Co., 1955, 1 Cir., 221 F.2d 586, 587)

The view thus expressed finds pragmatic support in the fact that the authorized recorder cannot sue, ordinarily, although, in addition to payment of royalties to copyright owners and to recording artists, he may be required, as a condition of recording, to make payment of various trust funds for the benefit of musicians and performers. (See Note, Copyright, 'Neighboring Right', 1958, 43 Cornell Law Quarterly, 476, 484-485)

By recognizing the right to recovery from 'sellers', these decisions aid copyright protection. So I can find no validity in the argument that a distinction be drawn between the 'manufacturers' cases and the 'sellers' cases, or that the trial of the 'sellers' cases be deferred until the 'manufacturers' cases are decided.

As to the motion for summary judgment, I adhere to what I said in the prior opinion in the companion case. Harms, Inc., v. Tops Music Enterprises, Inc., supra, 160 F.Supp. at page 85. A restudy of the affidavits leads me to the conclusion that there is no issue as to liability. For the documents before the court show clearly (1) title of the plaintiff to the songs; (2) liability for unauthorized use through the sale by these defendants of records published, without permission of the copyright owners, by Tops Music Enterprises, Inc.

There is also evidence in the affidavits that Tops Music Enterprises, Inc., which produced these unauthorized records, following the decision in Shapiro, Bernstein & Co. v. Goody, supra, entered into an agreement to indemnify the stores which purchased and sold the records. So there is absent even the argument of lack of knowledge pleaded in F. W. Woolworth v. Contemporary Arts, supra, and which the Supreme Court rejected in a brief paragraph which has already been quoted. And the 'seller' defendants are represented by the 'manufacturers' attorneys. So there is evidently no conflict of interest.

Hence the rulings above made.

PRESTIGE FLORAL, SOCIETE ANONYME, A. E. DeCamp and A. J. Fristot,
Plaintiffs,

v.

CALIFORNIA ARTIFICIAL FLOWER COMPANY, (Inc.) and Calart (Inc.),
Defendants

UNITED STATES DISTRICT COURT FOR THE SOUTHERN DISTRICT OF NEW YORK

201 F. Supp. 287

January 5, 1962

Kane, Dalsimer & Kane, New York City, for plaintiffs, Philip Dalsimer, and John Kurucz, New York City, of counsel.

Barlow & Barlow, Providence, R.I., Herbert B. Barlow, Jr., Providence, R.I., of counsel, and Keith, Bolger, Isner & Byrne, New York City, for defendants, Thomas J. Byrne, Jr., New York City, of counsel.

Judge Feinberg

OPINION

This is a motion for a preliminary injunction. Plaintiff Prestige Floral, Societe Anonyme, ('Prestige') filed its complaint on June 22, 1961, alleging copyright infringement under 17 U.S.C. § 101 and seeking a permanent injunction, damages, and other relief. Jurisdiction is vested in this Court by 17 U.S.C. § 112 and 28 U.S.C. § 1338. The article allegedly infringed is a molded polyethylene flower in the form of a Charles lilac.[1]

---

[1] The complaint also included a second count for infringement of a copyrighted

Defendant California Artificial Flower Company (Inc.) ('California') is a Rhode Island corporation and defendant Calart (Inc.) is a New York corporation. Both defendants have an office and a place of business at 225 Fifth Avenue, New York City. Defendants filed their answer on July 10, 1961. Beginning early in August 1961, settlement discussions were held intermittently. These proved abortive and on October 30, 1961, plaintiff noticed its motion for a preliminary injunction returnable on November 14, 1961. Thereafter, affidavits were submitted to the Court by plaintiff Prestige and by defendants. In addition, a hearing was held on December 11, 1961,[2] at which various exhibits were introduced and three witnesses testified: Donald A. Paulsen, an officer of D. Arnold Associates, exclusive distributor in this country for Prestige's artificial flowers; Edward R. Hughes, an expert on thermoplastic materials and molding; and Michele D'Agnillo, the principal of defendant corporations. From the affidavits, the exhibits, and the testimony of witnesses, and giving effect to my judgment as to the credibility of the witnesses where appropriate, I find the facts as hereinafter set forth.

Prestige is a French corporation engaged in designing, creating and manufacturing molded polyethylene flowers. Prestige has pioneered in the artificial flower field and enjoys a reputation for products of high quality and as a leader in the creation of new styles. Prestige created as an original work of art a sculptured lilac, made out of polyethylene, and first published this work on or about September 19, 1959. On or about September 22, 1960, a replica of the lilac was deposited by Prestige with the Copyright Office together with its application for copyright registration of the article as a sculpture, Class G. Thereafter, copyright registration No. Gp 25925 was issued.

Prestige's copyright lilac has at all times since publication had the copyright notice 'PRESTIGE FLORAL' molded on the long stem of the lilac near its base and on the underside of one of its leaves. A new version of the lilac was introduced into this country in the spring of 1961. This flower had similar copyright notices on the stem and leaf. The later version

---

artificial geranium. Plaintiffs on this second cause of action are A. E. DeCamp and A. J. Fristot. At the hearing on the preliminary injunction, defendants stipulated to entry of a preliminary injunction with regard to the geranium, reserving their rights for trial on the suit for a permanent injunction.

[2] In the few weeks prior to the hearing there were conferences between the Court and counsel regarding procedural matters and the practicality of getting testimony from a witness in France. Proposed findings of fact and conclusions of law were to be submitted by December 18, 1961; the date was later advanced to December 21, 1961.

of the lilac differed from the original only by the inclusion of additional foliage on the main stem and is sufficiently similar to the earlier model to be covered by copyright registration No. Gp 25925.

Defendant California is well known in the artificial flower market offering a line of over seven hundred flowers and fruits. Some of its items are made in Rhode Island and others are imported. Defendants have offered for sale and sold artificial lilacs which Prestige claims infringe its copyright. The allegedly infringing lilacs were imported by defendant from a company in Hong Kong which admits making a copy of another artificial flower of French origin. Prior to ordering the lilacs from Hong Kong, defendants had knowledge of Prestige's lilac and, in fact, had tried to order a small supply of them early in January 1961 from Prestige's distributor in New York. Copying of artificial flowers in Hong Kong is well known in the trade.

Artificial lilacs are a seasonable item in greatest demand during the early spring. The season for lilacs begins in January and lasts through Easter. In November and December most wholesalers will decide which items they will carry during the spring season. Prestige's exclusive distributor in this country has conditioned its acceptance of Prestige's lilacs on Prestige's success in stopping the importation of 'pirated duplicates * * * from Hong Kong.' If this is not stopped, the distributor reserves the right to cancel its order. The lilac sold by defendants is offered at a price substantially lower than that of the Prestige lilac.

I

It is settled in copyright infringement cases that a preliminary injunction should issue when the plaintiff makes a prima facie showing that his copyright is valid and that the defendant has infringed. H. M. Kolbe Co. v. Armgus Textile Co., 279 F.2d 555 (2 Cir. 1960); Houghton Mifflin Co. v. Stackpole Sons, Inc., 104 F.2d 306, 307 (2 Cir.) cert. denied 308 U.S. 597, 60 S.Ct. 131, 84 L.Ed. 499 (1939); Trifari, Krussman & Fishel, Inc. v. Charel Co., 134 F.Supp. 551, 554 (S.D.N.Y.1955).

Initially, defendants have raised several questions as to the validity of plaintiff's copyright. First, they attack the copyright generally, claiming that there is not sufficient artistry in the creation of artificial flowers to justify copyright protection. Second, they raise various narrower objections to the copyright, including claims that the copyright notice on plaintiff's flowers was defective and that plaintiff has not produced a specimen of the alleged copyrighted lilac.

In connection with the broad attack on the copyright, 17 U.S.C. § 4 provides:

'The works for which copyright may be secured under this title shall include all the writings of an author.'

17 U.S.C. § 5 provides that the application for registration shall specify to which of various enumerated classes the work in which copyright is claimed belongs. Plaintiff's application specified Class G, covering works of art, as the applicable class.[3] The basic question, therefore, is whether plaintiff's artificial flower is copyrightable as a work of art.

A recent comprehensive report of the Register of Copyrights[4] summarized pertinent court decisions on copyrightability as follows:

'It is well established, by a long line of court decisions, that in order to be copyrightable under the statute a work must meet the following requirements:

'(a) The work must be in the form of a 'writing,' i.e., it must be fixed in some tangible form from which the work can be reproduced.

'(b) The work must be a product of original creative authorship. Two interrelated elements are involved here: originality and creativity.

'(1) The work must be original in the sense that the author produced it by his own intellectual effort, as distinguished from merely copying a preexisting work. It need not be novel (as a patentable invention must be); in theory at least, it could be precisely the same as a preexisting work as long as it was created by the author independently.

'(2) The work must represent an appreciable amount of creative authorship.'[5]

The parties have not cited any cases involving artificial flowers. However, there are closely analogous situations which indicate that plaintiff's artificial flower may properly be the subject of a copyright. In Peter Pan Fabrics, Inc. v. Candy Frocks, Inc., 187 F.Supp. 334 (S.D.N.Y.1960), this Court granted a preliminary injunction in an infringement action where the copyrighted work of art was a floral design for a dress fabric. The Court pointed out (at 187 F.Supp. 336) that 'Obviously, floral patterns are in the public domain, but plaintiff has contributed enough originality in the designs to qualify them as distinguishable variations.'[6] Similarly, in F. W. Woolworth Co. v.

---

[3] The statutory description of the class in 17 U.S.C. § 5(g) is 'Works of art; models or designs for works of art.' See 37 C.F.R. § 202.10.

[4] Copyright Law Revision, House Comm. on the Judiciary, 87th Cong., 1st Sess. (Comm.Print 1961). This report is the culmination of a program of scholarly studies by the Copyright Office preparatory to a general revision of the copyright law.

[5] Ibid, p. 9.

[6] In Scarves by Vera, Inc. v. United Merchants & Mfgrs., Inc., 173 F.Supp. 625, 627

Contemporary Arts, Inc., 193 F.2d 162 (1 Cir.1951), aff'd 344 U.S. 228, 73 S.Ct. 222, 97 L.Ed. 276 (1952), copyright protection was afforded to statutes of a '**Cocker spaniel** in Show Position' sold commercially. In its opinion, the Court of Appeals for the First Circuit said (193 F.2d at 164):

'It is the well established rule that a copyright on a work of art does not protect a subject, but only the treatment of a subject. * * * The proposition was elaborated by Mr. Justice Holmes in Bleistein v. Donaldson Lithographing Co. * * * wherein with respect to cromolithographs of a circus scene prepared for advertising purposes he said: 'But even if they had been drawn from the life, that fact would not deprive them of protection. The opposite proposition would mean that a portrait by Velasquez or Whistler was common property because others might try their hand on the same fact. Others are free to copy the original. They are not free to copy the copy. * * * The copy is the personal reaction of an individual upon nature. Personality always contains something unique. It expresses its singularity even in handwriting, and a very modest grade of art has in it something irreducible, which is one man's alone. That something he may copyright * * *.' Here the 'something irreducible' * * * was shape. * * * It means the proportion, form, contour, configuration, and conformation, perhaps the latter in details too subtle for appreciation by anyone but a fancier, of the dog represented by the sculptured work of art.'

In Mazer v. Stein, 347 U.S. 201, 74 S.Ct. 460, 98 L.Ed. 630 (1954), the question raised was whether statuettes used as bases for electric lamps were protected by the copyright of the original models. The statuettes were of Balinese dancers. The Supreme Court held that use in industry would not bar or invalidate the copyrights.

One of the studies upon which the Report of the Register of Copyrights, supra, was based pointed out the following on the recent trend in copyrighting three-dimensional objects:

'The courts in recent years, particularly since Mazer v. Stein, are beginning to realize the validity of the copyright approach and are gradually overcoming their hesitation to hold, expressly or impliedly, that a three-dimensional object is a 'writing.' Perhaps the Copyright Office anticipated this development by changing its regulation with regard to the definition of the term 'work of art.' Prior to 1949 three-dimensional objects, intended primarily for commercial use, were not ordinarily granted registration. On the contrary, applicants were advised that 'protection of productions of the industrial arts, utilitarian in purpose and character, even if artistically made

---

(S.D.N.Y.1959), this Court noted that 'Obviously, fish, sailor suits and ice cream parlor trappings are in the public domain,' but silk screen paintings of these subjects used in the manufacture of blouse materials were protected.

or ornamented, depends upon action under the patent law.' However, in 1949 section 202.8 of the Regulations was changed so as to make registrable the artistic features of jewelry, enamel, glassware, tapestries, and other similar materials. Such registration was to cover only the artistic aspects, as distinguished from 'the mechanical or utilitarian' aspects. When the validity of this regulation was challenged in Mazer v. Stein, the Register of Copyrights, as amicus curiae, took the position that the new regulation actually reflected the previous practice of the Office. The brief said in this regard -- that the Copyright Office has consistently since 1909 -- and even before then -- registered works like the one in this case following the clearly stated mandate of Congress.

'In August, 1956, the Copyright Office issued regulations which, in greater detail than ever before, explicitly describe what can be registered. These regulations do not talk in terms of 'writings' but do require that any object offered for registration meet at least minimal standards of originality and creativity, as well as fall within one of the classes enumerated in section 5 of the copyright statute.'[7]

Applying these principles and analogous decisions to the instant case, it would seem that though a flower, like a dog, is a creation of nature, a likeness of it may be copyrighted. This conclusion seems particularly justified when the creation of the likeness involves, in the words of the Woolworth case, supra, numerous and detailed decisions as to 'proportion, form, contour, configuration, and conformation.' Plaintiff's expert testified at length as to the 'series of determinations' that had to be made by the creator of plaintiff's artificial flowers. Since plaintiff's lilac reflects originality and a substantial degree of skill and independent judgment, it is a proper subject for copyright. Mazer v. Stein, supra; Alfred Bell & Co. v. Catalda Fine Arts, 191 F.2d 99 (2 Cir.1951).

II

Defendants also press narrower objections to the copyright notice. Defendants first contend that the notices are insufficient because they cannot be seen by the naked eye. The notice on the stem though is clearly visible to the naked eye. The notice on the leaf, however, is considerably more difficult to make out. That it is on the underside of a leaf would not of itself seem objectionable. Coventry Ware, Inc. v. Reliance Picture Frame

---

[7] Study No. 3, The Meaning of 'Writings' in the Copyright Clause of the Constitution, pp. 100-101, Subcommittee on Patents, Trademarks, and Copyrights, Senate Committee on the Judiciary, 86th Cong., 1st Sess. (Comm.Print 1960); also published as Note, 31 N.Y.U.L.Rev.1263, 1303 (1956).

Co., 288 F.2d 193, 195 (2 Cir.) cert. denied 368 U.S. 818, 82 S.Ct. 34, 7 L.Ed.2d 24 (1961); Scarves by Vera, Inc. v. United Merchants & Mfgrs., Inc., supra. The notice can be seen by the naked eye although 'close examination is required to locate it.' Trifari, Krussman & Fishel, Inc. v. Charel Co., supra. Even if this were not so, I find from the affidavits and evidence before me that plaintiff has made a prima facie case that, before engaging in the sale of their lilacs, defendants had actual notice of plaintiff's copyright. Under these circumstances, I do not believe that difficulty in discerning the notice on the leaf should of itself prevent the granting of a preliminary injunction if plaintiff is otherwise entitled to it. Trifari, Krussman & Fishel, Inc. v. B. Steinberg-Kaslo Co., 144 F.Supp. 577, 581 (S.D.N.Y.1956); accord, Peter Pan Fabrics, Inc. v. Martin Weiner Corp., 274 F.2d 487, 490 (2 Cir.1960).

Second, defendants urge that '* * * there is a strong possibility that the copyright here in suit is invalid because of a postdated notice thereby claiming a date a year too late, and thereby claiming a year more for monopoly. * * *' It should be noted that although apparently no date was necessary on plaintiff's flower, Fleischer Studios v. Ralph A. Freundlich, Inc., 73 F.2d 276, 278 (2 Cir.1934) the legend 'MOD. DEPOSE 1961' did appear on the stem of plaintiff's later lilac,[8] although the publication date was 1959.[9] Defendants cite in support of their position Baker v. Taylor, 2

---

[8] On plaintiff's Exhibit D (the earlier model) the notice appears on the stem in the following form:
PRESTIGE FLORAL 1959 MOD. DEPOSE and on the underside of a leaf in the following form:
PRESTIGE FLORAL 1959 MODELE DEPOSE
On Plaintiff's Exhibit C (the later model), the notice appears on the stem in the following form:
PRESTIGE FLORAL MOD. DEPOSE 1961
and on the underside of a leaf in the following form:
PRESTIGE FLORAL 1959 MODELE DEPOSE

[9] Defendants also contend in submitting proposed finding of fact No. 4 that plaintiff admitted that its earlier lilac was on sale in 1958, one year prior to the date of publication stated in the Certificate of Registration (plaintiff's Exhibit A at the hearing). This is apparently based upon a statement by Mr. Paulsen on December 11, 1961, that plaintiff's earlier lilac was introduced into this country 'approximately 3 years ago.' (Tr., p. 13) However, on cross-examination, Mr. Paulsen indicated that the first items received from Prestige Floral were 'extremely close to the date of the copyright.' (Tr., p. 35), by which I assume he meant September 1959, and I find that plaintiff has made a prima facie case that the date of publication was actually 1959, not 1958. Cf. also 17 U.S.C. § 209, 210 to the effect that the statement in

Fed.Cas. 478, No. 782 (C.C.S.D.N.Y.1848) and American Code Co. v. Bensinger, 282 Fed. 829, 836 (2 Cir.1922). While it may be possible to limit the effect of these cases,[10] it would seem that they are inapplicable on the facts of the instant case. Defendants do not contend that the notice on the leaf was inaccurate although, as noted, they claim it is not sufficiently legible. Since the notice on the leaf and the notice on the steam differ as to date, this may be confusing. But I do not believe that plaintiff's copyright notice is thereby rendered so affirmatively misleading as to justify invalidating the copyright. The decisions upon which defendants rely require at least this likelihood. National Comics Publications v. Fawcett Publications, 191 F.2d 594, 602 (2 Cir.1951). Further, I do not find on the record now before the Court that defendants were in fact misled.

Defendants also argue that plaintiff did not produce a specimen of the lilac filed in the Copyright Office, and that plaintiff has failed to prove exactly what is covered by its copyright. On the affidavits and evidence before me, however, I feel this contention is incorrect and that plaintiff has made a prima facie showing. The affidavits submitted include one by plaintiff's trial counsel that he personally supervised the application for the copyright registration and submitted a three-dimensional replica of the copyrighted work. While it is true that the Copyright Office has been unable to locate the deposited work in its files, the affidavit of plaintiff's counsel, the colloquy in Court between respective counsel and the stipulation thereon[11] and the testimony of Mr. Paulsen[12] all support the conclusion that the lilacs produced in Court by plaintiff are specimens of what was copyrighted.

---

plaintiff's Certificate of Registration is 'prima facie evidence of the facts stated therein.'

[10] In Baker v. Taylor, there was more than a mistake, because plaintiffs there knew of the error before publication and did not trouble to correct it; the statement in Bensinger is a dictum. See Heim v. Universal Pictures Co., 154 F.2d 480, 490 (2 Cir. 1946), indicating that these cases still represent the law; but cf. Peter Pan Fabrics, Inc. v. Martin Weiner Corp., supra, 274 F.2d 490; Ziegelheim v. Flohr, 119 F.Supp. 324, 328 (S.D.N.Y.1954); Trifari, Krussman & Fishel, Inc. v. B. Steinberg-Kaslo Co., supra, 144 F.Supp. 581.

[11] Tr., pp. 11-12.

[12] Tr., pp. 13-15, 35.

III

In addition to validity of the copyright, it is, of course, essential for plaintiff to make a prima facie case of infringement. I find from the affidavits and evidence that defendants had access to the copyrighted lilac. Arc Music Corp. v. Lee, 296 F.2d 186 (2 Cir.1961). Also, plaintiff's expert testified at length about the similarity between plaintiff's and defendants' lilacs and the extreme unlikelihood that such similarity was brought about by chance. It is true that the test for copying cannot be stated with precision. Thus, in Peter Pan Fabrics, Inc. v. Martin Weiner Corp., supra, 274 F.2d at 489, Judge Learned Hand stated:

'The test for infringement of a copyright is of necessity vague. In the case of verbal 'works' it is well settled that although the 'proprietor's' monopoly extends beyond an exact reproduction of the words, there can be no copyright in the 'ideas' disclosed but only in their 'expression.' Obviously, no principle can be stated as to when an imitator has gone beyond copying the 'ideas,' and has borrowed its 'expression.' Decisions must therefore inevitably be ad hoc. In the case of designs, which are addressed to the aesthetic sensibilities of an observer, the test is, if possible, even more intangible. No one disputes that the copyright extends beyond a photographic reproduction of the design, but one cannot say how far an imitator must depart from an undeviating reproduction to escape infringement. In deciding that question one should consider the uses for which the design is intended, especially the scrutiny that observers will give to it as used. * * * However, the ordinary observer, unless he set out to detect the disparities, would be disposed to overlook them, and regard their aesthetic appeal as the same.'

Applying the test which rests on the intended use of the copyrighted article, and basing my conclusion upon the affidavits and evidence before me and on my own comparison of the flowers, I find that the allegedly infringing lilacs are copies of plaintiff's lilac and that the claimed variations between them do not sufficiently differentiate them.

Defendants have also contended that plaintiff has not shown sufficient likelihood of immediate irreparable injury to justify the granting of a preliminary injunction. While no detailed proof of such harm is required on this motion, Rushton v. Vitale, 218 F.2d 434, 436 (2 Cir.1955), plaintiff has made out a prima facie case -- and I do so find -- that unless afforded preliminary relief, it will suffer immediate substantial and irreparable injury.[13]

---

[13] See Peter Pan Fabrics, Inc. v. Brenda Fabrics, Inc., 169 F.Supp. 142 (S.D.N.Y.1959).

Therefore, for the reasons set forth above, I conclude that plaintiff has made a prima facie case that it has validly copyrighted the artificial flower in issue, that defendants have been selling or offering for sale lilacs copied from plaintiff's lilac, that this infringes plaintiff's copyright, that defendants' various contentions are lacking in merit, and that plaintiff will suffer immediate irreparable injury unless granted preliminary relief. Consequently, plaintiff's motion for a preliminary injunction should be and hereby is granted as to both defendants.

Settle order on notice on the first cause of action. The findings and conclusions required by Rule 52(a), Fed.Rules Civ.Proc., 28 U.S.C., are contained in this opinion. Plaintiff must furnish security in the amount of $ 10,000 to defendants.

BLAZON, INC.,
Plaintiff,

v.

DeLUXE GAME CORP.,
Defendant

No. 65 Civ. 697

UNITED STATES DISTRICT COURT
FOR THE SOUTHERN DISTRICT OF NEW YORK

268 F. Supp. 416

May 11, 1965

Davis, Hoxie, Faithfull & Hapgood, New York, New York, Ely, Goldrick & Flynn, Cleveland, Ohio, Albert L. Ely, Jr., Cleveland, Ohio, of counsel, for plaintiff.

Arnold Fein, New York, New York, for defendant.

District Judge Tenney

MEMORANDUM OPINION

Plaintiff moves herein for a preliminary injunction to restrain defendant from further infringing plaintiff's copyrighted work. The complaint as drawn avers a cause of action for copyright infringement and for unfair competition. The alleged infringing item is defendant's hobby horse named "Thunder" which plaintiff asserts infringes upon its copyrighted hobby horse "War Cloud". Jurisdiction of this Court is invoked under Section 1338(a) and (b) of Title 28 of the United States Code (28 U.S.C. § 1338(a), (b) (1962).

Plaintiff's complaint is predicated on the assumption that the horse displayed in defendant's showroom and seized pursuant to a writ of seizure dated March 8, 1965, is the alleged infringing item. It is clear, however, that the seized and displayed item is in fact plaintiff's own horse, admittedly bought by defendant and displayed by it in its showroom.

It is further not disputed that defendant repainted plaintiff's item and in the process painted over the copyright notice, and, in addition, it appears that plaintiff's trademark was replaced with its own. While that much is not disputed, there is much dispute as to the reasons for defendant's actions, the use to which the item was put, and statements made by defendant's salesmen with respect to the item.

Insofar as the horse seized and displayed is concerned, it is clear that plaintiff cannot, based on that use of the item, ground an action for copyright infringement.

It is clear that before there can be infringement there must be both an averment and some proof of copying (Affiliated Enterprises, Inc. v. Gruber, 86 F.2d 958 (1st Cir. 1936); see Nimmer, Copyright § 137.1 (1963)), and as a matter of logic there can be no copying in the case at bar where the horse seized and alleged to copy "War Cloud" is in fact "War Cloud", nor is there an infringement upon any of plaintiff's other protected rights by reason of the display of the copyrighted work. For a full discussion of possible rights protected, see Appendix "A", hereto.

Furthermore, if it can be held that the display of "War Cloud" by defendant constituted a copying of "War Cloud" and/or a violation of any other rights, and therefore an infringement of the copyright, there is no showing of any harm, much less irreparable harm, by denying the motion for the injunction. While it cannot be doubted that after a prima facie showing is made by plaintiff of copyright validity and infringement, plaintiff need not make a detailed showing of danger of irreparable harm (Rushton Co. v. Vitale, 218 F.2d 434 (2d Cir. 1955)), nonetheless, as Professor Nimmer points out, "[the] Court may nevertheless deny a preliminary injunction if the plaintiff's damages appear to be trivial [Consumers Union of United States, Inc. v. Hobart Mfg. Co., 189 F. Supp. 275 (S.D.N.Y.1960)] * * * or possibly if the plaintiff fails to indicate a sufficient likelihood of immediate irreparable injury to satisfy the granting of such relief. [See Platt & Munk Co. Inc. v. Republic Graphics, Inc., 218 F. Supp. 262 (S.D.N.Y.1962), modified, 315 F.2d 847 (2d Cir. 1963)]". Nimmer, supra, § 157.2 at 698. In the case at bar the model of "War Cloud" that was displayed has been seized, and accordingly there can be no further infringement by its continued display. In addition, there is no indication nor averment by plaintiff that defendants will buy another "War Cloud" and display it in place of the seized horse.

However, if we broadly construe plaintiff's complaint, there can be read therein an alternative but more substantial allegation of copyright infringement. For plaintiff asserts that defendant's hobby horse "Thunder" infringes plaintiff's copyrighted horse "War Cloud" and this can be construed as averring that "Thunder", whether it be the horse seized by the Marshal, or the horse displayed in photographs furnished by defendant's counsel to the Court and to plaintiff, infringes on "War Cloud". It is admitted that the horse in the photographs was also on display in defendant's showrooms. Accordingly, we must now ascertain whether "Thunder" as portrayed in the picture is an infringing work.

Of necessity, the first item to be decided is the validity of plaintiff's copyright.

While defendant questions whether a hobby horse is entitled to copyright protection since all hobby horses flow from an effort to simulate real horses (Gurbst Affidavit, Mar. 29, 1965, at 12), it is no longer subject to dispute that statutes or models of animals or dolls are entitled to copyright protection, see e.g., F. W. Woolworth Co. v. Contemporary Arts, Inc., 193 F.2d 162 (1st Cir. 1951) (model of a dog in a "show" position); Rushton Co. v. Vitale, 218 F.2d 434 (2d Cir. 1955) (chimpanzee); Ideal Toy Corp. v. Adanta Novelties Corp., 223 F. Supp. 866 (S.D.N.Y.1963) ("Tammy" doll), and accordingly a model horse, per se, is copyrightable.

Plaintiff has annexed to his complaint the registration certificate covering "War Cloud". Section 209 of the Copyright Act (17 U.S.C. § 209 (1952)) provides that the registration certificate issued by the copyright office "shall be admitted in any court as prima facie evidence of the facts stated therein." This in effect means that a plaintiff, in a copyright infringement action based on a statutory copyright, is entitled to a prima facie presumption of originality since among the facts to be set forth in the certificate is a statement of the author of the work and "authorship presumptively connotes originality." Remick Music Corp. v. Interstate Hotel Co., 58 F. Supp. 523, 531 (D.Nebr.1944), aff'd, 157 F.2d 744 (8th Cir. 1946); see Drop Dead Co. v. S. C. Johnson & Son, Inc., 326 F.2d 87, 92 (9th Cir. 1963), cert. denied, 377 U.S. 907, 84 S. Ct. 1167, 12 L. Ed. 2d 177 (1964).

Defendant does not directly attack the originality of "War Cloud." At a number of points in the affidavits submitted in opposition to the motion, defendant does infer that perhaps "War Cloud" is based on one of its (defendant's) prior hobby horse models, "Flash". Thus, for example, in the Affidavit of Herbert Gurbst, Vice President of defendant corporation (dated March 25, 1965), he avers: "During the years 1963 to 1964 plaintiff has copied exactly from defendant and sold a number of lines of hobby horses. Plaintiff may very well have based its 'War Cloud' model, subject of this motion, on copies of defendant's models." Id. at 12.

At the hearing, defendant produced prior models of its hobby horse line and compared them with other models of plaintiff's line, attempting to show that plaintiff had on prior occasions copied its models from defendant's. However, no specific attempt was made demonstrating how by reason of the copying of these other models, plaintiff had copied "War Cloud" as well. A similar veiled inference appears at page 13 of the same

Gurbst Affidavit wherein he asserts that "[under] these circumstances [one of defendant's former employees having been hired by plaintiff] it is not surprising that plaintiff's 'War Cloud' has the characteristic appearance of defendant's 'Flash'. [1] (See Affidavit of Milton Henry, at page 3. "It is also immediately evident on visual inspection that plaintiff modeled its 'War Cloud' after defendant's 'Flash'.")

1

Is this a sufficient attack on the originality of "War Cloud"? I think not.

"[With] respect to the issue of plaintiff's originality upon introduction of the certificate of registration * * * the burden shifts to the defendant to prove that plaintiff copied from a prior source and hence was not original. Mere denial by the defendant, unsupported by evidence, is not sufficient to overcome the prima facie presumption of plaintiff's originality." Nimmer, supra, at § 139.2 at 602. And "[proof] that plaintiff copied from prior works should involve the same elements as are required to establish copying by the defendant, i.e., access and similarity." Id. at 602, n. 235.

The fact that plaintiff took a matter admittedly in the public domain, (i.e., a horse) does not in and of itself   preclude a finding of originality, since plaintiff may have added unique features to the horse, enlarged it and made it sufficiently dissimilar from defendant's horse as to render it copyrightable to plaintiff. See Doran v. Sunset House Distrib. Corp., 197 F. Supp. 940, 941 (S.D.Calif.1961), aff'd, 304 F.2d 251 (9th Cir. 1962) (Santa Claus); Alva Studios, Inc. v. Winninger, 177 F. Supp. 265 (S.D.N.Y.1959) (Replica of Rodin's "Hand of God" in a reduced size); and cases cited supra at 421.

In addition, the thrust of defendant's affidavits, while seemingly discussing originality, are directed more to the matter asserted in its counterclaim (i.e., that one of defendant's former employees transmitted trade secrets to plaintiff, which presumably assisted it in the production of "War Cloud" and that, accordingly, a trust should be impressed on plaintiff's copyright), rather than to an attack on the originality per se of "War Cloud" insofar as it relates to the question of copyright. Accordingly, the affidavits will be so construed on the instant motion.

Thus in view of the failure of proof by the defendant, and in view of the disposition of the within motion, for the purposes of the present proceeding the Court will assume the originality of "War Cloud" and that plaintiff's copyright is valid and subsisting.

---

[1] I might observe parenthentically that "War Cloud" has the characteristics of a real live horse, as well.

While copyright validity has thus been assumed, copyright infringement cannot also be assumed. Plaintiff must show copying to sustain his burden of proof. Direct evidence of copying is rarely available, since the cases are few wherein there is direct testimony by a witness that he saw defendant copying plaintiff's item. "Therefore copying is ordinarily established indirectly by the plaintiff's proof of access and substantial similarity." Nimmer, supra, § 141.2 at 613.

On the issue of access, it is admitted by defendant that it bought "War Cloud" and displayed it. However, there is no proof as to when "War Cloud" was bought and, more importantly, as to what stage of development "Thunder" was in when "War Cloud" was bought by defendant, allegedly to demonstrate merely how a hobby horse would look in defendant's unique frame, since the model of "Thunder" on display next to "War Cloud" was too heavy to be mounted in the frame.

On the other hand, plaintiff avers that it first published "War Cloud" on March 17, 1964, a full year prior to its display by defendant, and from this fact it may be presumed that, at any point in that year, defendant had an opportunity to view plaintiff's item. There is a conflict of authority as to the burden plaintiff must carry to show access. Some courts have defined access as the actual viewing and knowledge of work by the person who composed defendant's work. See Nimmer, supra, at § 142.1 n. 35, and cases cited therein. These cases reason that the opportunity to view creates an inference of access which in turn creates an inference of copying. Professor Nimmer, however, in his treatise, submits that the proper test to be applied, and the more just test in terms of plaintiff's burden of proof, is to regard a "reasonable opportunity to view as access in itself and not merely as creating an inference of access." Id. at 615 (see id. at n. 39.) In view of the latter more liberal test, I am of the opinion that access has prima facie been shown. Accordingly, we now proceed to the more substantial aspect of plaintiff's case, upon which it has not sustained its burden, namely, proof of substantial similarity. See, generally, Nimmer, supra § 143, and its subdivisions.

Defendant asserts, and it is uncontradicted, that it has not produced a hobby horse named "Thunder". The only thing that has been produced, as of this point, is a plaster model of "Thunder" weighing approximately one hundred pounds which, due to its size and weight, has not been produced in court.[2] It has, however, produced photographs of the plaster model.

---

[2] In view of that fact and of the other sharply disputed facts presented by the respective affidavits as to what transpired when counsel appeared before Judge Cannella, and what was said at the time the subpoena to produce the model in court was served, plaintiff's motion to cite defendant for contempt in failing to so produce the model cannot be decided on this disputed record. See Stringfellow v.

"War Cloud" was produced in court and the Court has in its possession photographs of "War Cloud" annexed to the writ of seizure.

In approaching the question of substantial similarity it must be borne in mind that the figure is a horse and that, accordingly, since both items are copies of horses, some similarity is inevitable. See Ideal Toy Corp. v. Adanta Novelties Corp., 223 F. Supp. 866, 868 (S.D.N.Y.1963).

It is a well established rule of law that a copyright on a work of art does not protect a subject (i.e., a horse) but only the treatment of a subject. See, e.g., Stephens v. Howells Sales Co., 16 F.2d 805, 808 (S.D.N.Y.1926). This proposition was elaborated by Justice Holmes in Bleistein v. Donaldson Lithographing Co., 188 U.S. 239, 249-250, 23 S. Ct. 298, 47 L. Ed. 460 (1903) wherein with respect to cromolithographs of a circus scene prepared for advertising purposes, he said:

"But even if they had been drawn from the life, that fact would not deprive them of protection. The opposite proposition would mean that a portrait by Velasquez or Whistler was common property because others might try their hand on the same face. Others are free to copy the original. They are not free to copy the copy. Blunt v. Patten; 2 Paine 397, 400. Fed.Cas.No.1,580. See Kelly v. Morris, L.R. 1 Eq. 697; Morris v. Wright, L.R. 5 Ch. 279. The copy is the personal reaction of an individual upon nature. Personality always contains something unique. It expresses its singularity even in handwriting, and a very modest grade of art has in it something irreducible, which is one man's alone. That something he may copyright * * *."

By reason of the fact that defendant has not as yet made any infringing items, save the plaster model, and the inability to produce it in court, I must weigh the question of similarity based on the photographs submitted. While Mr. Chapman, Treasurer of plaintiff corporation, in his affidavit in support of the motion (dated March 15, 1965) lists ten features common to both "War Cloud" and what he thought was "Thunder", it seems clear that he in fact was comparing "War Cloud" to the seized "War Cloud", for in his deposition, a part of which is set forth in defendant's brief at page 5, he states that he did not examine the plaster model of "Thunder" on display in defendant's showroom. In opposition, defendant sets forth some sixteen differences which it contends are substantial between "Thunder" and "War Cloud".

The closest case that I have been able to find raising a somewhat similar problem is F. W. Woolworth Co. v. Contemporary Arts, Inc., 193 F.2d 162 (1st Cir. 1951), wherein the copyrighted item was a model of a **cocker**

Haines, 309 F.2d 910 (2d Cir. 1962); 4 Barron & Holtzoff § 2428 at 387-88 (1951).

spaniel in a "show" position.

In that case, the Court took particular note of the proportion, form, contour, configuration and conformation of the model rather than the coloring and standard stylized position of a dog in that particular stance as being matters of importance insofar as the distinctness of the copyrighted item was concerned.

On the issue of infringement, the Court stated as follows:

"There is ample evidence in the record that the plaintiff's dog and the Woolworth one embody the identical intellectual or artistic conception of a dog of the breed involved in show attitude. Moreover, this evidence is strongly supported by visual comparison. It is true that a dog with short hair on the head, neck and upper two thirds of the body is represented in the plaintiff's statuettes, whereas the dog in the Woolworth model is represented as having long hair on the body and neck. This difference, however, is unimportant, for on ample evidence the court below found that the representation of long hair on the Woolworth model could readily have been accomplished, and was in fact accomplished, by etching in wavy lines on a plaster master model made from one of the plaintiff's plaster statuettes. What is highly, if not conclusively, significant of copying is the fact that the plaintiff's and the defendant's statuettes are identical in proportion, and so far as we can see with inexpert eyes in conformation, and furthermore the configuration of the curls and folds of the long hair represented on the under body and the feathering represented on the legs of the plaintiff's statuette are shown as asymmetrical, and the defendant's statuette shows the identical lack of symmetry in these respects. Thus there is ample evidence that one model was copied from the other." Id. at 165-166.

In addition, in that case there was expert testimony on the issue of conformation.

In contrast, in the case at bar, plaintiff has relied on affidavits rather than live proof. There has been no expert testimony. The comparison of the animals of necessity must be done on the basis of photographs. Plaintiff's affidavits highlighting the similarity between the hobby horses in fact set forth the similarity between two models of the same horse.

Does the Court have enough before it upon which to invoke the extraordinary remedy of a preliminary injunction? Bearing in mind the subject matter involved[3] and the fact that in this area the line dividing

---

[3] As was observed by Chief Judge Ryan in Alva Studios, Inc. v. Winninger, 177 F. Supp. 265, 267 (S.D.N.Y.1959): "Where the principal elements of design of plaintiff's copyrighted work and of defendant's allegedly infringing article are taken, as a common source, from an object in the public domain, mere resemblance will not justify a finding of infringement."

originality, similarity and copying is thin at best, I think not. See Ideal Toy Corp. v. Adanta Novelties Corp., 223 F. Supp. 866, 868 (S.D.N.Y.1963); cf., Ideal Toy Corp. v. Sayco Doll Corp., 302 F.2d 623, 625 (2d Cir. 1962) (Dissenting opinion per Clark, J.).

"The granting of a preliminary injunction 'is an exercise of a very far-reaching power, never to be indulged in except in a case clearly demanding it.' * * * 'It is a cardinal principle of equity jurisprudence that a preliminary injunction shall not issue in a doubtful case. Unless the court be convinced with reasonable certainty that the complainant must succeed at final hearing the writ should be denied.'" Nadya, Inc. v. Majestic Metal Specialties, Inc., 127 F. Supp. 467 (S.D.N.Y.1954).

Since I do not have sufficient information before me upon which to make the requisite findings, I am constrained to hold that plaintiff has not sustained its burden of proof and, accordingly, the motion for a preliminary injunction is denied.

I next proceed to plaintiff's claim of unfair competition.

Accepting the factual averments in the affidavits of plaintiff as true (as will be noted, infra, they are very hotly disputed), the following picture emerges.

Plaintiff asserts that defendant bought one of plaintiff's horses, painted it over thereby erasing plaintiff's copyright notice, changed the trademark thereon to defendant's trademark and thereafter displayed the horse in its showrooms and solicited orders on it, representing that the horses to be delivered were the same as the model displayed. [4] (Affidavit of Patrick J. Flaherty, Mar. 29, 1965.)

While the propriety of these actions, if proven, may be subject to question, they do not constitute unfair competition, and even assuming, arguendo, that such a cause of action were made out, the facts are so in dispute that the grant of a preliminary injunction under these circumstances would be an improper exercise of this Court's equity powers.

It appears that what is involved herein is a "reverse" palming-off situation. In the usual case a defendant presents its product in such a way as to give the impression that it is plaintiff's product, thus palming off its product as that of another. Midwest Plastics Corp. v. Protective Closures Co., 285 F.2d 747 (10th Cir. 1960). In the case at bar, defendant has reversed the sequence and palmed off plaintiff's product as its own. Is this

---

[4] 4 In its complaint, drawn on the theory that the seized "War Cloud" was really "Thunder", plaintiff averred that this seized model was being palmed off as plaintiff's, deceiving the public "into believing that the plagiarizing work is the copyrighted work." Complaint Para. 8. This theory has, of course, now been changed in the light of subsequently developed facts.

an actionable wrong?

It has now been definitively held by the Court of Appeals for this Circuit that state law (in this case New York law) governs an unfair competition claim resting upon the doctrine of pendent jurisdiction alone, as well as a claim resting both on pendent jurisdiction and diversity of citizenship. Flexitized, Inc. v. National Flexitized Corp., 335 F.2d 774, 780-781 (2d Cir. 1964).

In Pic Design Corp. v. Sterling Precision Corp., 231 F. Supp. 106 (S.D.N.Y.1964), defendant bought certain items from plaintiff through an intermediary, removed their identifying markings, replacing them with its own, and resold the items to the customer.[5] Id. at 113.

Chief Judge Ryan initially limited International News Service v. Associated Press, 248 U.S. 215, 235, 39 S. Ct. 68, 63 L. Ed. 211 (1918) to its particular facts, thereby following that line of authority which has been less than enthusiastic with the broad sweep of that decision.[6]

"It is to be noted, however, that the International News Service case has not been given the scope and effect such language [at page 235 of 248 U.S., 39 S. Ct. 68 and quoted at page 113 of Judge Ryan's decision] would seem to demand. Subsequent cases exhibit a lack of judicial enthusiasm for a full extension of this doctrine; e.g., Speedry Products Inc. v. Dri Mark Products, Inc., 2 Cir., 271 F.2d 646 (1959)." 231 F. Supp. at 113; see Handler, Product Simulation: A Right or a Wrong, 64 Colum.L.Rev. 1183 (1964).

Then, in reliance on Mastro Plastics Corp. v. Emenee Indus., Inc., 16 A.D.2d 420, 228 N.Y.S.2d 514, 517 (1st Dep't), aff'd without opinion, 12 N.Y.2d 826, 236 N.Y.S.2d 347, 187 N.E.2d 360 (1962), Chief Judge Ryan held that "[we] are unable to find any actionable wrong at common law under the facts of this case insofar as defendants' actions in purchasing items from plaintiff for resale are concerned." 231 F. Supp. at 114. [The Court then proceeded to discuss, on the facts presented, a possible violation of the Lanham Act, 15 U.S.C. § 1125(a) (1963).]

In the Mastro Plastics case, supra, the New York courts denied any common law right of action in a case where a defendant bought bongo

---

[5] 5 In the case at bar, however, defendant is only accused of using plaintiff's item as a display and sample and taking orders on it. There is no allegation that defendant is buying plaintiff's horses en masse and selling them to customers.

[6] 6 The International News Service case held actionable the defendant's issuing of plaintiff's news compilations as its own, thus applying the common law doctrine of unfair competition "to misappropriation as well as misrepresentation, to the selling of another's goods as one's own - to misappropriation of what equitably belongs to a competitor." Schechter Poultry Corp. v. United States, 295 U.S. 495, 532, 55 S. Ct. 837, 844, 79 L. Ed. 1570 (1935).

drums from plaintiff, removed plaintiff's trademarks and identifying characteristics, replaced them with its own and used them as a sample to the trade of its own brand of bongos. As is obvious, the facts are almost indistinguishable from those in the case at bar. The Court, in denying relief, held as follows:

"Title to these chattels which plaintiff had put on unrestricted general sale and for which defendant paid plaintiff's price had passed to defendant. By reason of such title defendant has as much right to sell and use them for the purposes of sale as it would an exact reproduction of the plaintiff's drums made by itself. A workable distinction between a right to use in the channels of trade an original to which title had been acquired and an exact reproduction is not easily drawn.

In removing the plaintiff's trade-mark from the chattels to which defendant had acquired title, defendant did precisely what it should have done to avoid unfair competition before using them as samples in trade, because, although its right to resell or use for the purposes of trade the drums made by plaintiff is clear, it had no such right to use the plaintiff's trade-mark in furtherance of its own trade or promotion (cf. Lanvin Parfums Inc. v. Le Dans, Ltd., 9 N.Y.2d 516, 215 N.Y.S.2d 257, 174 N.E.2d 920; Bourjois Sales Corp. v. Dorfman, 273 N.Y. 167, 7 N.E.2d 30, 110 A.L.R. 1411).

Placing its own trade-mark on the drums is quite a different thing from misusing the plaintiff's trade-mark. If defendant has the right to reproduce and sell reproductions of plaintiff's drums it had a correlative right to put its trade-mark on the chattel it proffered to the public; and, indeed, the reverse situation exists from that which would have occurred if the defendant had left plaintiff's trade-mark on the drums.

The use of its own trade-mark amounted to a representation that defendant and not the plaintiff stood behind the sample chattel and behind the chattels bought in reliance on the sample. This is the antithesis of palming off and the plaintiff demonstrates no actionable rights in the defendant's use of its own trade-mark on a product it bought to use in promoting its own products." Id. 228 N.Y.S.2d at 517.

On appeal, the Court of Appeals affirmed the lower court's decision but granted plaintiff leave to serve an amended complaint based on 15 U.S.C. § 1125(a) (1963) for a preliminary injunction.

While these decisions are persuasive, I would prefer to rest my denial of the motion not on the absence of a cause of action for unfair competition, but rather on an insufficiency of proof. In the Mastro case, for example, the Court's opinion was based in part on the fact that plaintiff had not secured a patent or copyright on the drums, and accordingly "[what] it [defendant] could thus reproduce [without fear of copyright or patent infringement] and sell it could use as samples of what it would produce and sell." 228 N.Y.S.2d at 516. Similarly, in the Pic case, supra, there was no discussion as to whether the items bought were covered by a patent.

In addition, in Midwest Plastics Corp v. Protective Closures Co., 285 F.2d 747 (10th Cir. 1960), cited above, one of the averments was that the defendants had bought quantities of the plaintiff's products and resold them to its customers. Id. at 749. And while the thrust of the opinion revolves around the normal palming-off situation, at least one of the cited cases involved reversed palming off, and the Court cited the following language in its opinion: "'Deceit is the basis of an action of this character. The principle underlying unfair trade practice cases is that one manufacturer or vendor is palming off his merchandise as that of another * * * or that he is vending the products of another as his own * * *.' Reynolds & Reynolds v. Norick, 10 Cir., 114 F.2d 278, 281." Id. at 750. See Pic Design Corp. v. Sterling Precision Corp., supra, 231 F. Supp. at 113.

Moreover, while International News Service v. Associated Press, 248 U.S. 215, 39 S. Ct. 68, 63 L. Ed. 211 (1918) has been limited, there is language therein particularly applicable to the instant case. 248 U.S. at 241-42, 39 S. Ct. 68. The scope of the wrong was similarly expressed in the opinion of Mr. Justice Holmes, who disagreed not as to the impropriety of the action nor as to the necessity of some relief, but rather as to the scope of the relief granted. 248 U.S. at 247, 39 S. Ct. 68. See also A. L. A. Schechter Poultry Corp. v. United States, 295 U.S. 495, 531-532, 55 S. Ct. 837, 79 L. Ed. 1570 (1935).

Accordingly, a review of the sharp conflict as to the facts is warranted.

Plaintiff's position, as set forth above, is that defendant's sales representative, one Irving Sircus, quoted prices on the seized "War Cloud" and was accepting orders on it. (See Affidavit of Patrick J. Flaherty, Mar. 29, 1965; Affidavit of Thomas E. Chapman, Mar. 29, 1965.)

In opposition, defendant submits the affidavit of Herbert Gurbst, its Vice President, wherein he asserts that "Defendant's plaster model of its 'Thunder' horse so displayed weighs approximately 100 pounds, much too heavy to be placed in the metal frames in which hobby horses usually weighing 10 to 15 pounds are displayed, sold and used by children. Such a weight might cause the frame to collapse. In any event, it would make it impossible to demonstrate the movement of defendant's hobby horse and its position in relation to the frame. * * * Defendant did not yet have a polyethylene sample of its 'Thunder' model for display but wished to be able to demonstrate the size and position of a polyethylene horse, the size of its 'Thunder' model and its position in defendant's unique frame." (Gurbst Affidavit, March 29, 1965, at 3-4.) Accordingly, the plaintiff's model "War Cloud" was purchased and painted over and was placed adjacent to the plaster model of "Thunder".

Gurbst further avers as follows:

"I was present during the Toy Fair and engaged in selling on behalf of defendant. I also conducted sales meetings and instructed defendant's sales personnel and was present during much of their selling. Prospective customers were shown defendant's plaster model and told that this was the hobby horse which defendant would manufacture and sell. The only reference made to the plaintiff's hobby horse modified and set in defendant's frame as aforesaid was to indicate to prospective customers the mode and manner in which defendant's horse would appear in the frame. * * *

* * * Plaintiff's horse modified by defendant for demonstration purposes was not offered for sale by defendant." Id. at 4-5.

Similarly, Irving Sircus, the individual who is accused of having taken the orders on "War Cloud" initially, asserted in his affidavit that he did not know Flaherty, to whom the representations were allegedly made, and did not meet him on the day alleged, and in support submits his appointment sheet for that date. He further averred that

"[in] accordance with the instructions of defendant's Vice President, Herbert S. Gurbst, at a sales meeting, the Saturday prior to March 3, 1965, in attempting to sell defendant's 'Thunder' model hobby horse, I demonstrated defendant's plaster model exhibited in defendant's showroom. I told the customers that this was the hobby horse which defendant would produce and sell.

The only reference I made to plaintiff's hobby horse 'War Cloud', exhibited nearby defendant's plaster model, in defendant's unique frame, was to say that defendant's horse would fit and ride in defendant's frame substantially in the same manner. At no time did I state that defendant was selling plaintiff's 'War Cloud' or that defendant's model was a 'knock-off' of plaintiff's 'War Cloud', as alleged by Mr. Flaherty. I did not say to anyone, in reference to plaintiff's horse, 'This is our new model - isn't it a beauty,' as asserted by Mr. Flaherty. Nor did I ever state to him or anyone else that plaintiff's horse was 'our new model' or 'our new horse.'

At all times, I made clear to the customers, and to all who questioned me, that the horse to be manufactured and sold by defendant was in its 'Thunder', to be modeled after the plaster model exhibited in the showroom." (Sircus Affidavit, April 9, 1965, 2-3.)

There is similar conflict as to whether the plaster model of "Thunder" was displayed adjacent to or even in the same area as "War Cloud". (Compare Chapman Affidavit, March 30, 1965, at 2, with Gurbst Affidavit, March 29, 1965, at 5.)

Based on the sharp conflict of facts in the affidavits, it is impossible to even attempt to ascertain whether, assuming that certain actions, if proved, would constitute actionable unfair competition, the horse was put to such an improper use. In view of this sharp conflict, I am unable to permit the invocation of the equity powers of this Court and permit the imposition of such a drastic remedy on such a minimal showing.

"Where sharp issues of fact are presented it is apparent that the case is not a fit one for preliminary relief and the resolution of the disputed issues must await trial. [Citing cases.]" Heyman v. Ar. Winarick, Inc., 166 F. Supp. 880, 883 (S.D.N.Y.1958); see General Elec. Co. v. American Wholesale Co., 235 F.2d 606, 608-609 (7th Cir. 1956).

Finally, plaintiff, in its supplemental memorandum of law, for the first time asserts a cause of action based on an alleged violation of Section 1125(a) of Title 15 of the United States Code (the Lanham Act) (15 U.S.C. § 1125(a) (1963)). In its complaint, plaintiff neither alleges that defendant violated this section nor even sets forth factual averments from which such violation can be inferred, though not specifically pleaded. Moreover, the "newly acquired facts" upon which plaintiff bases this assertion were known to it as of March 29, 1965, and no motion was made or attempted, though there surely was sufficient time to do so, to amend the complaint to add a cause of action for a violation of Section 1125(a). On that basis alone I would be disposed to deny its motion for a preliminary injunction predicated on a violation of that section.

However, even assuming arguendo that the complaint had been amended and the matters set forth in the supplemental memorandum of law incorporated therein, there would still be both an insufficiency of pleading and proof to warrant the issuance of a preliminary injunction.

Section 1125(a) of Title 15 of the United States Code in pertinent part provides:

(a) Any person who shall affix, apply, or annex, or use in connection with any goods * * * a false designation of origin * * * including words or other symbols tending falsely to describe or represent the same, and shall cause such goods or services to enter into commerce, and any person who shall with knowledge of the falsity of such designation of origin * * * cause or procure the same to be transported or used in commerce or deliver the same to any carrier to be transported or used, shall be liable to a civil action by any person * * * who believes that he is or is likely to be damaged by the use of any such false description or representation."

As is obvious from the language italicized in the above citation, the only actionable wrong proscribed by the statute is the false designation of origin of a product and the causing of its subsequent entry into interstate commerce.

The word "origin" has now been definitively held to refer not merely to geographical origin, but in addition, to origin of source or manufacture as well. Federal-Mogul-Bower Bearings, Inc. v. Azoff, 313 F.2d 405, 408 (6th Cir. 1963).

However, the requirement of the statute that the goods upon which the false designation appears must enter into interstate commerce is not to be lightly taken since it is jurisdictional in nature. Miles Lab., Inc. v. Frolich, 195 F. Supp. 256, 257-258 (S.D.Cal.), aff'd, 296 F.2d 740 (9th Cir. 1961) (Per curiam), cert. denied, 369 U.S. 865, 82 S. Ct. 1030, 8 L. Ed. 2d 84 (1962). See Mogul-Bower Bearings, Inc. v. Azoff, supra. Even causing one item with false designation to enter into commerce is sufficient. Drop Dead Co. v. S. C. Johnson & Son, Inc., 326 F.2d 87, 93 (9th Cir. 1963), cert. denied, 377 U.S. 907, 84 S. Ct. 1167, 12 L. Ed. 2d 177 (1964). But for pleading purposes there must at least be that minimal connection and, a fortiori, there must be some proof of such connection on a motion for a preliminary injunction.

The term "used in commerce" is defined in the statute as follows:

For the purposes of this chapter a mark shall be deemed to be used in commerce (a) on goods when it is placed in any manner on the goods or their containers or the displays associated therewith or on the tags or labels affixed thereto and the goods are sold or transported in commerce and (b) on services when it is used or displayed in the sale or advertising of services and the services are rendered in commerce, or the services are rendered in more than one State or in this and a foreign country and the person rendering the services is engaged in commerce in connection therewith.

In the case at bar the only allegation is that defendant replaced plaintiff's trademark with defendant's in violation of Section 1125(a) and that the horse was on display in defendant's showroom in New York. However, there is no averment herein that the seized "War Cloud" with the false designation entered into interstate commerce subsequent to the time that the trademark was changed. It is obvious that, having been seized, the article cannot now enter into interstate commerce. In short, even accepting all of plaintiff's assertions as true, there is no statement either express or implied that the seized "War Cloud" at any time was caused to enter into interstate commerce.

"There is no allegation that after the making of any misrepresentation in regard to the goods any of the defendants caused such goods to enter into commerce or transported or used them in commerce, even though an allegation of such subsequent connection of the goods with commerce is an essential element of the cause of action created by the Act. It is true that 'commerce' as used in the Act is defined broadly as 'all commerce which may lawfully be regulated by Congress.' 15 U.S.C.A. § 1127. This definition, though broad, is not all-inclusive. Business essentially local in nature is still outside the scope of its terms in the absence of some relationship to interstate commerce sufficient to bring it within the limits of Congressional power. The complaint does not allege such a relationship nor any facts nor circumstances from which such a relationship can be inferred."

Samson Crane Co. v. Union Nat'l Sales, Inc., 87 F. Supp. 218, 221 (D.Mass.1949), aff'd, 180 F.2d 896 (1st Cir. 1950) (Per curiam).

While, in the case at bar, the defendant company obviously deals in interstate commerce, it is the transportation of the item with the mark on it rather than the general scope of business which would appear to be determinative under the statute, and, as noted, the item itself has never entered into interstate commerce and was never transported therein.

Moreover, even if we were to construe the statute as applying to goods which, though not themselves individually having false designations, were sold and entered into commerce as a result of the intrastate display of the seized "War Cloud" with the false designation and therefore "affecting commerce", (see Drop Dead Co. v. S. C. Johnson & Son, Inc., 326 F.2d 87, 94 (9th Cir. 1963), cert. denied, 377 U.S. 907, 84 S. Ct. 1167, 12 L. Ed. 2d 177 (1964); Stauffer v. Exley, 184 F.2d 962, 966 (9th Cir. 1950); Mastro Plastics Corp. v. Emenee Indus, Inc., 14 N.Y.2d 498, 248 N.Y.S.2d 223, 197 N.E.2d 620 (1964); see also Aluminum Fabricating Co. of Pittsburgh v. Season-All Window Corp., 160 F. Supp. 41, 45-46 (S.D.N.Y.1957), aff'd, 259 F.2d 314 (2d Cir. 1958)) [7], an injunction could not issue thereon in view of the sharp conflict as to the use made of the horse. The same considerations necessitating the denial of an injunction on a claim of unfair competition apply here as well. (See 428, supra.)

---

[7] While Mastro, supra, presents a closely analogous problem, in that case there seemed to have been no dispute that sales were made and goods shipped in commerce as a result of the display of the item with false designation, whereas in the case at bar there is no such showing. In addition, as distinguished from Mastro, in the instant case there is no allegation that defendant's products were inferior in quality to plaintiff's, (see George O'Day Associates, Inc. v. Talman Corp., 206 F. Supp. 297, 300 (D.R.I.), aff'd sub nom. O'Day Corp. v. Talman Corp., 310 F.2d 623 (1st Cir. 1962), cert. denied, 372 U.S. 977, 83 S. Ct. 1112, 10 L. Ed. 2d 142 (1963)), an allegation which has been said to be the very essence of a Section 1125(a) Lanham Act violation. Note, Development in the Law, Competitive Torts, 77 Harv.L.Rev. 888, 907-08 (1964).

To be distinguished from the instant case is Pic Design Corp. v. Sterling Precision Corp., 231 F. Supp. 106 (S.D.N.Y.1964), relied upon so heavily by plaintiff, wherein there was proof, at a trial on the merits, that there had been an order by a customer and a receipt by him of one of plaintiff's items, shipped by defendant after the removal of all designation. In that case there was no question of sale, use in commerce, and/or a use "affecting commerce", whereas in the case at bar, aside from the unsupported and contradicted assertions of plaintiff, there is a total failure of proof on this critical point.

In summation, I find myself unable to issue an injunction on: (a) a claimed copyright infringement, by reason of an inability to determine the issue of similarity, i.e., insufficiency of proof; (b) unfair competition by reason of the sharply conflicting and contradictory factual averments in the affidavits of the respective parties; and (c) violation of the Lanham Act, by reason of an insufficiency of pleading and proof and the same conflict as to the facts noted in subdivision (b) above.

Accordingly, on the basis of the facts before me or the lack thereof, the motion for a preliminary injunction is denied.

In addition to its motions for a preliminary injunction, plaintiff also moves herein to dismiss defendant's amended conterclaim.

Rule 15(a) of the Federal Rules of Civil Procedure provides in part that "[a] party may amend his pleading once as a matter of course at any time before a responsive pleading is served * * *."

In the case at bar the summons and complaint for copyright infringement and unfair competition were served on March 8, 1965, and the answer and counterclaim were served by defendant's original counsel on March 12, 1965. Plaintiff moved to dismiss this counterclaim by a motion served on March 16, 1965.

Thereafter, different counsel were substituted by defendant, and the deposition of plaintiff's Treasurer was commenced. On March 26, 1965, an amended answer and counterclaim for unfair competition was served, within twenty days of the service of the summons and complaint.

Defendant was entitled to serve under the Rules an amended pleading as a matter of right prior to service by plaintiff of a responsive pleading, and no such responsive pleading has been filed. Plaintiff's motion to dismiss the counterclaim was not such a responsive pleading and thus did not terminate plaintiff's right to amend under Rule 15(a). Breier v. Northern California Bowling Proprietors' Ass'n, 316 F.2d 787, 789 (9th Cir. 1963) and cases cited therein.

Accordingly, I will now proceed to the merits of plaintiff's motion to dismiss, addressed to the amended counterclaim.

On a motion to dismiss, the averments of the pleading attacked must, of course, be accepted as true. 2 Moore, Federal Practice Para. 12.08 (2d ed. 1964).

The thrust of defendant's counterclaim is to impress a trust on plaintiff's copyright by reason of the appropriation from defendant of valuable trade secrets which enabled plaintiff to produce the copyrighted "War Cloud".

"The hobby horse body copyrighted by plaintiff was created as a result of plaintiff's misappropriation of defendant's trade secrets in conspiracy with defendant's former employee, Kovacs, who, while in defendant's employ, participated in the creation of the design of the hobby horse copyrighted by plaintiff and reproduced those designs for plaintiff and revealed other of defendant's designs and trade secrets." (Defendant's Memorandum of Law at 9.) Defendant thus asserts that one of its employees, to whom were revealed many secret processes respecting the method, mode and sources of materials for molds and sculpting services, was induced by plaintiff to terminate his services with defendant, and to betray these secrets relating to design of hobby horses to plaintiff. These secrets included the "process of rotational casting embodying the use of powdered polyethylene [alleged to be] * * * unique in the manufacture of hobby horse bodies and [which] represented confidential information and a trade secret * * *." (Amended Answer Para. Ninth.) Similarly, in the second amended counterclaim, defendant alleges that by reason of the confidential nature of his (Kovacs') employment, defendant's President showed to him certain porcelain statues of horses, the features of which were to be embodied into the design of a hobby horse body, and that this information was also given to plaintiff by Kovacs and subsequently embodied in "War Cloud". By reason of all these acts, defendant seeks to impress a trust on plaintiff's copyrighted horse.

Insofar as the remedy is concerned, if plaintiff has a cause of action the imposition of a trust is one of the remedies which might be imposed. Colgate-Palmolive Co. v. Carter Prod., 230 F.2d 855, 865 (4th Cir.), cert. denied, 352 U.S. 843, 77 S. Ct. 43, 1 L. Ed. 2d 59 (1956).

Plaintiff, in its brief in opposition, admits the propriety of the claim insofar as it arises out of the same transaction or series of transactions as plaintiff's claim, thus being a proper counterclaim. (Plaintiff's Brief in support of motion to dismiss at page 7.) However, based on two recent Supreme Court decisions, Sears Roebuck & Co. v. Stiffel Co., 376 U.S. 225, 84 S. Ct. 784, 11 L. Ed. 2d 661 (1964), and Compco Corp. v. Day-Brite Lighting, Inc., 376 U.S. 234, 84 S. Ct. 779, 11 L. Ed. 2d 669 (1964), plaintiff asserts that defendant has not set out a claim upon which relief can be granted.

Plaintiff argues that "due to the failure of defendant to allege that defendant's alleged copied designs were patented or copyrighted (as they in fact are not) under Sears Roebuck and Co. v. Stiffel Co. * * * and Compco

Corp. v. Day-Brite Lighting, Inc. * * * plaintiff would have had a perfect right to copy such alleged designs * * *." (Plaintiff's Brief, supra, at page 3.)

The holdings of both cases is best summed up as follows:

"Today we have held in Sears, Roebuck & Co. v. Stiffel Co., (supra) that when an article is unprotected by a patent or a copyright, state law may not forbid others to copy that article. To forbid copying would interfere with the federal policy, found in Art. I, § 8, cl. 8, of the Constitution and in the implementing federal statutes, of allowing free access to copy whatever the federal patent and copyright laws leave in the public domain. Here Day-Brite's fixture has been held not to be entitled to a design or mechanical patent. Under the federal patent laws it is, therefore, in the public domain and can be copied in every detail by whoever pleases."

Compco Corp. v. Day-Brite Lighting, Inc., 376 U.S. at 237-238, 84 S. Ct. at 782.

What effect do these cases have on the trade secret doctrine?

In the very recent case of Titelock Carpet Strip Co. v. Klasner, 142 U.S.P.Q. 405 (Cal.Super.Ct. July 24, 1964), the defendant not only copied plaintiff's machine in "practically all details" (ibid.) but was a former employee who had gained access to the premises under the guise of seeking to purchase parts of plaintiff's machine as scrap, when in fact he intended to use these parts for purpose of reconstruction "and physically [appropriated] from the plaintiff's plant some of the parts which went into the assembling of the defendant's first machine." (Ibid.) Although acknowledging that "many hundreds of hours of effort" went into plaintiff's project before he had produced an economically effective machine and that the defendant had obtained "for free" the advantage of all of this experimental effort, cost and time expenditure, the plaintiff was left without relief aside from a $250. recovery, the cost of the misappropriated scrap parts. Citing Sears and Compco, supra, the Court held defendant's conduct "if a wrong" to be actionable only under the patent laws. Cf., Angell Elevator Lock Co. v. Manning, 348 Mass. 623, 205 N.E.2d 245, (Mass.Sup.Jud.Ct., March 2, 1965.)

In Servo Corp. of America v. General Elec. Co., 337 F.2d 716 (4th Cir. 1964), cert. denied, 383 U.S. 934, 15 L. Ed. 2d 851, 86 S. Ct. 1061 (1965), plaintiff corporation in its complaint sought recovery for infringement of three patents and for unjust enrichment. The Court of Appeals, on appeal, held the two patents involved in the appeal invalid, but nonetheless sustained a cause of action for unjust enrichment, based on improper appropriation of trade secrets by defendant.

It appears from the opinion that plaintiff corporation had a confidential relationship with the Southern Railway Company during plaintiff's installation and testing of its "hot box detector" on Southern's tracks in

Salisbury, North Carolina.

In breach of this confidental relationship, one of Southern's officers accompanied defendant's engineers to Salisbury where members of the party photographed the installation, brought back with them Southern's drawings of the installation, and examined a diagram of the installation made by plaintiff; and the court below confirmed the master's finding that defendant, as a result of the trip, "'gleaned and copied ideas belonging to Servo * * *.'" Id. at 722.

The Court of Appeals initially stated the traditional pre-Sears rule, that "where a holder of a trade secret imparts to another in confidence and that other person then appropriates it for his own use, equitable remedies may be invoked to remedy the wrong. That it is not necessary that the trade secret be covered by patent was made explicit by the early and oft-quoted case of Booth v. Stutz Motor Car Co. of America, 56 F.2d 962 (7 Cir. 1932)." Id. at 723.

The Court then distinguished Sears thusly:

"Because of the confidential relationship which was betrayed here by Southern, this case is distinguishable from Sears, Roebuck & Co. v. Stiffel Co., 376 U.S. 225, 84 S. Ct. 784, 11 L. Ed. 2d 661 (1964). In that case the action was grounded upon state law which gave a remedy for copying resulting in confusion as to the source of manufacture. In that case the Court held that a manufacturer whose design and mechanical patents are invalid for want of invention cannot under state unfair competition law obtain an injunction against copying its product, nor an award of damages for such copying, as such use of state law conflicts with the federal government's power to grant patents. The Court went on to hold that an unpatented article being in the public domain may be freely copied as the federal patent law had preempted the field from state action. This case, however, is one of unjust enrichment through breach of a confidential relationship, and the remedy is derived from the court's power to award general equitable relief. In Saco-Lowell Shops v. Reynolds, supra, [4 Cir.,] 141 F.2d [587] at page 598, we held:

'[Whether] the [inventor's ideas] were covered by patent or not, he was entitled to protection against their use by one to whom he had disclosed them in the course of a confidential relationship.'" Id. at 724-725.

After quoting the Restatement of Torts § 757(c) (1939) to reject the defendant's argument that the secrets were obtained not from plaintiff but from Southern, the Court held that "General Electric and Southern were in pari delicto and General Electric may not escape liability in a court of equity." Id. at 725.

The Court then stated:

"Several cases have held that a businessman who hires his rival's former employee and induces the employee to divulge the rival's trade secrets imparted in confidence may be required to respond in damages. A. O. Smith Corp. v. Petroleum Iron Works Co. of Ohio, 73 F.2d 531 (6 Cir. 1934). modified on another point, 74 F.2d 934 (6 Cir. 1935); Herold v. Herold China and pottery Co., 257 F. 911 (6 Cir. 1919). The facts here vary; the principle remains constant. General Electric learned that which it needed to know through Southern, and both parties knew that their concerted activities were in violation of the confidence reposed in Southern by Servo. Under the circumstances the plaintiff is entitled to recover of the defendant the reasonable value of the data acquired and utilized by it in unfair competition with the plaintiff. See International News Service v. Associated Press, 248 U.S. 215, 39 S. Ct. 68, 63 L. Ed. 211 (1918)." Ibid.

It is axiomatic that a pleading should not be dismissed if by any construction it states a claim upon which relief can be granted. See 2 Moore, Federal Practice Para. 12.08 (2d ed. 1964).

In view of the Servo decision, I am of the opinion that the amended counterclaim as drawn does state a claim upon which relief could be granted.

In addition, in view of the state of flux in which this area of the law is presently embroiled in light of the Sears and Compco decisions[8] I would be loath to dismiss a pleading until the exact guidelines of those decisions are definitively set.

In view of that fact, plaintiff's motion to dismiss the counterclaim is denied.

The motions are disposed of as noted herein.

So ordered.

---

[8] See, e.g., Symposium-Product Simulation: A Right or Wrong, 64 Colum.L.Rev. 1178 (1964) which includes articles by Daphine R. Leeds (id. at 1179), Milton Handler (id. at 1183), Walter J. Derenberg (id. at 1192), Ralph S. Brown (id. at 1216); Note, Unfair Competition Protection After Sears & Compco, 40 N.Y.U.L.Rev. 101, 108 nn. 66, 67 (1965).

Donald DAVIS, Plaintiff,

v.

E. I. DuPONT de NEMOURS
& COMPANY, Batten, Barton, Durstine & Osborn, Inc., Columbia Broadcasting System, Inc., Talent Associates, Ltd., David Susskind, Jacqueline Babbin and Audrey Gellen,
Defendants

UNITED STATES DISTRICT COURT
FOR THE SOUTHERN DISTRICT OF NEW YORK

249 F. Supp. 329

January 20, 1966

O'Brien, Driscoll & Raftery, New York, New York, for plaintiff; Paul D. O'Brien and Milton M. Rosenbloom, New York, New York, of counsel.

Coudert Brothers, New York, New York, for defendants; Carleton G. Eldridge, Jr., and Eugene L. Girden, Stephen S. Singer, New York, New York, of counsel.

FEINBERG, District Judge.

OPINION

This proceeding grows out of a 1960 telecast of "Ethan Frome," which was shown on 162 television stations. The court has already held that the telecast infringed plaintiff Donald Davis's copyright in a dramatization of Edith Wharton's classic novel. Davis v. E. I. DuPont de Nemours & Co., 240 F. Supp. 612 (S.D.N.Y.1965). The proceeding now to fix damages raises the ultimate issue of what damages would be "just" under the applicable section of the Copyright Act, 17 U.S.C.A. § 101(b).

Davis v. E. I. DuPont de Nemours & Co., supra, contains a full discussion of the tangled copyright history of various versions of "Ethan Frome," the abortive negotiations before the offending telecast and the nature of the copyright infringement. The findings set forth in that opinion will not be repeated but should be regarded as incorporated herein. The facts that should be singled out in this proceeding to fix damages are, briefly, as follows. Defendants are E. I. DuPont de Nemours & Company ("DuPont"), sponsor of the infringing telecast; Batten, Barton, Durstine & Osborn, Inc. ("BBDO"), DuPont's advertising agency; Columbia Broadcasting System, Inc. ("CBS"), the network over which the program was televised; Talent Associates, Ltd. ("Talent"), producer of the telecast; David Susskind ("Susskind"), the Talent officer in charge of the production; and Jacqueline Babbin ("Babbin") and Audrey Gellen ("Gellen"), Talent employees who prepared the script. The infringing telecast occurred on February 18, 1960, as "The DuPont Show of the Month" over the facilities of CBS. Not more than twenty per cent of the program was pre-recorded on video tape; the balance was broadcast live. In the two months prior to the telecast, plaintiff Davis formally notified defendants twice that if they went ahead with the proposed television performance of "Ethan Frome" without his consent, they would be committing a deliberate copyright infringement.

CBS transmitted the infringing program from New York over 162 stations each of which telecast the program to its own specific audience. Almost all of the stations showed the program simultaneously. The fact that a few did not[1] has been ignored by the parties in urging their respective contentions and will be disregarded by the court. Each station was located in a different city; the locations ranged across the entire nation.[2] The total viewing audience for the program was over 17 million people.[3] Each local station broadcast not only the infringing program but also commercials transmitted to it by CBS for which the station received payment. [4] DuPont, through its advertising agency, BBDO, retained and exercised ultimate power to determine the content of the program. DuPont sought nationwide coverage for the program through its dealings with CBS.[5] CBS made arrangements with those of its affiliated stations which agreed to broadcast the program when it was received from CBS. Each station had the choice of rejecting the proposed program.[6] A few stations were owned and operated by CBS; [7] the others were independently owned and operated,

---

[1] See Plaintiff's Exhibit (hereinafter cited as "Pl. Ex.") 35.

[2] Ibid.

[3] Stipulation on damage hearing, dated June 14, 1965 (hereinafter cited as "Stipulation"), p. 7.

[4] Pl. Ex. 39; Stipulation, pp. 14-15.

[5] Stipulation, pp. 6-7.

[6] Stipulation, pp. 5-6.

[7] Joint letter of counsel to court, dated June 16, 1965, p. 2.

but were contractually affiliated with CBS.[8]

The damage issues here are raised within the legal framework of 17 U.S.C. § 101(b), which, in its present form, is an ambiguous hodgepodge of improvisations. This section states as follows:

If any person shall infringe the copyright in any work protected under the copyright laws of the United States such person shall be liable:
* * *

(b) * * * To pay to the copyright proprietor such damages as the copyright proprietor may have suffered due to the infringement, as well as all the profits which the infringer shall have made from such infringement, and in proving profits the plaintiff shall be required to prove sales only, and the defendant shall be required to prove every element of cost which he claims, or in lieu of actual damages and profits, such damages as to the court shall appear to be just, and in assessing such damages the court may, in its discretion, allow the amounts as hereinafter stated, but in case of a newspaper reproduction of a copyrighted photograph, such damages shall not exceed the sum of $200 nor be less than the sum of $50, and in the case of the infringement of an undramatized or nondramatic work by means of motion pictures, where the infringer shall show that he was not aware that he was infringing, and that such infringement could not have been reasonably foreseen, such damages shall not exceed the sum of $100; and in the case of an infringement of a copyrighted dramatic or dramatico-musical work by a maker of motion pictures and his agencies for distribution thereof to exhibitors, where such infringer shows that he was not aware that he was infringing a copyrighted work, and that such infringements could not reasonably have been foreseen, the entire sum of such damages recoverable by the copyright proprietor from such infringing maker and his agencies for the distribution to exhibitors of such infringing motion picture shall not exceed the sum of $5,000 nor be less than the sum of $250, and such damages shall in no other case exceed the sum of $5,000 nor be less than the sum of $250, and shall not be regarded as a penalty. But the foregoing exceptions shall not deprive the copyright proprietor of any other remedy given him under this law, nor shall the limitation as to the amount of recovery apply to infringements occurring after the actual notice to a defendant, either by service of process in a suit or other written notice served upon him.
First. In the case of a painting, statue, or sculpture, $10 for every

---

[8] The other stations had network contracts with CBS which gave them the first option to broadcast programs offered by the network. Pl. Ex. 38; Stipulation, pp. 3, 6.

infringing copy made or sold by or found in the possession of the infringer or his agents or employees;

Second. In the case of any work enumerated in section 5 of this title, except a painting, statue, or sculpture, $1 for every infringing copy made or sold by or found in the possession of the infringer or his agents or employees;

Third. In the case of a lecture, sermon, or address, $50 for every infringing delivery;

Fourth. In the case of a dramatic or dramatico-musical or a choral or orchestral composition, $100 for the first and $50 for every subsequent infringing performance; in the case of other musical compositions $10 for every infringing performance.

The parties have stipulated that because the "rules of law and evidence render difficult proof of plaintiff's actual damages, if any, and proof of profits, if any, of the defendants" due to the infringing telecast, plaintiff relies solely upon the "in lieu of" provisions quoted above,[9] commonly referred to as the statutory damage provisions. Accordingly, plaintiff does not claim and has not proved actual damages or profits and seeks to recover only such damages under the above quoted statutory language "as to the court shall appear to be just." Plaintiff argues that this amount is $211,500, computed in a manner set forth below, and, in any event, can be no less than $40,500. Defendants contend that damages can be no higher than $8,150 and should be fixed at a lower figure.

The basic issues before the court are: (1) whether the 1960 telecast by 162 stations was one "infringement" by these defendants or 162, thereby determining whether the minimum statutory damage is $250 or $40,500; (2) if there was only one infringement, whether the maximum damage is the $5,000 limit set forth in 17 U.S.C. § 101(b), or whether this is inapplicable because defendants had "actual notice" of the copyright claim; and (3) in any event, at what figure "just" damages should be fixed.

I

The statutory damage provisions provide a minimum of $250 and a maximum of $5,000 for each infringement. Plaintiff contends that there were 162 infringements of his copyright and therefore the minimum damage must be 162 times $250, or $40,500. Defendants claim that there was only one infringement of the copyright and the applicable minimum is accordingly only $250. Whether a simultaneous network telecast by many stations constitutes more than one infringement is remarkably unclear. As

---

[9] Stipulation, p. 1.

is so often the case in copyright actions, although the issue raised is far reaching in import, there are few, if any, decisions on point and none containing any extended discussion of the problem.[10]

Any careful analysis of the issue must begin with close examination of section 101(b). That section states that any person who infringes a copyright shall be liable to pay to the copyright proprietor damages due to "the infringement" as well as profits made by the infringer "from such infringement," or in lieu of actual damages and profits, such damages as appear just to the court. The limits on the "in lieu of," or statutory, damages are that they shall in no "case" exceed $5,000 or be less than $250, with an exception as to the maximum to be discussed below. The law is clear that an award as statutory damages of any amount from $250 to $5,000 for an infringement is within the discretion of the trial court.[11] In situations where repetitive infringement of a copyrighted work is probable, the statute suggests amounts ("yardstick amounts") to guide the court in the exercise of its discretion. Thus, the yardstick amounts for "a dramatic composition" like the Davis play infringed here are $100 for the first and $50 "for every subsequent infringing performance." Clearly, then, the statutory scheme contemplates that one "infringement" may nevertheless result in more than one "performance" and that in fixing damages for such infringement between the $250 minimum and the $5,000 maximum, the court may consider the number of infringing performances and the suggested yardstick amount for each one. Conversely, more than one performance does not require a finding of more than one "infringement" to each of which a minimum of $250 damages would apply.

On the first issue - whether the network telecast over 162 stations was one infringement by these defendants or 162 - the cases are not truly helpful. In Law v. National Broadcasting Co., 51 F. Supp. 798 (S.D.N.Y.1943), plaintiff sued for copyright infringement of a song which had been performed on radio on three occasions over a total of 218 stations. Through the National Broadcasting network, sixty-seven radio stations simultaneously broadcast the song the first time and, in two later years, sixty-six stations and eighty-five stations, respectively, broadcast it. The court did not discuss whether there were three or 218 infringements, but focused on the yardstick amount for infringing performances which, in

---

[10] See Shapiro, Bernstein & Co. v. H. L. Green Co., 316 F.2d 304, 305 (2d Cir. 1963).

[11] Douglas v. Cunningham, 294 U.S. 207, 210, 55 S. Ct. 365, 79 L. Ed. 862 (1935).

the case of a musical composition, is $10 for each performance.[12] It fixed damages at 218 times $10, or $2,180, rejecting defendants' argument that damages amounted only to $30 on the theory that each of the three network broadcasts should be considered only one yardstick performance. It is not clear whether the court regarded the three network broadcasts as one infringement or three (to which a minimum of $750 and a maximum of $15,000 would apply). It is clear, however, that the court did not regard each broadcast by each radio station as a separate infringement because it did not apply a multiplier of 218 to the statutory minimum of $250 to reach minimum damages of $54,500. The court's entire discussion of the point was as follows (51 F. Supp. at 799):

Under all the circumstances, I feel it to be only just and fair to assess against the defendants the sum of $10 for each infringing performance. In coming to this conclusion, I have taken into consideration that there were 85 performances after notice was given.

Plaintiff's composition was performed on three occasions by the NBC with chain hook-ups of 67, 66 and 85 stations, in all 218. Damages should be awarded on the theory that there were 218 performances, not three. Buck v. Jewell-La Salle Realty Co., 283 U.S. 191, 51 S. Ct. 410, 75 L. Ed. 971.

In Buck v. Jewell-LaSalle Realty Co., 283 U.S. 191, 51 S. Ct. 410, 75 L. Ed. 971 (1931) (Jewell-LaSalle I), relied upon by the court in Law, a radio station played two copyrighted songs without permission. A hotel in the same city, through a master receiving radio set, picked up the songs and transmitted them simultaneously by wire throughout public areas and many private rooms of the hotel. Buck, as president of the American Society of Composers and Publishers ("ASCAP"), sued the owner of the radio station and Jewell-LaSalle Realty Co., owner of the hotel, for an injunction and damages for copyright infringement.[13] The Supreme Court, in response to a question certified to it by the Court of Appeals for the Eighth Circuit, held that the acts of the hotel in making available to its paying guests through loudspeakers in hotel rooms an audible rendition of a copyrighted musical composition constituted a performance of the composition within the meaning of 17 U.S.C. § 1(e). This section defines the scope of a copyright proprietor's exclusive performing rights in musical compositions. The Court was faced with the argument that since the radio station was liable for the unauthorized performance of the copyrighted song, the hotel

---

[12] See p. 332 supra for statutory language.

[13] See Buck v. Duncan, 32 F.2d 366 (W.D.Mo.1929), rev'd with respect to infringement by radio after certification sub nom. Buck v. Jewell-LaSalle Realty Co., 51 F.2d 726 and 730 (8th Cir. 1931).

could not be liable too. Responding to this contention, the Court stated (283 U.S. at 198, 51 S. Ct. at 411):

But nothing in the Act circumscribes the meaning to be attributed to the term "performance," or prevents a single rendition of a copyrighted selection from resulting in more than one public performance for profit. While this may not have been possible before the development of radio broadcasting, the novelty of the means used does not lessen the duty of the courts to give full protection to the monopoly of public performance for profit which Congress has secured to the composer. Compare Kalem Co. v. Harper Bros., 222 U.S. 55, 63 [32 S. Ct. 20, 56 L. Ed. 92]. No reason is suggested why there may not be more than one liability.

Jewell-LaSalle I was authority for the holding in Law that there could be 218 performances growing out of three network broadcasts. However, Jewell-LaSalle I did not deal with the issue of whether a simultaneous broadcast over many stations is more than one "infringement" under 17 U.S.C. § 101(b), as well as more than one "performance."

Shortly after the decision in Law, another case in this court arose out of a simultaneous broadcast by two radio stations. In Select Theatres Corp. v. Ronzoni Macaroni Co., 59 U.S.P.Q. 288 (S.D.N.Y.1943), plaintiffs were the copyright proprietors of the play, "Death Takes A Holiday," in its original Italian form and in its English versions. Various episodes illegally copied from the plays were broadcast at different times over a New York radio station owned by defendant International Broadcasting Corporation. This station transmitted the episodes to another radio station in Philadelphia, owned by defendant William Penn Broadcasting Corporation, which broadcast each episode simultaneously.[14] On the issue pertinent here, the court regarded the simultaneous broadcasts by the New York and Philadelphia stations as two separate series of infringements. E.g., for three broadcasts by each station of episodes from the Italian version, judgments were entered for two separate sums of $750 (three times $250), one against International Broadcasting Corporation and the other against William Penn Broadcasting Corporation.[15] Presumably, the Ronzoni court regarded each broadcast over the two stations as entitling the plaintiff to minimum damages of $500 (two times $250), each station to pay plaintiff $250. Unless controlling significance is given to the fact that both stations were actually sued in Ronzoni and only the network was sued in Law, the two

---

[14] See Findings of Fact and Conclusions of Law, Select Theatres Corp. v. Ronzoni Macaroni Co., Civil No. 10-216, S.D.N.Y., May 29, 1944.

[15] Id. at 10; Order of the Court, Select Theatres Corp. v. Ronzoni Macaroni Co., June 7, 1944, at 3. Two similar judgments with respect to broadcasts of seventeen additional episodes infringing one English version were entered for $4,250 against each station.

cases appear inconsistent; e.g., a radio broadcast in Law over sixty-seven stations resulted in statutory damages of $10 a performance (or $670), rather than sixty-seven times $250. However, again in Ronzoni there was no discussion of the problem; the only authority cited on the point was Jewell-LaSalle I and Society of European Stage Authors & Composers, Inc. v. New York Hotel Statler Co., 19 F. Supp. 1 (S.D.N.Y.1937). Jewell-LaSalle I has already been discussed, supra. In Statler, as in Jewell-LaSalle I, defendant hotel used a master receiving set, picked up a broadcast of a song, and replayed it through speakers in private rooms of the hotel. The hotel sought to distinguish Jewell-LaSalle I because, inter alia, the original broadcast it picked up from station WJZ was licensed to that station by the copyright owner. However, the court held the hotel liable for copyright infringement. The case is not significant for the basic issue under examination here.

There have been other Supreme Court copyright cases in which the issue may have been present but was either not raised or not decided. Thus, in the language quoted from Jewell-LaSalle I, supra,[16] the Court referred to Kalem Co. v. Harper Bros., 222 U.S. 55, 63, 32 S. Ct. 20, 56 L. Ed. 92 (1911). In that case, the owner of the copyright on the book "Ben Hur" sued the Kalem Company, a producer and distributor of motion pictures. Defendant Kalem did not exhibit the allegedly offending motion picture itself but had distributed it to theaters throughout the country, where the film had been shown over 500 times.[17] Plaintiff sought only injunctive relief, which was granted by the trial court. On appeal, the decree was affirmed both by the circuit court, 169 Fed. 61 (2d Cir. 1909), and the Supreme Court, 222 U.S. 55, 32 S. Ct. 20, 56 L. Ed. 92 (1911). The chief issue in the Supreme Court was whether the showing of the film constituted an infringement of the copyright by Kalem; none of the courts in that litigation dealt with the question of whether Kalem was liable in damages for a series of infringements (at least one by each theater).[18]

The statutory damage provisions of 17 U.S.C. § 101(b) were scrutinized by the Supreme Court in Jewell-LaSalle Realty Co. v. Buck, 283 U.S. 202, 51 S. Ct. 407, 75 L. Ed. 978 (1931) ("Jewell-LaSalle II"), which grew out of the same lower court litigation as Jewell-LaSalle I, supra, and was decided the same day. In Jewell-LaSalle II, the claimed copyright infringement was by a

---

[16] P. 334 supra.

[17] Transcript on Appeal, p. 35, Harper & Bros. v. Kalem Co., 169 F. 61 (2d Cir. 1909).

[18] Cf. Universal Pictures Co. v. Harold Lloyd Corp., 162 F.2d 354, 378 (9th Cir. 1947) (apparently neither plaintiff nor court considered argument that showings of the offending film in each of 6,636 theaters constituted separate infringements).

live rendition given by an orchestra at the LaSalle Hotel, rather than by the pickup and replay of a radio broadcast.[19] The hotel admitted this infringement, leaving the trial court with the sole question of whether to award minimum damages of $250 or $10. The court awarded the larger sum. Buck v. Duncan, 32 F.2d 366, 368 (W.D.Mo.1929). Defendant argued in the Supreme Court that since there was only one unauthorized performance of the song in question, plaintiffs were entitled to only $10 statutory damages, relying upon the yardstick amount quoted above.[20] The Supreme Court held that the minimum damage for the infringement was $250 and that the yardstick amount of $10 for every infringing performance could be applied in the discretion of the court only when the number of infringing performances exceeded twenty-five. As previously noted, in Jewell-LaSalle II, only the hotel orchestra was involved, and there was no rebroadcast of a radio program. Obviously, therefore, the Court had no occasion to deal with the question of whether there was more than one infringement, which would require application of more than $250 minimum damages.

In Jewell-LaSalle II, the Court relied upon its earlier decision in L. A. Westermann Co. v. Dispatch Printing Co., 249 U.S. 100, 39 S. Ct. 194, 63 L. Ed. 499 (1919). That case involved newspaper publication of six separately copyrighted pictorial illustrations. The Court found seven infringements. Five of the infringements consisted of reproduction in defendant's newspaper on five different occasions of a different copyrighted illustration. Of significance here, the Court found two additional infringements because defendant twice published (twenty-six days apart) plaintiff's sixth copyrighted illustration. Accordingly, the Court held that a minimum of $250 damages for each of the seven infringements had to be awarded. The Court explained (249 U.S. at 105-106, 39 S. Ct. at 195):

The statute says that the liability thus defined is imposed for infringing "the copyright in any" copyrighted "work." The words are in the singular, not the plural. Each copyright is treated as a distinct entity, and the infringement of it as a distinct wrong to be redressed through the enforcement of this liability. Infringement of several copyrights is not put on the same level with infringement of one. On the contrary, the plain import of the statute is that this liability attaches in respect of each copyright that is infringed. Here six were infringed, each covering a

---

[19] See 283 U.S. 202 at 203, 51 S. Ct. 407 ("orchestral performance"). This is more clearly brought out by references to "Count 7 of Case No. 1207" in Buck v. Duncan. 32 F.2d 366, 368 (W.D.Mo.1929), and "the seventh count" in Buck v. Jewell-LaSalle Realty Co., 51 F.2d 730 (8th Cir. 1931).

[20] See p. 332 supra.

different illustration. Thus there were at least six cases of infringement in the sense of the statute. Was there also another? The illustration covered by one of the copyrights was published on two separate occasions, each time in a different advertisement. There was no connection between the two advertisements other than the inclusion of the same illustration in both. Each was by a different advertiser and was published at his instance and for his benefit. The advertisers were not joint, but independent, infringers, neither having any connection with what was done by the other. By publishing their advertisements, the defendant participated in their independent infringements. In these circumstances, we think the second publication of the illustration must be regarded as another and distinct case of infringement. Whether it would be otherwise if that publication had been merely a continuation or repetition of the first, and what bearing the "third" and "fourth" subdivisions of § 25 [now § 101], before quoted, would have on the solution of that question, are matters which we have no occasion to consider now. They are mentioned only to show that no ruling thereon is intended.

The language of the Supreme Court focusing on the seventh infringement is significant here. The Court pointed out that the sixth illustration "was published on two separate occasions, each time in a different advertisement." It also stressed that there was no connection between the advertisements or the advertisers who placed them. Under these circumstances, the Court concluded that the second publication of the illustration "must be regarded as another and distinct case of infringement." However, it expressly left open for future decision whether the result would be the same if the second publication "had been merely a continuation or repetition of the first," having in mind the yardstick amounts.

After the decision in Westermann, a number of courts faced the problem of whether succeeding publications each constituted a separate "infringement" for the purpose of computing minimum damages. It has been suggested that although these decisions seem, upon superficial examination, to conflict with each other, they actually show the following consistent pattern:[21] if the interval between succeeding publications is merely a matter of days, the courts will consider all the publications as one infringing transaction, which requires application of one minimum damage award; conversely, if the time lag between succeeding publications is longer, then each publication will be viewed as a separate infringement requiring separate minimum damages.[22] It has also been suggested that the nature of

---

[21] See Nimmer, Copyright § 154.32 at 689 (1964).

[22] Compare, e.g., Gordon v. Weir, 111 F. Supp. 117 (E.D.Mich.1953), aff'd per curiam, 216 F.2d 508 (6th Cir. 1954) (e.g., publications "during February" one

the business transaction giving rise to the infringement is significant, implying that a single integrated business transaction would result in one infringement, while separate and distinct transactions would result in more than one.[23]

The most recent decision in the Supreme Court construing the statutory damage provisions is F. W. Woolworth Co. v. Contemporary Arts, Inc., 344 U.S. 228, 73 S. Ct. 222, 97 L. Ed. 276 (1952). In that case, suit was brought for infringement of a copyrighted work of art entitled "**Cocker spaniel** in Show Position." Plaintiff, assignee of the copyright, made small sculptures and figurines among which were statues of a **cocker spaniel**, and marketed them chiefly through gift and art shops. Defendant Woolworth bought 1,524 **cocker spaniel** statues from a

---

infringement); Doll v. Libin, 17 F. Supp. 546 (D.Mont.1936) (publications on April 17, 19, 22 and 24 and May 5), (Contra, Advertisers Exchange, Inc. v. Bayless Drug Store, Inc., 50 F. Supp. 169 (D.N.J.1943) (separate infringements for publications on April 2 and 3).) with, e.g., Burndy Engineering Co. v. Sheldon Service Corp., 127 F.2d 661 (2d Cir. 1942) (time intervals of publications varied from three weeks to over six months. Record on Appeal, p. 275); Harry Alter Co. v. A. E. Borden Co., 121 F. Supp. 941 (D.Mass.1954) (three publications in 1945, 1948 and 1950, respectively); Eliot v. Geare-Marston, Inc., 30 F. Supp. 301 (E.D.Pa.1939) (two publications in May 1936 and January 1937, respectively).

[23] In Cory v. Physical Culture Hotel, Inc., 14 F. Supp. 977, 985 (W.D.N.Y.1936), aff'd, 88 F.2d 411 (2d Cir. 1937), the court stressed that:

> Each issue of the magazine was a separate and distinct set-up involving a new and independent arrangement of copy and advertising matter and a printing based on a separate and distinct order in each case, unrelated to the order for any preceding edition or printing.

Although the court held that each separate printing "constituted a separate infringement," it left open whether this required application of separate minimum and maximum limits to the seven infringements involved in that case. Ibid. Cf. Gordon v. Weir, 111 F. Supp. 117, 123 (E.D.Mich.1953), aff'd per curiam, 216 F.2d 508 (6th Cir. 1954) (operating methods of plaintiff examined to justify finding of only one infringement for several publications); Doll v. Libin, 17 F. Supp. 546 (D.Mont.1936) (five copyrighted advertisements published after contract expired constituted one infringement); Cravens v. Retail Credit Men's Ass'n, 26 F.2d 833, 836 (M.D.Tenn.1924) (infringing replacement pages in a loose-leaf book not separate infringements).

different source and distributed them through thirty-four Woolworth stores. These statues had been illegally copied from plaintiff's verson, although Woolworth was not aware of this. The issue before the Supreme Court was whether the trial court had properly allowed statutory damages in the amount of $5,000, even though there was proof that Woolworth's gross profit on the sale of the dogs was under $900. Woolworth argued in the Supreme Court that it was error to apply the statutory damage maximum because actual profits in a lesser amount had been proved. Affirming, the Court held (7-2) that such proof did not foreclose the trial court from using the statutory damage provisions and in its discretion awarding maximum damages. The dissent disagreed and characterized the $5,000 award as a "manifestly unjust exaction." Both the majority and dissenting opinions assumed that the minimum and maximum damages for only one infringement were applicable.

Turning from Supreme Court and other copyright cases to analogies from other fields of law seems unfruitful. Thus, common law definitions of joint tortfeasors - in themselves frequently inconsistent - are of limited utility in construing an act where complex wrongs and remedies are intertwined and unique.[24] The analogy of mass media defamation, though tempting, is unhelpful for the same reason and, in addition, raises more problems than it solves.[25]

Thus, a review of the cases indicates that there is no binding precedent in point on the issue of whether a network telecast over 162 stations constitutes one infringement or 162. At the trial court level, Law v. National Broadcasting Co., supra, and Select Theatres Corp. v. Ronzoni Macaroni Co., supra, involved simultaneous radio broadcasts but reached inconsistent results. In the Supreme Court, the problem of multiple infringement was implicit in the Kalem case, where a motion picture distributor was held liable as a contributory infringer for the public exhibition of films in various theaters, but no issue of damages was dealt with in the litigation. In Westermann, the Supreme Court recognized, but

---

[24] See Note, Joint and Several Liability for Copyright Infringement: A New Look at Section 101(b) of the Copyright Act, 32 U.Chi.L.Rev. 98, 118-121 (1964).

[25] See 1 Harper & James, Torts § 5.16 (1956). If anything, the single publication rule, formulated in part to prevent a multiplicity of suits from springing out of a single set of defamatory activities, suggests that a simultaneous network telecast should be considered a single infringement by the network and these co-defendants. But apparently, borrowing the single publication rule would still leave unanswered the question of under what circumstances separate stations could be sued individually. See Developments in the Law - Defamation, 69 Harv.L.Rev. 875, 947-950 & 948 n. 516 (1956); consider also id. at 950-951.

did not deal with, the question of whether a second publication which was "merely a continuation or repetition of the first" would be another infringement. Since then, in cases involving publishing and printing rights, some courts have regarded as significant the interval between publications or have examined the nature of the business transaction giving rise to the infringement. If the theory of those cases is applied to performing rights, it suggests that a simultaneous telecast by many stations over one network gives rise to only one infringement. In any event, it is accurate to describe the case law as inconclusive.

With this in mind, it is appropriate again to focus on the statute, with particular reference to its legislative history. The statutory language has been analyzed above, and it was there concluded that 17 U.S.C. § 101(b) clearly contemplates that several performances may amount to only one "infringement." The minimum of $250 and the maximum of $5,000 for any infringement and the yardstick amounts have remained unchanged since the general revision of the Copyright Act in 1909. Since then, two additional damage provisions have been enacted dealing with infringement by a medium of mass communication. After the litigation in Kalem, supra, which decided that a motion picture could violate the copyright on a novel, the Act was amended in 1912. The amendment provided that in the case of innocent infringement by means of motion pictures embodying a nondramatic or undramatized copyrighted work, the statutory damages should not exceed $100, and for similar infringment of a dramatic work "the entire sum" of damages recoverable by a copyright proprietor from a "maker of motion pictures and his agencies for distribution thereof to exhibitors" should not exceed $5,000.[26] This amendment has been characterized as "intended to rectify" the Supreme Court decision in Kalem[27]. Another limitation of the statutory damage provisions was added

---

[26] Pub.L. No. 303, 62d Cong., 2d Sess., 37 Stat. 489 (1912). This language, which presently appears in 17 U.S.C. § 101(b), is quoted at p. 331 supra. The same amendment also added the provision lifting the $5,000 maximum when written notice is given.

[27] See Warner, Radio and Television Rights § 163 at 650 (1953):

> This provision was intended to rectify the Supreme Court's decision in Kalem Co. v. Harper, where the exhibition of the motion picture by 10,000 innocent exhibitors resulted in 10,000 separate infringing performances.

As indicated above (p. 335), the courts in the various stages of the Kalem case did not discuss whether more than one "infringement" was involved.

in 1952 to cover damages for infringement by radio of nondramatic literary works.[28] This section, which has been placed in 17 U.S.C. § 1(c), rather than in section 101(b), provides that:

The damages for the infringement by broadcast of any work referred to in this subsection shall not exceed the sum of $100 where the infringing broadcaster shows that he was not aware that he was infringing and that such infringement could not have been reasonably foreseen; * * *.

While there has been no other applicable legislation, the issue posed by the instant case has not gone unnoticed by those expert in the field. Thus, in one of the studies recently published under the auspices of the Register of Copyrights,[29] it was pointed out that "it is not clear how many infringements are involved when a copyrighted work * * * [is] used in successive editions or broadcasts, or in simultaneous broadcasts," and that "there is therefore good reason for some uncertainty about the extent of statutory liability for multiple infringements * * *."[30] Moreover, there have been proposals in Congress in the past few decades to clarify the situation. However, none of these bills was enacted. More recently, there has been a series of hearings and conferences which may lead to further revision of the copyright law. The most recent bill under examination is apparently designed to put a limit of $20,000 on possible liability for simultaneous infringing telecasts,[31] although there is conflict in testimony at the hearings

---

[28] Pub.L. No. 575, 82d Cong., 2d Sess., 66 Stat. 752 (1952).

[29] Subcomm. on Patents, Trademarks, and Copyrights, Sen. Comm. on the Judiciary, 86th Cong., 2d Sess., Copyright Law Revision Study No. 23 (studies hereinafter cited as, e.g., "Study No. 23"), Brown, The Operation of the Damage Provisions of the Copyright Law: An Exploratory Study 77-80 (Comm. Print 1958).

[30] Id. at 79-80. See also id. at 81, referring to the limitation in section 1(c) of $100 for certain infringements by radio:

With respect to the determination of multiple infringements by a network broadcast, will the $100 limitation be controlling, or will "the infringing broadcaster" be held to refer to each outlet? If there are multiple infringements in such a situation, would each outlet have to be sued separately, precluding recovery from the network for all the claimed infringements?

[31] Various earlier legislative proposals are discussed in Study No. 22 at 20-29 (1956) and Study No. 25 at 149-52 (1958). The latest bill is S. 1006, H.R. 4347, H.R. 5680, H.R. 6831, H.R. 6835, 89th Cong., 1st Sess. § 504(c) (1965), reprinted in House Comm. on the Judiciary, 89th Cong., 1st Sess., Copyright Law Revision, Part 6, Supplementary Report of the Register of Copyrights on the General Revision of the U.S. Copyright Law: 1965 Revision Bill 274 (Comm. Print 1965)

as to the advisability of doing so.[32]

None of this, of course, resolves the question of how section 101(b) in its present form should be interpreted. The 1912 and 1952 amendments, putting limits on possible multiple liability for motion pictures and radio broadcasts under certain circumstances, might be urged as a recognition that the law requires piling minimums upon each other in those analogous situations (such as network telecasts) where Congress has not acted. However, the legislative history of the 1912 amendment, at least, indicates that it was enacted not in apprehension of multiple infringements; rather, it was designed to prevent excessive awards based on numerous yardstick performances in movie theaters apparently assumed to be involved in only one infringement.[33] In addition, for the limited significance of later statutes in construing an earlier one, see SEC v. Capital Gains Research Bureau, Inc., 375 U.S. 180, 199-200, 84 S. Ct. 275, 11 L. Ed. 2d 237 (1963). On the other hand, the specter of multiple infringements occasioned by the advance of technology in motion pictures, radio and television has existed for quite a while. It can be plausibly argued that one reason for congressional inaction is an awareness that the courts are reluctant to construe the statute as requiring an automatic multiplication of minimum liabilities. Thus, the Register of Copyrights has recently pointed out: [34]

We believe that the danger of exorbitant awards in multiple infringement cases is more theoretical than real. In a few cases involving multiple infringements - e.g., where various items in a copyrighted

---

(hereinafter cited as "Copyright Revision, Part 6"); see id. at 136-138.

[32] Compare House Comm. on the Judiciary, 88th Cong., 2d Sess., Copyright Law Revision, Part 4, Further Discussion and Comments on Preliminary Draft for Revised U.S. Copyright Law 136, 148-149, 164 (Comm. Print 1964); House Comm. on the Judiciary, 89th Cong., 1st Sess., Copyright Law Revision, Part 5, 1964 Revision Bill with Discussions and Comments 201-202, 269 (Comm. Print 1965); Copyright Revision, Part 6 at 136-138. Although some of these comments were specifically directed to legislative proposals made in 1964, they are equally applicable to the 1965 bill.

[33] S.Rep. No. 906, H.R.Rep. No. 756, 62d Cong., 2d Sess. (1912) (identical reports); 48 Cong.Rec. 8288-8291 (1912) (remarks of Representative Townsend, sponsor of the amendment).

[34] House Comm. on the Judiciary, 87th Cong., 1st Sess., Register of Copyrights, Copyright Law Revision Report 105 (Comm. Print 1961) (hereinafter cited as "Register's Report").

merchandise catalog were reproduced in a series of infringing catalogs - the courts have used this formula of multiplying the number of infringements by $250, but they did so to reach a result they thought just. We know of no case in which the court has felt constrained to use this formula where the resulting total was considered excessive. The present statute, however, is not clear on this point. It is conceivable that a court might construe the statute as requiring the use of this formula in multiple-infringement cases.

Legislative intent is often elusive; frequently, that best that a court can do is make an educated guess. Here, the statute is over half a century old and was enacted long before any Congressman ever heard of a nationwide telecast. Under such circumstances, a judgment as to what Congress meant (or would have meant had the problem been posed) is even more tentative. Taking all of the above into consideration, it appears that the legislative history of the statute, like the case law, is not determinative of the issue presented here. However, section 101(b), in clearly providing that many performances of a copyrighted work may result in only one infringement, indicates that it does not require a mechanical adding together of 162 simultaneous telecasts to produce 162 separate infringements.

With neither conclusive precedents nor legislative guidance, the competing policies underlying the contending positions of the parties become more significant. Under the copyright law, plaintiff is undoubtedly entitled to protection for his independent creation, but the protection should be appropriate.[35] The Copyright Act should certainly not be lightly interpreted in a manner likely to produce ridiculous results.[36] Thus, if an innocent but nonetheless infringing network played even a portion[37] of a copyrighted melody only once on a network broadcast of 200 stations, plaintiff's construction of section 101(b) would require the network to pay a minimum of $50,000 (200 times $250). Is the risk of such an outlandish result required, however, to protect adequately a copyright in a work of more substantial value, such as the infringed play in this case? In other words, is there a real danger that unless the multiple-infringement theory is mandated, the $5,000 maximum for one infringement will work hardship

---

[35] See generally Chafee, Reflections on the Law of Copyright, 45 Colum.L.Rev. 502, 506-14 (1945).

[36] For an example of how courts anxious to avoid awarding enormous multipleminimum statutory damages have found more attractive alternatives, see Shapiro, Bernstein & Co. v. Bleeker, 224 F. Supp. 595, and 243 F. Supp. 999 (S.D.Cal.1963 and 1965, respectively).

[37] See Warner, op. cit. supra note 27, § 154 at 573-575, § 163 at 663, and authorities cited therein.

on the copyright proprietor of a very valuable work? As a practical matter, the answer is probably not. The statutory damage provision (including the maximum) only applies where plaintiff is unable to prove actual damages and profits. In many instances, a plaintiff will be able to offer such proof.[38] Moreover, if a radio or television network has written notice of a copyright claim, then the maximum of $5,000 for each infringement does not apply. In other words, if such notice has been given, a multiplication of infringements to pile up high minimum statutory damages and (by hypothesis) a more equitable damage figure is not necessary because the court is not bound by the maximum of $5,000.[39] In view of advance announcement of network program schedules, it seems likely today that notice will usually have been served when a network broadcasts a program infringing a quite valuable copyrighted work. Thus, the significance of a failure to find multiple infringements in this case is materially lessened by the holdings in Points II and III, infra.

Plaintiff points out that the statutory damage provisions have a deterrent, as well as a compensatory, purpose and argues that a finding of multiple infringements is necessary "to discourage wrongful conduct." See F. W. Woolworth Co. v. Contemporary Arts, Inc., 344 U.S. 228, 233, 73 S. Ct. 222, 97 L. Ed. 276 (1952).[40] However, the cases neither minimize the compensatory statutory purpose nor indicate that deterrence should be carried to an extreme by converting a $250 incentive to sue into a windfall. Id. at 231, 73 S. Ct. 222; see L. A. Westermann Co. v. Dispatch Printing Co., 249 U.S. 100, 108, 39 S. Ct. 194, 63 L. Ed. 499 (1919). Requiring a mechanical application of a rule of multiple minimum damages for each network broadcast or telecast could, as indicated above, at times have absurd results. On the other hand, retaining flexibility with respect to minimum damages would not destroy the deterrent effect of any award since it would rarely, if ever, as a practical matter, require a court to undercompensate a plaintiff. Plaintiff's deterrence argument really applies only to the case of a deliberate infringer who has not received written notice, a case unlikely to occur often where a network proposes to broadcast a valuable copyrighted work. As pointed out above, if an infringer has been notified properly, the court needs no compulsory

---

[38] Cf. Universal Pictures Co. v. Harold Lloyd Corp., 162 F.2d 354, 368-370 (9th Cir. 1947) (suggesting actual damages can be proven without great difficulty).

[39] See Points II and III infra for a discussion of the authorities.

[40] Plaintiff also cites Douglas v. Cunningham, 294 U.S. 207, 55 S. Ct. 365, 79 L. Ed. 862 (1935), and Peter Pan Fabrics, Inc. v. Jobela Fabrics, Inc., 329 F.2d 194 (2d Cir. 1964).

multiple-infringement rule, since it is not bound by the $5,000 maximum in fixing a damage award with sufficient deterrent force. The only remaining situation involves an infringer who has acted innocently - without knowledge or reason to know he has infringed a copyright. Here plaintiff's argument based on deterrence yields an utterly anomolous result. A multiple-minimum damage rule could not possibly deter the infringer who has no reason to know he is violating another's copyright. But such a rule would leave the court no choice but to assess arbitrary and potentially enormous minimum damages against such a nonculpable defendant. Any discretion remaining in the court to fix a "just" award could only be characterized as emasculated.

Plaintiff also argues that a simultaneous telecast is similar to the unauthorized showing of plaintiff's play in 162 theaters, in which event plaintiff could sue each theater separately and recover at least the minimum of $250 from each. Some similarities doubtless exist, as do some differences. Thus, stage performances in 162 theaters would not normally be simultaneous or occur as part of the same business transaction. The cases analyzed above[41] indicate that these may be crucial dissimilarities. In other words, the analogy begs the question since the very issue to be decided is whether multiple performances are, in the words of the Supreme Court in Westermann (249 U.S. at 106, 39 S. Ct. at 195), "merely a continuation or repetition of the first." Defendants argue that a more compelling analogy is found in the sale of one day's edition of a newspaper in many cities which, under the authorities, would amount to only one infringement, not many.[42] Moreover, assuming arguendo that plaintiff could indeed recover minimum damages from each broadcasting station individually, that does not imply a fortiori that the network or other defendants named in this suit should be held for this multiplied amount. In many instances of copyright violations there are numerous secondary infringers, whose acts when considered separately may each constitute an infringement, e.g., shops which sell an infringing book. But, to continue with this example, it does not seem that by suing the publisher alone, the copyright holder can collect as minimum statutory damages the amount he

---

[41] See notes 21-23 supra.

[42] Defendants' Brief in Opposition to and in Mitigation of an Award of Damages (hereinafter cited as "Def. Brief in Opposition"), pp. 8-10. Defendants cite for this point Westermann, supra; Cory v. Physical Culture Hotel, Inc., 14 F. Supp. 977 (W.D.N.Y.1936), aff'd, 88 F.2d 411 (2d Cir. 1937), and Schellberg v. Empringham, 36 F.2d 991 (S.D.N.Y.1929). Cf. Douglas v. Cunningham, 294 U.S. 207, 55 S. Ct. 365, 79 L. Ed. 862 (1935) (384,000 copies of Sunday edition of the Boston Post sold by many news vendors regarded as one infringement).

might have obtained had he elected to go to the trouble and expense of suing every bookseller who was also an infringer.[43]

The fact of the matter is that the contrasting analogies emphasize but do not solve the problem. On balance, it seems preferable, for the purpose of applying the statutory damage provisions, to regard the simultaneous network telecast here as one infringement by the network and these co-defendants, rather than many. This preserves flexibility, avoids the possibility of a ridiculous and injurious award in other cases and is the result at least suggested by the cases and the statute. It leaves open conceptually perplexing questions, e.g., whether telecasts separated by a few days or longer constitute one infringement,[44] whether recovery from a network of "in lieu of" damages forecloses subsequent recovery from an individual station for its profits from the infringement, to what extent an initial suit against an infringing station (for actual damages or profits, or for "in lieu of" damages) would affect subsequent suits against other stations or the network. However, these need not now be decided; it is hoped that the present legislative concentration on copyright revision will result in an amendment of the statute clearly resolving all problems in this area. In any event, I hold that the simultaneous network telecast over 162 stations in this case constituted only one infringement by these defendants, so that the minimum damages to be applied need not be $40,500, but only $250.

II

Having held that the network telecast of "Ethan Frome" was only a single infringement, the next issue is whether there is a $5,000 maximum on damages.

Section 101(b) sets that limit for one infringement but also states that:

[The] limitation as to the amount of recovery [shall not] apply to

---

[43] The discussion in text is by no means meant to imply that plaintiff here could in fact recover $250 minimum damages in each of 162 suits. See Note, Monetary Recovery for Copyright Infringement, 67 Harv.L.Rev. 1044, 1051-1052 (1954). See also Mura v. Columbia Broadcasting System, Inc., Civil No. 60-2787, S.D.N.Y., April 28, 1965.

[44] It is true that a few of the telecasts in the instant case were not simultaneous. See note 1 supra and accompanying text. However, an assumption arguendo that these were separate infringements with a required minimum damage of $250 for each telecast is not significant because the damage award fixed in Point III infra is much higher than the total of these minimums.

infringements occurring after the actual notice to a defendant, either by service of process in a suit or other written notice served upon him.

In the former opinion in this case, it was noted that (240 F. Supp. at 617):

In December 1959 and January 1960, Davis formally notified defendants that if they went ahead with the proposed television performance of "Ethan Frome" based upon the Deutsch screenplay, without the consent of Davis, they would be committing a deliberate copyright infringement.

The basis for this finding was a fivepage letter, dated December 23, 1959, and a telegram, dated January 27, 1960, sent by plaintiff's attorneys to defendants. The letter admonished defendants that:

If the telecast contains any material which was not in the original novel but is in the Davis dramatization, we will presume that this resulted from access to the famed and established dramatization, and will thereby establish that this constitutes a copyright infringement.[45]

The telegram reiterated this warning, stating:

PLEASE BE ADVISED ON BEHALF OF DONALD DAVIS AND MATHEWS DAVIS, INC. THE COPYRIGHT OWNERS OF THE DRAMATIZATION OF ETHAN FROME AND SUPPLEMENTING OUR LETTER OF DECEMBER 23 (1) THAT THE SCREEN PLAY WRITTEN BY HELEN DEUTSCH BEING ADAPTED FOR THE DUPONT TELECAST IS BASED UPON THE DAVIS PLAY (2) THAT COLUMBIA SUCCESSOR TO WARNERS HAS NO RIGHT TO LICENSE A LIVE TELECAST (3) THE DUPONT SHOW IS BILLED AS A LIVE TELECAST AND ALL OF ITS CONTRACTS WITH THE WRITERS AND PLAYERS AND OTHERS ARE FOR A LIVE TELECAST (4) YOUR HAVING HAD WRITTEN NOTICE THE PLAGIARISM OF THE DAVIS DRAMATIZATION WOULD CONSTITUTE A DELIBERATE COPYRIGHT INFRINGEMENT AND THE DAMAGES UNDER THE COPYRIGHT LAW ARE $250 TO $5,000 FOR EACH TELECAST AND THIS BEING A DELIBERATE INFRINGEMENT IS NOT COVERED BY INSURANCE (5) LIKEWISE MRS. TYLER BY HER ACTS HAS EXTENDED THE ORIGINAL EDITH WHARTON DRAMATIZATION CONTRACT TO THE RENEWAL PERIOD AND CANNOT GRANT A LICENSE FOR A LIVE TELEVISION

---

[45] Pl. Ex. 18.

[TELECAST] WITHOUT THE CONSENT OF THE DAVISES.[46]

The issue is whether these warnings were "actual notice to a defendant, either by service of process in a suit or other written notice served upon him." Once again, there is a dearth of authority directly on point. In Advertisers Exchange, Inc. v. Hinkley,[47] plaintiff's copyrighted advertising material was published twenty-nine times in a local newspaper after the expiration of a contract for the use of the material between plaintiff and defendant, "the proprietor of a small grocery store." Plaintiff sought damages of $94,569, based upon the 94,569 published copies of the twenty-nine issues of the newspaper. The trial court characterized this claimed sum as "a ridiculous amount."[48] Similarly outraged, the appellate court regarded the claim as "an attempt * * * to magnify and inflate * * * damages to an unconscionable great sum of money * * *." [49] In affirming the award below of only $312, the court of appeals held alternatively that although a letter gave the infringer notice, the $5,000 limitation applied because "there was no law suit of which he had notice and he was not then 'a defendant' within the contemplation of the statute." [50] Although the court's concern with the possibility of excess damages was understandable, this interpretation of the notice provision of section 101(b) seems unduly restrictive. By specifying that written notice other than service of process will suffice, Congress has quite surely indicated that one need not already have become a defendant for written notice to be effective. No reason has been pointed out why Congress would have intended to shield an infringer who has been given full written notice until after the arbitrary point in time when the copyright owner has been able to draw up and file a complaint against him. See generally, Nimmer, Copyright § 154.2 at 685-86 (1964). I conclude that a letter or telegram may be sufficient written notice to lift the $5,000

---

[46] Pl. Ex. 20. Defendants Babbin and Gellen were not personally notified by plaintiff's written communications, but, as indicated in the earlier opinion, they were made aware of plaintiff's claim. 240 F. Supp. 612 at 617 n. 21, 620.

[47] 101 F. Supp. 801, 806 (W.D.Mo.1951), aff'd, 199 F.2d 313 (8th Cir. 1952), cert. denied, 344 U.S. 921, 73 S. Ct. 388, 97 L. Ed. 710 (1953).

[48] 101 F. Supp. at 805-806.

[49] 199 F.2d at 316.

[50] Id. at 315.

maximum set forth in section 101(b), and that such notice was given here.[51]

Defendants make various contentions that the letter and telegram were somehow legally deficient as notice. However, their arguments - including a claim that their freedom of speech is being unconstitutionally violated [52] - are without merit. The violation by defendants in this case was willful in the sense that they knew they were taking a calculated risk. It was not the situation envisioned recently by the Report of the Register of Copyrights where "a television network may receive a notice alleging infringement on the eve of a scheduled broadcast when it is too late to defer the program pending an investigation of the claim." [53] Plaintiff's letter was mailed over seven weeks before the telecast, and his telegram was sent over three weeks before. Moreover, they were both preceded by abortive negotiations between plaintiff and Susskind. [54] The day before the telecast, DuPont wrote plaintiff's attorneys to say that, on the basis of an investigation it had directed BBDO to make following plaintiff's telegram, DuPont had concluded that no infringement was involved. [55] Clearly, then, defendants had sufficient time to act on the notice they received.

Having found that each defendant, except Babbin and Gellen, received timely and sufficient written notice, CBS, DuPont, Talent, Susskind, and BBDO may be held jointly and severally liable for damages in excess of $5,000. Babbin and Gellen may be held liable only to the extent of $5,000.

III

Thus, the ultimate issue before the court is what damages "appear to be just." On the facts of this case, the possible range of discretion is broad, since the $250 minimum for one infringement (see Point I, supra) is too small, and the $5,000 maximum does not apply (see Point II, supra). With these two limits inapplicable, as might be expected, the suggestions of the parties are far apart.

---

[51] Cf. Universal Pictures Co. v. Harold Lloyd Corp., 162 F.2d 354, 371 (9th Cir. 1947), containing possible dictum that actual notice is sufficient even though there was no written notice at all.

[52] Def. Brief in Opposition, p. 17

[53] Register's Report at 105; see Study No. 23 at 78 (1958).

[54] Pl. Ex. 18, p. 1.

[55] Pl. Ex. 23.

Plaintiff urges that damages be fixed at $211,500[56] based upon the following computation: $30,000 as a figure "reasonably reflecting damages" to plaintiff, added to $40,500, as a figure "reasonably reflecting profits," and in lieu thereof a minimum of $250 multiplied by 162 separate infringements to make a total of $70,500 which, in turn, should be tripled "as a deterrent."[57] Defendants suggest, as indicated in Point II supra, that the $5,000 limit for one infringement applies. However, in the event this contention is rejected, as it has been, defendants alternatively argue that "just" damages should be determined by the yardstick amounts of $100 for the first performance and $50 for each additional performance,[58] for a total of $8,150.

Plaintiff's contention that a minimum of $40,500 must be included in the damage figure because there were 162 separate infringements has already been dealt with in Point I supra, and rejected. Moreover, short shrift should be made of his argument that whatever figure is fixed as damages should be trebled to serve as "a deterrent." Plaintiff relies by analogy on patent and antitrust law in arguing that Congress has there determined "what formula would constitute a deterrent."[59] However, the trebling of damages there is done pursuant to specific congressional authorization or command,[60] notably absent here. Plaintiff cites no judicial precedent for the proposition that the court has such authority. Moreover, even if by some stretch of the imagination trebling, as proposed by plaintiff, were within the court's authority, I emphatically reject the notion that the suggested astronomical figure would on these facts be "just."

Having rejected plaintiff's extreme position, it must still be determined what "just" damages are. The first question is whether the yardstick amounts must be followed once the $5,000 maximum is exceeded. Defendants refer to the yardstick amount of $50 a performance but have not argued that the court must follow the yardstick and find damages of $8,150. In fact, defendants alternatively suggest that the court look to "the infringed work's true market value for the use made," [61] although by a

---

[56] 56 Plaintiff's Brief in Support of an Award for Damages (hereinafter cited as "Pl. Brief in Support"), p. 24.

[57] 57 Ibid. In Plaintiff's Reply Brief, p. 17, he asks for similar sums based on damages of $1,000 to $1,500 per network station or one penny for each of the 17 million estimated viewers of the telecast.

[58] 58 See statutory language quoted at p. 332 supra.

[59] 59 Pl. Brief in Support, p. 24.

[60] 60 35 U.S.C. § 284; 15 U.S.C. § 15. Plaintiff also cites 17 U.S.C. § 1(e), which allows trebled royalties of 6 cents per mechanical reproduction of a musical composition under certain circumstances. Plaintiff's Reply Brief, p. 5.

[61] 61 Def. Brief in Opposition, p. 28.

process of apportionment and argument defendants by this route reach a value of less than $5,000. The cases abound with statements that the yardstick amounts are discretionary and need not be followed by the courts.[62] However, these have generally been made in the context of an award where the statutory minimum of $250 and maximum of $5,000 both applied. Thus, in Douglas v. Cunningham, 294 U.S. 207, 55 S. Ct. 365, 79 L. Ed. 862 (1935), the issue was whether the trial court had erred in awarding $5,000 for the publication in some 384,000 copies of a Sunday edition of the Boston Post of an article infringing plaintiffs' copyrighted story. In holding the award proper, the Court said (294 U.S. at 210, 55 S. Ct. at 366):

The trial judge may allow such damages as he deems to be just and may, in the case of an infringement such as is here shown, in his discretion, use as the measure of damages one dollar for each copy, - Congress declaring, however, that just damages, even for the circulation of a single copy, cannot be less than $250, and no matter how many copies are made, cannot be more than $5000. In the Westermann and LaSalle cases it was held that not less than $250 could be awarded for a single publication or performance. It follows that such an award, in the contemplation of the statute, is just. The question now presented is whether it can be unjust, according to the legislative standard, to use the prescribed measure, - $1 per copy, - up to the maximum permitted by the section. As the Westermann Case shows, the law commits to the trier of facts, within the named limits, discretion to apply the measure furnished by the statute provided he awards no more than $5,000. He need not award $1 for each copy, but, if upon consideration of the circumstances he determines that he should do so, his action can not be said to be unjust. In other words, the employment of the statutory yardstick, within set limits, is committed solely to the court which hears the case, and this fact takes the matter out of the ordinary rule with respect to abuse of discretion. This construction is required by the language and the purpose of the statute.

Thus, it seems clear that use of the yardstick amounts up to and including $5,000 is discretionary. However, whether they can be disregarded when the $5,000 limit is inapplicable poses more difficulty. The case law is again scanty. Two courts refused to follow the yardstick amounts because the damage so computed was too high even though the

---

[62] E.g., Advertisers Exchange, Inc. v. Hinkley, 199 F.2d 313, 316 (8th Cir. 1952), cert. denied, 344 U.S. 921, 73 S. Ct. 388, 97 L. Ed. 710 (1953); Hartfield v. Peterson, 91 F.2d 998, 1001 (2d Cir. 1937); Russell & Stoll Co. v. Oceanic Elec. Supply Co., 80 F.2d 864 (2d Cir. 1936) (dictum); see Nikanov v. Simon & Schuster, Inc., 144 F. Supp. 375, 380 (S.D.N.Y.1956), aff'd, 246 F.2d 501 (2d Cir. 1957).

violation occurred after notice. In Sebring Pottery Co. v. Steubenville Pottery Co., 9 F. Supp. 384 (N.D.Ohio 1934), the yardstick damages (at one dollar a copy) for violating plaintiff's copyright in an advertising card or circular would have been over $39,000. The court approved a master's recommendation that statutory damages be fixed at $2,500, the amount at which plaintiff had offered to settle the case before an accounting had been ordered. In Turner & Dahnken v. Crowley, 252 F. 749 (9th Cir. 1918), defendant, with notice, had distributed 7,000 copies of plaintiff's copyrighted song and had been held liable for $7,000 in damages at one dollar per copy, the yardstick amount. The appellate court reduced the damage award to $560, a figure it characterized as "a fair estimate" of plaintiff's damage,[63] although plaintiff had offered no proof of actual loss or of profits. In Schellberg v. Empringham, 36 F.2d 991 (S.D.N.Y.1929), the court allowed statutory damages of $8,000 for 8,000 copies of an infringing book, at the yardstick amount of one dollar per copy. It is not clear whether the basis for awarding over $5,000 was statutory notice or an assumption that the two editions of the offending book constituted two infringements so that the maximum damage limit was $10,000. Research discloses no case where the statutory damage award for one infringement was over $5,000 and exceeded the yardstick amount.[64]

All of this leaves the matter unsettled. The Supreme Court's reference to "within set limits" in Douglas v. Cunningham, supra, may indicate discretion to ignore the yardstick amounts only when damages are fixed at or under $5,000. On the other hand, if the yardstick amounts may be disregarded to reach lesser damages, logically they may be disregarded to fix higher damages. The statutory language, after all, directs the court to award "such damages as to the court shall appear to be just." The nub of the difficulty is that once the $5,000 maximum is disregarded because of notice, the court is on an uncharted sea, unless it adheres to the yardstick amounts. By hypothesis, there is in this situation no proof - or inadequate proof - of plaintiff's damages or defendants' profits. The yardstick amounts at least then provide something definite to turn to. But, it should be noted that one of the reasons given above for construing a network telecast as only one infringement was to give a court flexibility rather than bind it to an unrealistic massing of $250 minimums.[65] Requiring rigid adheren[65]ce in

---

[63] 252 F. at 754.

[64] Cf. Nikanov v. Simon & Schuster, Inc., 144 F. Supp. 375, 380 (S.D.N.Y.1956), aff'd, 246 F.2d 501 (2d Cir. 1957) (damages of $5,000, higher than yardstick amount, awarded).

[65] See p. 341 supra.

every case to yardstick amounts fixed in 1909 is inconsistent with this approach; it can hardly be justified when dealing with radio or television performances reaching a far larger audience than then envisioned. Although, as just suggested, the Supreme Court may have meant to imply in Douglas v. Cunningham that a trial court has no discretion to depart from the yardstick amounts above $5,000, its discussion is certainly subject to a contrary interpretation, one supporting the view taken here. The Court stated that "the employment of the statutory yardstick, within set limits, is committed solely to the court which hears the case, and this fact takes the matter out of the ordinary rule with respect to abuse of discretion." Rather than implying that a trial court has no authority to exceed the yardstick amounts over $5,000, the Court may simply have meant that if a trial court did go higher, its award would be subject to "the ordinary rule with respect to abuse of discretion." This interpretation seems sound; it enables the trial court to assess fair statutory damages in such a case as this, while protecting the infringer against unreasonable awards by substituting for the statutory yardstick closer appellate review.

After much reflection, I conclude that a court has the discretion to depart from the yardstick amounts, even if the $5,000 limit is inapplicable, and can depart upward as well as downward. This upward discretion should be used most sparingly and only when the yardstick amounts produce a clearly inadequate damage award for a violation of plaintiff's copyright. I have no doubt that this is such a case.

The question of what to look to here in fixing damages still remains. In awarding statutory damages under the $5,000 maximum for the infringement of a photograph by the printing of 16,000 copies, Judge Learned Hand stated:

Under section 25b(2), Comp.St.1913, § 9546 [now section 101(b)], these numbers [16,000 copies] would exceed the maximum, but I shall not take them as a basis of damages in any event, as I cannot think it has any relation to actual damages. I shall rather try to estimate Gross' actual damages, without observing the rules of evidence, as though the issue had to be proved like other such issues, and allowing myself considerable latitude in speculation. This is, as I understand the duty laid upon the court by section 25b: In place of the old penalties the court is to estimate damages, but to estimate them within the sums given, without the limitations of usual legal proof. I think the whole course of copyright law shows a recognition of the difficulty of making legal proof of damages, and that, in substituting for rigid penalties the discretionary power of the court, we must assume that a plaintiff should not fail for lack of proof. I must assess the damages, all things considered, by the best inference I can make, even when I cannot have much basis for certainty, even when the plaintiff would fail, were the issue tried before a jury. [66]

Some of the facts already in this record or logically inferable are as follows: In 1959, defendant Talent paid $15,000 to the heirs of Edith Wharton for a license to use the original story. [67] In 1942, Warner Brothers paid $17,500 for the motion picture rights, [68] although no motion picture was ever subsequently made. The Davis play, excluding the Broadway production of about thirty years ago, has not been in demand or a financially successful work. [69] In 1959, plaintiff may possibly have been willing to pay $30,000 for the re-purchase from Columbia Pictures of the motion picture rights, but the highest offer he ever actually made was $10,000. [70] Plaintiff himself suggests that "the sum of $30,000 might reasonably reflect the price plaintiff could expect to receive for a one-shot live television performance of his play." [71] Defendants "speculate that the unapportioned market value of the Davis play for a single network broadcast lies somewhere in an area less than a figure between $17,500 and $10,000." [72] However, both plaintiff and defendants then veer off sharply from this middle area of $30,000 to $10,000-$17,500. Plaintiff urges that since he had larger plans for his dramatization in the motion picture field, the value of the play destroyed by the telecast was far in excess of $30,000. But the plans were nebulous, at least on this record. Plaintiff also suggests use of a measure of "a profit of a single penny for each of the 17,000,000 viewers of the infringing telecast," or $1,000 to $1,500 per station as the worth to defendant advertisers.[73] However, these possibilities are too fanciful even "allowing myself considerable latitude in speculation." See Gross v. Van Dyk Gravure Co., as quoted, supra. Conversely, defendants argue that the Davis play's "true market value," whatever it may be, should be halved, citing Sheldon v. Metro-Goldwyn Pictures Corp., 309 U.S. 390, 60 S. Ct. 681, 84 L. Ed. 825 (1940); Orgel v. Clark Boardman Co., 301 F.2d 119 (2d Cir.), cert. denied, 371 U.S. 817, 83 S. Ct. 31, 9 L. Ed. 2d 58 (1962), and Alfred Bell & Co. v. Catalda Fine Arts, Inc., 86 F. Supp. 399 (S.D.N.Y.1949), aff'd, 191 F.2d 99 (2d Cir. 1951). Those cases all dealt with the question of whether a copyright infringer's profits should not be apportioned "so as to give to the owner of the copyright only that part of

---

[66] As quoted in Gross v. Van Dyk Gravure Co., 230 Fed. 412, 413 (2d Cir. 1916), affirming Judge Hand.

[67] Defendants' Exhibit (hereinafter cited as "Def. Ex.") A

[68] Pl. Ex. 15.

[69] See Stipulation, pp. 18-21.

[70] Id. at 18-20.

[71] Pl. Brief in Support, p. 16.

[72] Def. Brief in Opposition, p. 33.

[73] Plaintiff's Reply Brief, p. 17.

the profits found to be attributable to the use of the copyrighted material as distinguished from what the infringer himself has supplied * * *." See Sheldon, 309 U.S. at 396, 60 S. Ct. at 682. Since those decisions all involved proof of an infringer's actual profits, they are not applicable here where it is impossible to prove, or a fortiori apportion, defendants' profits. [74] Defendants' final argument that plaintiff would be "unjustly enriched" unless any "just" award is reduced by half is similarly without merit. [75]

Accordingly, after a review of the entire record, I find that the damages which "to the court appear to be just" under the circumstances of this case amount to $25,000. In reaching this conclusion I have taken into account plaintiff's undoubted injury, plaintiff's notice to defendants prior to infringement, and all of the other facts and arguments advanced by the parties. Defendants have objected to the admission of certain evidence, which I have admitted for the purpose offered, but these objections are not significant; my finding would be the same whether the evidence is in the record or not.

To summarize: I find that the network telecast over 162 stations was one infringement by these defendants, that the $5,000 maximum does not apply, and that plaintiff is entitled to an award of damages of $25,000. The foregoing constitutes the court's findings of fact and conclusions of law in accordance with Fed.R.Civ.P. 52(a). A decree, in accordance with these findings, may be settled on notice.

---

[74] Stipulation, p. 1.

[75] Def. Brief in Opposition, p. 32

GARDENIA FLOWERS, INC.,
Plaintiff,

v.

JOSEPH MARKOVITS, INC.,
Defendant

No. 62 Civil 1713

UNITED STATES DISTRICT COURT
FOR THE SOUTHERN DISTRICT OF NEW YORK

280 F. Supp. 776

February 26, 1968

Fink & Pavia, New York, New York, for plaintiff, Jerome Bauer, Mineola, New York, of counsel.

Julian T. Abeles, New York, New York, for defendant, John S. Clark, Robert C. Osterberg, New York, New York, of counsel.

Levet, District Judge.

OPINION

OPINION, FINDINGS OF FACT AND CONCLUSIONS OF LAW

Plaintiff, Gardenia Flowers, Inc. ("Gardenia"), alleges infringement of seven copyrighted artificial flower corsages and a claim of unfair competition.

Both liability and damages on the copyright infringement claim were submitted; on the unfair competition claim, liability was tried but any question of resulting damages thereon was reserved.

THE COMPLAINT

The complaint alleges seven causes of action to the effect that plaintiff is the proprietor of a copyright in a specified "original work of art," to wit, an artificial corsage and that defendant, Joseph Markovits, Inc. ("Markovits"), "in infringement of said copyright * * * has made or caused to be made, published and offered for sale copies of the copyrighted work of art," copyrights in suit being dated and identified as follows:

Artificial Single Rose Corsage-Sep. 26, 1961,
Class G, No. Gp 30585;
Artificial Double Gardenia Corsage-Sep. 26, 1961,
Class G, No. Gp 30587;
Artificial Single Gardenia Corsage-Sep. 26, 1961,
Class G, No. Gp 30589;
Artificial Daisy Corsage-Sep. 26, 1961,
Class G, No. Gp 30795;
Artificial Rosebud Corsage-Sep. 26, 1961,
Class G, No. Gp 30797;
Artificial Carnation Corsage-Sep. 26, 1961,
Class G, No. Gp 30798;
Artificial Single Camellia Corsage-Sep. 26, 1961,
Class G, No. Gp 30588.

In an eighth cause of action, it is alleged in substance that Markovits "contacted plaintiff's original manufacturer of each of said works of art and induced such manufacturer to terminate its business relationship with plaintiff in favor of" Markovits; that infringing copies of plaintiff's said "works of art are being made" for Markovits "from the same molds as plaintiff's copyrighted works were originally made," and are being sold by Markovits without plaintiff's copyright notice; that "such activities * * * has [sic] resulted in the confusion of government agencies, thereby preventing their proper application of the law to the benefit and protection of the plaintiff;" that the "infringement of plaintiff's copyrighted works of art" has "caused damage to plaintiff by confusing the trade, detracting from plaintiff's reputation, and loss of sales, thereby constituting acts of unfair competition with plaintiff;" that plaintiff's "copyrighted works of art are well known in the trade as having originated with plaintiff" and that the "copying" by Markovits "results in confusion in the trade and of the public, such that the trade and the public believe and will believe that * * *" the "infringing articles originated with plaintiff, thus damaging plaintiff and creating a loss of business"; and that Markovits' acts "of copying; and its deliberate attempt to trade upon plaintiff's good will, its reproduction of plaintiff's originally created works of art, are acts of copyright infringement and unfair competition * * *."

Plaintiff bases jurisdiction upon the ground that the Copyright Law of the United States is directly involved in the first seven causes of action and upon the ground that the eighth cause of action asserts a claim of unfair competition as a substantial and related claim under the Copyright Law.

After hearing the testimony of the parties, examining the exhibits, the pleadings and the proposed findings of fact and conclusions of law submitted by counsel, this court makes the following Findings of Fact and Conclusions of Law:

FINDINGS OF FACT

1. The court has jurisdiction of the subject matter and of the parties in this action.

2. Plaintiff and defendant are corporations incorporated under the laws of the State of New York, engaged in the business of importing and distributing artificial flowers.

3. In June 1961, Snyder, president of Gardenia, visited the factory of Italspring, a manufacturer of artificial flowers located in Milan, Italy; examined certain sample corsages previously manufactured by Italspring; furnished Italspring with other samples Snyder had obtained from various sources and requested Italspring to supply him with samples of the artificial corsages later involved in this suit. None of the corsages involved in this suit (Pl. Ex. 3-9) were created by the skill, labor or judgment of Snyder (220, 237-242; [1] Deft. Ex. H, dep. of Termini, pp. 1-4; Pl. Ex. 31).

4. Snyder organized the plaintiff company twenty-two years ago. Before that time he had worked in the artificial flower industry for nineteen years (41, 42).

5. On or about June 20, 1961, plaintiff placed an order with Italspring for various items, among them copies of the artificial corsages involved in this suit, and in a letter dated July 5, 1961, instructed Italspring that every such item ordered by Gardenia should carry a notice of copyright in Gardenia's name, irrespective of the authorship of such items (265-268; Pl. Ex. 30, 31).

6. During Snyder's stay in Milan, Italy in June 1961, and at his request, Italspring agreed to invoice shipments of artificial corsages to plaintiff at 70% of the actual price thereof for the purpose of allowing plaintiff to evade payment of customs duty based on true value (see Deft. Ex. H, dep. of Termini, pp. 4, 5; Pl. Ex. 31, 36, 41; Deft. Ex. F).

7. Plaintiff's president brought samples of the corsages he ordered from Italspring to New York in July 1961. After his arrival, plaintiff packaged these samples in acetate boxes with bows attached (345-347; Pl. Ex. 40).

---

[1] Numbers in parentheses not otherwise identified refer to pages in the stenographer's minutes of the trial.

8. Customers to whom the samples were shown were sold substantial numbers of corsages by plaintiff in July 1961. A sale of 5,000 dozen of the corsages had been consummated by July 5, 1961 (140, 376, 377; Pl. Ex. 31).

9. At the time of this first publication of the corsages, a purported copyright notice appeared on paper tags through which the stems of the corsages were slipped (253, 254, 340, 341, 378; Pl. Proposed Finding of Fact No. 18).

10. On September 26, 1961, plaintiff obtained Certificates of Registration for artificial corsages as follows:

Artificial Single Rose Corsage, Class G, No. Gp 30585 (Pl. Ex. 3);
Artificial Double Gardenia Corsage, Class G, No. Gp 30587 (Pl. Ex. 4);
Artificial Single Gardenia Corsage, Class G, No. Gp 30589 (Pl. Ex. 5);
Artificial Daisy Corsage, Class G, No. Gp 30795 (Pl. Ex. 6);
Artificial Rosebud Corsage, Class G, No. Gp 30797 (Pl. Ex. 7);
Artificial Carnation Corsage, Class G, No. Gp 30798 (Pl. Ex. 8);
Artificial Single Camellia Corsage, Class G, No. Gp 30588 (Pl. Ex. 9).

11. In each of the applications for registration of claim to United States copyright in said artificial corsages filed by plaintiff in the Copyright Office, it is stated that plaintiff is the author thereof, that the work, the subject of the claim, was first published on July 7, 1961 in the United States; but said applications do not reveal any previous publication of component parts thereof or the utilization of old matter therein (Pl. Ex. 3-9).

12. Plaintiff's copyright claim in each of said artificial corsages is confined to the arrangement of the flowers therein, and it does not cover the individual component parts thereof (65, 66).

13. The artificial corsages involved in this case consisted of arrangements of flowers which were common and traditional in the flower industry at the time of plaintiff's claim of copyright. The arrangements in the corsages were old styles, lacking in both creativity and originality, and plaintiff's president had been aware of the existence of such arrangements in natural and cloth corsages prior to the time of its claimed copyrights (86, 87, 227-230, 233-237, 322-344).

14. Italspring ceased doing business with plaintiff in October 1961 because it preferred not to risk the consequences of performing its agreement with plaintiff to invoice shipments of the artificial floral corsages at 70% of the true value thereof (Deft. Ex. H, dep. of Termini, p. 5).

15. Defendant did not order any plastic artificial corsages from Italspring until January 22, 1962, approximately three months after Italspring ceased doing business with plaintiff (392, 395; see Pl. Proposed Finding of Fact 33).

16. Some time prior to May 1962, defendant sold to Woolworth

corsages it purchased from Italspring which were similar to those ordered from Italspring by plaintiff. Certain of these corsages were purchased from Woolworth by employees of plaintiff (355-357, 369-375; Pl. Ex. 25-28).

17. Some of the corsages purchased by plaintiff's employees from Woolworth contained defendant's label, and some did not (361, 362, 372, 374).

18. Imprints of plaintiff's name had been scraped from the stems of the corsages purchased by plaintiff's employees, and the prior existence of such imprints is noticeable only upon extremely close examination (Pl. Ex. 25-28).

19. Plaintiff has failed to prove by a fair preponderance of the credible evidence that defendant misrepresented any of the corsages sold to be the goods of plaintiff.

20. The plaintiff has failed to prove by a fair preponderance of the credible evidence that (1) it had any exclusive agreement with Italspring to supply Gardenia with the artificial corsages which are the subject matter of this suit (Pl. Ex. 36, 44; 123-128, 146, 147, 150); or (2) that defendant had any knowledge of any exclusive contract or agreement of Italspring with plaintiff (144, 145, 146, 147, 150, 389); or (3) that defendant induced Italspring to cease to sell to plaintiff (383-390).

21. Plaintiff has failed to prove by a fair preponderance of the credible evidence that defendant committed any acts of unfair competition in respect to the corsages at issue here.

DISCUSSION

A. The Copyright Issue

The issue upon which plaintiff's infringement claims must stand or fall is that of the validity of the copyrights it obtained upon the arrangements of flowers in the artificial corsages. Clearly, there may be infringement of copyrighted works of art by reproduction of the objects themselves. Mura v. Columbia Broadcasting System, Inc., 245 F. Supp. 587 (S.D.N.Y.1965).

Plaintiff introduced its Certificates of Registration of the copyrights relating to the artificial corsages, and under 17 U.S.C. § 209 these are prima facie evidence of the facts stated therein. Initially, therefore, the burden is upon defendant to produce sufficient evidence to overcome this presumption of validity. National Institute, Inc. v. Nutt, 28 F.2d 132 (D.Conn.1928), aff'd, 31 F.2d 236 (2nd Cir. 1929).

Proof by defendant of facts contrary to those stated in the Certificate of Registration, however, shifts the burden of overcoming such evidence to plaintiff. Hirsch v. Paramount Pictures, Inc., 17 F. Supp. 816 (S.D.Cal.1937); Werner Co. v. Encyclopaedia Britannica Co., 134 F. 831

(3rd Cir. 1905); see also Stuff v. E. C. Publications, Inc., 342 F.2d 143 (2nd Cir. 1965), cert. denied, 382 U.S. 822, 86 S. Ct. 50, 15 L. Ed. 2d 68 (1965). The burden of proof may be shifted back to a plaintiff even upon those issues over which the Register may have exercised its discretion, for such exercise is subject to judicial review. Bailie v. Fisher, 103 U.S.App.D.C. 331, 258 F.2d 425 (1958). Here defendant offered evidence sufficient to place the burden of proving the validity of his copyrights upon the plaintiff. This burden plaintiff has not met.

With regard to works of art, 37 CFR § 202.10 states:

"(a) * * * This class includes published or unpublished works of artistic craftsmanship, insofar as their form but not their mechanical or utilitarian aspects are concerned, such as artistic jewelry, enamels, glassware, and tapestries, as well as works belonging to the fine arts, such as paintings, drawings and sculpture. * * * [and] (b) In order to be acceptable as a work of art, the work must embody some creative authorship in its delineation or form."

Creative authorship is required as a matter of definition in this class of works subject to copyright; without it there can be no work of art. See Nimmer on Copyright § 19.1 (1964). The requirement of creativeness is separate and distinct from authorship or originality. "Where creativity refers to the nature of the work itself, originality refers to the nature of the author's contribution to the work." Nimmer, supra, § 19.2.

The standard for determining that degree of creativity necessary to constitute a work of art is not high. But though the boundaries may be generous, there are, nevertheless, limits beyond which courts cannot accord objects the status of work of art. See, e.g., Bailie v. Fisher, supra. Plaintiff has conceded that its claims are limited to the arrangements of the flowers in the corsages. No claim is made that the component parts thereof are covered.

With respect to the arrangements in question, however, plaintiff's president testified that he did not create anything new. On the contrary, he admitted that before his trip to Italy he had seen flowers arranged with ferns, corsages with a lily of the valley, a carnation bud with gardenias, daisies with ferns in a bouquet, and rosebud corsages with a fern attached. He had seen these arrangements made both with natural and cloth components (227-234). Furthermore, plaintiff's president acknowledged that the rosebud corsages with a fern attached, the rose and bud with lilies of the valley and ferns, the double gardenia with lilies of the valley and ferns, as well as the full-blown camellia and bud with a lily of the valley and fern were all "traditional" flower arrangements for corsages (234-237). There is no evidence of creativity in plaintiff's flower arrangements.

That degree of creativity necessary to define objects as works of art is not supplied through innovations which are solely utilitarian or mechanical. 37 CFR § 202.10(a); Mazer v. Stein, 347 U.S. 201, 74 S. Ct. 460, 98 L. Ed. 630 (1954). Thus, the fact that plaintiff may have been responsible for adding certain practical features to the component parts of the flower arrangements, which facilitated their assembly and eliminated the need for certain manufacturing operations, does not overcome the absence of creativity inherent in the arrangements. Likewise, plaintiff's decision to use plastic material for fabrication of the articles may have added certain utilitarian advantages, such as durability or color retention over natural or cloth materials, but this, too, does not constitute the creativity required for copyright purposes.

The lack of creativity in the corsages herein involved is fatal to plaintiff's claims regarding the validity of its copyrights and infringements thereof.

Lack of creativity, however, is not the only fault to be found with plaintiff's corsages. They also are lacking in originality,[2] and it is elementary that no work is entitled to copyright protection unless it is "* * * original, in that the author has created it by his own skill, labor, and judgment." Stuff v. La-Budde Feed & Grain Co., 42 F. Supp. 493, 495 (E.D.Wis.1941).

"The 'originality' requirement for copyrightability is not onerous." Peter Pan Fabrics, Inc. v. Acadia Company, 173 F. Supp. 292, 299 (S.D.N.Y.1956), aff'd, 274 F.2d 487 (2nd Cir. 1960). Indeed, it has been held that: "* * * practically anything novel can be copyrighted. * * * 'No matter how poor artistically the "author's" addition, it is enough if it be his own'. * * *" Dan Kasoff, Inc. v. Novelty Jewelry Co., 309 F.2d 745, 746 (2nd Cir. 1962). Moreover, it has been said that "originality in this context 'means little more than a prohibition of actual copying.'" Rushton v. Vitale, 218 F.2d 434, 435 (2nd Cir. 1955).

As with the question of creativity, though, the fact that only minimal standards need be applied does not prevent the court from concluding as a matter of fact that works may lack even the modicum of originality required. When the copyright claimant has added nothing of his own to a work, then copyright protection must be denied. See Nimmer, supra, § 19.2.

Much of the same reasoning which led this court to the determination that plaintiff's corsages were devoid of creativity applies with equal force to its claim of originality. Applying the standard in Sieff v. Continental Auto

---

[2] 2 To some extent this deficiency may be more vital then an absence of creativity. The requirement of originality applies universally, while creativity must be given special consideration only for the purposes of Class G works due to its definitional function therein. See Nimmer, supra, §§ 10 and 19.1.

Supply, 39 F. Supp. 683, 688 (D.Minn.1941), that "* * * sameness or similarity is determined by the eye of the ordinary observer," it cannot be said that plaintiff's works represent anything new.

Once more it must be noted that plaintiff's claims relate only to the arrangements of the components of the corsages and not the component parts themselves. These arrangements, which consisted primarily of placing flowers and flower buds upon a background of ferns and leaves, were old traditional styles in the flower industry and they had existed in both natural and cloth corsages well before the time the works at issue appeared in plastic (Finding of Fact 13).

Cases relied upon by plaintiff do not support the premise that its arrangements of flowers in the corsages are sufficiently original to be protected by copyright. Concededly, reproductions of creations of nature such as Balinese dancers, **cocker spaniels** and even artificial flowers themselves have been given copyright protection where they represented some originality in their treatment of the subject. See Mazer v. Stein, supra; Contemporary Arts, Inc. v. F. W. Woolworth Co., 93 F. Supp. 739 (D.Mass.1950), aff'd, 193 F.2d 162 (1st Cir. 1951); Prestige Floral, Societe Anonyme v. California Artificial Flower Co., 201 F. Supp. 287 (S.D.N.Y.1962). The copyright claims here, however, do not represent creations of nature but merely patterns of arranging floral components for decorative purposes, and plaintiff has shown no originality in the patterns of arrangements it chose. Furthermore, the fact that flower arrangements may have been given copyright protection when incorporated into fabric designs is not relevant, for in such cases the originality required is inherent in the reduction of three dimensional objects to a two dimensional presentation on cloth. See, e.g., Peter Pan Fabrics, Inc. v. Candy Frocks, Inc., 187 F. Supp. 334 (S.D.N.Y.1960).

Plaintiff's argument that requisite originality is demonstrated by slight irregularities of details in the component parts of the flower arrangements, which may be noticed only upon extremely close observation, is also of no avail. The originality of the component parts is not at issue here, but, more important, even a botanist's inspection which might reveal an unusual vein pattern in some of the leaves or abnormal stem configurations would be irrelevant. Considering, arguendo, that some small details of the component parts of the plastic corsages may be somewhat dissimilar to natural components, still it cannot be said that such variances affect the arrangements of the components or the overall impression made by the complete corsages when viewed by the eye of an ordinary observer. In any event, there was no proof that such minor variations of detail were not present in the artificial cloth corsages which antedated plaintiff's creations.

Finally, it must be noted that originality is not proved merely because plaintiff may have had the idea to produce artificial corsages made out of a new plastic material. There can be no copyright on an idea. Baker v. Selden, 101 U.S. 99, 25 L. Ed. 841 (1879); Uneeda Doll Co. v. P & M Doll Co., 353 F.2d 788 (2nd Cir. 1965).

"The purpose of the copyright law is to protect creation, not mechanical skill." Shapiro, Bernstein & Co., Inc. v. Miracle Record Co., Inc., 91 F. Supp. 473, 475 (N.D.Ill.1950). Here there is no doubt that the corsages were completely lacking in creativity and originality. The arrangements of components in these corsages are no different from the arrangement of components in artificial and natural corsages which had been common and traditional in the trade for many years before plaintiff's were produced, and plaintiff's president admitted familiarity with such common and traditional arrangements of corsage components during his long experience in the flower business (Findings of Fact 4, 13).

For these reasons, the copyrights claimed by plaintiff upon the corsages herein involved are invalid.

In addition to the intrinsic defects in plaintiff's works which render its claimed copyrights invalid, there is a further reason for which copyright protection must be denied. Publication with proper notice of copyright is the essence of compliance with the Copyright Act, and publication without such notice amounts to a dedication to the public sufficient to defeat all subsequent efforts at copyright protection. 17 U.S.C. § 10; Universal Film Mfg. Co. v. Copperman, 212 F. 301 (S.D.N.Y.), aff'd, 218 F. 577 (2nd Cir.), cert. denied, 235 U.S. 704, 35 S. Ct. 209, 59 L. Ed. 433 (1914); Fleischer Studios, Inc. v. Ralph A. Freundlich, Inc., 73 F.2d 276 (2nd Cir. 1934), cert. denied, 294 U.S. 717, 55 S. Ct. 516, 79 L. Ed. 1250 (1935).

The first publication of the corsages in question occurred during the early part of July 1961, shortly after plaintiff's president brought samples of the corsages to the United States from Italy. These samples were shown to customers who placed substantial orders with plaintiff for future delivery of the plastic corsages. Indeed, a sizeable customer order was accepted by plaintiff two days before the date of publication which appears on its Certificates of Copyright Registration (Pl. Post Trial Brief, p. 32). Purported copyright notices were on removeable paper tags which were slipped onto the stems of the samples (Finding of Fact 9).

These notices were insufficient to prevent dedication of the corsages to the public, for the law is clear that notices which appear on paper tags attached to articles do not meet the requirement of affixation in 17 U.S.C. § 10. See Trifari, Krussman & Fishel, Inc. v. B. Steinberg-Kaslo Co., 144 F. Supp. 577 (S.D.N.Y.1956); Peter Pan Fabrics, Inc. v. Dixon Textile Corporation, 188 F. Supp. 235 (S.D.N.Y.1960); cf. 37 CFR § 202.2(b)(9).

In answer to this, plaintiff asserts that its use of paper tags is proof that it "sought to comply" with the provisions of the Copyright Act, and the defect in notice should be excused, presumably by the savings clause in 17

U.S.C. § 21. This statute, however, does not apply when a defect in notice is the result of a mistake of law, Wildman v. New York Times Co., 42 F. Supp. 412, 413 (S.D.N.Y. 1941); and it also fails to excuse defective forms of notice which were deliberately selected and used by the copyright claimant. Advertisers Exchange, Inc. v. Anderson, 144 F.2d 907 (8th Cir. 1944).

Additionally, plaintiff claims that the entire range of activities which took place in July 1961 constituted merely a limited publication that did not divest it of any copyright protections. With this argument I also do not agree.

A limited publication is one which communicates a work "* * * to a definitely selected group and for a limited purpose, without the right of diffusion, reproduction, distribution, or sale * * *." White v. Kimmell, 193 F.2d 744, 746 (9th Cir. 1952). Though plaintiff's customers might be considered a selected group since they must all have been retail flower sellers, it cannot be said that plaintiff's publication of the corsages was for a limited purpose. The customers whose orders were accepted by plaintiff were never subject to any limitations on their rights to distribute or sell the corsages. Obviously, the only purpose for which such customers purchased the corsages was to resell them.

Cases cited by plaintiff relate to the distribution of samples for the purpose of enabling the recipients to place future orders, to distributions for the purpose of record "plugging," or distributions for the purpose of soliciting backers for future theatrical productions. Such authorities are not relevant to the facts of this case, since the customers here had already placed orders with the plaintiff which it had accepted. Furthermore, those of plaintiff's cases which suggest that there can be no general publication unless the author so intends, represent a minority view only. I agree with the prevailing view which holds that an intentional surrender is in no sense necessary to the forfeiture of a copyright. See National Comics Publications v. Fawcett Publications, 191 F.2d 594 (2nd Cir. 1951). Plaintiff's publication of the corsages in the manner described amounted to a dedication to the public.

Thus, for all of the reasons stated, the copyright infringement claims of the plaintiff are dismissed. It is unnecessary at this time to consider defendant's allegations of unclean hands and material omissions in its Certificates of Registration on the part of plaintiff.

B. Unfair Competition

In connection with its copyright infringement claims, plaintiff has alleged a claim of unfair competition. The gist of this is that the defendant induced Italspring to terminate its business relationship with plaintiff and to sell defendant corsages made from plaintiff's molds-although with defendant's name tag on said corsages. Further, it alleges that defendant sold these to plaintiff's customers so as to lead the customers to believe that the same originated with plaintiff.

Sharing in the goodwill of an unprotected article "* * * is the exercise of a right possessed by all-and in the free exercise of which the consuming public is deeply interested." Kellogg Co. v. National Biscuit Co., 305 U.S. 111, 122, 59 S. Ct. 109, 115, 83 L. Ed. 73, rehearing denied, 305 U.S. 674, 59 S. Ct. 246, 83 L. Ed. 437 (1938). "In our freely competitive economy, there is no vested and indefeasible right to monopolize customers." Corica v. Ragen, 140 F.2d 496, 498 (7th Cir. 1944).

The owner of property may sell to whom he chooses. Locker v. American Tobacco Co., 195 N.Y. 565, 88 N.E. 289 (1909); Federal Trade Commission v. Raymond Bros.-Clark Co., 263 U.S. 565, 44 S. Ct. 162, 68 L. Ed. 448 (1924), and in the absence of an exclusive sales contract with plaintiff, Italspring breached no duty by selling to defendant.

The proof as to defendant's alleged inducement to Italspring to terminate its business relationship with plaintiff is insufficient. There is no proof, other than an unsupported statement of plaintiff's president, that Italspring had agreed to sell the corsages to plaintiff exclusively (see Finding of Fact 20), and the fact that defendant placed orders larger than plaintiff's is immaterial. No liability falls upon defendant just because Italspring, for its own reasons (Findings of Fact 6, 14), ceased to sell corsages to plaintiff. Furthermore, defendant placed no orders with Italspring until three months after Italspring terminated its business relationship with plaintiff (Finding of Fact 15).

The only contracts proved by plaintiff between itself and Italspring were mere orders for the delivery of corsages, and though Italspring's refusal to fill plaintiff's order may give rise to some liability on the part of Italspring, there can be no liability of the defendant herein absent any causal relationship.

The second part of plaintiff's unfair competition claim alleges that defendant palmed off plaintiff's corsages as its own. Indeed, the essence of the wrong of unfair competition lies in the sale of the goods of one manufacturer or vendor for those of another or under such conditions as may lead the purchaser to think they are the goods of another. Lewis v. Vendome Bags, 108 F.2d 16 (2nd Cir. 1939), cert. denied, 309 U.S. 660, 60 S. Ct. 514, 84 L. Ed. 1008 (1940).

Conceding, however, that under certain circumstances, particularly by reason of prior use, unfair competition may exist without infringement of a copyright, Sally Chain Stores, Inc. v. Sally's Fur Studio, Inc., 40 F. Supp. 445 (E.D.Mich.1941), that condition is not present here. Palming off, or the fair likelihood of it, is not shown by production or sale of plaintiff's uncopyrightable corsages which defendant may be deemed to have caused, since plaintiff had no exclusive right to produce or use them. See Airolite Co. v. Fiedler, 147 F.2d 496 (2nd Cir.), cert. denied 326 U.S. 726, 66 S. Ct. 32, 90 L. Ed. 431 (1945). Mere copying of plaintiff's corsages does not constitute unfair competition. See Day-Brite Lighting, Inc. v. Sandee Manufacturing Co., 286 F.2d 596 (7th Cir. 1960).

There is no proof whatever that defendant sold any corsages to anyone upon a representation that they were produced by plaintiff, and, in any event, no purchaser would be injured by purchase of defendant's corsages since they were identical to plaintiff's. In addition, when plaintiff's employees purchased defendant's corsages from a Woolworth store they found that all references to "Gardenia Flowers" had been scraped from the corsages (Finding of Fact 18). Such obliteration of plaintiff's name was proper inasmuch as it diminished chances of possible confusion and is some evidence that defendant's corsages were not sold upon misrepresentations that they were plaintiff's products

Plaintiff has failed to prove its claim of unfair competition, and this cause of action is dismissed.

CONCLUSIONS OF LAW

1. The court has jurisdiction over the subject matter and of the parties herein.

2. The arrangements embodied in the artificial corsages herein involved are copies of old arrangements which were common and traditional in the flower industry and were known to be so by plaintiff at the time it filed applications for the copyright thereof. Plaintiff has failed to meet the burden of proving that such arrangements possessed even a modicum of creativity and originality and, hence, the copyrights of said corsages are invalid.

3. Purported copyright notices on paper tags which were slipped onto the stems of the corsages at the time of their first publication did not meet the requirement of affixation in 17 U.S.C. § 10, and such publication resulted in a dedication of the corsages to the public sufficient to defeat all subsequent efforts at copyright protection.

4. Plaintiff's copyright infringement claims are dismissed.

5. Plaintiff has failed to prove by a fair preponderance of the credible

evidence that defendant induced Italspring to terminate its business relationship with plaintiff or that defendant palmed off plaintiff's corsages as its own.

6. Plaintiff's claims of unfair competition are dismissed.

7. Plaintiff's claims were not so lacking in merit as to constitute bad faith and, accordingly, defendant's demand for an award of attorney's fees is hereby denied.

8. Defendant Joseph Markovits, Inc. is entitled to judgment herein dismissing the complaint with costs.

Settle order on notice.

ART ROGERS,
Plaintiff,

v.

JEFF KOONS and
SONNABEND GALLERY, INC.,
Defendants

No. 89 Civ. 6707 (CSH)

UNITED STATES DISTRICT COURT
FOR THE SOUTHERN DISTRICT OF NEW YORK

777 F. Supp. 1

February 22, 1991

District Judge Charles S. Haight, Jr.

OPINION

MEMORANDUM OPINION
AND ORDER

Following entry of this Court's Memorandum Opinion and Order dated December 10, 1990, familiarity with which is assumed, plaintiff made a timely motion for reargument pursuant to Civil Rule 3(j) of this Court.[1] Upon consideration, the motion for reargument is granted, and judgment for infringement will enter against defendant Sonnabend Gallery, Inc.

I am not at all certain that Sonnabend is vicariously liable for Koon's infringement under Shapiro, Bernstein & Co. v. H.L. Green Co., 316 F.2d 304, 137 U.S.P.Q. (BNA) 275 (2d Cir. 1963), the case plaintiff relies upon for that theory of liability. Vicarious liability, the Second Circuit said in Shapiro, "depends upon a detailed examination of the relationship between" the primary infringer (in this case Koons) and the one sought to be held

---

[1] There is no basis for defendants' characterization of the motion as one under Rule 59, Fed.R.Civ.P.

vicariously liable (in this case Sonnabend). 316 F.2d at 306. In Shapiro the defendant held vicariously liable operated a chain of retail stores. The primary infringer operated the phonograph record departments at concessionaire in those stores, and sold records which infringed the copyrights of plaintiffs, proprietors of musical compositions. The store owner, defendant H.L. Green Co., Inc. exacted from its concessionaire a licensing agreement which provided that the concessionaire's employees were to "abide by, observe and obey all rules and regulations promulgated from time to time by H.L. Green Company, Inc. . . ." Green also had the authority, in its "unreviewable discretion," to discharge any concessionaire employee believed to be conducting himself improperly. Ibid. In those particular circumstances, the Second Circuit regarded Green as bearing a closer resemblance to "the proprietor or manager of a dance hall leasing his premises to or hiring" an infringing dance band (vicariously liable), as opposed to a "landlord leasing his property at a fixed rental to a tenant who engages in copyright-infringing conduct on the leased promises" (not vicariously liable). Id. at 307.

In the case at bar, Sonnabend did not exercise that degree of supervision and control over Koons that Green did over its infringing concessionaire. As far as the dance hall cases go, the arguments fairly cut both ways. Neither party at bar cites an art gallery case, nor have I found one, which leads me to comment with Judge Kaufman in Shapiro upon the surprising dearth of squarely applicable precedents in "a business setting so common that the dearth of precedents seems inexplicable," id. at 305.

However, Sonnabend was unquestionably a seller of Koons' infringing sculptures. I agree with Rogers that Sonnabend is accordingly a direct infringer under F.W. Woolworth Co. v. Contemporary Arts, Inc., 344 U.S. 228, 97 L. Ed. 276, 73 S. Ct. 222, 95 U.S.P.Q. (BNA) 396 (1952). Woolworth sold **cocker spaniel** statuettes which, without Woolworth's knowledge, infringed the plaintiff's copyright. Woolworth was held liable as a direct infringer.

Counsel for Sonnabend argues that Woolworth did not address the point at issue. It is the fact that the Supreme Court granted certiorari "limiting the issues to the measure of recovery, as to which conflict appears among the lower courts." 344 U.S. at 229 (footnotes omitted). However, in its recitation of the facts, the court stated unequivocally:

Unbeknown to Woolworth, these dogs had been copied from respondent's and by marketing them it became an infringer. Ibid.

I must regard that statement either as something the Court tossed off without thinking about it, or as a statement of what the Court conceived to be applicable copyright law. I adopt the latter interpretation. See also Justice

Black's dissent at 234: "The earthenware dogs found to infringe respondent's copyright were bought by F.W. Woolworth Company in good faith at a total cost of $ 914.40."

Judge Goettel of this Court expressed the same principle more recently in Kieselstein-Cord v. Accessories By Pearl, Inc., 489 F.Supp. 732, 737, 206 U.S.P.Q.2d (BNA) 439 (S.D.N.Y.) reversed on other grounds, 632 F.2d 989, 208 U.S.P.Q.2d (BNA) 1 (2d Cir. 1980):

The fact that defendant did not copy the Winchester Buckle but instead allegedly bought unauthorized copies from a manufacturer without notice to defendant of the copyright does not affect the validity of the copyright or defendant's liability for infringement. If defendant has should the unauthorized copies, which he admits, defendant's liability -- given a valid copyright -- is established. The infringer's claimed lack of knowledge of the copyright affects only damages, not basic liability and injunctive relief.

(footnote omitted).

In the case at bar, Sonnabend was identified as the seller on the sales invoices for the sculptures, and realized 50% of the infringing profits. I think that Sonnabend is a directly infringing seller within the principle of law articulated in Woolworth. This Court's prior Memorandum Opinion and Order is amended accordingly.

It is SO ORDERED.

KING RECORDS, INC., Plaintiff,

v.

KENNETH R. BENNETT d/b/a KRB MUSIC COMPANIES and KRB MUSIC COMPANIES, INC.,

Defendants.

UNITED STATES DISTRICT COURT FOR THE MIDDLE DISTRICT OF TENNESSEE NASHVILLE DIVISION

Case No. 3-00-0299

438 F. Supp. 2d 812

June 20, 2006

JOHN T. NIXON, SENIOR JUDGE. Magistrate Judge Griffin.

OPINION

MEMORANDUM

Plaintiff King Records, Inc. ("King" or "Plaintiff") filed a three-count Complaint against Defendants Kenneth Bennett ("Bennett"), d/b/a KRB Music Companies and KRB Music Companies, Inc. ("KRB," and together with Bennett, "Defendants") alleging, among other things, copyright infringement in violation of the Copyright Act, 17 U.S.C. § 101 et seq. of numerous re-recordings of popular songs. Count I alleges the copyright infringement of a musical composition entitled "Don't Fall Asleep at the Wheel." Count II alleges copyright infringement of twenty-one sound recordings. Count III alleged the unlawful duplication of forty noncopyrightable sound recordings protected under the common law, including claims of unfair competition, conversion, and unjust enrichment, as well as violations of Tenn. Code. Ann. § 39-14-139 and the Lanham Act, 15 U.S.C. § 1125(a).

A bench trial was conducted between July 21, 2003, and July 25, 2003.[1] At the start of trial, Plaintiff sought the dismissal without prejudice of the claims in Count III pursuant to Rule 41(a)(2) of the Federal Rules of Civil Procedure, to which Defendant objected requesting dismissal with prejudice. (See Doc. No. 199, Trial Tr. I at 6, 28-29.) The Court reserved ruling on Plaintiff's motion (Id. at 29), and no evidence was presented regarding the claims in Count III. Each party submitted their proposed findings of fact and conclusions of law (Doc. Nos. 209, 210).

In addition to the ultimate issue, also pending before the Court are the parties' motions in limine and post-trial motions. These are addressed in the contemporaneously filed Memorandum Order. For the reasons set forth below, the Court ENTERS JUDGMENT in favor of Plaintiff and AWARDS Plaintiff $ 170,000.

I. MATERIAL FACTS

King is a Tennessee corporation with its principal place of business in Nashville, Tennessee at 1900 Elm Hill Pike. Prior to September 21, 2001, King was known as Gusto Records, Inc. ("Gusto"). Gayron C. "Moe" Lytle ("Lytle") is the president and sole shareholder of King. King is in the music industry and causes to be manufactured, sells and licenses music records.

Defendant KRB is an Indiana corporation with its principal place of business in Brentwood, Tennessee. Defendant Bennett is KRB's president and sole owner. KRB's primary business is "rack jobbing," which entails placing display fixtures in retail stores and using service representatives to refurbish the inventory in those fixtures. The business at issue in this case is KRB's "rack jobbing" of cassettes and compact discs at Big Lots, a retail store with approximately 1,300 outlets across the country. KRB has been in business for seventeen years and has been the exclusive supplier of music products to Big Lots for most of those seventeen years. Prior to the end of 2002, Big Lots was KRB's biggest customer.

A. COUNT I -- MUSICAL COMPOSITION "DON'T FALL ASLEEP AT THE WHEEL"

On January 5, 1982, John Riggs and Gary Lumpkin entered into an agreement transferring their rights in the musical composition "Don't Fall Asleep at the Wheel" to Power Play Music (Division of Gusto Records,

---

[1] This case was previously assigned to Judge Echols. Due to a criminal matter in Judge Echols' Court, this case was reassigned to the undersigned three days prior to trial. (See Doc. No. 184.)

Inc.) & Moe's Music, located at 1900 Elm Hill Pike, Nashville.[2] In addition to the agreement, Messrs. Riggs and Lumpkin executed an agreement entitled "Transfer of Copyright" in which they transferred to Power Play Music (A Division of Gusto Records, Inc.) "all right, title and interest in and to the copyright and all exclusive rights comprised in the copyright, without limitation in the musical composition . . . Don't Fall Asleep at the Wheel." (Pl. Ex. 6.) Lytle testified that the original authors of the song created it for Gusto.

Ten years later, a musical composition copyright was registered with the United States Copyright Office ("Copyright Office") in the words and music of "Don't Fall Asleep at the Wheel," effective December 18, 1992. The copyright claimant on the original registration is Power Play Music, Inc., located at 1900 Elm Hill Pike in Nashville. There is no evidence in the record that a corporation entitled Power Play Music, Inc. existed in 1992. There is, however, evidence that a Tennessee corporation entitled Power Play Publishing Company was incorporated on April 11, 1988, and its charter was amended on October 10, 2001 to reflect a name change to Power Play Music, Inc. Lytle was the president and sole shareholder of Power Play Publishing Company, and continues to be the president and sole shareholder of Power Play Music, Inc.

Lytle testified that the copyright claimant should have been "Power Play Music (A Division of Gusto Records, Inc.)" and that the reference to "Power Play Music, Inc." on the registration was a mistake. In an attempt to correct the error on the registration, Lytle executed a series of assignments purporting to assign the copyright in "Don't Fall Asleep at the Wheel" to Gusto, which is now known as Plaintiff King. These assignments utterly fail to create any clarity; instead, riddled with error, they simply enhance the confusion surrounding the copyright claimant of "Don't Fall Asleep at the Wheel."

First, on April 7, 2000, Lytle executed an "Assignment of Copyright" in which GML, Inc. ("GML"), another company of which Lytle is the sole shareholder and an officer, purported to be the "sole owner" of the copyright registration of "Don't Fall Asleep at the Wheel." GML transferred its "rights" to Gusto even though there is no evidence that GML had any rights in "Don't Fall Asleep at the Wheel" to assign to Gusto. This assignment was signed by notary public Carolyn McMinn ("McMinn"). McMinn also completed a "Document Cover Sheet For Recordation of Documents United States Copyright Office." McMinn affirmed that the information she provided on the recordation cover sheet was "a true and

---

[2] A musical composition includes the music and lyrics written by the composer. The copyright in a musical composition is governed by 17 U.S.C. § 106.

correct representation of the accompanying document." The recordation cover sheet, which was recorded with the Copyright Office on October 2, 2000, is not a true and correct representation of the assignment because it incorrectly explains that the assignment is from Power Play Music, Inc. to Gusto, whereas the assignment is actually from GML to Gusto.

Second, again on April 7, 2000, Lytle executed and McMinn notarized another "Assignment of Copyright" in which Power Play Music, Inc. purported to be the "sole owner" of the copyright registration of "Don't Fall Asleep at the Wheel," and assigned its "rights" to Gusto. There is no evidence that this assignment was recorded with the Copyright Office. There is also no evidence that a company by the name of Power Play Music, Inc. existed on April 7, 2000. This is underscored by the fact that this assignment does not include the standard language in the preamble regarding the state in which Power Play Music, Inc. is incorporated. There is evidence that such a company came into existence on October 10, 2001. As it stands, however, this assignment involves a non-existent company purporting to have rights in "Don't Fall Asleep at the Wheel," and attempting to assign those rights to Gusto.

Third, on April 16, 2001, Steven Kountzman ("Kountzman"), purported Vice President of Power Play, Inc., executed a third "Assignment of Copyright," which McMinn notarized. In this assignment, Power Play Music, Inc. (not Power Play, Inc.) purported to be the "sole owner" of the copyright registration of "Don't Fall Asleep at the Wheel," and assigned its "rights" to Gusto. There is no evidence that this assignment was recorded with the Copyright Office. There is also no evidence that a company by the name of Power Play, Inc. or Power Play Music, Inc. existed on April 16, 2001. This is underscored by the fact that this assignment does not include the standard language in the preamble regarding the state in which Power Play Music, Inc. or Power Play, Inc. are incorporated. While there is evidence that Power Play Music, Inc. came into existence on October 10, 2001, there is no evidence that Power Play, Inc. ever existed or now exists. This assignment, therefore, involves two non-existent companies, one or both of which are claiming ownership in "Don't Fall Asleep at the Wheel," and attempting to assign their rights to Gusto.

To add to this confusion, Gusto (now known as Plaintiff King) acknowledged in response to Defendants' First Set of Interrogatories, that it was not the registered copyright owner of "Don't Fall Asleep at the Wheel" on August 18, 2000. It was not until June 20, 2003 that Plaintiff provided a supplemental response stating that it was the registered copyright owner of "Don't Fall Asleep at the Wheel." This response was apparently based on Plaintiff's incorrect belief that at least one of the three assignments described above involved the rightful owner of "Don't Fall Asleep at the Wheel" properly assigning its rights to Gusto.

B. LIABILITY

Thus far, Plaintiff has proved ownership and copyright infringement of the Titles. The next issue is who must be held liable for this infringement and under what theory of infringement. There are several types of infringement: direct, contributory and vicarious infringement. Furthermore, an officer of a corporation may be held individually liable under corporate veil piercing law.

1. Defendant KRB

KRB is a direct infringer. "Liability for direct infringement arises from the violation of any one of the exclusive rights of a copyright owner. 17 U.S.C. § 501(a). The owner of copyright in a musical composition [or sound recording] has the exclusive right to, and to authorize others to, reproduce [and] distribute . . . the copyrighted composition [or sound recording]. 17 U.S.C. §§ 106, 114." Bridgeport Music, Inc. v. Rhyme Syndicate Music, 376 F.3d 615, 621 (6th Cir. 2004). One can be a direct infringer even when one is unaware that he or she is selling product that infringes on another's copyright. See F.W. Woolworth Co. v. Contemporary Arts, Inc., 344 U.S. 228, 73 S. Ct. 222, 97 L. Ed. 276 (1952); see also Rogers v. Koons, 777 F. Supp. 1 (S.D.N.Y. 1991), aff'd, 960 F.2d 301 (2d Cir.), cert. denied, 506 U.S. 934, 113 S. Ct. 365, 121 L. Ed. 2d 278 (1992). In F.W. Woolworth Co., Woolworth purchased sculptures of **cocker spaniel**'s from a third party. 344 U.S. at 229. "Unbeknown to Woolworth, these dogs had been copied from [plaintiff's]." Id. Notwithstanding Woolworth's lack of knowledge that the sculptures had been copied, the Supreme Court found them to be liable for direct infringement by the mere fact that they marketed and sold the sculptures.

KRB reproduced and distributed "Don't Fall Asleep at the Wheel," "Patches," and "When a Man Loves a Woman," pursuant to the Peachtree Agreement. KRB did so presuming it had a valid license from Peachtree to reproduce and distribute these Titles. KRB distributed the remaining nineteen Titles after purchasing finished product from Red Dog Express, Creative Sound and Golden Circle. KRB did not know that these third parties did not have the right to license or sell these Titles. Notwithstanding KRB's lack of knowledge, KRB is still directly liable for its reproduction and/or distribution of these Titles pursuant to 17 U.S.C. § 501(a). Id.

2. Defendant Bennett

Plaintiff argues that Bennett should also be held individually liable for the copyright infringement of the twenty-two Titles under the theories of contributory and vicarious infringement. Defendants do not address this argument directly, but state that Bennett should not be held individually liable because Plaintiff has not proved facts sufficient to pierce the corporate veil.

It is important to

> [n]ote the distinction between being liable as a related defendant and liability through various theories of corporate law. For instance, utter dominance of one corporation by another could lead to direct liability under an alter ego theory. By contrast, related defendants become liable indirectly, either via the . . . category of corporate liability or through theories of vicarious liability, contributory infringement . . . . The boundaries between these categories are fluid. Nonetheless, the distinction between them should be drawn when possible.

3 Nimmer on Copyright, § 12.04[A][1], at 12-76. In this case, the Court finds that Bennett is individually liable under the theory of vicarious infringement. [3]

"A defendant can be held vicariously liable if he enjoys a direct financial benefit from the infringing activity and 'has the right and ability to supervise' the infringing activity." Rhyme Syndicate Music, 376 F.3d at 621. Bennett was the primary decision maker for almost every aspect of KRB's business. Importantly, at the time the Titles were purchased, Bennett decided which products were purchased from third parties and sold at Big Lots. In addition, Bennett was the only corporate officer on behalf of KRB who was involved in the negotiations with Peachtree. As a whole, Bennett was in charge of operating KRB, made all final decisions, and was ultimately responsible for anything that happened at KRB. This is consistent with his

---

[3] 16 Plaintiff has not proven the factors required to pierce the corporate veil. Similarly, Plaintiff has not shown the requisite knowledge for contributory infringement. "Contributory infringement occurs when one, 'with knowledge of the infringing activity, induces, causes, or materially contributes to the infringing conduct of another.'" Bridgeport Music, Inc. v. Rhyme Syndicate Music, 376 F.3d 615, 621 (6th Cir. 2004). As the Court notes in its discussion of willful infringement, KRB did not have knowledge that it was engaging in infringing activity. A fortiori, Bennett could not have known that he was engaging in infringing activity. Thus, the contributory infringement avenue is precluded.

position as sole shareholder and president of KRB. As a result, he had the right and ability to supervise the infringing activity. In addition, Bennett enjoys a direct financial benefit from the infringing activity because, as sole shareholder, he retains any profit produced by the company. Consequently, Bennett is vicariously liable for KRB's copyright infringement of Plaintiff's Titles.

C. DAMAGES

1. Statutory Damages

A copyright owner may elect to recover an award of statutory damages in lieu of actual damages and profits at any time before final judgment is rendered. 17 U.S.C. § 504(c)(1). The Copyright Act permits a minimum award of $ 750 and a maximum award of $ 30,000 for each copyrighted work infringed. Id. "District courts have wide discretion in setting damages within the statutory range set forth in § 504(c)(1)." Disney Enters., Inc. v. Farmer, 427 F. Supp. 2d 807, 2006 WL 962577, at *6 (E.D. Tenn. 2006). This statutory scheme is "'designed not solely to compensate the copyright owner for losses incurred, but also to deter future infringement.'" Johnson v. Jones, 149 F.3d 494, 504 (6th Cir. 1998) (quoting F.W. Woolworth Co., 344 U.S. at 233).

Liability for copyright infringement does not turn on the infringer's mental state because "a general claim for copyright infringement is fundamentally one founded on strict liability." Bridgeport Music, Inc. v. 11C Music, 154 F. Supp. 2d 1330, 1335 (M.D. Tenn. 2001) (citation omitted). For purposes of damages, however, the infringer's mental state is important, as damages may be increased or decreased based on an infringer's knowledge of infringement. Thus, if the plaintiff proves that the infringement was willful, statutory damages may be awarded up to $ 150,000 per copyrighted work infringed. 17 U.S.C. § 504(c)(2). On the other hand, if the defendant proves that the infringement was innocent, the award may be reduced to $ 200. 17 U.S.C. § 504(c)(2).

"Willful" and "innocent" have specialized meanings under the Copyright Act. On the one hand, willful infringement means conduct that the defendant knows constitutes copyright infringement. "[O]ne who has been notified that his conduct constitutes copyright infringement, but who reasonably and in good faith believes the contrary, is not 'willful' for these purposes. But one who 'recklessly disregards' a copyright holder's rights, even if lacking actual knowledge of infringement, may be subject to enhanced damages." 4 Nimmer on Copyright, § 14.04[B][3][a], at 14-78-14-79, quoted in Princeton Univ. Press v. Mich. Document Servs., Inc., 99

F.3d 1381, 1392 (6th Cir. 1996).[4] On the other hand, the Copyright Act explains that innocent infringement occurs when "the infringer was not aware and had no reason to believe that his or her acts constituted an infringement of copyright." 17 U.S.C. § 504(c)(2). To prove "innocent" infringement, the defendant has the burden of showing that he or she had a good faith belief that his or her infringing conduct did not amount to infringement, and that the good faith belief was reasonable. 4 Nimmer on Copyright, § 14.04[B][2][a], at 14-74.

Courts may consider several factors in awarding statutory damages including:

'the expenses saved and profits reaped by the defendants in connection with the infringements, the revenues lost by the plaintiffs as a result of the defendants' conduct, and the infringers' state of mind whether willful, knowing, or merely innocent.' In awarding statutory damages, courts may also consider 'the goal of discouraging wrongful conduct.' . . . The option of electing statutory damages is especially appropriate where 'the information needed to establish an exact measure of actual damages is within the infringers' control and often is not fully disclosed.'

Disney Enters., Inc., 427 F. Supp. 2d 807, 2006 WL 962577, at *6 (citations omitted). Plaintiff argues that an analysis of these factors demonstrates willful infringement because Defendants knew they were infringing or at least should have known and recklessly disregarded Plaintiff's intellectual property rights, warranting an increase in damages of up to $ 150,000 per copyrighted work infringed.

a. Expenses Saved and Profits Reaped by Defendants

In this case, it is virtually impossible from the evidence presented to determine the expenses saved and the profits reaped by the Defendants in connection with the infringements. To begin with, Defendants have no record of purchasing, manufacturing or selling approximately eleven of the sound recordings in Count II. With regard to two sound recordings ("Patches" and "When a Man Loves a Woman") Defendants' records show that 2,100 cassettes were manufactured, but Defendants do not have any sales records. With regard to the remaining nine Titles, Defendants' records

---

[4] 17 It is important to note that the new rule enunciated by the Sixth Circuit regarding copyright infringement of sound recordings does "not play any role in the assessment of concepts such as 'willful' or 'intentional' in cases that are currently before the courts or had their genesis before this decision was announced." Dimension Films, 410 F.3d at 804-05.

reveal they reproduced or purchased them from third parties and then sold to Big Lots as much as 5,977 or as little as 600 of each Title. Using these figures, Defendants calculated that their net profit from the sale of the nine Titles is under $ 2,000.

Defendants raise numerous reasons for the low sales figures. Defendants claim that cassette sales represented a small percentage of total sales for KRB and dollar cassette product represented an even smaller percentage of sales. Vice President of KRB, Patrick Hayes ("Hayes"), testified that other than seasonal promotions for Christmas or Halloween and the like, for the years 1999, 2000 and 2001, sales of cassette tapes represented less than twenty percent of KRB's sales. No documentary evidence was presented to support Hayes' testimony. Similarly, no evidence was presented regarding the percentage of cassette tape sales in the years prior to 1999.

Defendants contend that they could not provide more sales information regarding the twenty-two Titles because many of them were purchased as part of pre-packs or closeouts and individual song titles were not noted in their accounting system. Defendants admitted that when buying miscellaneous closeout product from third parties, they would not necessarily know each and every title that was received due to the small quantity of the product. This process, Defendants argue, explains why its records do not show sales of certain of the Titles.

In contrast, Plaintiff argues that the true sales figure is much higher because from 1999 to 2001, Defendants' average yearly gross sales were between $ 32,625,107 and $ 34,800,114. Defendants stated that sales of cassettes represented approximately 20% of its sales; therefore, average yearly gross sales of cassettes were between $ 6,525,021 and $ 6,960,022. Plaintiff asserts that there is no way to extrapolate how much of this amount relates to the Titles at issue. Plaintiff contends that contrary to Defendants' explanations, a more pernicious reason lies beneath the lack of sales records for the Titles. Plaintiff asserts that Defendants pre- and post-lawsuit conduct not only has precluded Plaintiff from showing Defendants' actual expenses and profits, but is also indicative of intentional copyright infringement warranting an increase in damages.

i. Defendants' Pre-Lawsuit Conduct

Plaintiff contends that Defendants intentionally have developed an accounting system that does not track which products have been bought or sold in order to hide illegal activity. Plaintiff goes one step further and alleges that Defendants, and almost all the third parties with whom they do business, have colluded to create a fraudulent accounting system that permits Defendants to reproduce and distribute illegal copies of music product.

The cast of characters involved in the alleged illegal scheme to conduct copyright infringement include KRB's lawyer, William Tucker ("Tucker"); Theresa Peitsmeyer ("Pietsmeyer"), a former KRB employee who now runs Requin, a company that manages KRB's accounting system, Navision; Robert Ciotti ("Ciotti"), the principal of Distributors Copyright Maintenance Service ("DCMS"), which performed KRB's royalty accounting; KRB's external auditor, Greg Welch ("Welch"); Timothy O'Meara ("O'Meara"), the principal of Level Two, a warehouse company that stored KRB product that was received and distributed, and that received the cassette tapes returned by Big Lots. In essence, Plaintiff attacks almost anybody who had any contact with KRB as actively participating in a complex scheme to sell illegally copied music product to the public. There is little more than speculation to support Plaintiff's theory of deception.

1. Tucker

Plaintiff argues that Tucker's lack of experience in intellectual property matters coupled with his minimal due diligence in drafting the Peachtree Agreement is evidence of fraud. Plaintiff contends that Tucker should have reviewed all the contracts by which Horner acquired the rights to the titles that were being licensed to KRB in the Peachtree Agreement. Tucker reviewed some eight to ten contracts, but relied on KRB to conduct the remaining due diligence. It is unclear whether these eight to ten contracts related to a number of recordings or whether each contract related only to a single recording. If these contracts related to numerous recordings, it is possible that Tucker reviewed the documents that related to most of the recordings Horner was conveying to Bennett through the Peachtree Agreement. The evidence is simply too murky for this Court to make any conclusion with certainty.

Next, Plaintiff asserts that Tucker should have been skeptical about Horner's willingness to license songs by popular artists for twenty-five years for $ 50,000. Plaintiff, however, did not present any evidence of how much a licensing agreement regarding re-recordings of older songs would normally be worth. Furthermore, KRB was responsible for paying mechanical licenses and royalties pursuant to the Peachtree Agreement, which may have been a factor in negotiating the price. This Court, therefore, cannot say whether the purchase price was so unusually low to indicate fraud.

Lastly, Plaintiff points out that the Peachtree Agreement identified the first Classic Sound Lawsuit. Plaintiff asserts that the Peachtree Agreement included the same master recordings that were being litigated in the Classic Sound Lawsuit. As we have seen, that does not appear to be the case with two of the three Titles, "Don't Fall Asleep at the Wheel" and "When a Man

Loves a Woman," that KRB obtained from the Peachtree Agreement. It is possible, but has not been proved with any degree of certainty, that the master recording for "Patches" may be the same in the Classic Sound Lawsuit and the Peachtree Agreement. In any event, Plaintiff chastises Tucker for not further researching the Classic Sound Lawsuit before and after the Peachtree Agreement was executed. Had Tucker performed further research into the Classic Sound Lawsuit, he would only have discovered that ownership of "Patches" was being contested. As there is no evidence that the master recording of "Patches" is the same in both the Classic Sound Lawsuit and the Peachtree Agreement, the Court cannot say with certainty that Tucker acted with reckless disregard of Plaintiff's copyrights of that sound recording.

Notwithstanding the Classic Sound Lawsuit, Horner specifically warranted in the Peachtree Agreement that no claims or legal actions existed to prevent the licensing of the recordings to KRB. While additional research may have revealed that this representation may not have been accurate, the failure to conduct additional research does not amount to intentional fraud. Furthermore, while these facts demonstrate that Tucker's and Bennett's actions were perhaps on the cusp of reckless disregard of the ownership of the recordings in the Peachtree Agreement, the Court is not satisfied that the evidence pushes them firmly over.

Finally, the Court notes that by the time the Classic Sound Lawsuit was settled in August 1999 in Plaintiff's favor, Lytle had already made vague accusations to Bennett that the latter was illegally exploiting Plaintiff's Titles that were allegedly involved in the Classic Sound Lawsuit. Lytle, however, did not inform Bennett of the settlement. Nor did Horner. Therefore, KRB did not have notice that the Classic Sound Lawsuit was settled in Plaintiff's favor.

2. Pietsmeyer

Plaintiff also makes vague allegations of wrongdoing by Pietsmeyer. First, Plaintiff repeatedly notes that Pietsmeyer's company, Requin Accounting, is paid approximately $ 492,000 a year to manage the Navision accounting software system. Plaintiff contends that running Navision is essentially a data entry service and that Requin does not even employ a certified public accountant. Plaintiff asserts that in light of Pietsmeyer's prior salary of $ 54,000 per year when she was a KRB employee, her income through Requin of $ 492,000 per year is a considerable jump and is evidence of fraudulent activity. There is not a shred of evidence to support this accusation. Plaintiff has presented no proof as to how Pietsmeyer and her company Requin can or have manipulated Navision to produce incorrect information. Similarly, there is no proof that the lack of an accountant employed at Requin leads to the integrity of the accounting information to be compromised. Finally, Plaintiff has no support for its contention that payment of $ 492,000 to Requin is unduly high. There is no evidence that the cost of operating Requin is so minimal that Pietsmeyer receives most of the $ 492,000 directly. Even if she did earn that much, Plaintiff has not demonstrated how the payment of a high salary leads to accounting fraud.

Plaintiff also argues that Pietsmeyer failed to produce relevant documents in violation of Plaintiff's subpoena. Plaintiff argues that when relevant documents are not produced, and the party with the documents resists production, the Court must make a negative inference that these documents would have been harmful to that party's case. Plaintiff already filed a motion to compel Pietsmeyer to produce the requested documents with a federal district court in Indiana. The district court denied the motion to compel. Having failed to win its motion to compel, Plaintiff cannot now make the argument that Pietsmeyer improperly resisted or failed to respond to Plaintiff's discovery requests.

3. Ciotti

Ciotti was in charge of obtaining mechanical licenses, but he failed to do so for the musical composition "Don't Fall Asleep at the Wheel." Defendants admit that Ciotti failed to obtain such a license. "Don't Fall Asleep at the Wheel" was released on a KRB cassette entitled "Truck Drivin' Son of a Gun" in 1996. The cassette included a total often songs. Prior to the release, Ciotti obtained a mechanical license with respect to one of the songs, but did not obtain mechanical licenses for the remaining nine. After the release, Ciotti obtained licenses for eight of the songs, but failed to obtain one for "Don't Fall Asleep at the Wheel." Ciotti testified that he searched with the Harry Fox Agency, all performance rights societies (ASCAP, BMI, SESAC), the Internet and various other sources. Even though Ciotti was unable to locate the publisher of the composition, he calculated the mechanical royalties at the statutory rate for all sales of "Don't Fall Asleep at the Wheel" so that KRB could pay the publisher once its identity was discovered. Such royalties amount to $ 988.54 from 1996 through June 30, 2000. Ciotti testified that it was standard industry practice to obtain licenses after the release of the product.

Plaintiff points to Ciotti's lack of knowledge concerning where the royalties were deposited or accrued as evidence that KRB was not actually accruing the royalties. This allegation is unsupported by any evidence. Ciotti himself was not required to pay royalties, KRB was. Further, Ciotti testified that he was only responsible for informing KRB how much they were required to pay in royalties. Other than these allegations regarding Ciotti, Plaintiff did not demonstrate that KRB did not accrue royalties.

Plaintiff further argues that "industry custom" of obtaining mechanical licenses post-release is not a defense to infringement. In Cherry River Music Co. v. Simitar Entm't, Inc., 38 F. Supp. 2d 310, 318-20 (S.D.N.Y. 1999), the court stated that an alleged infringer could not rely on industry custom of obtaining mechanical licenses after the release of the album. Indeed, 17 U.S.C. § 115(b) is crystal clear that if a negotiated mechanical license is not obtained or notice of a compulsory mechanical license is not filed or served within thirty days after making, and before distributing the work, the making and distribution of the work is actionable as an act of infringement. While the industry custom of obtaining the mechanical license after the release is acceptable, notice of the request for the mechanical license must be served or filed within thirty days after making and before distributing the work. In this case, no notice was provided because Ciotti could not find the publisher of this particular recording of "Don't Fall Asleep at the Wheel."

Plaintiff asserts that as Defendants should have, at minimum, provided notice of an intent to seek a mechanical license before distributing "Don't Fall Asleep at the Wheel" and failed to do so, Defendants are liable for willful infringement. The statute, however, only says that such conduct is actionable infringement and does not require a finding of willful infringement. Similarly, this case is not like Cherry, in which the court found willful infringement. 38 F. Supp. 2d at 318-20. In that case, the court, relying on expert testimony, found that although it may be "industry custom" for a music publisher to grant mechanical licenses freely in order to maximize their royalty revenues, such custom was inapplicable in that case because the co-copyright owner was a non-music publisher. Id. That non-music publisher had a strong interest in denying mechanical licenses because it manufactured and sold a compact disc that included the copyrighted music at issue in the case. Id. Thus, a grant of a mechanical license to another party could reduce sales of its own compact disc. Id.

In this case, there is evidence that the industry custom was to obtain a mechanical license after the release of the product. In fact, Defendants obtained a majority of the mechanical licenses for the songs on "Truck Drivin' Son of a Gun" by Ferlin Husky, the cassette which included "Don't Fall Asleep at the Wheel," after the release of the cassette. None of the other music publishers objected to the practice and freely granted the mechanical license post-release. In contrast to Cherry, there is no evidence that Plaintiff continues to sell its album "Greatest Hits of Ferlin Husky." Indeed, the evidence would suggest that Plaintiff no longer sells this album, as the copy that was provided to the Court is in the form of an LP, which in the current iPod generation is obsolete. Regardless, when Plaintiff met with Bennett in 1997 he indicated that he wanted to conduct business with Bennett and KRB. Therefore, unlike the plaintiff in Cherry, in this case, the Plaintiff likely would have granted a mechanical license. In conclusion, although the Court does not condone this industry custom, and it is certainly not a defense to liability, the Court declines to use it as evidence of willful infringement to increase damages.

4. Welch

Next in the line of attack is Welch, KRB's external auditor and a certified public accountant. Plaintiff contends that Welch did not perform an accurate audit and did little more than check math based on documents provided by KRB. The crux of Plaintiff's argument is that Welch relied on documents provided by KRB in performing his audit and did not request certain documents or information regarding royalty payments. Plaintiff did not present any evidence to demonstrate that Welch's audit was inconsistent with general auditing and accounting principles. As a result, Plaintiff's accusations that Welch's audit was poorly performed, or worse, was in violation of audit and accounting principles and practices are unsubstantiated.

5. O'Meara

With regard to O'Meara, this Court is unable to fathom Plaintiff's underlying complaint. Plaintiff implies that it is suspicious why O'Meara's company, Level Two prepared and maintained accurate records related to the receiving and distributing of KRB products, but did not have accurate records of the product returned by Big Lots. Presumably Plaintiff is complaining that by having inaccurate records regarding the returned product, O'Meara was assisting KRB in obfuscating evidence regarding sales of the Titles at issue in this case. No evidence was presented at trial to support this suspicion. On the contrary, Plaintiff's suspicion is facially unreasonable as it is unclear why KRB would require O'Meara to painstakingly record 800,000 cassette tapes that could not be sold, as cassette tapes are -- like LPs -- obsolete.

Further, Plaintiff sought to rely on O'Meara's deposition at trial. Defendants filed a motion in limine to preclude Plaintiff's use of O'Meara's deposition based on the fact that O'Meara was within this Court's subpoena power. See Fed. R. Civ. P. 32(a)(3)(D) (permitting use of deposition of non-party witness at trial in limited circumstances if witness is unavailable). Plaintiff requests this Court to "presume" that O'Meara's testimony would have been harmful to Defendants due to their motion in limine. Plaintiff conveniently forgets that it resolved Defendants motion in limine by agreement. Moreover, Plaintiff did not follow the Federal Rules of Civil Procedure because it failed to subpoena O'Meara to testify at trial. Therefore, it cannot now request any negative inference.

ii. Defendants' Post-Lawsuit Conduct

Plaintiff argues that statutory damages and an increased award for willful infringement are warranted because Defendants' discovery conduct not only made it impossible to prove actual damages, but also reflects Defendants' state of mind as intentional infringers. "Statutory damages [are] . . . appropriate . . . [when] the information needed to establish an exact measure of actual damages is within the infringers' control and often is not fully disclosed." Microsoft Corp. v. Sellers, 411 F. Supp. 2d 913, 921 (E.D. Tenn. 2006), (citing Yurman Design, Inc. v. PAJ, Inc., 93 F. Supp. 2d 449, 462 (S.D.N.Y. 2000) ("Statutory damages have been made available to plaintiffs in infringement actions precisely because of the difficulties inherent in proving actual damages and profits, as well as to encourage vigorous enforcement of the copyright laws.")).

Plaintiff cites numerous instances of discovery conduct by Defendants as supportive of an increased award of damages. Plaintiff contends that a higher award is required because Defendants: (1) served misleading discovery responses regarding the time period Defendants reproduced and/or distributed the Titles at issue; (2) ignored orders from both the Court and the Magistrate Judge regarding the cassette inspection; (3) improperly redacted relevant information from documents that were produced; (4) destroyed relevant documents throughout the course of litigation; (5) refused to produce relevant and responsive information; and (6) offered a great deal of testimony at trial that contradicted deposition testimony.

With regard to the misleading discovery responses, the Magistrate Judge found:

In response to the plaintiff's written discovery, the defendants had previously responded that, other than that specifically provided, the defendant had not dealt in the titles at issue in this case 'at any time.' It was not until the deposition of Mr. Bennett on July 15, 2002, that the plaintiff learned that 'at any time' did not mean 'at any time.' Unbeknownst to the plaintiff, 'at any time' meant from December 4, 1997 through February 11, 2000, the time period asserted by the plaintiff in its complaint during which the defendants allegedly infringed the plaintiff's copyrights. . . . Whether intentional or not, the defendants clearly misled the plaintiff.

(Doc. No. 76.) Similarly, the Magistrate Judge expressed frustration with Defendants' failure to timely commence the cassette inspection. (Doc. No. 113.) Nevertheless, the Magistrate Judge noted in considerable detail that although Plaintiff was misled by Defendants' discovery responses regarding sales information, Plaintiff had "not acted as diligently as it could have to schedule any necessary discovery." (Doc. No. 76 at 8.) Thus, the Magistrate Judge concluded that "both sides bear responsibility for the predicament in which Plaintiff finds itself . . . ." (Id. at 14.)

With regard to the delayed inspection, while primarily faulting

Defendants, the Magistrate Judge did note logistical details delayed the inspection. (Doc. No. 113 at 6.) These details, the Magistrate Judge said, were not addressed adequately in the Court's order requiring the inspection. (Id.)

Therefore, like the Magistrate Judge, this Court does not find it appropriate to increase damages due to discovery obstacles which, primarily caused by Defendants, were exacerbated by the Plaintiff and the Court itself. The Court also notes that at the time of the cassette inspection Defendants were changing counsel. While this does not excuse the delay, it eliminates Plaintiff's assertion of deliberate misconduct, further precluding an increase in damages. [5][18]

At this point, the Court finds it necessary to make some general remarks about discovery in this case. While Defendants could have been more forthcoming during discovery, the Court does not find that their discovery behavior indicates an intentional obfuscation of actual expenses and profit records. Discovery in this case was very contentious. However, Defendants were not the only ones who contributed to the contention. As the Magistrate Judge already noted, Plaintiff's did not conduct timely discovery. In addition, Plaintiff's current complaint about not receiving sales information is a repetition of the argument already made before the Magistrate Judge. (See Doc. No. 97 (noting that "plaintiff contends that the defendants have not produced accurate records of sales of the titles at issue in this case").) There, in response to Plaintiff's complaints, the Magistrate Judge gave the Plaintiff the opportunity to have an independent certified public accountant review Defendants' vendor files from April 4, 1997 to December 31, 1997. "Depending on the results of such a review, the Court indicated that it would consider expanding a subsequent review to post 1997 vendor files." (Id. at 3.) Plaintiff, however, declined to have an independent certified public accountant conduct the review of Defendants' 1997 vendor files. Plaintiff did so believing that "such review was

---

[5][18] The remaining discovery issues raised by Plaintiff are dealt with in the contemporaneously issued Memorandum Order denying Rule 37 sanctions. For the reasons that the Court denies sanctions, it also declines to increase damages. Similarly, the Court finds no merit in Plaintiff's argument that Defendants offered a great deal of testimony at trial that contradicted deposition testimony. Other than for Bennett, Plaintiff's do not detail which deposition testimony conflicts with trial testimony to indicate Defendants' mendaciousness. With regard to Bennett's testimony, the Court does not find that it significantly differs from his deposition testimony.

unnecessary and would be unproductive because an independent [certified public accountant] would not be familiar enough with the documents at issue to make meaningful findings . . . ." (Id. at 4-5.) Instead, Plaintiff sought the production of vendor files, as well as general ledgers or subledgers from 1997 to December 2002. (Id. at 4.) The Magistrate Judge denied Plaintiff's request finding that there was insufficient reason to amend its previous ruling to permit an independent review of 1997 vendor files, with the possibility of an expansion to post 1997 files. Having declined to use the opportunity the Magistrate Judge provided, Plaintiff cannot now complain that the information needed to establish actual damages was within the infringers' control and not fully disclosed. The Magistrate Judge gave Plaintiff every opportunity to discover information relating to sales.

Further, Plaintiff makes a general complaint that third parties related to Defendants did not produce relevant documents that they acknowledged existed. Although it is clear that Plaintiff was not satisfied with the documents these third parties produced, except for Pietsmeyer, Plaintiff did not file a motion to compel production of the documents. As already noted, Plaintiff's motion to compel Pietsmeyer to produce documents was denied. Furthermore, Plaintiff has not explained how additional documents by other third parties would have assisted Plaintiff's calculation of actual damages. For these reasons, Plaintiff's complaints are now untimely and unfounded.

Finally, the Court notes that Plaintiff also resisted discovery and engaged in inappropriate litigation conduct. Plaintiff did not permit Defendants to inspect the sixteen-track master recordings until ordered to by Judge Echols. (Doc. No. 176). Most egregious in this Court's view is the fact that Plaintiff conducted extremely broad discovery regarding sixty-two titles, then during opening arguments without any prior notice to the Court or to Defendants, Plaintiff sought to dismiss without prejudice fully two-thirds of the titles from the lawsuit. In sum, both sides were at fault for the discovery disputes and the Court declines to make a finding that produces a windfall for Plaintiff just because its conduct was "slightly" better than that of Defendants.

b. Revenues Lost by Plaintiff or Harm to Plaintiff

Next in the analysis of statutory damages is whether Plaintiff can show that it lost revenue as a result of, or was harmed by, Defendants' sales. Plaintiff argues that because Plaintiff did not know how many copies of the Titles Defendants sold, Plaintiff cannot show lost revenue. Nevertheless, Plaintiff did not make any showing of lost revenue, even with the information it did have. Nor did Plaintiff explain how it was harmed. Plaintiff stated that KRB product was inferior and would deter consumers from purchasing legitimate King product. Plaintiff, however, did not present any evidence that it continues to sell its albums containing the

Titles. Indeed, as already noted, the evidence appears to show the contrary. Plaintiff submitted its albums in the form of obsolete LPs suggesting that it no longer sells these albums. Therefore, there was no evidence that the sale of Defendants' product reduced sales of Plaintiff's product. Further, there is no way that a consumer could tell that the inferior KRB product was actually Plaintiff's product. Thus, it is unlikely that a consumer would not purchase Plaintiff's product (if it is still available to the public) because it had previously purchased KRB's product and did not like it. Moreover, Lytle testified that he had never granted a mechanical license for these sound recordings in the past. Lytle did not say that he would have required a compulsory mechanical license as opposed to a negotiated license. Thus, it is unclear whether Plaintiff would have earned the statutory rate if Defendants had obtained a mechanical license. The only concrete harm Plaintiff has shown is the cost of litigating this lawsuit.

c. Defendants' State of Mind

Knowledge that one is infringing on, or reckless disregard of, another's intellectual property rights constitutes willful infringement and warrants increased damages. Notice that one is infringing on another's product is persuasive evidence of willful infringement. Video Views, Inc. v. Studio 21, Ltd., 925 F.2d 1010, 1021 (7th Cir. 1991), overruled on other grounds by Fogerty v. Fantasy, Inc., 510 U.S. 517, 114 S. Ct. 1023, 127 L. Ed. 2d 455 (1994); Chi-Boy Music v. Charlie Club, Inc., 930 F.2d 1224, 1227-28 (7th Cir. 1991). When the "infringer is provided oral or written notice of its infringing conduct by the copyright owner, yet 'pass[es] the matter off as a nuisance[,]'" the court may find willful infringement. Video Views, Inc., 925 F.2d at 1021. In other words, "one who undertakes a course of infringing conduct may neither sneer in the face of the copyright owner nor hide its head in the sand like an ostrich." Id.; see also Chi-Boy Music, 930 F.2d at 1227.

In Video Views, Inc., the Court considered the exact issue that is present in this case: the quality of the notice. 925 F.2d at 1021. In that case, the plaintiff notified the defendant in writing of plaintiff's rights in some of the films involved in the lawsuit. Id. However, the two films that were found to have been infringed were not specifically listed in the letter. Id. Based primarily on this lack of specificity in the notice letter the Seventh Circuit affirmed the district court's decision that the infringement of the two films was not willful. In contrast, in Chi-Boy Music, the Seventh Circuit affirmed the district court's finding of willful infringement becaus the letter provided specific notice of infringement. Chi-Boy Music, 930 F.2d at 1227.

i. Pre-Lawsuit Notice

In the present case, Plaintiff argues that Lytle informed Bennett numerous times that KRB was infringing Plaintiff's Titles, but Defendants continued to reproduce and distribute the Titles. Plaintiff contends that

Lytle's conversation and letters with Bennett constitute sufficient notice to warrant a finding of willful infringement. The Court disagrees.

In the 1997 meeting, Lytle made vague accusations to Bennett of infringement. At the time, Lytle confined his allegations of infringement to the Classic Sound catalogue, which apparently included the same titles as those in the Peachtree Agreement. Nevertheless, Lytle did not provide Bennett with any specific titles that he believed were being infringed.

This oral notice was followed by a written letter, dated February 3, 1998. The letter did not clarify matters. Instead, Lytle simply made the broad allegation that KRB was "handling bootleg copies of G.M.L./Gusto's masters." By the time he wrote the letter, Lytle had already purchased all of KRB's product that is at issue in this case. Nevertheless, Lytle did not furnish Bennett with a list of the allegedly infringing product or any evidence to prove his ownership of the Titles. Bennett, in turn, did not simply ignore the letter, but responded in writing. Bennett stated that Lytle's oral concerns "never reached a specific statement . . . of any particular violation." Bennett also pointed out that Lytle's letter did not "raise any specific issue." Bennett legitimately stated that he could not provide a further response without additional, specific information. Although Lytle had bought all of the allegedly infringing KRB product at this point, and knew which titles he believed Bennett was infringing, he did not respond to Bennett's request. As a result, the quality of the notice was so poor that Bennett could not know which of Plaintiff's Titles he was allegedly infringing.

Importantly, even if this Court were to find that Lytle's allusion to the Classic Sound catalogue provided Bennett with sufficient notice of infringement, such notice would potentially only extend to "Don't Fall Asleep at the Wheel," "When a Man Loves a Woman," and "Patches," which Bennett obtained from the Peachtree Agreement. There is absolutely no notice -- not even vague notice -- from Lytle that the other nineteen sound recordings were being infringed.

Plaintiff further contends that Bennett was on notice, or at least should have known, that he was infringing on Plaintiff's copyrights because he was aware of the Classic Sound Lawsuit. There is no doubt that Bennett knew of the Classic Sound Lawsuit, but he did not know and could not have known, that Horner's claim to ownership of the titles in the Peachtree Agreement was invalid because the lawsuit was not settled until August 1999. Even then, neither Lytle nor Horner informed Bennett of the settlement. Thus, Bennett's view that Lytle was attempting to use him as a "pawn" in the litigation and was not making a legitimate claim of ownership was reasonable. Even if, as Plaintiff asserts, Bennett should have conducted further research with Horner to determine the ownership status of the titles in the Peachtree Agreement, it is not clear that Bennett would have received an honest answer from Horner. Also, as the Court has already noted, the Classic Sound Lawsuit would only have revealed an issue of ownership over "Patches" because "Don't Fall Asleep at the Wheel" was not a part of that lawsuit or the subsequent Classic Sound lawsuits, and the recording for "When a Man Loves a Woman" was a David Johnson recording, not Plaintiff's.

There is no evidence that Defendants knew or should have known that Red Dog Express, Creative Sounds or Golden Circle were illegally selling Plaintiff's Titles. Defendants were aware that the principals of these companies were not particularly reliable, but that is not sufficient to demonstrate that Defendants should have known Red Dog Express, Creative Sounds or Golden Circle were selling illegal product.

In a similar case, the Ninth Circuit held that the fact that Defendants should have known that they did not have clear title to certain master tapes did not compel a finding of willful infringement. Grateful Dead Prods. v. Auditory Odyssey, 1996 U.S. App. LEXIS 1626, No. 94-56258, 1996 WL 19210, at * 1-2 (9th Cir. Jan. 18, 1996). In this case, while Defendants could have been more diligent in purchasing music product from third parties, and they perhaps should have known that the Peachtree Agreement was "too good to be true," the Court finds that their actions amount to negligence and nothing more.

Looking at the facts as a whole, the Court does not find that there is sufficient notice to constitute willful infringement.

ii. Post-Lawsuit Notice

Plaintiff also suggests that KRB continued to sell the Titles after the filing of the Complaint. To support this suggestion, Plaintiff points to the fact that it found small quantities of six of the sound recordings during the inspection of the cassettes returned from Big Lots in 2002. The presence of the six sound recordings in returned product, argues Plaintiff, indicates that these sound recordings continued to be sold two years after the initiation of the lawsuits and two years after KRB received explicit notice that it was allegedly infringing Plaintiff's copyrights. The evidence presented suggests otherwise.

As soon as the Complaint was filed, Bennett and his employees issued "freeze" memoranda informing all employees to stop purchasing and selling the titles identified in the Complaint. These memoranda included a freeze of the titles identified in the Complaint in the Navision system. Similarly, KRB informed its independent service representatives that serviced the music racks in the Big Lots stores to remove the titles identified in the Complaint from the display racks. The only evidence that these instructions were disobeyed or ignored is the presence of the Titles in the cassette inspection.

Plaintiff had sixty days in which to inspect 800,000 cassettes. Plaintiff complained numerous times to this Court that Defendants were delaying the cassette inspection. Nevertheless, once it began the inspection, Plaintiff did not utilize the entire time provided, and satisfied itself with a fifteen-day inspection. During these fifteen days, Plaintiff inspected approximately ten percent of the cassettes or approximately 80,000 cassettes and found very small quantities of six sound recordings at issue in this case. Plaintiff found one cassette of each of the following Titles: "Ain't Got No Home" by Clarence Henry, "The Mountain's High" by Dick & Dee Dee, and "Venus in Blue Jeans" by Jimmy Clanton; three cassettes of "The Coasters" by Charlie Brown; eight cassettes of "Bottle of Wine" by Jimmy Gilmer; and seventy-four cassettes of "Keep Searchin'" by Del Shannon. Plaintiff did not find any other Titles at issue in the present lawsuit.

Plaintiff wants this Court to assume that the presence of de minimis amounts of infringing material is evidence of post-lawsuit sales. Defendants, however, argue that these small amounts were bound to be in the returned product because notwithstanding their instructions, some cassettes were not going to be removed from the racks or Big Lots did not send the cassettes back when the service representatives removed the cassettes from the racks. The Court finds Defendants' explanation more plausible. Due to the fact that there were 1,300 Big Lots stores, a large number of service representatives involved and sixty-two titles initially identified in the Complaint, it is entirely possible, indeed probable, that 100% of the allegedly infringing KRB product identified in the Complaint was not removed from Big Lots stores. Defendants also pointed out that certain of the cassettes returned by Big Lots were several years old, suggesting that Defendants had not supplied them to Big Lots recently. Other than cassettes found in the inspection, there is no other evidence to support Plaintiff's argument that Defendants continued to sell product bearing titles identified in the Complaint. [6][19]

d. Goal of Discouraging Wrongful Conduct

Finally, in awarding statutory damages, the Court may also consider "the goal of discouraging wrongful conduct." Disney Enters., Inc., 427 F. Supp. 807, 2006 WL 962577, at *6. In this case, Defendants have been in business for seventeen years. Unlike Plaintiff, there is no evidence that Defendants

---

[6] 19 Plaintiff argues that the only other evidence that would reveal post-Complaint sales are the matrices. However, as the matrices were destroyed during the lawsuit, Plaintiff could not present any proof of post-Complaint sales. This argument is unavailing for the reasons set forth in the contemporaneously filed Memorandum Order denying Plaintiff's sanctions motion, among other things.

have been involved in any copyright infringement lawsuits other than the present one. Similarly, Defendants have sold 15,000 titles in the past. This lawsuit began with sixty-two titles and now only relates to twenty-two titles; a very small percentage of the Defendants' product. Moreover, Plaintiff essentially admitted that the real culprits in this case are the third parties from which Defendants obtained Plaintiff's Titles. These third parties are the ones who misrepresented their ownership in the Titles to Defendants. While this does not diminish Defendants' liability, it does bear favorably for Defendants in the damages analysis.

e. Amount of Statutory Damages Award

In conclusion, there is very little evidence regarding Defendants' expenses and profits and Plaintiff's loss of revenue or harm. This is partly due to Defendants' recalcitrance during discovery in providing sales figures, although the Court also notes that Plaintiff's had an opportunity to obtain actual damages figures through a review of Defendants' vendor files by an independent certified public accountant. Moreover, the Court finds that Defendants did not have knowledge that they were infringing on Plaintiff's copyrights. Keeping in mind the lack of actual damages information, the lack of willful infringement, the parties' discovery conduct and the goal of discouraging future infringement, the Court finds it appropriate to impose damages of $ 10,000 per copyrighted work infringed. For the reasons already outlined, the Court declines to impose the maximum statutory award or impose any increased damages for willfulness.

2. Copyrighted "Work"

The next question is what constitutes a copyrighted work because "for the purpose of computing statutory damages, the relevant unit is not the number of infringements but the number of infringed 'works.'" UMG Recordings, Inc. v. MP3.com, Inc., 109 F. Supp. 2d 223, 225 (S.D.N.Y. 2000). Plaintiff argues that each musical composition and sound recording is a separate copyrighted work. Therefore, Plaintiff seeks statutory damages for each of the twenty-two Titles at issue in this case. The caselaw does not support Plaintiff's request.

The House Report discussing statutory damages states "Where the suit involves infringement of more than one separate and independent work, minimum statutory damages for each work must be awarded." See H.R. Rep. No. 94-1476, 2d Sess. at 162 (1976), reprinted in 1976 U.S.C.C.A.N. 5659, 5778 (emphasis added). While the Copyright Act does not define the term "work," the Copyright Act considers "all the parts of a compilation . . . [to] constitute one work[,]" even if the constituent parts of the compilation are copyrightable in their own right. See 17 U.S.C. § 504(c)(1); see also 4 Nimmer on Copyright, § 14.04[E][1], at 14-91 (noting that "[t]his result clearly follows if there is but a single copyright owner of all of the 'parts.'"). The House Report "makes clear . . . that, although they are regarded as independent works for other purposes, 'all the parts of a compilation or derivative work constitute one work'" for purposes of determining an award of statutory damages. See H.R. Rep. No. 94-1476, 2d Sess. at 162, reprinted in 1976 U.S.C.C.A.N. at 5778.

UMG Recordings, Inc. addressed the same situation this Court faces. In that case, the court found that the defendant had copied compact discs containing multiple songs. 109 F. Supp. 2d at 225. Each compact disc containing the multiple songs was registered as a compilation on a single registration. Id. As the songs were registered as a compilation, the court, pursuant to the congressional mandate, awarded a single statutory damage award per compilation. In doing so, the Court explicitly declined to grant an award per song. Id.; see also TeeVee Toons, Inc. v. MP3.com, Inc. 134 F. Supp. 2d 546, 548 (S.D.N.Y. 2001) ("[T]he Court [in UMG Recordings, Inc.] held that the statute precluded an individual plaintiff who owned the copyrights on both the individual sound recordings that made up each of the CDs in issue and the compilation that comprised the CD itself from recovering more than a single award of statutory damages per CD.").

The Fourth Circuit came to a similar conclusion in Xoom. The issue addressed in Xoom was whether a plaintiff could obtain an award for the compilation, as well as an award for the underlying preexisting works contained therein in which plaintiff also owned the copyright. 323 F.3d at 285. The court answered in the negative stating that § 504(c)(1) only permitted one award because plaintiff's registration of the infringed product covered the product in its entirety and the underlying preexisting works contained therein. Id. Thus, the court concluded that a plaintiff holding a copyright in a compilation could only receive one award of statutory damages for copyright infringement of that compilation. Id.

In contrast, the First Circuit has noted:

Under regulations promulgated by the Copyright Office, the copyrights in multiple works may be registered on a single form, and thus considered one work for purposes of registration, see 37 C.F.R. § 202.3(b)(3)(i)(A), while still qualifying as separate "works" for purposes of awarding statutory damages. We are unable to find any language in either the statute or the corresponding regulations that precludes a copyright owner from registering the copyrights in multiple works on a single registration form while still collecting an award of statutory damages for the infringement of each work's copyright.

Gamma Audio & Video, Inc. v. Ean-Chea, 11 F.3d 1106, 1117 (1st Cir. 1993). Following this logic, the First Circuit held that four episodes of a twenty-four episode television series registered on a single form constituted four separate "works." Id. Thus, infringement of the four episodes warranted four awards of statutory damages. Id. at 1117-18; see CoStar Group Inc. v. Loopnet, Inc., 164 F. Supp. 2d 688, 709-12 (D. Md. 2001), aff'd 373 F.3d 544 (4th Cir. 2004) (noting that critical fact in deciding whether one or multiple awards of statutory damages should be awarded depends on whether registration is of multiple works on a single form or of a compilation).

In order to register multiple works on a single form, however, the copyright claimant must clearly identify each work being registered. In CoStar Group Inc., the plaintiff argued that it should receive multiple awards, one for each photograph infringed. 164 F. Supp. 2d at 711. The district court declined to do so finding that the photographs were not separate works registered on a single form, but instead were compilations. Id. at 711-12. The determining factor in the court's decision was the fact that the photographs were not individually identified on each application. Id. Rather, the registration simply identified the material to be copyrighted as "photographs." Id. The court stated that the "bare reference to 'photographs' only has the efficacy as a description of the work to be copyrighted if it was made with reference to the other elements being copyrighted -- the compilation." Id.

In the present case, there are seventeen copyright registrations for the twenty-two Titles at issue in the case. This is because the three Ferlin Husky sound recordings -- "Gone," "Wings of a Dove," and "Fallen Star" -- were registered with the Copyright Office on a single registration under the title "Favorites of Ferlin Husky," with the catalogue number SD-3018. Similarly, the four Mary Wells sound recordings -- "My Guy," "The One Who Really Loves You," "You Beat Me to the Punch," and "Two Lovers" -- were registered with the Copyright Office on a single registration under the title "Dobie Gray and Mary Wells . . Greatest Hits," with the catalogue number PO 313.

There is no doubt that these registrations constitute compilations and not registrations of separate works on a single form. First, Plaintiff concedes that it registered these songs as compilations. Second, the individual sound recordings are not listed on the registrations. The registration lists the title of the albums and the fact that the registration covers sound recordings, but does not list the individual sound recordings. The fact that the label copy deposited with the Copyright Office identifies the individual sound recordings does not change the registration from a compilation to that of multiple separate works on a single form. Third, the Court notes that this case strongly resembles UMG Recordings, Inc. in which the court found that registration of an album constitutes a registration of a compilation even though it contains multiple sound recordings that can be registered separately. 109 F. Supp. 2d at 224-25. Thus, the Court holds that these two registrations are compilation registrations and a separate statutory award is not warranted for each sound recording contained therein. [20] As seventeen "works" containing the twenty-one sound recordings have been infringed, the Plaintiff is awarded $ 10,000 per work for a total of $ 170,000.

3. Statute of Limitations

Defendants argue that the statute of limitations bars recovery of damages which accrued more than three years before April 3, 2000, the date of the filing of this lawsuit. The Copyright Act provides that "[n]o civil action shall be maintained under the provisions of this title unless it is commenced within three years after the claim accrued." 17 U.S.C. § 507(b). Generally, courts have permitted a civil action as long as one instance of infringement occurs within the three year statutory period. See Bridgeport Music, Inc. v. Chrysalis Songs, 2002 U.S. Dist. LEXIS 26200, No. 3:01-0701 (M.D. Tenn. Dec. 2, 2002) (Higgins J.) ("A claim for copyright infringement . . . accrues at the time that the infringement upon which the suit is based occurred. If such infringement occurred within three years prior to the filing, the action will not be barred even if prior infringements by the same party as to the same work are barred because they occurred more than three years previously.") The law is murkier, however, as to whether a plaintiff can recover damages on both the infringement that occurred within the statutory period and infringements that occurred three years prior to the commencement of the action. See 3 Nimmer on Copyright, § 12.05[A], at 12-148.8-12-148.10.

In the present case, it is clear that one instance of infringement occurred during the statutory period because KRB, through Big Lots, offered the Titles for sale and Lytle purchased each of the twenty-two Titles at issue during a period spanning from December 1997 to February 1998. As this action could have been commenced at any time before December 2000, by commencing it in April 2000, Plaintiff was well within the statutory period. The sole issue, therefore, is the extent of damages the Plaintiff can recover. Had Plaintiff sought actual damages, the statute of limitations would have

---

[7] [20] Other than the registrations for "Don't Fall Asleep at the Wheel," "Fraulein," "Amazing Grace," and possibly "Take This Job and Shove It," it appears to the Court that the remaining registrations are also compilation registrations. Nevertheless, it is unnecessary for the Court to decide the status of the remaining registrations because only one sound recording on each of them has been infringed in this lawsuit. Thus, whether the registrations are considered compilations and a constituent part has been infringed, or the registrations are that of separate works and one work on each registration has been infringed, the result is the same: one statutory award for each.

been an issue. Under an actual damages analysis, the Court would have been required to decide whether Plaintiff could recover for infringements occurring three years prior to the commencement of this lawsuit. Plaintiff, however, sought to recover statutory damages instead of actual damages. Therefore, it is irrelevant how many instances of actual infringement occurred. It is sufficient that one instance of infringement occurred during the statutory period. As one instance of infringement did occur during the statutory period, Plaintiff is entitled to statutory damages.

In any event, Judge Echols already ruled that the statute of limitations should be equitably tolled. (See Doc. No. 82.) Judge Echols noted that there are five factors to consider when determining the appropriateness of equitably tolling a statute of limitations period. (See id. at 6.) One of the most important factors is plaintiff's lack of notice or lack of constructive knowledge of the filing requirement. (Id.) In considering plaintiff's notice, the court must review the plaintiff's reasonableness in remaining ignorant of the legal requirement for filing his or her claim. (Id.) Judge Echols found that Plaintiff had no knowledge and was not chargeable with any knowledge of Defendants' alleged copyright infringement until December 1997. (Id. at 8.) Similarly, he found that "Plaintiff was totally reasonable in its ignorance of the legal need to file a claim prior to December 1997." (Id.)

Defendants challenged Judge Echols' ruling immediately after it was issued and requested that he reconsider. (Doc. No. 84.) Defendants argued that contrary to Judge Echols' ruling, equitable tolling is inappropriate in this case because Plaintiff did have knowledge of the infringing activity more than three years prior to the commencement of thd lawsuit. Defendants point to Lytle's February 3, 1998 letter to KRB in which Lytle stated:

I have had people check your Big Lot stores that you rack and continue to find illegal copies of my masters that apparently you are selling to them. As time goes on, there seems to be more.

I have told you on the phone two or three times over the past year and a half. I tried to talk to you in my office about the situation and you got very defensive. I should have known, when you refused to let me see and copy a Classic Sound catalog that you had, that you had no intentions of trying to stop handling bootleg copies of G.M.L./Gusto's masters.

From the letter, it is entirely unclear what exactly Lytle communicated to Bennett "on the phone two or three times over the past year and a half." The inference is that Lytle told Bennett that KRB was allegedly illegally exploiting Plaintiff's product. According to the letter, these telephone conversations occurred a year-and-a-half prior to the letter, i.e. in mid-1996. Judge Echols' denied the motion to reconsider stating "[w]hile this letter is evidence that Plaintiff may have been aware of the alleged infringing conduct more than three years prior to filing its Complaint, this is an issue of fact to be determined [at trial]." (Doc. No. 100 at 2) (emphasis added).

Other than this letter, there is no evidence that Plaintiff was aware of the infringement since mid-1996. At trial, Bennett testified that Lytle had contacted him telephonically once, but could not recall the date of the phone call. Moreover, Bennett did not testify about any details of the call. Therefore, it is unclear if Lytle accused him of infringement at that time. Similarly, Lytle testified that he "talked to [Bennett] on a few occasions on the phone and after I went out to the stores and seen myself that he was copying my tapes and selling them, I set up a meeting for him to come to my office, which he agreed to do." Lytle did not testify when the phone calls occurred or what he said to Bennett, although his testimony implies that he alluded to KRB's copyright infringement of Plaintiff's Titles. Lytle, however, also testified that in his early contact with Bennett, Lytle was trying to convince Bennett to purchase music product from Lytle and his companies. Thus, it is possible that the phone calls did not involve allegations of infringement.

In any event, it appears that until December 1997, when Lytle first purchased cassettes from Big Lots, Lytle himself did not know whether KRB was infringing on Plaintiff's Titles. Instead, Lytle had a vague notion that KRB may be infringing on his company's product. Just as this Court has already concluded that this February 3, 1998 letter was too vague to give Bennett notice of infringement, the Court also finds that it is ambiguous about what Lytle knew about the alleged infringement and when he knew it. The Court finds that Lytle's "suspicions" of infringement that "possibly" dated back to mid-1996 are too conjectural to hold that Lytle had the requisite knowledge to preclude the tolling of the statute of limitations. In sum, there is insufficient evidence to overturn Judge Echols' prior factual and legal determination that the statute of limitations should be equitably tolled, and the Court declines to do so. The statute of limitations does not prevent Plaintiff from obtaining an award of statutory damages per copyrighted work infringed.

D. ATTORNEY FEES

Plaintiff requests an award of attorney fees. The Copyright Act provides that the district court may, in its discretion, award costs, including reasonable attorney fees, to the prevailing party. 17 U.S.C. § 505. It is well-settled that a plaintiff will be considered a prevailing party "for attorney's fees purposes if [the plaintiff] succeed[s] on any significant issue in litigation which achieves some of the benefit the parties sought in bringing the suit. . . ." Hensley v. Eckerhart, 461 U.S. 424, 433, 103 S. Ct. 1933, 76 L. Ed. 2d 40 (1983) (citations omitted). As the Supreme Court teaches, awarding attorney fees to the prevailing party in copyright cases is entirely within the Court's discretion. Fogerty, 510 U.S. at 533 (emphasis added). While there "is no precise rule or formula for making" a decision regarding attorney fees, a district court is required to exercise "equitable discretion." Id. at 534. In doing so, the Supreme Court condoned the use of non-exclusive factors such as "frivolousness, motivation, objective unreasonableness (both factual and in the legal components of the case) and the need in particular circumstances to advance considerations of compensation and deterrence." Id. at 534 n. 19 (citations omitted). These factors are to be applied with the purpose of the Copyright Act in mind. Id.

In this case, even though the Court did not accept all the legal theories that Plaintiff propounded, it is clearly the prevailing party, as judgment is being entered in its favor and it is receiving monetary damages. Nevertheless, the Court -- in its discretion -- declines to award attorney fees. When this case commenced, it involved sixty-two titles. On the first day of trial without explanation or notice to this Court or to the Defendants, Plaintiff requested the dismissal without prejudice of claims relating to forty of the titles in Count III. Plaintiff conducted laborious and contentious discovery spanning three years. Much of this discovery focused on the titles in Count III. To grant attorney fees when Plaintiff dropped two-thirds of the case at the beginning of trial would impermissibly condone Plaintiff's conduct. As the Magistrate Judge noted, Plaintiff did not conduct discovery in an efficient manner and the dismissal of Count III at the start of trial is indicative of Plaintiff's lack of preparation.

While the Court acknowledges that it is rare for a prevailing party to be denied attorney fees in a copyright case, it is certainly not a case of first impression. Indeed, the Sixth Circuit resoundingly affirmed a district court's denial of attorney fees due to both parties' discovery misconduct. See Ronald Mayotte & Assocs. v. MGC Bldg. Co., 1998 U.S. App. LEXIS 15149, No. 97-1483, 1998 WL 385905, *1 (6th Cir. July 1, 1998) (finding that both "parties behaved so irresponsibly that the court was unable to calculate a reasonable fee.")

III. CONCLUSION

In sum, Defendants have INFRINGED Plaintiff's copyrights in the twenty-two Titles at issue in this case. Defendants are JOINTLY and SEVERALLY LIABLE for the infringement. JUDGMENT IS ENTERED in FAVOR OF PLAINTIFF and the Court AWARDS Plaintiff $ 10,000 for each copyrighted work infringed for a total of $ 170,000. The Court DENIES Plaintiff's request for attorney fees and both parties are to bear their own costs.

STOCKART.COM, LLC, Plaintiff,

v.

CARAUSTAR CUSTOM PACKAGING GROUP, INC., et al., Defendants.

Civil Action No. RDB 05-2509

UNITED STATES DISTRICT COURT FOR THE DISTRICT OF MARYLAND

240 F.R.D. 195

October 17, 2006

District Judge Richard D. Bennett

OPINION

MEMORANDUM OPINION

Currently pending is Plaintiff Stockart.com, LLC's Motion for Leave to Take Early Discovery and Defendants Caraustar Custom Packaging Group (Maryland), Inc. and Caraustar Custom Packaging Group, Inc.'s Motion to Strike Paragraphs 14, 19, 20, & 21 of the Amended Complaint. This Court has jurisdiction over this matter pursuant to 28 U.S.C. §§ 1331, 1332, and 1338. The parties' submissions have been reviewed and no hearing is necessary. See Local Rule 105.6 (D. Md. 2004). For the reasons that follow, Plaintiff's Motion for Leave to Take Early Discovery is GRANTED and Defendants' Motion to Strike Paragraphs 14, 19, 20, and 21 of the Amended Complaint is DENIED with respect to Paragraphs 14 and 19 and GRANTED with respect to paragraphs 20 and 21.

BACKGROUND

Plaintiff Stockart.com, LLC ("Plaintiff" or "Stockart") is a Colorado limited liability corporation engaged in online image licensing. (See Am. Compl. P 7.) Defendant Caraustar Custom Packaging Group, Inc. ("Caraustar (Ohio)") is in the business of digital imaging and package design. (Id. at P 11.) Its subsidiary, Caraustar Custom Packaging Group (Maryland), Inc. ("Caraustar (Maryland)") manufactures and sells paper products. (Id. at P 12.)

Stockart alleges that Caraustar (Ohio) obtained possession of one of Stockart's copyrighted images, "Pizza Man Image JJ0A0602", on or about March 18, 2003.[1] (Id. at P 11.) Stockart contends that Caraustar (Ohio) distributed the copyrighted image to Caraustar (Maryland), who "produced" more than one million pizza boxes with a copy of the pizza man image on the boxes and then sold those boxes to Defendants Acme Paper & Supply Co., Inc. and John Does 1-500. (Id. at PP 14-16.) These unknown defendants and Acme allegedly re-sold the pizza boxes "to food establishments who used them to package pizza sold at retail to consumers." (Id. at P 14.) Stockart represents that "[w]hen the names of said John Does are discovered, they will be properly named by amendment of this Amended Complaint." (Id.)

The procedural history of this case is described in the Memorandum Opinion issued by this Court on August 1, 2006. (See Paper No. 35 p. 2.) In that Opinion, this Court stayed this action pending resolution of Stockart's Motion to Set Aside Default in the United States District Court for the Western District of North Carolina ("the North Carolina Action"). (Id. at pp. 4-5.) On August 1, 2006, the Court in the North Carolina Action issued an order granting Stockart's Motion to Dismiss for Lack of Personal Jurisdiction. (See Paper No. 37 Ex. A.) Accordingly, on August 16, 2006, this Court granted Stockart's unopposed Motion to Lift Stay. (See Paper No. 38.)

On August 16, 2006, Stockart filed its Motion for Leave to Take Early Discovery. (Paper No. 41) On September 8, 2006, Caraustar (Maryland) and Caraustar (Ohio) filed their Motion to Strike Paragraphs 14, 19, 20, & 21 of the Amended Complaint. (Paper No. 44).

DISCUSSION

I. Motion for Leave to Take Early Discovery.

Stockart requests leave to serve the following interrogatory on Caraustar

---

[1] Stockart represents that "[a]ll authorized publications of Plaintiff's work have been published with copyright notice" and "Plaintiff has registered its claims of copyright in and to the Pizza Man Image." (Am. Compl. PP 9-10.) Stockart attached to the Amended Complaint a copy of a Certificate of Registration, effective June 6, 2005, that the United States Copyright Office issued in connection with "Pizza Man Image # JJ0A0602". (Id. at Ex. A.)

(Maryland):

Identify the name, and address, and telephone number of each person, firm, or entity to whom Caraustar (including its parent, divisions, or subsidiaries), have sold products bearing the pizza man image which is the subject of this case, and state the type and number of units of products sold, and the price paid in respect of each such product.

(Paper No. 41 p. 1.) The purpose of this discovery is to identify and bring into this action the Defendants that are currently named in the Amended Complaint as John Does 1-500. (Id.)

As a preliminary matter, it appears that John Does 1-500 may be liable to the extent that they distributed Stockart's copyrighted "pizza man" image without authorization. First, there is no question that the unauthorized distribution of a copyrighted work constitutes copyright infringement. See, e.g., Hotaling v. Church of Jesus Christ of Latter-Day Saints, 118 F.3d 199, 203 (4th Cir. 1997) ("[D]istributing unlawful copies of a copyrighted work does violate the copyright owner's distribution right and, as a result, constitutes copyright infringement."). Second, Plaintiff notes that the Supreme Court in F.W. Woolworth Co. v. Contemporary Arts, Inc., 344 U.S. 228, 73 S. Ct. 222, 97 L. Ed. 276 (1952) clearly established that distributing unlawful copies of a copyrighted work constitutes copyright infringement even where a party is unaware that he is distributing matter that infringes on another's copyright. In that decision, Woolworth purchased sculptures of **cocker spaniels** from a third party. Notwithstanding Woolworth's lack of knowledge that the sculptures had been copied, the Supreme Court found Woolworth to be liable for direct infringement by the mere fact that Woolworth marketed and sold the sculptures. Id. at 229 ("Unbeknown to Woolworth, these dogs had been copied from respondent's and by marketing them it became an infringer.");[2]

---

[2] The Woolworth decision remains binding precedent upon this Court. See King Records, Inc. v. Bennett, 438 F. Supp. 2d 812 (M.D. Tenn. 2006) (applying Woolworth); Rogers v. Koons, 777 F. Supp. 1 (S.D.N.Y. 1991) (same), aff'd, 960 F.2d 301 (2d Cir.), cert. denied, 506 U.S. 934, 113 S. Ct. 365, 121 L. Ed. 2d 278 (1992). Although the Woolworth decision has been cited numerous times by the United States Court of Appeals for the Fourth Circuit and United States District Courts within the Fourth Circuit, it has never been cited for the proposition that distributing unlawful copies of a copyrighted work constitutes copyright infringement even where a party is unaware that he is distributing matter that infringes on another's copyright. See, e.g., Superior Form Builders, Inc. v. Dan Chase Taxidermy Supply Co., Inc., 74 F.3d 488, 496 (4th Cir. 1996) (citing Woolworth for the proposition that "recovery is not limited to gross profit from infringement; court may consider all facts"), cert. denied, 519 U.S. 809, 117 S. Ct. 53, 136 L. Ed. 2d 16 (1996).

see also 4 Nimmer § 13.08 ("In actions for statutory copyright infringement, the innocent intent of the defendant will not constitute a defense to a finding of liability.") (footnote and citations omitted).

This Court notes that the Caraustar entities do not oppose early discovery in principle, just the particular discovery sought in this case:

Caraustar opposes Plaintiff Stockart.com's Motion for Leave to Take Early Discovery, not because Caraustar is opposed to early discovery, but because Caraustar is opposed to the disclosure of the highly-confidential information sought by Stockart.com before the entry of an appropriate protective order, and because Caraustar is opposed to Stockart.com's intended use of that highly-confidential information.

(Paper No. 45 (emphasis added).) This Court finds that the Caraustar entities have failed to support their objections to the discovery sought by Stockart. First, Caraustar does not explain how the information sought "would violate the terms of any protective order entered in this case." (Id. at p. 4.) Second, without citing any support, Caraustar claims that Stockart's motion is improper because "[i]f there is any liability stemming from use or sales of products bearing the pizza-man image by Caraustar's customers, that liability would likely revert back to Caraustar." (Paper No. 45 p. 3.) However, as noted above, Stockart appears to have correctly pointed out that John Does 1-500 may be directly liable to the extent that they distributed the copyrighted "pizza man" image without authorization. It follows that any resulting liability would be jointly and severally shared between Caraustar (Maryland) and John Does 1-500.[3]

In sum, Plaintiff's motion for early discovery appears appropriate in light of F. W. Woolworth Co. v. Contemporary Arts, Inc., 344 U.S. 228, 73 S. Ct. 222, 97 L. Ed. 276 (1952). Moreover, Defendants Caraustar (Maryland) and Caraustar (Ohio) do not object to early discovery in principle and this Court rejects Caraustar's other objections to the discovery sought by Stockart. Accordingly, Plaintiff's Motion for Leave to Take Early

---

[3] As one treatise points out:

Where two or more persons have joined in or contributed to a single infringement of a single copyright, they are all jointly and severally liable. . . . Suppose, further, that D without authority distributed the plaintiff's motion picture to A, B, and C. Although A, B, and C are not jointly or severally liable each with the other, D will be jointly and severally liable with each of the others. There will, therefore, be three sets of statutory damages which may be awarded, as to each of which D will be jointly liable for at least the minimum of $ 250. However, D's participation will not create a fourth set of statutory damages.

4 Nimmer § 14.04[E][2][d] (footnotes and citations omitted).

Discovery is GRANTED.[4]

II. Motion to Strike Paragraphs 14, 19, 20, & 21 of the Amended Complaint.

Defendants Caraustar (Maryland) and Caraustar (Ohio) move to strike a portion of paragraph 14, and the entirety of paragraphs 19-21 of the Amended Complaint. (See Paper No. 44.) These paragraphs concern pre-litigation discussions between the parties and the basis for Caraustar's decision to initiate the North Carolina Action. (See Am. Compl. PP 14, & 19-21.) The Caraustar entities object to these paragraphs because they "allege actions that are outside the scope of the copyright dispute and are highly and unreasonably prejudicial towards Caraustar." (Id. at p. 2.)

As the parties' papers acknowledge, motions to strike pleadings or a portion thereof are governed by Fed. R. Civ. P. 12(f). [5] The Fourth Circuit has noted that motions brought under this Rule are typically disfavored:

Rule 12(f) motions are generally viewed with disfavor "because striking a portion of a pleading is a drastic remedy and because it is often sought by the movant simply as a dilatory tactic." 5A A. Charles Alan Wright & Arthur R. Miller, Federal Practice & Procedure § 1380, 647 (2d ed.1990).

Waste Mgmt. Holdings, Inc. v. Gilmore, 252 F.3d 316, 347 (4th Cir. 2001); see also Talbot v. Robert Matthews Distributing Co., 961 F.2d 654, 664-65 (7th Cir. 1992) (noting that allegations may be stricken under Rule 12(f) if the matter bears no possible relation to the controversy or may cause the objecting party prejudice).

This Court will deny Defendants Caraustar (Maryland) and Caraustar (Ohio)'s motion with respect to the relevant portion of paragraph 14 and paragraph 19. Based on the present record, this Court cannot state with certainty that the conduct alleged in these paragraphs bears no possible relation to Stockart's claim for willful infringement under 17 U.S.C. §

---

[4] This Court has considered Plaintiff's request for attorney's fees. (See Paper No. 47 p. 8.) That request, however, is DENIED.

[5] Fed. R. Civ. P. 12(f) provides:

Motion to Strike. Upon motion made by a party before responding to a pleading or, if no responsive pleading is permitted by these rules, upon motion made by a party within 20 days after the service of the pleading upon the party or upon the court's own initiative at any time, the court may order stricken from any pleading any insufficient defense or any redundant, immaterial, impertinent, or scandalous matter.

504(c). In addition, to the extent that these allegations are directed at Stockart's request for an award of punitive damages under 17 U.S.C. § 504, the parties have not addressed the matter of punitive damages in sufficient detail.[6] This Court will, however, grant Caraustar's motion with respect to paragraphs 20 and 21. These paragraphs contain allegations that have no bearing on the controversy that is presently before this Court and are based exclusively on the North Carolina Action, e.g., "Caraustar Maryland, backed by a billion dollar company, commenced the law suit in North Carolina to harass Plaintiff. . . ." (Am. Compl. P 21.) This Court notes that Stockart did not appear in the North Carolina Action until after an entry of default was issued in that case. In sum, this Court finds that Paragraphs 20 and 21 are immaterial and impertinent under Fed. R. Civ. P. 12(f). Accordingly, Caraustar (Maryland) and Caraustar (Ohio)'s Motion to Strike is DENIED with respect to the relevant portion of Paragraph 14 and Paragraph 19 and GRANTED with respect to Paragraphs 20 and 21 of the Amended Complaint.[7]

CONCLUSION

For the reasons stated above, Plaintiff's Motion for Leave to Take Early Discovery is GRANTED and Defendants's Motion to Strike Paragraphs 14, 19, 20, and 21 of the Amended Complaint is GRANTED-IN-PART and DENIED-IN-PART. A separate Order follows.

Dated: October 17, 2006
/s/ Richard D. Bennett
United States District Judge

---

[6] Caraustar does not address whether punitive damages are appropriate under 17 U.S.C. § 504. In addition, the case relied on by Plaintiff for the proposition that punitive damages are available under § 504--TVT Records v. Island Def Jam Music Group, 262 F. Supp. 2d 185 (S.D.N.Y. 2003)--has been limited by other courts. See, e.g., Calio v. Sofa Express, Inc., 368 F. Supp. 2d 1290, 1291 (M.D. Fla. 2005); see also 4 Nimmer § 14.02[C][2]. Finally, neither party addresses the extent to which the United States Court of Appeals for the Fourth Circuit has considered this matter. Cf. Nintendo of Am., Inc. v. Aeropower Co., 34 F.3d 246, 251 (4th Cir. 1994); Superior Form Builders, 74 F.3d at 496-97.

[7] This Court rejects Stockart's argument that the Caraustar entities have waived their right to file a motion to strike under Fed. R. Civ. P. 12(g). The record reflects that Caraustar has not filed a prior motion under Rule 12. (See Paper Nos. 10 & 28 (requesting that this Court dismiss, stay, or transfer this action based on principles of federal comity).)

3
US CUSTOMS TAXES

Earthenware and Paper Mache

Tax cases about whether reproductions made in large quantity can be works of art and whether objects made for adults can be toys.

WM. S. PITCAIRN CORP.
v.
UNITED STATES

C. D. 1277, Protest 131121-K
against the decision of the collector of customs
at the port of New York

UNITED STATES CUSTOMS COURT, THIRD DIVISION

25 Cust. Ct. 145

October 5, 1950

Benjamin A. Levett (Meyer Ohlbaum of counsel) for the plaintiff.

David N. Edelstein, Assistant Attorney General (Richard E. FitzGibbon and Harold L. Grossman, special attorneys), for the defendant.

Before CLINE, EKWALL, and JOHNSON, Judges.

JUDGE CLINE

OPINION

CLINE, Judge:

This is a protest, arising at the port of New York, against the collector's assessment of duty on china and earthenware figurines, at 45 per centum ad valorem under paragraph 212 of the Tariff Act of 1930, as modified by the trade agreement with the United Kingdom, T.D. 49753, on those made of china, and at 50 per centum ad valorem and 10 cents per dozen pieces under paragraph 211 on those made of earthenware. It is claimed that the articles are properly dutiable at 20 per centum ad valorem under paragraph 1547 (a) as "Works of art * * * statuary, sculptures, or copies, replicas, or reproductions thereof, valued at not less than $ 2.50." The claim is limited to those articles shown by the appraiser's return to be of a value of $ 2.50 or more each. All other claims in the protest have been abandoned.

The court expresses appreciation of the excellent briefs supplied by counsel for both parties.

The pertinent provisions of the tariff act are as follows:

PAR. 211. Earthenware and crockery ware composed of a nonvitrified absorbent body, including white granite and semiporcelain earthenware, and creamcolored ware, terra cotta, and stoneware, including * * * statues, statuettes, * * * and all other articles composed wholly or in chief value of such ware; * * * painted, colored, tinted, stained, enameled, gilded, printed, ornamented, or decorated in any manner, and manufactures in chief value of such ware, not specially provided for, 10 cents per dozen pieces and 50 per centum ad valorem.

PAR. 212 [as modified by the trade agreement with the United Kingdom, T. D. 49753]. China, porcelain, and other vitrified wares, including chemical porcelain ware, composed of a vitrified nonabsorbent body which when broken shows a vitrified or vitreous, or semivitrified or semivitreous fracture, and all bisque and parian wares, including * * * statues, statuettes, * * * and all other articles composed wholly or in chief value of such ware (except sanitary ware and parts and fittings therefor); any of the foregoing containing 25 per centum or more of calcined bone:
* * * *

Painted, colored, tinted, stained, enameled, gilded, printed, or ornamented or decorated in any manner, and manufactures in chief value of such ware, not specially provided for:
* * * *

Other 45% ad val.

PAR. 1547. (a) Works of art, including (1) paintings in oil or water colors, pastels, pen and ink drawings, and copies, replicas, or reproductions of any of the same, (2) statuary, sculptures, or copies, replicas, or reproductions thereof, valued at not less than $ 2.50, and (3) etchings and engravings, all the foregoing, not specially provided for, 20 per centum ad valorem.

#***#

Frederick Thomas Daws stated in his deposition that he is an artist and sculptor specializing in the painting and modeling of dogs and other animals; that he studied at the Lambeth School of Art in London and is a life-long student of animal life at the Zoological Society of London; that he has exhibited pictures and models at the Royal Academy of Arts in London, the Salon of Paris, the Walker Art Gallery, Liverpool, the Bristol Academy, and the Royal Society of British Artists, London; that he has produced models of dogs and other animals for Doulton since 1930 or 1931, many from life, some from ideas of his own, and some from suggestions by

Doulton; that he modeled the following figures involved herein:

English Setter and Pheasant	No. 2529	**Cocker spaniel**	No. 1078
English Setter	1051	**Cocker spaniel**	1036
Rough Haired Terrier	1014	**Cocker spaniel**	1037
Cocker and Pheasant	1029	Irish Setter	1056

The witness stated that each of the above was modeled in clay or wax and then cast in plaster; that two of the plaster models were delivered to Doulton, one in full color as it was to appear when produced in china, to serve as a guide for the artist employed by Doulton when working on the china model, the second copy remaining unpainted from which to make molds for production in pottery. The witness stated that he has never worked as an employee of Doulton but has his own studio; that he has done work for rendering in pottery for no other firm; that the figures are works of art since they are the inception of a professional sculptor and every detail from the modeling to the finished original is his work as a professional artist.

#***#

The intent of Congress in limiting the entry at a low rate of duty to certain artistic productions was to encourage the importation of works of the free fine arts and at the same time to protect American producers of articles belonging to the decorative and industrial arts. Tutton v. Viti, 108 U.S. 312, 27 L. Ed. 737, 2 S. Ct. 687; Frei Art Glass Co. v. United States, 15 Ct. Cust. App. 132, T. D. 42214; Lazarus, Rosenfeld & Lehmann v. United States, 2 Ct. Cust. App. 508, T. D. 32247. A distinction is made between what is done in a sculptor's studio by his own hand or under his eye and what is done by workmen in a marble shop. Tutton v. Viti, supra.

In accordance with that purpose, it has been held that reproductions made in large quantities in factories are not works of art. Lazarus, Rosenfeld & Lehmann v. United States, supra; O. O. Friedlaender Co. v. United States, supra; A. N. Khouri & Bro. v. United States, 1 Cust. Ct. 92, C. D. 27; John P. Daleiden Co. v. United States, 50 Treas. Dec. 679, Abstract 707.

In the instant case it appears that during 1949 Doulton produced an average of 15,254 figures a month; that the average production per week per artist was 20.1 figures; that the average number of persons trained to paint figures employed during 1949 was 176; that the average annual salary of such employees was £ 513 for males and £ 237 for females; that in some cases over 100 reproductions of a figure were made. The report of customs agent Simms (defendant's collective exhibit 25) shows that plaintiff usually carries a few dozen of each figure in stock, as high as 4 dozen of the popular figures and 1 or 2 dozen of the less popular ones. The record shows further that retail establishments carry about six of each figure in stock and that they are billed, ordered, and cataloged by stock numbers.

From this, we conclude that these articles are not artistic productions of the type Congress intended by the words "works of art" but belong to the class of decorative arts, which was defined in United States v. Perry, 146 U.S. 71, 36 L. Ed. 890, 13 S. Ct. 26, as follows (p. 75):

2. Minor objects of art, intended also for ornamental purposes, such as statuettes, vases, plaques, drawings, etchings, and the thousand and one articles which pass under the general name of bric-a-brac, and are susceptible of an indefinite reproduction from the original. [Emphasis supplied.]

Plaintiff claims that the provision in paragraph 1547 (a), excluding sculptures valued at less than $ 2.50, denoted an intention by Congress to broaden the scope of the paragraph so as to include works of art not in the domain of the free fine arts or such works of art as were produced in commercial quantities. This contention has been answered in The Friedlaender Co. v. United States, 64 Treas. Dec. 247, T. D. 46637, where the court said (p. 254):

From the foregoing statement it is clear that the conference committee considered the amendment as removing from the possibility of classification as works of art all sculptures and statuary, not specially provided for, which are valued at not less than $ 2.50 and relegated them to classification according to the component material of chief value, and not that it was liberalizing the term "works of art" nor in any manner reducing the standard for classification thereunder.

For the foregoing reasons, we hold that the merchandise herein is not classifiable as "statuary, sculptures, or copies, replicas, or reproductions thereof, valued at not less than $ 2.50" under paragraph 1547 (a) of the Tariff Act of 1930, but is properly dutiable as found by the collector at 45 per centum ad valorem under paragraph 212, as modified by the trade agreement with the United Kingdom, T. D. 49753, on the china figures, and at 50 per centum ad valorem and 10 cents per dozen pieces under paragraph 211 on those made of earthenware. The protest is overruled and judgment will be rendered accordingly.

WM. S. PITCAIRN CORP.

v.

UNITED STATES

No. 46631

UNITED STATES COURT OF CUSTOMS AND PATENT APPEALS

1 C.A.D. 458 ; 39 C.C.P.A. 15

June 5, 1951

B. A. Levett (Meyer Ohlbaum of counsel) for appellant.

David N. Edelstein, Assistant Attorney General (Joseph F. Donohue, special attorney, of counsel), for the United States.

Before GARRETT, Chief Judge, and JACKSON, O'CONNELL, JOHNSON, and WORLEY, Associate Judges

OPINION

GARRETT, Chief Judge, delivered the opinion of the court:

This is an appeal from the judgment of the United States Customs Court, Third Division, overruling the protest of the importer whereby recovery is sought of a portion of the duties assessed and collected at the port of New York City on certain (1) earthen and (2) china, or porcelain, figures, often called figurines or statuettes, imported from England. Certain types of clay form the basic ingredients of the articles which have no utility, having been designed for purely ornamental purposes. They are hereinafter more particularly described with respect to their creation, composition and what they represent. Since they fall squarely within the dictionary definitions of figurine we shall usually so designate them. All are embraced within the term ceramics.

The earthen figurines of the first type were classified under paragraph 211 of the Tariff Act of 1930, with duty assessment at 10 cents per dozen pieces and 50 per centum ad valorem, and those of the second type, composed of china or porcelain, under paragraph 212 of that act as modified by the reciprocal trade agreement with the United Kingdom, T.D. 49753, 74 Treas. Dec. 253, 263, with duty assessment at 45 per centum ad valorem.

The pertinent provisions of the respective paragraphs read:

Par. 211. Earthenware and crockery ware composed of a nonvitrified absorbent body, including white granite and semiporcelain earthenware, and cream-colored ware, terra cotta, and stoneware, including * * * statues, statuettes, * * * and all other articles composed wholly or in chief value of such ware; * * * painted, colored, tinted, stained, enameled, gilded, printed, ornamented, or decorated in any manner, and manufactures in chief value of such ware, not specially provided for, 10 cents per dozen pieces and 50 per centum ad valorem.

Par. 212. [as modified by the trade agreement with the United Kingdom, T.D. 49753.] China, porcelain, and other vitrified wares, including chemical porcelain ware, composed of a vitrified nonabsorbent body which when broken shows a vitrified or vitreous, or semivitrified or semivitreous fracture, and all bisque and parian wares, including * * * statues, statuettes, * * * and all other articles composed wholly or in chief value of such ware (except sanitary ware and parts and fittings therefor); any of the foregoing containing 25 per centum or more of calcined bone:

* * * * * * *

Painted, colored, tinted, stained, enameled, gilded, printed, or ornamented or decorated in any manner, and manufactures in chief value of such ware, not specially provided for:

* * * * * * *

Other . . . 45% ad val.

The claim on behalf of appellant is that both classes of figurines are subject to duty assessment at only 20 per dentum ad valorem, because classifiable under paragraph 1547(a) of the 1930 Tariff Act, -- specifically under that clause of the paragraph which reads:

Par. 1547. (a) Works of art, including * * * statuary, sculptures, or copies, replicas, or reproductions thereof, valued at not less than $ 2.50, * * *, not specially provided for, 20 per centum ad valorem.

At the outset we are confronted by a disagreement of counsel with respect to the scope of the issue before us. This, we think, can be better understood after the facts are recited.

Much evidence was introduced on behalf of both parties, including exhibits illustrative of the merchandise, the testimony of numerous witnesses and some documentary exhibits.

#***#

We fully realize that not everything modeled by a sculptor thereby becomes a sculpture, or a work of art, within the common meaning of the terms, which, in the absence of defining phraseology, is also the statutory meaning, and we have given careful study to the arguments of counsel for the Government, in the light of the numerous decisions which they cite, against holding the originals in this case to have been sculptures, but we are not convinced of the soundness of their position.

The fact that suggestions as to subject matter to be represented by the figurines were made at times to the sculptors by the art director of Doulton & Co., Ltd., does not, in out opinion, detract from the originality of the sculptor's work.

For example, the witness Daws evidently was familiar with many types of dogs, and if the art director ordered the figure of, say, a **Cocker spaniel** in a certain position he modeled one from his own knowledge and observation of the breed and its motions and appearance, or perhaps from life. On the same basis, the witness Harradine in forming his diminutive figures of persons, we think did original work even when he was carrying out general suggestions made to him.

We have not commented upon the Work of those who painted the articles because the primary interest here revolves about the sculpture. The evidence is clear, however, that a high order of skill is displayed in the decoration of the figurines.

We have studied the evidence of the expert witnesses called on behalf of the Government whose testimony was to the effect that the involved figurines are not works of art. We think it evident that they approached the subject as artists -- we do not question their ability as such -- rather than from the standpoint of congressional intent in the matter of levying tariff duties.

The Congress did not create the new law embraced in paragraph 376 of the 1913 tariff act idly, nor has it been retained idly. The amendment as to valuation adopted by the Congress which passed the 1930 Act is believed to have a significance which aids in interpreting the paragraph. That phraseology has not been considered by us previously.

The Congress obviously intended that some forms of statuary and sculpture and copies, replicas, or reproductions of same should be classifiable under paragraph 1547(a), supra. If figurines, such as those here involved, are held not to be so classifiable, it seems to us the paragraph will be greatly mutilated even if not wholly emasculated.

No identification of originals as distinguished from copies is made among the figurines here involved, nor in the protest. So, upon the record, all should pay duty at the rate of 20 per centum ad valorem.

For the reasons stated, the judgment of the United States Customs Court is reversed and the case is remanded for further proceedings in conformity with this decision.

WILSON'S CUSTOMS CLEARANCE, INC.

v.

UNITED STATES

Protests 65/19189 and 65/19211
against the decision of the collector of customs at the port of New York

UNITED STATES CUSTOMS COURT,
FIRST DIVISION

59 Cust. Ct. 36

July 19, 1967

Gurson L. Schweller for the plaintiff.

Carl Eardley, Acting Assistant Attorney General (Glenn E. Harris and Andrew P. Vance), for the defendant.

Before WATSON and BECKWORTH, Judges, and OLIVER, Senior Judge

JUDGE OLIVER

OPINION

OLIVER, Judge: The cases at bar which were consolidated at the time of trial relate to importations of articles invoiced as "papier mache dogs" or "papier mache ware." Duty was assessed at the rate of 35 per centum ad valorem under item 737.40 of the Tariff Schedules of the United States. Plaintiff claims that the imported articles are properly classifiable under item 256.75 of said tariff schedules at the rate of 8.5 per centum ad valorem as articles of papier mache. Various other claims mentioned in the protests were not pressed at trial or in the plaintiff's brief and are deemed abandoned. The official papers accompanying the protests were received into evidence without being marked.

The pertinent statutory provisions appear as follows:

Schedule 7, part 5, subpart E, headnotes 1 and 2:

1. The articles described in the provisions of this subpart (except parts)

shall be classified in such provisions, whether or not such articles are more specifically provided for elsewhere in the tariff schedules, but the provisions of this subpart do not apply to --

* * *

2. For the purposes of the tariff schedules, a "toy" is any article chiefly used for the amusement of children or adults.

Item 737.40:

Toy figures of animate objects (except dolls):

Not having a spring mechanism:

* * *

Not stuffed:

* * *

Other   35% ad val.

Schedule 2, part 4, subpart D, headnote 1:

1. This subpart covers articles of pulp, of papier-mache, of paper, or of paperboard, not provided for elsewhere in this schedule or in schedule 7.

Item 256.mkd TArticles, of pulp, of papier-mache, of paper, or of paperboard, or of any combination thereof, not specially provided for:

* * *

Of papier-mache   8.5% ad val.

The imported merchandise as represented by plaintiff's exhibits 1 and 2 was accurately described in the Government's brief as follows:

Each exhibit consists of a dog-like figure, approximately 10 inches long, with a detachable head that is inserted into an opening in the neck portion of the body by means of a hook and an eye that are attached to the outside of the head and the inside of the neck respectively. There is a metal weight attached to the head, and a collar around the neck. Plastic eyes and nose are attached to the head of each figure. The exhibits have a suede-like finish, Plaintiff's Illustrative Exhibit 1 being black and gray, while Plaintiff's Illustrative Exhibit 2 is brown. When the head of the figure is subjected to a force acting against it the resulting movement, corresponding to the hook swinging through the eye, is that of a dog nodding its head.

Plaintiff's first witness was Mr. Theodore Royffe, owner and sole employee of Royffe Continenal, Inc., the actual importer in this case.[1] He testified that pursuant to negotiations with Korlis, Ltd., of Englewood, New Jersey, he went to Japan and arranged to have the instant merchandise manufactured. The entries involved cover three kinds of dogs, shepherd,

---

[1] At the outset of the trial, the Government moved and the court granted its motion to quash a subpoena duces tecum served the day before trial on the Regional Commissioner of Customs in New York to produce inter alia certain entry papers covering importations of similar items by a New Jersey importer.

dachshund, and **cocker spaniel**, and they are all produced by the same Japanese manufacturer. Exhibit 1 represents a shepherd and exhibit 2 a **cocker spaniel**.

The witness further stated that he sold the items exclusively to automotive stores or wholesalers who sell to automotive outlets, such as Rep Boys in Philadelphia, Western Tire in Chicago, E.J.B. Products in New York, and Korlis, Ltd., in New Jersey.He had seen this merchandise, and similar merchandise, used on the inside rear of automobiles, mounted on the bck shelf and plainly visible. He had never seen it used by a child and thought the presence of the hook to hold the head on, as well as the "toxic" nature of the material used, made it dangerous for youngsters.

On cross-examination, the witness testified that, besides papier mache, the items contained a weight of lead, some plastic, and cardboard.

Mr. Eric J. Browner of E.J.B. Products testified as plaintiff's second witness. He stated that his business was that of a general importer and that he had purchased items represented by exhibits 1 and 2 from Royffe Continental, Inc. He sold 120 dozen of them to Times Square Automotive which he characterized as a store dealing in supplies, gadgets, and accessories for automobiles. He also remembered selling them to two automotive jobbers, one in Providence and the other in Los Angeles. He had never sold them to toy stores. On many occasions, he had observed similar articles displayed in the rear of cars and he had never seen them any place else.

Plaintiff argues that the fact that these imports have been sold exclusively to automotive outlets and never to toy stores and that the witnesses Royffe and Browner observed them in use only as automobile ornaments is sufficient to show they are not articles chiefly used to amuse children or adults. The Government, on the other hand, argues that plaintiff's evidence is too limited to show the articles are not chiefly used by children, much less by adults, and that, in any event, plaintiff has failed to establish its claimed classification on the issue of chief value.

With the advent of the new Tariff Schedules of the United States, the definition of the term "toy" was changed to include articles used by adults. Under the definition appearing in paragraph 1513 of the Tariff Act of 1930, it was necessary to determine two things, namely, by whom is the article used and for what purpose. United States v. Calhoun, Robbins, & Co., 21 CCPA 167, T.D. 46495. Although the first of these two determinations is now eliminated, the second subsists. With respect to this second determination, it had always been held that not everything a child used would be a toy but that the character of amusement involved was that derived from an item which is essentially a plaything. United States v. Louis Wolf & Co., 26 CCPA 243, C.A.D. 23; F.F.G Harper Co. v. United States,

63 Treas. Dec. 948, T.D. 46423. It follows, therefore, that Congress has broadened the toy provision to include articles that may be described as essentially playthings for adults. Apropos of this is the following observation of Mr. Russell N. Shewmaker, Assistant General Counsel to the United States Tariff Commission, made during a hearing conducted by the Tariff Commission concerning the revised scope of the toy provision in the new schedules (1960 Tariff Classification Study, Explanatory and Background Materials, schedule, 7, page 682):

There is also another factor which I think is important here as we work with this provision. There has been in recent years a growth in the leisure time activities of adults. The adults are finding more and more time to play and to amuse themselves with various pursuits and, as Mr. Lerch said, they may be acting like a child sometimes when they are doing it, but nevertheless they are being amused. We were trying to help the tariff to go with the age.

In the recently decided case of Fred Bronner Corp. v. United States, 57 Cust. Ct. 428, C.D. 2832, we had occasion to review a significant line of cases distinguishing between a toy and articles of ornamentation, decoration, or display. The distinction exists regardless of the age of the users. In the instant case, the sole testimony offered is to the effect that these items, similar to those previously imported by others, have found but one use and that is as ornaments or objects of display for the rear window of automobiles. Such testimony, however, as pointed out by defendant, is limited to local observations in this city. Moreover, as merchants or executives commercially handling these items, the witnesses' testimony has limited effect since they mostly sell to other and distant distributors, and they did not disclose a very intimate knowledge of ultimate distribution and sale. Klipstein v. United States, 1 Ct. Cust. Appls. 122, T.D. 31120; F. B. Vandegrift & Co., Inc. v. United States, 56 Cust. Ct. 103, C.D. 2617.

Nevertheless, as is especially true in toy cases, the sample merchandise can offer potent evidence on the question of use, and when in harmony with the other evidence of record, can permit the drawing of inferences as to use nationally. Fred Bronner Corp., supra. There is precedent under the two previous tariff acts for viewing sample evidence as sufficiently persuasive to rebut the presumption of correctness on a toy classification and to shift the burden to the defendant. United States v. The Halle Bros. Co., 20 CCPA 219, T.D. 45995; United States v. Borgfeldt & Co., 13 Ct. Cust. Appls. 620, T.D. 41461.

We are inclined to the view that the present case presents one of those occasions where the sample merchandise itself supplies the necessary persuasiveness to carry the issue for the plaintiff, at least when the presumptive correctness of the collector's classification stands unsupported. The presence of a sharp and rather easily exposed hook renders the merchandise patently unusable by children of tender years. As for those over puberty, the articles represent essentially passive, uncomical, almost nonmanipulatable, yet finely finished replicas of well-known dog species. As such they are eminently suitable for purposes of display or ornamentation, no matter where that may be, and substantially incapable of functioning as objects of play or amusement in any normal or intelligent use. It is not a question of their appearing more suitable for one use than another as was the case in Fred Bronner Corp., supra, but of their offering mute testimony of their substantial incapability of use as classified. This type of potent evidence when in harmony with all other evidence presented satisfies the court that a shift in burden on this issue has taken place.

To discharge its two-fold burden in this classification case, it was for the plaintiff to show that the merchandise is properly dutiable as claimed, that is, as articles of papier mache under item 256.75. Rule 9(f)(i) of the General Headnotes and Rules of Interpretation preceding the new tariff schedules provides that the term "of" when used to relate a material to articles under a tariff provision means articles wholly or in chief value of that material. In conjunction with this, General Interpretative Rule 10(f) provides:

an article is in chief value of a material if such material exceeds in value each other single component material of the article:

Aside from the testimony of the importer that he had observed the manufacture of these articles in Japan, the record here is completely lacking in evidence on this issue of component material of chief value. Unlike the efficacy of the sample on the issue of use, the presence of a rather substantial amount of lead, as well as unknown amounts of nonpaper materials, renders it unsuitable as a competent source on this value issue. Compare John S. Connor, Inc. v. United States, 54 Cust. Ct. 213, C.D. 2536. In this situation, therefore, it was incumbent upon the plaintiff to show the costs of the different components used in producing these articles.

It is well settled that the proper method of determining the component material of chief value of an article is to ascertain the costs of the separate parts or component materials to the manufacturer at the time they are ready to be assembled or combined into the article. [Commercial Adolfo S. Pagan, Inc., et al. v. United States, 48 Cust. Ct. 210, 216, C.D. 2337, and cases cited therein.]

Having failed to offer the proofs required to sustain its claim, we have no alternative but to overrule plaintiff's protests without affirming the collector's classification. Judgment will issue accordingly.

4
TOY BANKS

...and (as in the previous section) referring to toys, and statues, and differences between copyright and patent law, here are two cases that address all of these issues; in the first, toy banks are protected by copyright, but then the case is cited to withhold protection from model airplanes. As with the Cocker in Show Position, the aesthetic form is protected, but the natural functions of the form are not.

Royalty Designs, Inc. v. Thrifticheck Service Corp.,
204 F. Supp. 702 (1962)

Monogram Models, Inc. v. Industro Motive Corp
448 F.2d 284 (1971)

ROYALTY DESIGNS, INC.,
Plaintiff

v.

THRIFTICHECK SERVICE CORP.,
Defendant

UNITED STATES DISTRICT COURT
FOR THE SOUTHERN DISTRICT OF NEW YORK

204 F. Supp. 702

February 15, 1962

Samuel J. Stoll, Jamaica, N.Y., for plaintiff.

Maxwell E. Sparrow, New York City, for defendant; Mark H. Sparrow, New York City, of counsel.

JUDGE BRYAN

OPINION

Plaintiff Royalty Designs, Inc. (Royalty) is the owner of two copyright registrations (numbers Gp16890 and Gp16892) issued May 7, 1958 for plastic molded toy coin banks in the shape of dogs. One registration is for a bank in the shape of a Boxer and the other for a bank in the shape of a **Cocker spaniel**. Plaintiff has manufactured and sold its copyrighted banks since November, 1957. Copyright notice is stamped on a metal plug which fits securely into an opening on the bottom of the banks.

Royalty sues for infringement of its registrations alleging that some time in May, 1961 defendant Thrifticheck Service Corp. (Thrifticheck) began to manufacture and sell plastic molded toy banks in the shape of Boxer and **Cocker spaniel** dogs which were direct copies of its copyrighted banks. It claims that the only difference between its products and those of Thrifticheck is that its banks are flocked with a substance which gives the appearance of dog hair and defendant's are not.

Royalty now moves for a preliminary injunction restraining Thrifticheck during the pendency of the action from further infringing its copyrights and from distributing and selling the toy dog banks complained of, alleging that unless preliminary injunctive relief is granted it will suffer irreparable injury.

It submitted samples of its finished banks and samples of its banks before they are flocked as well as samples of defendant's finished banks. Comparison of the samples shows conclusively that the Thrifticheck banks are direct copies of the Royalty copyrighted banks. The size, proportions, features and expressions of the animals represented are almost identical, with only minor and insignificant variations. The noses of the Royalty dogs are smooth and are molded as part of the entire bank. In the original molding of the Thrifticheck banks the dog's muzzle is flattened and a separate, somewhat more defined nose piece is glued on. The eyes of the Royalty dogs are predominantly black with some white showing whereas the Thrifticheck eyes are all black.

Apart from these insignificant differences the only other difference is in the finish used by defendant. Plaintiff's dogs are flocked with a tan colored substance which resembles dog hair. Defendant's dogs are bare plastic but are painted or tinted a tannish color.

These differences are totally irrelevant to the purpose for which the design is intended. Every important detail of the Royalty designs appear in the Thrifticheck dogs. The breed, size, shape and expressions of the dogs and each part of their bodies are almost precisely the same. The paws, ears, tails and mouths are carbon copies. The wrinkles about the foreheads and mouths are identical. In every important respect defendant's banks are a direct verisimilitude of plaintiff's designs. The variations in the finish, nose and eyes and any slight differences in size are all totally insignificant. This is not an instance or mere accidental similarity. It necessarily must result from conscious and intentional copying.

This is borne out by Royalty's uncontroverted statement that Thrifticheck acquired its master molds from the same moldmaker who manufactured plaintiff's molds from its original designs.

Thrifticheck does not deny that it has copied. It defends on the grounds that (1) the copyrights are invalid because the notice of copyright has not been properly affixed to the produce, and (2) that Royalty has failed to establish its claim of irreparable injury and, therefore, is not entitled to a preliminary injunction.

If Royalty has valid copyrights which have not been lost by failure to affix proper notice as required by 17 U.S.C. §§ 10 and 19, then it is entitled to a preliminary injunction on a finding that defendant has infringed without a detailed showing of irreparable injury.

#***#

There is no doubt that copyright protection extends to Royalty's designs as productions of originality and novelty. See Rushton v. Vitale, supra. Royalty does not claim rights to all toy banks in the form of Boxer and **Cocker spaniel** dogs. Its copyrights are for the particular novel and original renditions created and designed by it, which are legitimate subjects of copyright registrations. Royalty by its treatment of the subjects has contributed something recognizably its own which is by no means trivial. See Alfred Bell & Co. v. Catalda Fine Arts, 191 F.2d 99 (2 Cir. 1951); F. W. Woolworth Co. v. Contemporary Arts, 193 F.2d 162 (1 Cir. 1951); aff'd 344 U.S. 228, 73 S.Ct. 222, 97 L.Ed. 276.

Therefore, if the notice of copyright on the metal disc at the bottom of its banks is properly affixed Royalty is entitled to a preliminary injunction. Though the discs themselves are not copyrighted, they are an integral part of the banks. Money is inserted into the bank through a slit in the top of the dog's head. A circular hole about an inch in diameter is molded into the bottom of the bank itself. The disc, which is marked clearly with Royalty's name, place of origin and notice of copyright, fits securely into the hole and prevents coins from falling out of the bank. It cannot fall out by itself and must be pried out with a flat object when the bank is emptied. The disc is firmly attached and is an essential part of the bank, and without it the product would not serve its purpose. The banks are sold with the disc securely inserted and it is so placed as to give adequate notice to anyone seeking to copy the article of the existence of the copyright. The method of affixing the notice amply satisfies the requirements of 17 U.S.C. §§ 10 and 19.

#***#

Therefore, I find that the Royalty copyrights for its Boxer and **Cocker spaniel** dog toy banks are valid and that it has made out a prima facie case of infringement of such copyrights by Thrifticheck. Under these circumstances the general statements by Royalty as to the irreparable damage it has and will continue to suffer as a result of this infringement are sufficient and the damages need not be detailed.

The motion for a preliminary injunction enjoining Thrifticheck pending the final determination of this action from making, publishing, distributing and selling the toy banks of which Royalty complains, or otherwise infringing the Royalty copyrights, numbers Gp16890 and Gp16892, is hereby granted.

Pursuant to Rule 65(c), Fed.Rules Civ.Proc., 28 U.S.C., Royalty will be required as a condition of the grant of injunctive relief, to give security in the sum of $ 2,500 for the payment of such costs and damages as may be incurred or suffered in the event that Thrifticheck is found to have been unlawfully enjoined.

This opinion constitutes my findings of fact and conclusions of law pursuant to Rule 52(a), F.R.C.P.

Settle order which conforms with Rule 65(d), F.R.C.P., on notice.

MONOGRAM MODELS, INC.,
Plaintiff-Appellee,

v.

INDUSTRO MOTIVE CORPORATION
and Henry G. Michael,
Defendants-Appellants

No. 21060

UNITED STATES COURT OF APPEALS
FOR THE SIXTH CIRCUIT

448 F.2d 284

September 17, 1971

Peck, Brooks and Kent, Circuit Judges.

BROOKS, Circuit Judge.

OPINION

This is an appeal by defendants-appellants, Industro Motive Corporation and Henry G. Michael, the corporation's president and major stockholder, from a judgment of the District Court holding that defendants infringed plaintiff-appellee's copyrights on two scale plastic model airplane kits. The District Court granted summary judgment for plaintiff, Monogram Models, Inc., permanently enjoining defendants from future infringing of plaintiff's copyrights. The question of damages and the personal liability of Henry Michael as president and major stockholder of defendant corporation were not resolved.

In granting summary judgment, the District Court drew certain legal and factual conclusions which it termed "general observations". First, the District Court held that plaintiff's plastic scale model airplanes were proper subject matter for copyright protection. Second, there was nothing "to attack the presumption of validity" of plaintiff's copyrights. Apparently, the Court was making reference to the statutory requisites for copyrightability, particularly the giving of proper notice of copyright on the model airplanes.

Third, that defendant's model airplanes were wholesale copies of plaintiff's airplanes and the factual posture of the case made summary judgment appropriate.

On this appeal defendant has challenged each of these holdings claiming that plastic scale model airplanes are not copyrightable but, if copyrightable, plaintiff failed to give proper notice of copyright, 17 U.S.C. §§ 10, 19, and, therefore, loses any protection it might have had. And that there are genuine issues of material fact, including whether defendant's model airplanes were plagiarized from plaintiff, which removes the case from the category where granting summary judgment would be proper. Defendant also contends it was error for the District Court to have granted only partial summary judgment thereby leaving the question of damages and the liability of Henry Michael unresolved. For reasons hereafter stated, we affirm the District Court's legal conclusion as to the copyrightability of plastic scale model airplanes, but reverse and remand for trial and resolution of certain factual disputes and questions.

Our disposition of this case reflects the fact that on the present record it is not possible to review any other question but the legal one respecting the copyrightability of scale plastic model airplanes. As regards the propriety of the grant of summary judgment, we hold this case has raised several genuine issues of material fact thereby making summary handling of the matter under Rule 56 Federal Rules of Civil Procedure impossible. Specifically, there appear to be conflicts raised over the infringement question by the opposing affidavits for summary judgment. See generally, Blumcraft of Pittsburgh v. Newman Brothers, Inc., 373 F.2d 905 (6th Cir. 1967). In considering the motions for summary judgment, the District Court had before it the pleadings, two sets of interrogatories, three affidavits and the airplane models. In one set of interrogatories, defendant had responded affirmatively to the general question whether it copied any component of either of plaintiff's models. Yet, in defendant's affidavit specific similarities between each company's models, which plaintiff claimed to be proof of plagiarism, were explained as technical or standard trade methods commonly used by all manufacturers of plastic model airplanes. While there was a general admission of copying, the fact that scale models were of the same actual airplanes and that similarities were explained in terms of common industrial practices tends to raise a genuine issue of fact as to whether the similarities were simple resemblances, being a natural by-product of the expression of identical ideas, or copyright infringement. Sunset House Distributing Corporation v. Doran, 304 F.2d 251, 252 (9th Cir. 1962); Alfred Bell and Company, Ltd. v. Catalda Fine Arts, Inc., 191 F.2d 99, 103 (2nd Cir. 1951); Ricker v. General Electric Company, 162 F.2d 141, 142 (2nd Cir. 1947).

Moreover, there appear to be other important factual disputes, such as the sufficiency of copyright notice and the extent of the subject matter protected by the copyright certificate, which were not specifically addressed but require development and resolution by the District Court. While it is recognized that once a copyright certificate is issued it is prima facie evidence of the facts stated therein, 17 U.S.C. § 209, Nimmer on Copyrights §§ 139.1, 139.2, and that initial publication was with sufficient copyright notice, Tennessee Fabricating Company v. Moultrie Manufacturing Company, 421 F.2d 279 (5th Cir. 1970), the presumption is clearly rebuttable, Rohauer v. Friedman, 306 F.2d 933 (9th Cir. 1962); Jerry Vogel Music Company v. Forster Music Publisher, 147 F.2d 614, 615 (2nd Cir. 1945). Since the burden of going forward shifts to the defendant following proof of issuance of the copyright, Blumcraft of Pittsburgh v. Newman Brothers, Inc., supra, 373 F.2d at 907; Rohauer v. Friedman, supra, 306 F.2d at 935, and as in this case there exists on the face of a copyright certificate ambiguity as to the extent of the subject matter protected, [1] as well as a specific affirmative attack on a copyright for lack of adequate notice, a defendant should be permitted the opportunity to introduce supporting evidence to satisfy the burden of going forward. Accordingly, we reverse and remand this action to the District Court for consideration and trial on the factual questions presented, among which are:

1. Did the registration for copyright filed by plaintiff and the copyright certificate cover the actual plastic model airplane and not simply the instruction sheet for assembly and the decorative container packaging the plastic pieces of the model airplane?

2. Was there sufficient and adequate legal notice of copyright on all the subject matter (instruction sheets, containers and plastic models) for which plaintiff seeks copyright protection?

3. Was there ever a period during which the alleged copyrighted subject matter was manufactured without copyright notice, [2] and if so was there an abandonment to the public domain?

4. If valid, were plaintiff's copyrights infringed by defendants' models?

Resolving whether scale plastic model airplanes are proper subject matter for copyright protection presents a unique problem in statutory construction. Section 4 of the Copyright Act (17 U.S.C. § 4) provides: "The works for which copyright may be secured under this title shall

---

[1] 1 See note 3 infra.

[2] 2 A basis for this question arises because it appears from the record that over two years elapsed between the first public sales of the model airplanes and filing for copyright protection.

include all the writings of an author." Then section 5 ("Classification of works for registration") provides:

The application for registration shall specify to which of the following classes the work in which copyright is claimed belongs:

(a) Books, including composite and cyclopedic works, directories, gazetteers, and other compilations.

(b) Periodicals, including newspapers.

(c) Lectures, sermons, addresses (prepared for oral delivery).

(d) Dramatic or dramatico-musical compositions.

(e) Musical compositions.

(f) Maps.

(g) Works of art; models or designs for works of art.

(h) Reproductions of a work of art.

(i) Drawings or plastic works of a scientific or technical character.

(j) Photographs.

(k) Prints and pictorial illustrations including prints or labels used for articles of merchandise]

(l) Motion-picture photoplays.

(m) Motion pictures other than photoplays.

The above specifications shall not be held to limit the subject matter of copyright as defined in section 4 of this title, nor shall any error in classification invalidate or impair the copyright protection secured under this title.

Plaintiff's two plastic model airplanes are called F-105 Thunderchief and A1-E Skyraider. The F-105 Thunderchief is registered in class (a) (Books, etc.) and the A1-E Skyraider is registered in class (g) (Works of Art, etc.).[3] The fact that these classifications are perhaps not accurate descriptions of the subject matter sought to be copyrighted apparently is of no consequence. 17 U.S.C. § 5; see also, Day-Brite Lighting, Inc. v. Sta-Brite Fluorescent Manufacturing Company, 308 F.2d 377 (5th Cir. 1962); Peter Pan Fabrics, Inc. v. Dan River Mills, Inc., 415 F.2d 1007 (2nd Cir. 1969); Bouve v. Twentieth Century Fox Film Corporation, 74 App.D.C. 271, 122 F.2d 51 (1941). It is a legitimate question as to how certain of the classifications, such as photographs, motion pictures and "Works of art; models or designs for works of art" can be reconciled as "writings of an

---

[3] The Certificate of Registration for the Thunderchief listed under the section for "Title" "F-105 THUNDERCHIEF, being a container and instruction sheet for the assembly of a scale model airplane and components thereof." The Certificate for the Skyraider listed under the section for "Title" "A1-E Skyraider" and under the "Nature of Work: section Scale Model Airplane."

author."[4] However, courts have held, either by assuming sub silentio or through the use of a legal fiction, that the phrase "writings of an author" is not to be literally construed so as to restrict the scope of copyrightable subject matter. Thus, there has been upheld copyright protection on "writings of an author" as far removed from a literal definition of "writings" and "author" as miniature statues of certain religious shrines, Allegrini v. DeAngelis, 59 F. Supp. 248 (E.D.Pa.1944), aff'd. 149 F.2d 815 (3rd Cir. 1945); miniature reproduction of Robins' "Hand of God", Alva Studios, Inc. v. Winninger, 177 F. Supp. 265 (S.D.N.Y.1959); a doll called Zippy in the form of a chimpanzee which appeared on the old Howdy Doody television program, Rushton v. Vitale, 218 F.2d 434 (2nd Cir. 1955); a filigreed room divider, Tennessee Fabricating Company v. Moultrie Manufacturing Company, 421 F.2d 279 (5th Cir. 1970); costume jewelry, Boucher v. DuBoyes, 253 F.2d 948 (2nd Cir. 1958); plastic Boxer and Cocker spaniel dogs used as coin banks, Royalty Designs, Inc. v. Thrifticheck Service Corporation, 204 F. Supp. 702 (S.D.N.Y.1962); red flat plastic bags with decoration and faces which when stuffed with crumpled newspapers become "fat life-sized dummy Santa Claus", Sunset House Distributing Corporation v. Doran, 304 F.2d 251 (9th Cir. 1962); a model hobby horse, Blazon, Inc. v. Deluxe Game Corporation, 268 F. Supp. 416 (S.D.N.Y.1965); a sculptured artificial lilac flower made of polyethylene, Prestige Floral, Societe Anonyme v. California Artificial Flower Company, 201 F. Supp. 287 (S.D.N.Y.1962) and the list goes on and on. From these and other cases it can be observed that "practically anything novel can be copyrighted", Dan Kasoff, Inc. v. Novelty Jewelry Company, 309 F.2d 745, 746 (2nd Cir. 1962) so long as it is "original". Mazer v. Stein, 347 U.S. 201, 214, 74 S. Ct. 460, 98 L. Ed. 630 (1953). In short, we feel compelled to affirm the holding that scale plastic model airplanes are proper subject matter for copyright protection.

The judgment of the District Court is vacated and the case is remanded for further proceedings consistent with this opinion.

---

[4] Since this appeal does not raise a constitutional challenge we only allude to the fact that there has been some probative concern expressed that the grant of Congressional power provided in Article I, § 8 of the Constitution is perhaps not as broad as has been exercised in the Copyright Act. See Mr. Justice Douglas' opinion in Mazer v. Stein, 347 U.S. 201 at 219, and note 5, 74 S. Ct. 460, 98 L. Ed. 630 (1953) of Mr. Justice Reed's majority opinion in Mazer v. Stein at 206-208, 74 S. Ct. at 464-466.

5
THE COCKER SPANIEL
IN BUSINESS

Two more tax cases (business deductions for dog related business), and another intellectual property case over grooming device Furminator.

Hall v. Commissioner,
1953 Tax Ct. Memo LEXIS 242; 12 T.C.M. (CCH) 564; T.C.M. (RIA) 53179, May 22, 1953

Smith v. Commissioner,
T.C. Memo 1971-122; 1971 Tax Ct. Memo LEXIS 209; 30 T.C.M. (CCH) 516; T.C.M. (RIA) 71122, May 27, 1971, Filed.

FURminator, Inc. v. Ontel Prods. Corp.,
429 F. Supp. 2d 1153; (2006)

Louis Hall and Joan P. Hall, Husband and Wife
v.
Commissioner.

Docket Nos. 37461, 40802.

UNITED STATES TAX COURT

12 T.C.M. (CCH) 564

May 22, 1953

Kenneth C. Tiffin, Esq., for the petitioners. Nathan M. Silverstein, Esq., for the respondent.

Judge Murdock

OPINION

Memorandum Findings of Fact and Opinion

The Commissioner determined deficiencies in income tax of $655.37 for 1947, $1,132.86 for 1948 and $971.14 for 1949 against the petitioners. The only issue for decision is whether losses sustained in raising dogs are deductible as losses from a business regularly carried on for profit.

Findings of Fact

The petitioners, husband and wife, filed joint returns for the taxable years with the collector of internal revenue for the District of Massachusetts.

Louis was graduated from Harvard in 1933 and thereafter did some graduate work in law and theology but received no degree in either. He entered the United States Navy in 1942 and continued in that service until 1944. He and Joan were married in 1945 and they considered how he could profitably occupy his time. He had never been employed or engaged in business, except for his service in the Navy, and he was unsuccessful in his efforts to obtain employment. He had income from trusts, interest and dividends of $5,379.48 for 1946, $4,881.14 for 1947, $16,010.96 for 1948 and $18,841.41 for 1949. He had had a little previous experience with dogs beginning in 1939, he liked dogs and he and Joan decided to go into the business of raising and selling **cocker spaniels** for profit. The breed was popular in England but relatively new in the United States.

They built a new garage on their residence property at Wayland, Massachusetts, and turned the old one-car garage into a one-room kennel and fenced in a large double run for dogs. The kennel had capacity for four litters a year. They continued to use those facilities until 1949 when they decided to acquire a more desirable place with more room for their **spaniels**. They purchased a place in Holliston, Massachusetts, on which there was a barn, containing five single dog pens, and a pony barn which they improved with a new foundation, a wing and running water outlets. They put a kitchen and eight pens in the pony barn. Each new pen could accommodate two dogs. They fenced in large runs adjacent to the kennels. Those kennels had capacity for sixteen litters a year. The improvements were completed in November 1949. They had equipment usual in such an establishment.

The petitioners devoted their full time to their dog business during the taxable years and did all of the work themselves, except a negligible amount. The **spaniels** required a great deal of attention.

They tried to have their kennels and dogs become widely and favorably known by exhibiting and winning in shows, by advertising, by joining Kennel Clubs and by helping the latter put on shows. Their dogs won many events at shows during the taxable years.

They kept no books for the dog business but kept a list of stud fees and sales receipts. Some expenses were paid by check, others in cash. Some items such as automobile, telephone, electricity and heat were prorated between business and personal expense.

The breeding dogs owned and litters whelped in the taxable years were as follows:

	1947	1948	1949
Matrons	2	3	3
Dogs	3	3	2
Litters	2	1	2

They could have had more litters in each year but sales did not justify more.

Each matron can have two litters a year and there are usually five or six pups in a litter. Puppies sell for from $65 to $75 each. The stud fee at the petitioner's kennels was $50. No dogs belonging to others were boarded.

The receipts, ordinary and necessary expenses and losses of the dog business were as follows during the years 1946 through 1949:

	1946	1947	1948	1949
Expenses	$2,447.48	$3,613.01	$4,887.17	$4,670.04
Receipts	525.00	310.00	105.00	819.77
Loss	$1,922.48	$3,303.01	$4,782.17	$3,850.27

Those losses were claimed as deductions on the returns.

The Commissioner, in determining the deficiencies, disallowed the losses from the operation of the kennels and explained that they "were not incurred in a trade or business, or in a transaction entered into for profit and, therefore, are not allowable deductions from gross income."

The petitioners entered into the dog business in 1945 and carried it on during the taxable years in good faith for the purpose of making a profit and in the belief that they could eventually realize a profit from the business.

Opinion

MURDOCK, Judge: The question here is whether these petitioners operated these kennels for personal reasons, in which profit was not essential, or strictly as a business for the realization of profits. That is a question of fact to be determined from the record before the Court. The Commissioner points to the consistent losses, Louis' love of dogs, his independent means to gratify it, the lack of records, and argues that this was not a business but a personal expense from which no one could reasonably expect a profit. He concedes that "an enterprise of this sort cannot be expected to yield profits from its inception * * *." Louis points to his modest income, his desire for gainful occupation, the long hours at hard work put in by him and Joan and their belief that they could, in time, make the business profitable after their kennels and the breed became better known. Of course, continued losses over a longer period could swing the balance the other way but there is a fair preponderance of the evidence in the present record in the petitioners' favor on which findings have been made.

The Commissioner's counsel argues that all of the expenses have not been substantiated. The deficiency notices indicate that the deductions were disallowed for the sole reason that there was no profit motive. The evidence, in view of this determination, justifies the allowance of the amounts claimed on the returns.

Decision will be entered under Rule 50.

Celeste B. Smith

v.

Commissioner.

Docket No. 5123-70 "SC"

UNITED STATES TAX COURT

T.C. Memo 1971-122

May 27, 1971.

:

Celeste B. Smith, pro se, Albany, Ga.
Shuford A. Tucker, for the respondent.

Judge Scott

OPINION

Memorandum Findings of Fact and Opinion

Respondent determined a deficiency in petitioner's income tax for the calendar year 1966 in the amount of $298.54.

The issue for decision is whether petitioner during the calendar year 1966 was engaged in the trade or business of operating a dog kennel so as to be entitled to a deduction for expenses or losses of that operation.

Findings of Fact

Some of the facts were orally stipulated and are found accordingly.

Celeste B. Smith, hereinafter referred to as petitioner, resided in Albany, Georgia at the time of the filing of her petition in this case. She filed her individual Federal income tax return for the calendar year 1966 with the district director of internal revenue at Atlanta, Georgia.

During the year 1966, petitioner lived in Albany, Georgia, and was employed as a full-time teacher in the Dougherty County, Georgia School System where she had been teaching for several years.

Petitioner's father had been a veterinarian, and petitioner gained some experience with dogs from working with him.

In 1962, while living in an apartment with other persons, petitioner purchased for $35 a female **cocker spaniel** as a pet. She had attended dog shows since 1960 but prior to 1966 had not shown any dog. In May 1964 petitioner bought a home and within a month enclosed with wire fencing a 12- by 15-foot space in the yard in which to keep her pet dog. Following the death of her father in January, 1965, petitioner received a little over $2,000 from an insurance policy. After receiving this sum, petitioner decided she was in a position to "operate a little bit more in the dog line." In July 1965 petitioner bought for $100 a 4-month-old **cocker spaniel** pup from a kennel that showed dogs. The pedigree on this pup was sufficient to permit entry of the dog in shows. Petitioner planned to use this male dog for stud for her female dog and to obtain stud fees for his services to other female dogs. Petitioner had unsuccessfully used three different male dogs in Albany in 1965 in an effort to get some pups from her female dog. This dog was not of the quality that would produce pups petitioner would plan to keep but she planned to sell the pups.

In 1966 petitioner improved the enclosure in her yard with a concrete floor, a covered roof, and walls on two of the four sides. Sleeping boxes for the two dogs were kept in the enclosure. The space was ample for two dogs and possibly could have been used for three dogs. Petitioner was of the opinion that a dog without championship status obtained through wins at shows would bring only $35 to $45 per stud service whereas a dog that had obtained championship status would bring $40 and up per service. Petitioner was also of the opinion that breeders would attend dog shows and observe males that might be available for stud service.

Beginning in January 1966 when her male dog was 9 months old, petitioner exhibited him at various dog shows. He was shown four times in Florida in January, once in Florida and once in Georgia in February, and three times in Georgia in March. In April he was shown once in Richmond and once in Baltimore. The dog was shown five times in Florida in June, three times in South Carolina in July, once in Tennessee in September, and twice in Georgia in November. The shows attended by petitioner were on weekends or holidays and therefore they did not interfere with her work as a teacher. The April shows in Richmond and Baltimore were during 517 petitioner's spring vacation. Petitioner continued to show the dog in 1967 and part of 1968 but the dog was never able to achieve championship status.

Petitioner had no employees to help with the dogs in 1966 and if she were away from home would board the dogs at a kennel.

On at least two occasions during 1966, petitioner advertised the male **cocker spaniel** as being available for stud. The advertisements were in local newspapers and were run for several consecutive days.

During 1966, petitioner attempted to use the male **cocker spaniel** in stud on four separate occasions, two   of which were with her female dog. On the first attempt the male did not complete his assignment and on the second two attempts the female did not conceive. He was used successfully with petitioner's female **cocker spaniel** in October resulting in a litter of nine pups born in December. All of the pups were sold as pets in the calendar year 1967 for a total amount of about $400.

In February 1966 petitioner arranged to purchase a female show quality **cocker spaniel** pup but before the date set for delivery the pup died of distemper.

At some time after 1966 petitioner changed her planned activities with dogs and decided not to keep any male dogs but to keep and breed females and sell the pups. At the time of the trial of this case, petitioner owned three females of breedable age, two of which had completed their championship, one 9-month-old male pup and two 3-month-old male pups which were for sale.

In September 1968 petitioner discovered that the male dog she had bought in July 1965 had a hereditary defect and dropped offering him for stud. Prior to making this discovery petitioner had received three stud fees for his services, two of $30 each and one in the form of a pup she sold for $50.

Petitioner in 1966 kept meticulous records of her receipts and expenses in maintaining the dogs and showing the male. The only revenue reported by petitioner on her 1966 income tax return from her kennel operations was the amount of $19.50, which was received as awards from shows. There was no income derived from stud fees or from the sale of pups in the calendar year 1966. Petitioner had the following expenses which she set forth on her return showing a resultant operating loss of $1,526.26:

Expense	Amount
Veterinary expense	$ 117.36
Feed	90.57
Advertising	15.39
Kennel supplies	97.00
Boarding fees	34.00
Phone calls	2.86
Show entry fees	120.00
Travel expense attending dog shows:	
Lodging	185.74
Auto expense - 8,383 miles at 10 cents per mile	838.30
Depreciation – Schedule	44.54
	$1,545.76

DEPRECIATION SCHEDULE

Asset	Acq'd	Cost	Life	Prior	Current
Kennel fencing	3-1-65	$200.00	15 years	11.10	$13.33
Kennel improvement	8-3-66	104.63	15 years	.00	4.64
Transport crate and pen	1-3-66	36.45	5 years	.00	7.29
Cocker spaniel (female)	6-1-65	100.00	7 years	7.14	14.28
Cocker spaniel (male)	1964	35.00	7 years	5.00	5.00
					$44.54

Respondent determined the deficiency in petitioner's income tax set forth in his statutory notice by disallowing the deduction claimed by petitioner for the year 1966 for the loss from operating her kennel.

Opinion

Petitioner contends that her efforts were directed at the establishment of a kennel with the intent of operating it as a profitable enterprise, that she did in fact operate the kennel with the usual techniques 518 associated with the business of a dog kennel, and that the expenses incurred are deductible.

It is respondent's position that petitioner was not engaged in the trade or business of operating a dog kennel for profit and that the most favorable view of petitioner's activities based on this record is that she hoped at some later time to engage in a kennel business and was taking steps during 1966 looking toward preparing herself to engage in such business.

Section 162, I.R.C. 1954, provides for the deduction of expenses incurred in the operation of a trade or business, and section 165(c) provides for deduction by an individual of losses incurred in a trade or business or in a transaction entered into for profit. Therefore, for petitioner to be entitled to deduct her expenses in connection with her dogs or the losses from her kennel operation in 1966, she must show that the operation was a trade or business or a transaction entered into for profit. One of the basic criterion of a "trade or business" is that it be operated for the purpose of making a profit. Hirsch v. Commissioner, 315 F. 2d 731, 736 (C.A. 9, 1963), affirming a Memorandum Opinion of this Court.

As we pointed out in Margit Sigray Bessenyey, 45 T.C. 261, 273-274

(1965), affirmed 379 F. 2d 252 (C.A. 2, 1967), a loss in a particular year or even a long history of losses is not conclusive that the operation was not conducted for the purpose of making a profit but this factor may be important in determining the purpose of the operation. In that case we also noted that while a taxpayer's expectation of profit from the operation must be bona fide it is not necessary that it be a reasonable expectation.

Whether a taxpayer actually possesses the requisite profit motive is a question of fact to be decided from a consideration of all of the evidence in a particular case. Hirsch v. Commissioner, supra. The fact that the operation is small and can be carried on by a person otherwise employed in a fulltime salaried position does not preclude the activity from being a trade or business entered into with the expectation of profit. However, the amount of time given to the undertaking and the motive of the taxpayer's efforts are factors to be considered. Kerns Wright, 31 T.C. 1264 (1959), affirmed 274 F. 2d 883 (C.A. 6, 1960).

Petitioner testified that she originally intended to obtain payments for the services of a stud dog which she hoped would obtain its championship. Although she did not specifically state that she intended in this manner to make a profit, her argument at the conclusion of the trial was that she did. However, when a taxpayer's claims or stated intent appears improbable in light of the other evidence of record, his intent must be determined from all the evidence with particular regard to his activities as compared to his claimed intent. Army Times Sales Co., 35 T.C. 688 (1961).

While petitioner kept accurate records of her income and expenses, her expenditures display a lack of concern for the economics of the operation. Petitioner's expenditures in showing her dog appear to be disproportionate to any return she could expect to receive from any difference in the stud fees received from a dog with championship status as compared to one without such status. Also, the continued showing of a dog which produced only minimal winnings is indicative of lack of profit motive. Likewise indicative of a lack of profit motive. is the keeping of a female not of show quality which had been bought for a pet and would produce pups which would sell at a lower price than pups from a show quality female.

Petitioner's vacillation in the objectives of her enterprise manifest a lack of preliminary exploration as to the profit potential of a small kennel business. The facts and circumstances as a whole demonstrate that petitioner's operation in 1966 was merely an avocational activity. Based upon the record before us we conclude that petitioner had no bona fide expectation of making a profit from the type of operation she was engaging in or planning to engage in during 1966. The weight of the evidence indicates that petitioner's activities were primarily in the nature of a hobby and were at most exploratory as to the business potential of operating a dog kennel for profit. We therefore conclude that petitioner has failed to show that in 1966 she had the requisite profit motive to be engaged in a trade or business of operating a dog kennel or that the expenditures she made in connection with her dogs were in a transaction entered into for profit. We hold on the basis of the facts in this record that petitioner is not entitled to deduct her claimed expenses or loss in the operation of her dog kennel in 1966.

Decision will be entered for respondent.

FURMINATOR, INC.,
Plaintiff,
v.
ONTEL PRODUCTS CORP., et al.,
Defendants.

No. 4:06-CV-23 CAS

UNITED STATES DISTRICT COURT
FOR THE EASTERN DISTRICT OF MISSOURI,
EASTERN DIVISION

429 F. Supp. 2d 1153

March 17, 2006, Decided,
April 19, 2006, Filed

CHARLES A. SHAW, U.S. DISTRICT JUDGE.

OPINION

REDACTED, NONCONFIDENTIAL VERSION OF FINDINGS OF FACT AND CONCLUSIONS OF LAW PREVIOUSLY ISSUED MARCH 17, 2006

This matter is before the Court on plaintiff FURminator, Inc.'s Motion for Preliminary Injunction on its claims of patent and trademark infringement. The defendants are Ontel Products Corporation, Linens 'N Things, Inc. (collectively referred to as "Ontel"),[1] Bamboo, a division of Munchkin, Inc., and Munchkin, Inc. (collectively referred to as "Munchkin"). The Court conducted an evidentiary hearing on February 14,

---

[1] Defendant Linens 'N Things offers for sale in this judicial district the alleged infringing product manufactured by defendant Ontel Products Corporation. These defendants assert a joint defense.

2006 and thereafter the parties submitted proposed findings of fact and conclusions of law. For the following reasons, the Court finds that plaintiff's motion for preliminary injunction should be denied in all respects.

FINDINGS OF FACT

A. FURminator's Patent Infringement Claim

The Porter Patent

1. Plaintiff FURminator, Inc. ("FURminator") is the listed assignee and owner of U.S. Patent No. 6,782,846 B1 ("the Porter Patent"). See Def. Munchkin Ex. A, Porter Patent, cover page.

2. The Porter Patent is titled "PET GROOMING TOOL AND METHOD FOR REMOVING LOOSE HAIR FROM A FURRY PET" and lists David and Angela Porter as the named inventors. See id.

3. The application for the Porter Patent was filed on May 30, 2000, and the Porter Patent issued on August 31, 2004. See id.

4. The invention disclosed and claimed in the Porter Patent involves putting a handle on a conventional clipper blade to perform a process known as "carding" or "deshedding." This process is described in column 1, lines 19-29 of the Porter Patent, which states:

> Some pet groomers have determined that a toothed blade removed from electric grooming sheers [sic] is effective for removing shed hair from a dog or cat. The toothed blade includes a relatively sharp blade edge with a plurality of relatively short, comb-like teeth extending from the edge. Although effective in removing shed hair, the size and shape of the toothed blade makes it difficult to hold while combing or passing the blade over the pet's fur. This difficulty fatigues a groomer's hands and arms, thereby limiting the time a groomer can groom pets in this manner.

See also id., Col. 2, ll. 41-54; Def. Munchkin Ex. C, Declaration of Paul Bryant, PP3-4; Def. Munchkin Ex. D, Declaration of C.J. McLaughlin, P3. The Porter Patent added an elongate handle to the toothed blade of the prior art to alleviate the fatigue problem. See Def. Munchkin Ex. A, Porter Patent, Col. 1, ll. 32-47, 56-61.

5. The grooming tool disclosed in the patent has an elongate handle portion 22 that extends generally along a handle axis X. See Def. Munchkin Ex. A, Porter Patent, Figure 1. A pet engageable portion 24 (described in the patent as an Oster A5 clipper blade) is secured to the handle portion. The pet engageable portion 24 (shown in Figure 4) includes a blade portion

30 and a plurality of teeth 32. The blade portion 30 includes a blade edge 34 with a number of different segments. The teeth 32 extend from the blade edge 34. See Def. Munchkin Ex. A, Porter Patent, Col. 2, ll. 25-47.

6. To remove loose hair from a pet, a user places the pet engageable portion 24 in engagement with the pet so that the teeth 32 are against the pet's coat in a manner so that the first planar surface 36 is generally perpendicular to the handle axis X (id., Col. 2, ll.s 55-58) and to the region of the pet's coat engaged by the teeth 32. Id., Col. 3, ll. 36-41. The user then pulls the handle portion 22 generally along the handle axis X while maintaining engagement of the teeth 32 with the pet's coat. Id.

7. FURminator promotes and sells, among other things, three deshedding products entitled "FURminator(R) small professional deShedding tool," "FURminator(R) medium professional deShedding tool" and "FURminator(R) large professional deShedding tool" (collectively, the FURminator tools). See Def. Ontel Ex. N (FURminator tool); Def. Munchkin Ex. L-N (FURminator tools); Def. Munchkin Ex. F, P9 (Porter Declaration); Joint Stipulation of Uncontested Facts, P2; D. Porter Dep. at 89:8-90:7.

8. All three FURminator tools have the same basic configuration--a fine-toothed metal comb or "blade" and an elongated handle attached at the centerline of the blade and perpendicular to it, like a small rake or hoe. The user places the blade against the pet's coat and then pulls the handle in a direction generally parallel to the longest dimension of the handle, which drags the blade through the fur so that the blade's teeth engage and remove the loose hair, like pulling a rake through a lawn covered with leaves. FURminator's instructions and infomercial show its tools being used in this manner. See Def. Ontel Ex. N (FURminator tool); Def. Ontel Ex. O (FURminator infomercial); Def. Munchkin Ex. L (FURminator tool); Def. Munchkin Ex. M (FURminator tool); Def. Munchkin Ex. N (FURminator tool); Plaintiff Ex. 40 (FURminator instructions).

9. FURminator sells its tools through two primary channels of distribution--first, by direct sales to professional dog groomers and other pet professionals such as breeders and veterinarians and second, through the QVC television shopping channel. Beginning in the fall of 2005, FURminator also briefly sold its tools through a television infomercial, but discontinued the infomercial in mid-December 2005. FURminator also sells its tools at PetSmart, a national pet specialty retail chain. FURminator's tools carry a retail price between $ 29.95 and $ 49.95. See Def. Ontel Ex. S (Hawthorn Direct Broadcast History); Def. Ontel Ex. T (chart of FURminator's ads and sales); Def. Munchkin Ex. F, PP10-12 (Porter Decl.); D. Porter Dep. at 17:16-18:25; 20:12-15; 21:5-22; 23:11-15; 26:2-9; 31:6-12; 32:17-34:22; 178:10-179:1; 168:10-18; A. Porter Dep. at 163:1-166:14.

The Accused Munchkin Product

10. Munchkin sells Munchkin's Bamboo(R) Dog de-shedding comb and Munchkin's Bamboo(R) Cat de-shedding comb, which are substantially identical in their configuration, differing only in size. See Def. Munchkin Exs. AA, EE, AAA, & NNN. Each includes a metal blade with an integrated comb. A padded grip portion is provided that is generally coplanar (along the same plane) with the plane in which the metal blade resides. See id.; see also Pl.'s Ex. 43, Bamboo de-shedding tool instruction manual.

11. The Munchkin products are used by holding the grip portion while passing the comb and blade over a pet's fur. See Pl.'s Ex. 43. The orientation of the groomer's hand and the motion of the tool while using the Munchkin products are substantially identical to those of the groomers practicing the admitted prior art "carding" process that is described in column 1, lines 19-28 of the Porter Patent. See id.

12. The Munchkin products do not have an elongate handle. See Def. Munchkin Exs. AA, EE, AAA, & NNN; McLaughlin Dep., Vol. I at 47:2 - 49:9; id., Vol. II at 86:15-24, Feb. 9, 2006; Preliminary Injunction Hearing Transcript ("Hearing Tr.") at 122:20 - 123:3, Feb. 14, 2006. To use the Munchkin products, a user would not pull the grooming tool along anything that could be described as an elongate handle axis. See Pl.'s Ex. 43; McLaughlin Dep., Vol. I at 47:2 - 49:9.

13. Munchkin was aware of the Porter Patent and specifically designed its product to avoid infringement of the Porter Patent, even eliminating from the final product a handle that was on a prototype to ensure non-infringement of the Porter Patent. See Def. Munchkin Ex. E, Declaration of Mark Hatherill, PP12-14 (including referenced exhibits); Hatherill Dep. at 120:17 - 121:8, Feb. 10, 2006. Munchkin made significant investment in such development of its accused products. See Def. Munchkin Ex. E, Hatherill Decl., P15.

14. Munchkin asserts it has sufficient assets to pay monetary damages for any alleged infringement by its accused products. See id., P18.

The Accused Ontel Product

15. Ontel promotes and sells, among other things, a carding or deshedding tool called the "Shed Ender TM Professional De-Shedding Tool" (the "Shed Ender"). See Def. Ontel Ex. A, PP22-24 (Murphy Decl.); Def. Ontel Ex. G, PP17, 20 (Anderson Decl.); Def. Ontel Ex. K, P23 (Khubani Decl.); Def. Ontel Ex. M (Shed Ender product).

16. The Shed Ender consists of a fine-toothed metal comb or "blade" and an elongated handle, but the handle is located at the end of the blade and parallel to it, like a knife or a comb with a handle. See Def. Ontel Ex. A, PP20 (Murphy Decl.); Def. Ontel Ex. G, PP22 (Anderson Decl.);

Murphy Dep. at 52:20-53:11; Def. Ontel Ex. M (Shed Ender product); Anderson Dep. at 56:4-15; Khubani Dep. at 46:12-17; 75:12-22.

17. Unlike the FURminator tools, the Shed Ender is used by placing the blade against the coat of a furry pet like a dog or cat and then pulling the handle in a direction generally perpendicular to the longest dimension of the handle. Ontel's instructions and infomercial show the Shed Ender being used in this manner, and in fact, pulling the Shed Ender's handle in a direction parallel to the longest dimension of the handle prevents the teeth of the metal comb from engaging the pet's fur and could injure the pet. See Def. Ontel Ex. A, PP20 (Murphy Decl.); Def. Ontel Ex. G, PP22-25 (Anderson Decl.); Def. Ontel Ex. P (Ontel infomercial); Def. Ontel Ex. VV (Shed Ender instructions); Murphy Dep. at 52:20-53:11; Khubani Dep. at 86:4-20; 87:11-15.

18. Ontel sells its product through retail stores such as Wal-Mart (mass retail), Walgreens and CVS (the top two mass drug retailers), Bed Bath & Beyond and Linens 'N Things (the top two specialty housewares retailers), and Doctor Leonard and Harriet Carter (the top two mass retail catalogs). Ontel also sells its product through a television infomercial. Ontel's product sells for a retail price of $ 9.99 to $ 14.99. See Def. Ontel Ex. K, PP16, 27 (Khubani Decl.); Def. Ontel Ex. III, page 2 (ONT 00605) (Ontel sales document); Khubani Dep. at 121:18-22.

Prior Art to the Porter Patent

19. Prior to the Porter Patent, groomers in the United States used toothed electric clipper blades and stripping knives to "card," "de-shed," or remove loose hair from animals without pulling hair that is not loose. See Def. Munchkin Ex. A, Porter Patent, Col. 1, ll. 19-29; Hearing Tr. at 120:11 - 122:3; McLaughlin Dep., Vol. I at 23:8 - 24:4; Def. Munchkin Ex. C, Bryant Decl., PP3-8.

20. Clipper blades with grips formed by masking tape were in public use in the United States more than one year prior to the filing date of the Porter Patent application. See Def. Munchkin Ex. C, Bryant Decl., PP3-8.

21. Stripping knives were in public use to perform carding more than one year before the filing date of the Porter Patent application. See id., PP5-6; Def. Munchkin Ex. D, McLaughlin Decl., PP3-6; McLaughlin Dep., Vol. I at 23:8 - 24:4; Def. Ontel Ex. D (FURminator video labeled FURminator 001029); Def. Munchkin Exs. GG, HH, JJ, KK, LL, MM, NN, PP, ZZ, FFF, GGG, HHH, III, JJJ, and KKK. The Porters were aware that stripping knives could be used to perform carding. See Def. Ontel Ex. D (FURminator video).

22. Angela Porter admitted that she knew stripping knives were on sale and were in public use in the United States more than one year before the filing date of the Porter Patent. See A. Porter Dep. at 49:6-9, Feb. 4, 2006.

23. Stripping knives are available in a number of different shapes and sizes, but all share the same basic configuration--there is a fine-toothed metal comb or "blade" and an elongated handle attached at the end of the blade and parallel to it, like a knife or a comb with a handle. Ontel's Shed Ender looks and works like a stripping knife. See Def. Ontel Ex. A, PP14, 16, 17, 19-20 (Murphy Decl.); Def. Ontel Ex. D (Winter 1997 Pet Stylist magazine blurb regarding carding); Def. Ontel Ex. G, PP12-26 (Anderson Decl.); Def. Ontel Ex. I (1996 - "Grooming the American **Cocker spaniel**" videocassette); Anderson Dep. at 38:3-5; 47:3-12.

24. When used for carding or deshedding, a stripping knife is used in exactly the same manner as the Shed Ender. The user places the blade against the fur and then pulls the handle in a direction generally perpendicular to the longest dimension of the handle. See Def. Ontel Ex. A, PP17, 20 (Murphy Decl.); Def. Ontel Ex. C ("Captivating Cockers" DVD); Def. Ontel Ex. D (Winter 1997 Pet Stylist Magazine); Def. Ontel Ex. G, PP12-19, 22-25 (Anderson Decl.); Def. Ontel Ex. P (Shed Ender infomercial); Murphy Dep. at 52:20-53:11; Khubani Dep. at 87:11-15.

25. Multiple prior art references disclose handles that are perpendicular to the working plane of the grooming tool. See, e.g., Def. Munchkin Ex. BB (U.S. Patent No. 441,135 to Clements); Def. Munchkin Ex. J (U.S. Patent No. 797,184 to Deneen); Def. Munchkin Ex. B, Porter Patent File History, at 350-57 (citing Clements and Deneen references as anticipatory prior art).

Disputed Claim Language and the Parties' Proposed Constructions
26. Claim 1 of the Porter Patent reads as follows:

1. A method of removing loose hair from a furry pet such as a dog or cat having loose hair and non-loose hair, the method comprising:
providing a grooming tool having an elongate handle portion extending generally along a handle axis, and a pet engageable portion secured to the handle portion, the pet engageable portion including a blade portion and a plurality of teeth, the blade portion including a blade edge, the teeth extending from the blade edge; placing the pet engageable portion in engagement with the pet;
pulling the handle portion generally along the handle axis while maintaining engagement of the pet engageable portion with the pet to cause the blade edge to engage the loose hair of the pet and pull it from the pet without cutting or pulling the non-loose hair from the pet.

Def. Munchkin Ex. A, Porter Patent, Col. 3, ll. 59 to Col. 4, line 7.
27. The parties dispute the meaning of multiple claim terms and phrases appearing in claim 1 and the two other independent claims of the Porter

Patent (claims 12 and 16), including the phrases "an elongate handle portion extending generally along a handle axis" and "pulling the handle portion generally along the handle axis."

28. FURminator proposes that the phrase "an elongate handle portion extending generally along a handle axis" be construed as follows: "a part designed to be held by a hand, and having more length than width, projecting generally along a reference line along which a handle extends (i.e., any of the following: a longitudinal handle axis, a lateral handle axis, or a transverse handle axis)." Joint Preliminary Claim Construction and Prehearing Statement at 3-5.

29. Munchkin proposes that the phrase "an elongate handle portion extending generally along a handle axis" be construed as follows: "a part [of the grooming tool] designed to be grasped by the hand, that is slender and long in proportion to its width, stretching out to its fullest length generally in the direction of a long axis of the handle." Id. at 14-16.

30. Ontel proposes that the phrase "an elongate handle portion extending generally along a handle axis" be construed as follows: "a grooming tool having a handle portion of more length than width that is stretched or spread out to greater or fullest length generally along a handle axis," with "handle axis" defined as "the axis defined by the longest dimension of the elongated handle." Id. at 26; see Ontel's Proposed Findings of Fact and Conclusions of Law P49.

31. FURminator proposes that the phrase "pulling the handle portion generally along the handle axis" be construed as follows: "the action of moving [the handle portion of] a comb or brush through hair mostly along the reference lines along which the handle extends." Joint Preliminary Claim Construction Statement at 3, 7-8.

32. Munchkin proposes that the phrase "pulling the handle portion generally along the handle axis" be construed as follows: "applying force to the handle portion so as to cause or tend to cause motion toward the source of the force generally in the direction of the long axis of the handle." Id. at 16-19.

33. FURminator proposes that the third step of claim 1, "pulling the handle portion generally along the handle axis while maintaining engagement of the pet engageable portion with the pet to cause the blade edge to engage the loose hair of the pet and pull it from the pet without cutting or pulling the non-loose hair from the pet," include the additional limitation of "as quickly and as effectively as the toothed blades disclosed in the Porter Patent." Id. at 7-8.

34. Munchkin proposes that the third step of claim 1 be construed as a step-plus-function element pursuant to 35 U.S.C. § 112, P6, wherein, to achieve the claimed function of engaging the loose hair of the pet and pulling it from the pet without cutting or pulling the non-loose hair from

the pet, the entire disputed phrase include the following: "(1) pulling the handle portion of a grooming tool having a pet engageable portion constructed as described in the specification (col. 2, l. 41 - col. 3, l. 49) and prosecution of the Porter Patent (Munchkin Ex. B, at 447) generally in the direction of the elongate handle axis while maintaining engagement of the pet engageable portion with the pet so that a first planar surface of the pet engageable portion is generally perpendicular to the region of the pet's coat; and (2) pulling the handle portion to cause a second planar surface of the pet engageable portion (that together with the first planar surface defines a blade edge) to trail the first planar surface." Id. at 20-22.

#***#

CONCLUSIONS OF LAW

A. FURminator's Patent Infringement Claim

Preliminary Injunction Standards

1.   Federal Circuit law controls the issuance of an injunction against alleged patent infringement under 35 U.S.C. § 283. See Hybritech, Inc. v. Abbott Labs., 849 F.2d 1446, 1451 n.12 (Fed. Cir. 1988).

2.   In a patent infringement case, the decision whether to issue a preliminary injunction is within the court's discretion. See Amazon.com, Inc. v. BarnesandNoble.com, Inc., 239 F.3d 1343, 1350 (Fed. Cir. 2001). "A preliminary injunction is a drastic and extraordinary remedy that is not to be routinely granted." National Steel Car, Ltd. v. Canadian Pac. Ry., Ltd., 357 F.3d 1319, 1324 (Fed. Cir. 2004) (internal quotations omitted).

3.   In deciding whether to grant or deny a plaintiff's motion for preliminary injunction, the court considers (1) whether plaintiff has demonstrated a reasonable likelihood of success on the merits; (2) whether plaintiff will suffer irreparable harm if an injunction is not granted; (3) whether the balance of hardships favors the grant of injunctive relief; and (4) whether and to what extent granting the injunction would have a positive impact on the public interest. See Oakley, Inc. v. Sunglass Hut Int'l, 316 F.3d 1331, 1338-39 (Fed. Cir. 2003).

4.   A court cannot grant a preliminary injunction unless a plaintiff establishes both a reasonable likelihood of success on the merits and the threat of irreparable harm. See Anton/Bauer, Inc. v. PAG, Ltd., 329 F.3d 1343, 1348 (Fed. Cir. 2003); Sofamor Danek Group, Inc. v. Dupuy-Motech, Inc., 74 F.3d 1216, 1223 (Fed. Cir. 1996).

5.   To demonstrate a likelihood of success on the merits, a plaintiff must show that (1) it will likely prove infringement of one or more of the patent claims at trial; and (2) any challenges to the validity of the patent lack

substantial merit. See Amazon.com, 239 F.3d at 1351; Anton/Bauer, 329 F.3d at 1348.

6.   Irreparable harm is presumed in a patent case only where a patent owner "establishes a strong showing] of likely infringement of a valid and enforceable patent." Pfizer, Inc. v. Teva Pharmaceuticals USA, Inc., 429 F.3d 1364, 1381 (Fed. Cir. 2005).

The Law of Claim Construction

7.   The first step in any infringement analysis involves construing the patent to determine the scope of its asserted claims. See Markman v. Westview Instruments, Inc., 52 F.3d 967, 976 (Fed. Cir. 1995) (en banc), aff'd, 517 U.S. 370, 116 S. Ct. 1384, 134 L. Ed. 2d 577 (1996). Claim construction is a matter of law reserved exclusively for the court. See Markman, 517 U.S. at 387. A court need not definitively construe the claims at the preliminary injunction stage, but must preliminarily construe the claim in order to determine whether the accused product infringes. See Purdue Pharma L.P. v. Boehringer Ingelheim GmbH, 237 F.3d 1359, 1363 (Fed. Cir. 2001).

8.   As the Federal Circuit recently articulated in its landmark decision in Phillips v. AWH, to determine the correct claim construction, a court must follow, first and foremost, the words of the patent claim itself. It is a bedrock principle of patent law that the claims define the invention that the patentee owns, and the court may neither add words to nor subtract words from the claims in the process of construing them. Phillips v. AWH Corp., 415 F.3d 1303, 1312 (Fed. Cir. 2005) (en banc); TechSearch, L.L.C. v. Intel Corp., 286 F.3d 1360, 1373 (Fed. Cir. 2002) (citing Perkin-Elmer Corp. v. Westinghouse Elec. Corp., 822 F.2d 1528, 1533 (Fed. Cir. 1987)).

9.   Claim terms "are generally given their ordinary and customary meaning." Phillips, 415 F.3d at 1312 (quoting Vitronics Corp. v. Conceptronic, Inc., 90 F.3d 1576, 1582 (Fed. Cir. 1996)). "The inquiry into how a person of ordinary skill in the art understands a claim term provides an objective baseline from which to begin claim interpretation." Id. at 1313.

10.   "Importantly, the person of ordinary skill in the art is deemed to read the claim term not only in the context of the particular claim in which the disputed term appears, but in the context of the entire patent, including the specification." Id.; Medrad, Inc. v. MRI Devices Corp., 401 F.3d 1313, 1319 (Fed. Cir. 2005) ("We cannot look at the ordinary meaning of the term . . . in a vacuum. Rather, we must look at the ordinary meaning in the context of the written description and the prosecution history.").

11.   "[T]he claims themselves provide substantial guidance as to the meaning of particular claim terms." Phillips, 415 F.3d at 1314. "In some cases, the ordinary meaning of claim language as readily understood by a person of skill in the art may be readily apparent even to lay judges, and

claim construction in such cases involves little more than the application of the widely accepted meaning of commonly understood words." Id.

12. The claims must, however, "be read in view of the specification, of which they are a part." Markman, 52 F.3d at 979. The specification "is always highly relevant to the claim construction analysis. Usually, it is dispositive; it is the single best guide to the meaning of a disputed term." Vitronics, 90 F.3d at 1582.

13. In addition to consulting the specification, the court "should also consider the patent's prosecution history, if it is in evidence." Markman, 52 F.3d at 980. "The prosecution history, which we have designated as part of the 'intrinsic evidence,' consists of the complete record of the proceedings before the PTO and includes the prior art cited during the examination of the patent." Phillips, 415 F.3d at 1317. "Like the specification, the prosecution history provides evidence of how the PTO and the inventor understood the patent. . . . Furthermore, like the specification, the prosecution history was created by the patentee in attempting to explain and obtain the patent." Id.

14. Courts may also rely on extrinsic evidence in construing claims. Extrinsic evidence is "all evidence external to the patent and prosecution history, including expert and inventor testimony, dictionaries, and learned treatises." Markman, 52 F.3d at 980.

15. "Within the class of extrinsic evidence, the court has observed that dictionaries and treatises can be useful in claim construction." Phillips, 415 F.3d at 1318. "Because dictionaries, and especially technical dictionaries, endeavor to collect the accepted meanings of terms used in various fields of science and technology, those resources have been properly recognized as among the many tools that can assist the court in determining the meaning of particular terminology to those of skill in the art of the invention." Id.

16. Similarly, expert testimony "can be useful to a court for a variety of purposes, such as to provide the background on the technology at issue, to explain how an invention works, to ensure that the court's understanding of the technical aspects of the patent is consistent with that of a person of skill in the art, or to establish that a particular term in the patent or the prior art has a particular meaning in the pertinent field." Id.

The Court's Preliminary Claim Construction

17. In this case, the key term requiring construction is handle axis, which appears in two longer clauses in claim 1 of the patent--"a grooming tool having an elongate handle portion extending generally along a handle axis" and "pulling the handle portion generally along the handle axis." Def. Ontel Ex. HH ('846 patent) (col. 3, ll. 62-63; col. 4, l. 3).

#****#

The Court's Analysis of the Preliminary Injunction Factors

57. FURminator has not demonstrated that it will likely prove infringement of any claim of the Porter Patent at trial. Munchkin and Ontel have established a clear case of non-infringement of the Porter Patent.

58. Further, given the lack of a strong showing on patent infringement, irreparable harm is not presumed and FURminator has failed to demonstrate that money damages are an inadequate remedy at law. See Def. Munchkin Ex. E, Hatherill Decl., P18.

59. Accordingly, FURminator is not entitled to a preliminary injunction on its patent claim, and the Court need not consider the remaining factors. See Amazon.com, 239 F.3d at 1350.

60. Nonetheless, the remaining factors, the public interest and the balance of the hardships, favor denying the injunction. The public interest in free and fair competition outweighs FURminator's private financial interests. The balance of the hardships supports denying the motion because Munchkin has taken care to avoid FURminator's patent and would be harmed if not allowed to sell its grooming products in the market. See Def. Munchkin Ex. E, Hatherill Decl., PP12-15 (including referenced exhibits); Hatherill Dep. at 120:17 - 121:8. Ontel would also be harmed in its reputation and customer relationships if not allowed to sell its grooming product in the market. See Def. Ontel Ex. K, PP32-40 (Khubani Decl.).

B. FURminator's Trademark Infringement Claim
#***#

Conclusion.

For the foregoing reasons, the Court concludes that plaintiff FURminator's motion for preliminary injunction should be denied on its claims for patent and trademark infringement, as plaintiff has not shown a likelihood of success on the merits or irreparable harm, and the balance of the hardships and the public interest weigh against the issuance of an injunction.

Accordingly,

IT IS HEREBY ORDERED that plaintiff FURminator's motion for preliminary injunction is DENIED. [Doc. 19]

CHARLES A. SHAW

UNITED STATES DISTRICT JUDGE
Dated this 17th day of March, 2006.

6
ACTUAL COCKER SPANIEL DOGS

Particularly 4th amendment searches and animal abuse cases, but also- is a woman who can take care of her cocker spaniel competent for trial? Is a cockapoo a service animal? Is an attack on one cocker spaniel justification for pit bull genocide?

1. B Amusement Co. v. United States, Cong., 148 Ct. Cl. 337; 180 F. Supp. 386,(1960)
2. United States v. Rodd, 38 F.3d 1221 (1994)
3. Tindall v. City of Grosse Pointe Park, CASE No. 98-71295, UNITED STATES DISTRICT COURT FOR THE EASTERN DISTRICT OF MICHIGAN, SOUTHERN DIVISION, 1999 U.S. Dist. LEXIS 11089, June 28, 1999, Decided , June 28, 1999, Filed
4. Haefner v. Schuyler, Civil Action No. 00-393-RRM, UNITED STATES DISTRICT COURT FOR THE DISTRICT OF DELAWARE, 2001 U.S. Dist. LEXIS 16507, October 11, 2001, Decided
5. Hudson v. Coleman, 347 F.3d 138 (2003)
6. Madruga v. County of Riverside, 431 F. Supp. 2d 1049 (2005)
7. Scannavino v. Fla. Dep't of Corr., 242 F.R.D. 662 (2007)
8. Cowart v. City of Eau Claire, 571 F. Supp. 2d 1005 (2008)
9. Am. Canine Found. v. City of Aurora, 618 F. Supp. 2d 1271 (2009)
10. Overlook Mut. Homes, Inc. v. Spencer, 666 F. Supp. 2d 850; (2009)
11. Hardman v. United States, Case No. 3:09-0589,Crim. Case No. 3:02-00179, UNITED STATES DISTRICT COURT FOR THE MIDDLE DISTRICT OF TENNESSEE, NASHVILLE DIVISION, 2010 U.S. Dist. LEXIS 43043, May 3, 2010, Filed
12. Fabrikant v. French, 722 F. Supp. 2d 249 (2010)

B AMUSEMENT COMPANY, ET AL.
v.
THE UNITED STATES

UNITED STATES COURT OF CLAIMS

Cong. No. 1-54

148 Ct. Cl. 337
180 F. Supp. 386

January 20, 1960

Whitaker, Judge, delivered the opinion of the court. Barksdale, District Judge, sitting by designation; Laramore, Judge; Madden, Judge, and Jones, Chief Judge, concur.

OPINION

This case is before the court pursuant to H.R. Resolution No. 475, 83d Congress, 2d Session, by which the court has been requested to determine whether plaintiffs have a legal or equitable claim against the United States, and the amount, if any, legally and equitably due thereon, and to report its conclusions to the House.

Plaintiffs sue to recover property losses and damages sustained by them as a result of a flood on the Missouri River in the vicinity of Kickapoo Bend south of St. Joseph, Missouri. The flood in question took place in March 1949 and resulted from the melting of an ice gorge which jammed the river in the vicinity of Iatan Bend. Plaintiffs' claims rest on the allegation that the ice gorge which caused the flood was in turn caused by certain pile dikes and revetments which had been negligently placed in the river by the Army Corps of Engineers for purposes of flood control and navigation.

The facts of the case show that the Missouri River in its natural state was a wide, meandering, braided stream which flowed through a flood plain or valley which varied in width from 2 1/2 to 10 miles. The channel was composed of numerous, shallow, interlaced streams of varying width separated by bars and islands. By the Act of January 21, 1927 (44 Stat. 1010, 1013), Congress approved a plan for the improvement of the Missouri for purposes of navigation. By the acts of August 30, 1935 (49 Stat. 1028, 1034) and March 2, 1945 (59 Stat. 10, 19), the original plan was expanded and modified to provide for both a larger and deeper navigable channel as well as a plan for flood control.

To carry out these plans, it was necessary that the Corps of Engineers narrow and stabilize the river channel. This approach is the only one that is feasible on a river such as the Missouri. It is an alluvial stream and the only way it can be harnessed is to use its inherent qualities. Thus, the depth of the navigable channel is maintained by allowing the river to scour the bottom. To accomplish this, the width of the river is first narrowed and stabilized within the flood plain by the process of accretion. This is done by the location of pile or trail dikes placed parallel to the river bank and surrounded by rock fill. The river gradually deposits sediment around these dikes and thus creates an effective dam which forces the river down the designed channel and keeps it from meandering over the entire flood plain.

At the time of the flood in 1949, the designed channel, in the area in question, was composed of three bends which formed an ox yoke. The middle link is Iatan Bend joined upstream by Oak Mill Bend and below by Kickapoo Bend. Running off from Oak Mill Bend and Iatan Bend were two natural chutes or depressions, there before the Corps of Engineers started on the project, which tended to allow the river water to bypass the designed channel. These chutes were called Oak Mill Chute, which ran off on the Kansas side, and Iatan Chute, which bypassed the channel on the Missouri side. To contain the river within the design channel the Corps of Engineers placed pile dikes at the head of both Oak Mill and Iatan Chutes. At the time of the flood in the winter of 1948-1949 these dikes were not sufficiently high to dam off all of the water running into the chutes and some did bypass the design channel.

On the inner or Kansas side of Iatan Bend at approximately mile 422, there was a submerged pile structure, designated 437.3L. This structure had originally been designed to contain the channel existing prior to the flood of 1943. After that flood, the river changed its course. The engineers then adopted the new course, but this left structure 437.3L, which was originally on the Missouri side, along the Kansas bank. The engineers saw no reason to remove the structure, but merely shortened it so that it protruded only a few feet into the new design channel, and not at all into the navigation portion of the channel. In this position, it supported the Kansas bank.

Along the outer side of Iatan Bend the engineers had constructed a long curving pile dike which paralleled the Missouri shore, which constricted the water, so that its scouring action produced the necessary depth for navigation. The 1948 hydrograph shows that there was a very good navigation channel proceeding around the bend ranging in depth from 6 to 26 feet.

The Missouri River has ice on it each year and this has been a factor in most of the early spring floods. In December 1948 the first ice block on the river was observed between mile 476.5 and 478.5 approximately 50 miles up the river from Iatan Bend. By January 5, 1949 the ice had moved downstream and lodged at mile 421 on Iatan Bend at the point where Oak Mill Chute returns to the main channel. By January 8, the ice at mile 421 moved downstream, but it continued to hold fast immediately upstream at mile 422, approximately at the location of the submerged structure 437.3L. Ice continued to form in the river and by January 11, 1949 a block of ice extended from mile 421 to mile 434.5. There were also four other blocks of ice further upstream at this time. On January 15 and 16 various blocks of ice moved downstream and gorged at mile 422. This gorge held fast and by January 31 the ice had extended up the river for some 100 miles.

There was little movement of the ice gorge after this time until March. In February, the engineers made an effort to dislodge it with explosives, which proved unsuccessful. In late February, the weather warmed and the tributary streams began to thaw and rise, some even flooded. The Corps of Engineers issued flood warnings daily and advised all residents that when the ice moved out water levels would be unpredictable.

On March 6, 1949, at 3:45 a.m. the lower end of the ice from mile 422 to mile 428 went out; at 8:00 a.m. the block from mile 428 to 430 went out; and by 9:30 a.m. the rest of the long jam began to move. It was at this time that the flooding occurred on plaintiffs' properties.

Plaintiffs base their legal claims on two theories: first, that the flooding constituted a taking compensable under the Fifth Amendment; or, second, that the flooding was a tort, damages for which are allowable under the Federal Tort Claims Act, 28 U.S.C. 1346(b). In the alternative, the plaintiffs say that they are equitably entitled to recover, since the defendant's negligent construction and maintenance of the dikes and revetments at Iatan Bend were the proximate cause of the ice gorge and, consequently, of their injury.

It seems clear from the record that plaintiffs do not have a legal claim against the United States. Certainly the defendant's actions do not constitute a taking under the Fifth Amendment. It is well settled that consequential damages form no basis for such a recovery. To constitute a taking there must be an intent on the part of the United States to take plaintiffs' properties, or, at least, an intention to do an act the natural consequences of which was to take the property. Here, however, the record clearly shows that the defendant's acts were designed to protect plaintiffs' private properties, not to take them; nor can it be said that the natural consequences of these acts would result in a taking of their properties for public use. Sanguinetti v. United States, 264 U.S. 146; Columbia Basin Orchard v. United States, 132 C. Cls. 445; Crites v. United States, 132 C. Cls. 544; Coates v. United States, 124 C. Cls. 806; Yazel v.

United States, 118 C. Cls. 59. One flooding does not constitute a taking and the plaintiffs have failed to show by their evidence that the flooding which occurred in 1949 will inevitably recur. This fact is essential to prove a taking. North Counties Hydro-Electric Co. v. United States, 138 C. Cls. 380, cert. denied 355 U.S. 882.

Nor have plaintiffs a legal claim under a tort theory of recovery. In providing for a broad plan of flood control on the Mississippi River and its tributaries, of which the Missouri River is one, Congress specifically provided that "No liability of any kind shall attach to or rest upon the United States from any damage from or by floods or flood waters at any place." 33 U.S.C. § 702c. This long established policy of non-liability is bottomed on public policy and not sovereign immunity, but, at any rate, it is a withdrawal of consent to be sued in such cases, if it can be said that such consent had previously been given. Grant v. Tennessee Valley Authority, 49 F. Supp. 564. We agree with the Eighth Circuit Court of Appeals that this section was not intended to be repealed by the enactment of the Federal Tort Claims Act. See National Mfg. Co. v. United States, 210 F. 2d 263, where the question is fully and ably discussed.

We come, then, to the final question before the court, which is whether the plaintiffs have an equitable claim against the United States. The word "equity" in this context is used in the sense of broad moral responsibility, what the Government ought to do as a matter of good conscience. Georgia Kaolin Co. v. United States, 145 C. Cls. 39, Gay Street Corp. v. United States, 130 C. Cls. 341. Under even this theory, however, defendant's liability must rest on some unjustified act or omission to act which caused plaintiffs' damage; otherwise any award would be a pure gratuity.

In reviewing the record, we do not believe that it shows the defendant was at fault. The ice gorge at mile 422 was caused by many factors over which the defendant had no control. The combination of weather, water velocity, stream gauge, and wind all contributed substantially to the formation of the jam. The facts show that the normal daily discharge of water passed St. Joseph, Missouri, some 20 or so miles upstream, which normally amounted to some 36,000 cubic feet per second, had dropped to only 6,880 c.f.s. on January 3, 1949, due to ice on the tributaries, low rainfall, and other factors. This unusually small flow, not only made the river shallower than usual, but also greatly reduced its velocity. This fact alone substantially contributed to the gorge, since the shallower and slower the water, the easier it is for it to freeze.

The plaintiffs say that the defendant caused the ice jam because it did not remove structure 437.3L from its place on the inner bank of Iatan Bend. We disagree. This structure did not cause the gorge. Its removal would not have prevented the inner bank of the bend from shoaling, which is inherent in an alluvial stream. The current being slow at the shoals, sediment is continually deposited and when the ice comes down the river it catches on these shoals and might create a jam, whereas swift water carries the ice on down the stream. This shoaling was, without doubt, one of the causes of the gorge, and there would have been shoaling at this point even if the defendant's structure 437.3L had been entirely removed.

Nor do we believe that the plaintiffs can complain because the pile dikes across the head of Oak Mill and Iatan Chutes did not completely block the flow of water into these old channels. The only practical way these channels could be effectively blocked was through the slow process of accretion, without incurring prohibitive expense. The defendant was not negligent because the river had not deposited enough sediment to form a dam.

Basically, plaintiffs' claims are bottomed on the theory that, if the defendant had made no effort to improve navigation and flood control on the Missouri, the ice would not have gorged in the particular spot that it did on Iatan Bend. This may or may not be true. However, we do not believe it is relevant. The United States has a constitutional right, even a duty, to improve navigation and protect against floods, for the benefit of all of its citizens who are affected thereby. To say that, if it does enter into plans of improvement, it will stand liable for damage regardless of negligence would be an absurd rule, and one contrary to the expressed will of Congress embodied in the provision quoted above, 33 U.S.C. § 702c. The general welfare of its citizens demands the Government's participation in these navigation and flood control projects; without it, the control of floods would be impossible.

We must conclude, on the basis of all the facts, that the United States is not equitably responsible for the plaintiffs' damages, since it is in no way at fault.

This opinion, together with the findings of fact which follow, will be certified to the Congress pursuant to House Resolution No. 475, 83d Congress, 2d Session.

It is so ordered.

ADDITIONAL FINDINGS OF FACT

#***#

(9) Plaintiff Donald Cox, R. F. D. 6, St. Joseph, Missouri, was owner of a lot in Buchanan County, described in the petition, and on which was located a house and tavern which suffered damage in the 1949 flood. He claims $ 5,240.32 for this damage, including loss of merchandise, moving of certain equipment, loss of business and loss of 2 **cocker spaniels**. It is found that the fair and reasonable value of his damage was $ 3,958.32. As

is true with most of the plaintiffs, the evidence about Mr. Cox's losses was based largely upon his own credible and uncontradicted testimony and not upon any documentary evidence or the evidence of experts. His records were destroyed in the flood of 1952. Much of the work of restoration he did himself. No allowance is made for the claimed loss of business, which is speculative and consequential, or for the loss of the 2 dogs, the cause of their disappearance being uncertain.

#***#

UNITED STATES OF AMERICA,

Plaintiff-Appellee,

v.

WILLIAM EDWARD RODD,

Defendant-Appellant.

UNITED STATES COURT OF APPEALS
FOR THE TENTH CIRCUIT

No. 94-3087

38 F.3d 1221

October 18, 1994, Filed

Before MOORE, REAVLEY, and ANDERSON, Circuit Judges.

JOHN PORFILIO MOORE

OPINION

ORDER AND JUDGMENT *

* This order and judgment is not binding precedent, except under the doctrines of law of the case, res judicata, and collateral estoppel. The court generally disfavors the citation of orders and judgments; nevertheless, an order and judgment may be cited under the terms and conditions of the court's General Order filed November 29, 1993. 151 F.R.D. 470.

William Rodd, defendant-appellant, conditionally pled guilty to violating 21 U.S.C. 841(a)(1), for his possession with intent to distribute 2.15 kilograms of cocaine. Mr. Rodd entered his conditional plea under Fed.R.Crim.P. 11(a)(2) after the district court denied his pretrial motion to suppress the cocaine found in his car. Mr. Rodd argues that the police lacked probable cause to arrest him and that the evidence found in the subsequent search of his car should have been suppressed. We affirm.

Mr. Rodd was arrested upon information provided to the Kansas City Police by Glen R. Jones, who volunteered to cooperate with the police after his arrest for possession of marijuana and cocaine. Mr. Jones informed the police that Mr. Rodd was his cocaine supplier, and that Mr. Rodd planned to travel to Kansas City from Florida with about 2 kilograms of cocaine. In his recorded statement to police, Mr. Jones described Mr. Rodd as a white male, approximately 40 years old and balding with a ring of hair. Mr. Jones added Mr. Rodd drove a blue Cadillac with a vinyl roof and Kansas license plates, and traveled with a blonde **cocker spaniel** dog. Mr. Jones thought that Mr. Rodd would be at the American Motel in Kansas City on Sunday, October 24, 1993, and that Mr. Jones expected delivery of the cocaine on Monday, October 25, 1993.

The police investigated Mr. Jones' story and confirmed that Mr. Rodd owned a 1986 Cadillac with Kansas license plates and that there was a reservation at the American Motel in the name of William Rodd for Saturday, October 23. The motel was placed under police surveillance beginning October 23.

At approximately 11:00 p.m. on October 24, Mr. Jones informed police Mr. Rodd was having car trouble and would not arrive in Kansas City until sometime the next day. Mr. Rodd made new reservations at the American Motel for October 25, 1993. Motel employees advised the police of Mr. Rodd's new itinerary.

The police renewed their surveillance of the motel on October 25, 1993. Mr. Rodd arrived at approximately 8:30 p.m. that night. The details provided by Mr. Jones about Mr. Rodd's appearance, car, and dog were confirmed by police observation. The police also confirmed with the desk clerk at the motel that he had registered under the name of William Rodd.

Mr. Rodd was arrested as he got out of his car in front of his assigned motel room. An officer read him his Miranda warnings and asked permission to search his car. Mr. Rodd verbally consented and also signed a written form consenting to the search. The search recovered approximately 2 kilograms of cocaine hidden underneath the back seat of the Cadillac.

We review factual findings made for the disposition of a suppression motion under a clearly erroneous standard and view the evidence in the light most favorable to the trial court's ruling. United States v. Eylicio-Montoya, 18 F.3d 845, 848 (10th Cir. 1994); United States v. Swepston, 987 F.2d 1510, 1513 (10th Cir. 1993). However, the ultimate question of the reasonableness of a seizure under the Fourth Amendment receives de novo review. 18 F.3d at 848; United States v. Perdue, 8 F.3d 1455, 1462 (10th Cir. 1993).

Police may arrest a person in public without a warrant if they have probable cause to believe that person committed a felony. United States v. Watson, 423 U.S. 411, 417-24, 46 L. Ed. 2d 598, 96 S. Ct. 820 (1976). The factual predicate necessary for the probable cause determination may be provided by information obtained from an informant and corroborated by police investigation. Illinois v. Gates, 462 U.S. 213, 76 L. Ed. 2d 527, 103 S.

Ct. 2317 (1983); Draper v. United States, 358 U.S. 307, 3 L. Ed. 2d 327, 79 S. Ct. 329 (1959); Jones v. United States, 362 U.S. 257, 4 L. Ed. 2d 697, 80 S. Ct. 725 (1960). In Gates, the Court held a flexible inquiry should be conducted to take into account an informant's veracity and reliability and the basis for the informant's knowledge. Thus, the test is not mechanically applied. "[A] deficiency in one may be compensated for, in determining the overall reliability of a tip, by a strong showing as to the other, or by some other indicia of reliability." 462 U.S. at 233.

The instant case introduces a slight variation in applying Gates. Mr. Jones, the informant, could have been found at least an accomplice to Mr. Rodd, if not a potential coconspirator, had he not decided to cooperate with the police. More commonly, probable cause cases with informants involve an anonymous tip or an informant who has worked with the police and proven reliable in the past.[1] However, the Gates analysis still applies to these facts.

Mr. Jones' status initially calls his veracity and reliability into question. Statements made by accomplices often are treated with some suspicion because their "interested" status may lead to bias, half-truths, or outright falsehoods. However, the detailed inside information he provided to police helps make up for this potential difficulty under the Gates totality of circumstances analysis. As in Gates, Mr. Jones' statement contained, "a range of details relating not just to easily obtained facts and conditions existing at the time of the tip, but to future actions of third parties ordinarily not easily predicted." 462 U.S. at 245. Combined with the corroboration of Mr. Jones' information provided by the independent police investigation, sufficient "indicia of reliability" exists so that his information could establish probable cause to arrest Mr. Rodd without a warrant.

Additionally, the Court's analysis in Draper is instructive. In holding an informant's tip gave the police probable cause to arrest Draper, the Court said: "[The police] had personally verified every facet of the information given him by [the informant] except whether petitioner had accomplished his mission and had the three ounces of heroin on his person or in his bag." Id. at 313.

The present case is similar. The police acted upon Mr. Jones' information by placing the American Motel under surveillance only after corroborating his story with independent investigation. Mr. Rodd was arrested only after the police also verified significant details about his

---

[1] See, e.g., Eylicio-Montoya (Identified prior informant); Draper (Same); Gates (Anonymous informant); Alabama v. White, 496 U.S. 325, 110 L. Ed. 2d 301, 110 S. Ct. 2412 (1990) (Same in the reasonable suspicion "Terry-stop" context).

physical appearance, his car, and his dog. The missing piece of the puzzle was whether Mr. Rodd did in fact bring cocaine with him from Florida to Kansas City as Mr. Jones had alleged was planned.

The difference in this case--that Mr. Jones was an accomplice rather than an anonymous tipster or prior police informant--is only a slight variation on a theme. The corroboration of Mr. Jones' story by police, and their personal observation of Mr. Rodd's arrival at the motel, places this case squarely alongside Draper and Gates. In both of those cases, the Court held that the informant's information combined with the corroboration established by independent police investigation provided sufficient probable cause for arrest. We reach the same conclusion here.

AFFIRMED.

Entered for the Court

John Porfilio Moore
Circuit Judge

MICHAEL E. TINDALL,

Plaintiff,

v.

CITY OF GROSSE POINTE PARK;

MATTHEW HAMBRIGHT; LT. D. HILLAR; OEO JOHN WALTERS; PSOD. KOLAR; SGT. JOHN KRETZSCHMAR; OEO ERIK ALLAN DAVIS; BRIAN BURSIEK; JUDITH GREENSTONE MILLER; BODMAN LONGLEY & DAHLING LLP; CLARK HILL, P.C.; BMW NORTH AMERICA, INC., a Delaware corporation; BMW FINANCIAL SERVICES, N.A., a Delaware corporation; JOHN and LUCY BROW, jointly and severally,

Defendants.

UNITED STATES DISTRICT COURT FOR THE EASTERN DISTRICT OF MICHIGAN, SOUTHERN DIVISION CASE No. 98-71295

1999 U.S. Dist. LEXIS 11089

June 28, 1999, Decided

AVERN COHN, UNITED STATES DISTRICT JUDGE.

OPINION

MEMORANDUM AND ORDER

I. Introduction

This is a 42 U.S.C. § 1983 action in which plaintiff Michael Tindall, Esq. (Tindall) is suing numerous defendants for alleged constitutional violations. The claims stem from an incident in which Matthew Hambright (Hambright), an ordinance enforcement officer for the City of Grosse Pointe Park, Michigan (the City), responded to a complaint by Tindall's neighbor that Tindall's dog was neglected. Tindall claims Hambright violated his rights secured by the Fourth Amendment to the United States Constitution when Hambright went into Tindall's backyard to check on the dog without a search warrant. Thereafter, Tindall claims, various officers and attorneys for the City, among others, conspired to deprive him of his constitutional right to access the courts. Tindall also claims that the City is liable for inadequate supervision and training.

Each of the defendants moves for summary judgment on the ground that Tindall's claims have no merit. Among other things, the defendants assert that Tindall's Fourth Amendment rights were not violated, that Tindall has not established a conspiracy to deprive him access to the courts, and that there is no evidence demonstrating a policy or custom of deliberate indifference. Defendants also move for sanctions pursuant to Fed. R. Civ. P. 11.

Oral argument is unnecessary. See E.D. Mich. L.R. 7.1(e)(2). Tindall's claims have no merit. Accordingly, defendants' motions for summary judgment will be granted. Defendants' motions for sanctions will be denied.

II. Facts

A. The Dogs

Tindall lived in a rented flat in an area of the City consisting of several rental properties that are "very close together." Tindall lived in the lower flat. Another tenant, with whom Tindall had virtually no contact, lived in the upper flat. Each had rights to use the backyard.

On June 29, 1996, Hambright drove to Tindall's residence to investigate a citizen complaint of animal neglect lodged by Lucy Brow (Brow), one of Tindall's neighbors. [1] Hambright knocked on Tindall's door; there was no response. Hambright then went around to the backyard to see if anyone was home. The backyard was not separated from the front yard by a fence or gate, and there were no barriers separating Tindall's backyard from the neighboring yards. Hambright saw Tindall's **cocker spaniel**, which was on a fifteen to twenty foot leash, sitting in the neighbor's backyard. Hambright observed that the dog had a bowl of dirty, "brownish" water, and a dish of old and decomposed dog food. The dog had only a plastic cage for shelter.

Brow came out to talk to Hambright, and informed him that the dog often sits on her lawn and driveway, and that it is frequently left outside without fresh food or water. Tindall, who had been watching Hambright and Brow from his flat, came outside and approached Hambright. Tindall

---

[1] Brow's complaint apparently was not the first complaint of animal neglect lodged against Tindall.

shouted obscenities and shook his fist at Brow and Hambright.

Hambright left the yard and contacted defendant police officer Erik Davis (Davis) for support. When Davis arrived, he obtained a witness statement from Brow and then confronted a hostile Tindall. After threatening to file a lawsuit if he was issued a citation, Tindall led Davis and Hambright to the backyard to view the conditions. Hambright then issued Tindall a citation for animal neglect. The citation was dropped, however, because defendant supervising officer D. Hillar (Hillar) and defendant city attorney Brian Bursiek (Bursiek)[2] issued a misdemeanor complaint against Tindall. The complaint was in four counts: animal cruelty; harboring a dog without a license; assault on another person; and disturbing the peace.

Three more complaints were lodged by Tindall's neighbors in October 1996. At that time, Tindall also had a **cocker spaniel** puppy; the dogs frequently would get tangled in the leashes, and the larger dog would drag the puppy around the backyard. Tindall was issued additional citations for animal neglect and dog at large, and the dogs were impounded.

With his trial on the misdemeanor complaint in Grosse Pointe Park Municipal Court approaching, Tindall filed motions to suppress and dismiss. The municipal court suppressed Hambright's initial observations in Tindall's yard, but denied Tindall's other motions. Tindall ultimately pled guilty to having a dog without a license and paid a fine. Bursiek dropped the other counts of the complaint largely because Brow had moved to Arizona.

B. The BMW

In November 1997, Davis ticketed a BMW parked near Tindall's home because the license plate had expired. A copy of the ticket was sent to defendant BMW Financial Services, N.A. (BMW Financial), which owned the vehicle. The vehicle was leased to Invest Financial Group, Inc. (IFG); Tindall was the president of IFG, and the main driver of the BMW. Tindall was in litigation in Oakland County Circuit Court with BMW Financial, which was seeking to repossess the BMW because the lease payments were in default.

In April 1997, while the charges were still pending in municipal court, Hillar checked the Law Enforcement Information Network (LEIN) and National Crime Information Center (NCIC) databases on Tindall. Bursiek faxed copies of the LEIN and NCIC reports to defendant Judith Greenstone Miller (Miller), an attorney with defendant Clark Hill P.C. (Clark Hill). Miller and Clark Hill represented defendant BMW Financial and defendant BMW North America, Inc. in the Oakland County action.

---

[2] Bursiek is an attorney with defendant Bodman, Longley and Dahling LLP.

III. Analysis

Tindall's claims against defendants are categorized as follows: illegal search of the backyard against Hambright and other police officers; conspiracy to deprive Tindall access to the courts; and inadequate supervision and training by the City. Defendants move for summary judgment and sanctions, arguing that the claims lack merit and Tindall filed this lawsuit solely to harass them. Under the Order of June 11, 1998, all state law claims were dismissed.

A. Summary Judgment

Summary judgment will be granted when the moving party demonstrates that there is "no genuine issue as to any material fact and that the moving party is entitled to a judgment as a matter of law." Fed. R. Civ. P. 56(c). There is no genuine issue of material fact when "the record taken as a whole could not lead a rational trier of fact to find for the non-moving party." Matsushita Elec. Indus. Co. v. Zenith Radio Corp., 475 U.S. 574, 587, 89 L. Ed. 2d 538, 106 S. Ct. 1348 (1986).

The Court must decide "whether the evidence presents a sufficient disagreement to require submission to a jury or whether it is so one-sided that one party must prevail as a matter of law." In re Dollar Corp., 25 F.3d 1320, 1323 (6th Cir. 1994) (quoting Anderson v. Liberty Lobby, Inc., 477 U.S. 242, 251-52, 91 L. Ed. 2d 202, 106 S. Ct. 2505 (1986)). In so doing, the Court "must view the evidence in the light most favorable to the non-moving party." Employers Ins. of Wausau v. Petroleum Specialties, Inc., 69 F.3d 98, 101 (6th Cir. 1995).

B. Illegal Searches

Hambright and the police officers that investigated the complaints of animal cruelty (hereinafter "officers") argue they are entitled to summary judgment on the illegal search claim because Tindall had no reasonable expectation of privacy in the area where his dogs were kept. Alternatively, the officers argue they are entitled to qualified immunity because it was not objectively unreasonable for the officers to enter Tindall's backyard to check on the dogs.

"It is well established that the protection provided by the Fourth Amendment extends to the 'curtilage' area of a house." United States v. Jenkins, 124 F.3d 768, 771 (6th Cir. 1997). "The concept of curtilage, unfortunately, evades precise definition." Id. at 772. As the Court of Appeals for the Sixth Circuit explained in Jenkins:

In United States v. Dunn, the Court elaborated upon these articulations and explained that curtilage questions should be resolved with reference to four factors: (1) "the proximity of the area claimed to be curtilage to the

223

home"; (2) "whether the area is included within an enclosure surrounding the home"; (3) "the nature of the uses to which the area is put"; and (4) "the steps taken by the resident to protect the area from observation by people passing by." The Court cautioned, however, that it was not announcing a rigid test. "Rather, these factors are useful analytical tools only to the degree that, in any given case, they bear upon the centrally relevant consideration-- whether the area in question is so intimately tied to the home itself that it should be placed under the home's 'umbrella' of Fourth Amendment protection."

Id. (citations omitted).

Assuming arguendo that the area in which Tindall's dogs were found constituted curtilage, the Court is satisfied that the conduct of the officers was not objectively unreasonable and thus they are entitled to qualified immunity. Under the doctrine of qualified immunity, government officials engaged in discretionary functions are generally "shielded from liability for civil damages insofar as their conduct does not violate clearly established statutory or constitutional rights of which a reasonable person would have known." Harlow v. Fitzgerald, 457 U.S. 800, 818, 73 L. Ed. 2d 396, 102 S. Ct. 2727 (1982). "The burden is on the plaintiff to allege and prove that the defendant official violated a clearly established constitutional right." Adams v. Metiva, 31 F.3d 375, 386 (6th Cir. 1994).

In the recent decision in Daughenbaugh v. City of Tiffin, 150 F.3d 594 (6th Cir. 1998), the Sixth Circuit found that the defendants were entitled to qualified immunity even though their search of the plaintiff's backyard was illegal under the Fourth Amendment. The Sixth Circuit held that the search was not objectively unreasonable in large part because the search took place before the Jenkins decision in 1997, which held that a backyard was curtilage under the circumstances. See id. at 603.

In this case, the purportedly illegal searches of Tindall's backyard took place prior to the Jenkins decision. Further, it is important to point out that Tindall had a reduced expectation of privacy in the backyard. The backyard was not included "within an enclosure surrounding the home," and he did not take any steps "to protect the area from observation" by passers-by or his neighbors. The backyard was not separated by a fence or gate, and there were no barriers separating Tindall's backyard from the neighboring yards, which were "very close together." Finally, Tindall did not have sole possession of the backyard; he shared it with the tenant in the upper flat, whom he barely knew.

The Court finds that it was not objectively unreasonable for Hambright and the other officers to enter the backyard to check on the dogs under the circumstances. Accordingly, the officers are entitled to qualified immunity. Further, to the extent Tindall claims that Bursiek "procured" the searches of Tindall's backyard, the claim lacks merit. There is no evidence of record to indicate that Bursiek had any knowledge of the searches until after the dogs were impounded.

C. Conspiracy Claims

Defendants assert that they are entitled to summary judgment on Tindall's claims that defendants conspired to deprive him of his rights to equal protection, due process, and access to the courts secured by the First and Fourteenth Amendments to the United States Constitution. The Court agrees.

The due process claim is made in connection with the access to the courts claim. Tindall says defendants conspired to violate his "right to free and unfettered access to the Courts, which right is protected by the First Amendment to the United States Constitution" by retaliating against him for threatening to sue defendants regarding Hambright's initial investigation of the animal neglect complaint. According to Tindall, defendants replaced the civil citation with the misdemeanor complaint to intimidate him so he would not sue.

There is no evidence of record establishing an agreed upon plan by any of the defendants to violate Tindall's constitutional rights. See Moore v. City of Paducah, 890 F.2d 831, 834 (6th Cir. 1989).[3] There is also no evidence of record establishing that Tindall's threat to file a lawsuit was a substantial or motivating factor in the decision to issue the misdemeanor complaint against Tindall. See, e.g., Barrett v. Harrington, 130 F.3d 246, 262 (6th Cir. 1997) (noting that a plaintiff must establish that protected speech was a substantial or motivating factor in the purportedly retaliatory action). The misdemeanor complaint was based on the statement of Brow and reports of Hambright and Davis. The record indicates that the officers' visits in October 1996 were based upon further citizen complaints of animal neglect. Bursiek also points out that he has absolute immunity in connection with issuing the misdemeanor complaint. See Buckley v. Fitzsimmons, 509 U.S. 259, 273, 125 L. Ed. 2d 209, 113 S. Ct. 2606 (1993)

---

[3] As stated in Moore:

A civil conspiracy is an agreement between two or more persons to injure another by unlawful action. Express agreement among all the conspirators is not necessary to find the existence of a civil conspiracy. Each conspirator need not have known all of the details of the illegal plan or all of the participants involved. All that must be shown is that there was a single plan, that the alleged coconspirator shared in the general conspiratorial objective, and that an overt act was committed in furtherance of the conspiracy that caused injury to the complainant.

890 F.2d at 834 (quoting Hooks v. Hooks, 771 F.2d 935, 943-44 (6th Cir. 1985)).

("Acts undertaken by a prosecutor in preparing for the initiation of judicial proceedings or for trial, which occur in the course of his role as an advocate for the State, are entitled to the protections of absolute immunity.").

Further, there is no basis for concluding that the searches for Tindall's name in the LEIN and NCIC databases violated Tindall's constitutional rights "because there is no constitutional right to privacy in one's criminal record." Cline v. Rogers, 87 F.3d 176, 179 (6th Cir. 1996) (finding plaintiff's claim that search of NCIC database violated his constitutional rights meritless).[4] Finally, there is no basis for an equal protection claim. Tindall has not established that he was treated differently than similarly situated individuals.

D. Policy of Inadequate Training and Supervision

Tindall's claim that the City had a policy or custom of inadequate training or supervision of its employees has no merit. "The inadequacy of police training may serve as the basis for § 1983 liability only where the failure to train amounts to deliberate indifference to the rights of persons with whom the police come into contact." City of Canton v. Harris, 489 U.S. 378, 388, 103 L. Ed. 2d 412, 109 S. Ct. 1197 (1989). To make out a claim, a plaintiff must "identify the policy, connect the policy to the city itself, and show that the particular injury was incurred because of the execution of that policy." Garner v. Memphis Police Dep't., 8 F.3d 358, 367 (6th Cir. 1993).

Tindall has not identified a policy or custom, or the lack thereof, to support the claim. Tindall also has not proffered evidence to support a claim of deliberate indifference. Accordingly, the claim is unfounded.

Further, Tindall's § 1983 claim that defendant Bodman, Longley and Dahling LLP, as attorneys for the City, failed to adequately train or supervise Bursiek is baseless. Because Bursiek did not violate Tindall's constitutional rights, the claim against Bodman, Longley and Dahling fails. See, e.g., Hancock v. Dodson, 958 F.2d 1367, 1376 (6th Cir. 1992) ("because the only City police officer present committed no constitutional violation, the City cannot be liable for failure to train its police officers").

E. Sanctions

Although this action appears to be an attempt to harass defendants,[5]

---

[4]   Tindall's claim that the searches violated his rights secured under the Michigan Constitution was dismissed under the Order of June 11, 1998.

[5] Defendants note that Tindall is litigious. Tindall recently filed a lawsuit in this Court against two Wayne County Circuit Judges and the Wayne County Sheriff,

the Court is not disposed to grant the motions for sanctions. The case was over-litigated by defendants as demonstrated by the number of papers filed, and as observed first-hand by the Court in supervising a room full of lawyers taking depositions at the courthouse. It certainly would have been more efficient and less costly had defendants cooperated by agreeing on a single lawyer to litigate this action in necessary appearances in court and in taking plaintiff's depositions.

IV. Conclusion

For the foregoing reasons, defendants' motions for summary judgment are GRANTED. Defendants' motions for sanctions are DENIED. This case is DISMISSED.

SO ORDERED.
AVERN COHN
UNITED STATES DISTRICT JUDGE
DATED: JUN 28 1999
Detroit, Michigan

---

among others, claiming they violated his constitutional rights in connection with his divorce proceedings and child support obligations.

DR. RICHARD HAEFNER, Plaintiff,

v.

CATHERINE SCHUYLER, Defendant.

Civil Action No. 00-393-RRM

UNITED STATES DISTRICT COURT
FOR THE DISTRICT OF DELAWARE

2001 U.S. Dist. LEXIS 16507

October 11, 2001, Decided

JUDGES: McKELVIE, District Judge.

OPINION

MEMORANDUM OPINION

This is a tort case. Plaintiff Dr. Richard Haefner is a United States citizen and California resident. Defendant Catherine Schuyler is a United States citizen and Delaware resident. On April 11, 2000, Haefner, proceeding pro se, filed his complaint in this case, asserting diversity jurisdiction under 28 U.S.C. § 1332. In his complaint, Haefner raises six claims against Schuyler: (i) assault; (ii) battery; (iii) intentional infliction of emotional distress; (iv) negligent infliction of emotional distress; (v) damage to property; and (vi) fraud and abuse of legal process.

On June 8, 2000, Schuyler moved to dismiss the complaint, pursuant to Federal Rules of Civil Procedure 8(c) and 12(b)(6), for failure to state a claim upon which relief can be granted. Schuyler argues that Haefner's complaint is barred by the doctrine of collateral estoppel because he was tried and convicted by the Court of Common Pleas of the State of Delaware of crimes against Schuyler that are directly related to his allegations in this case. On June 30, 2000, Schuyler moved for the court to impose sanctions on Haefner pursuant to Federal Rule of Civil Procedure 11, arguing that Haefner's complaint is frivolous and was filed for the sole purpose of harassing Schuyler.

This is the court's decision on Schuyler's motion to dismiss and motion for sanctions.

I. FACTUAL AND PROCEDURAL BACKGROUND

In the procedural context of a motion to dismiss, the court must assume that all of the facts alleged in the complaint are true. Schrob v. Catterson, 948 F.2d 1402, 1405 (3d Cir. 1991). Accordingly, this section first will set forth the facts as alleged by Haefner. However, because Schuyler's motion also raises the affirmative defense of collateral estoppel, pursuant to Federal Rule of Civil Procedure 8(c), the court will also set forth the factual and procedural record of Haefner's criminal trial.

The court thus draws facts from the following sources: Haefner's complaint, the State of Delaware v. Haefner trial transcript, the State of Delaware v. Haefner sentencing hearing transcript, the Court of Common Pleas of the State of Delaware for New Castle County Sentencing Report, and the Court of Common Pleas Restitution Opinion and Order.

A. Allegations of Haefner's Complaint

The disputed incident between Haefner and Schuyler occurred on January 6, 1998 at a parking lot in the Milltown Shopping Center. The altercation began when Schuyler scolded Haefner for leaving his fifteen year old blind **cocker spaniel** in a shopping cart outside of the Liquor World liquor store. According to Haefner's complaint, Schuyler, "without provocation or justification," approached him, beat on the door of his vehicle with a wine bottle and attempted to hit him on the face and head with the bottle. Haefner further alleges that Schuyler hit him on his arms and shoulders with the bottle and kicked him in the groin. Haefner asserts that he suffers from asthma and clinical depression and receives monthly disability checks from Social Security.

Haefner alleges that, following the incident, he called the police. The responding officer allegedly asked Haefner whether he would like to press charges against Schuyler, but he declined. No charges were brought against either Schuyler or Haefner at that time. According to the complaint, Schuyler then hired a third party to conduct an investigation of Haefner's background. From the investigation, Schuyler apparently learned that, approximately twenty-five years ago, Haefner had been charged with child molestation. Haefner was found not guilty of that charge and his record has been expunged. Haefner alleges that Schuyler then contacted the police and notified them that she would like to press charges. Haefner was thereafter charged with misdemeanor assault and misdemeanor criminal mischief.

B. Decision by the Court of Common Pleas of the State of Delaware for New Castle County

1. Haefner's Criminal Trial

On May 27, 1998, the Court of Common Pleas of the State of Delaware for New Castle County found Haefner guilty of assault in the third degree and criminal mischief. At Haefner's trial, the State set forth the following version of what happened on January 6, 1998 in the Milltown Shopping Center parking lot.

After exiting Liquor World, Schuyler observed a dog, that she believed was abandoned, sitting in a shopping cart. Schuyler approached the dog and noticed tags on it. She and an unknown female decided they would take the dog to a local veterinarian in an attempt to locate the owner.

After she placed her shopping bags in her Isuzu Trooper, Schuyler moved her vehicle closer to the dog. At about the time that Schuyler and the unknown female were about to remove the dog from the cart, plaintiff Richard Haefner, the dog's owner, exited Liquor World. Haefner allegedly yelled at Schuyler and the unknown female, stating that he was the dog's owner. A verbal argument then ensued between the three people.

Schuyler asserted that Haefner followed her after she attempted to extricate herself from the situation. Haefner then allegedly struck Schuyler's vehicle with a bottle. Harriet Stacey and Raymond Giordano, two witnesses to the event, stated in their police interviews that they observed Haefner hit Schuyler's vehicle.

Schuyler then allegedly told Haefner to get away from her car, and he proceeded to leave. At that time, Schuyler followed Haefner to his vehicle in an attempt to record his vehicle tag number. After Schuyler pulled up behind Haefner's vehicle, Haefner allegedly grabbed her neck and pulled her out of her vehicle. John Parks, another witness, stated in his police interview that Haefner did in fact grab Schuyler by the neck and pull her out of the vehicle.

Haefner then allegedly kicked and punched Schuyler with his fist. Witnesses, Raymond Simpson, April Wells, and Tinika Miller stated in their police interviews that they saw Haefner attack Schuyler. After the alleged attack, Schuyler dialed 911 from her cellular phone and received medical attention. She sustained injuries that included a dislocated jaw, loosening of teeth, contusions on her upper right lip and neck, and laceration to her mouth that required stitches.

The above version of the incident was corroborated by testimony from multiple witnesses, the Delaware State Police Investigation Report of January 6, 1998, and the Delaware State Police Investigation Supplement Report of January 16, 1998.

At trial, Haefner argued that the State's version of the incident was wrong. Haefner contended that Schuyler acted aggressively towards him and kicked him in the groin and that his actions against her were in self-defense. Haefner also alleged that Schuyler struck and damaged his vehicle, despite the fact that the responding police officer noted in his Police

Investigation Report that he found no indication of any damage to Haefner's vehicle.

2. Haefner's Sentencing

On June 29, 1998, the Court of Common Pleas held a sentencing hearing. For the charge of assault in the third degree, the court sentenced Haefner to incarceration for a term of one year, of which the balance was to be suspended after serving thirty days. This was to be followed by a one year period of Level II probation. Conditions of the probation included: 1) payment of restitution to Schuyler; 2) completion of an anger control program; 3) continuation of treatment for his mental health problems; and 4) no contact with Schuyler or her family. In addition, the court ordered Haefner to pay the costs of prosecution. For the charge of criminal mischief, the court sentenced Haefner to incarceration for one year, which was suspended immediately and to be followed by a period of one year of Level II probation.

At the sentencing hearing, Haefner accepted responsibility for his actions stating that "I do take responsibility for this incident" State of Delaware v. Haefner, CM No. 98-01-1788-1789, Hr'g Tr. at 185 (May 27, 1998).

3. Haefner's Restitution Hearing

On June 24, 1999, the Court of Common Pleas held a restitution hearing to determine the amount of recovery for Schuyler's out-of-pocket expenses, which Haefner would be required to pay to Schuyler as a condition of his probation. At the hearing, the court heard testimony from Schuyler, Haefner, various witnesses and the pre-sentence officer. The court received into evidence the Pre-sentence Report, which included Haefner's financial status and Schuyler's Victim Loss Statements. The Victim Loss Statements included an attached verification of loss sustained by Schuyler for personal injuries and property damage. Schuyler testified that as a result of the incident she had incurred out-of-pocket medical and auto repair fees to date of $ 3,504.00 and submitted evidence that an additional $ 325.53 in medical fees had been paid by her insurance company. Along with her Victim Loss Statement, Schuyler also presented documentation from two of her doctors that set forth the restorative dental work that was necessary to correct the trauma sustained as a result of Haefner's criminal conduct. The total estimated cost of the dental restoration was $ 37,920.00.

The court determined that Haefner proximately caused Schuyler's injuries and proximately caused damages to Schuyler's vehicle. The court also found that the medical expenses were reasonable and necessary. In making this determination, the court noted the severe extent of Schuyler's injuries:

[Schuyler] sustained severe injuries as a result of the January 6, 1998 incident, including a cut to her mouth requiring stitches and the loosening of teeth holding a plate in her mouth that now must be replaced. Her jaw was also dislocated to such a degree that she has been unable to chew solid food since the assault and caused her to lose weight in excess of 32 pounds. All of the projected dental work is restorative rather than cosmetic in nature and will take approximately two years to complete.

State of Delaware v. Haefner, CM No. 98-01-1788-1789, Restitution Op. and Order at 9 (June 25, 1999).

The court granted restitution to Schuyler in the amount of $ 3,504.00, the full amount of her submitted out-of-pocket expenses that arose from the incident. Based on an assessment Haefner's financial capabilities, the court ordered Haefner to pay at least $ 100.00 per month. The court concluded its order by noting that, pursuant to 11 Del. C. § 4104(d), it would retain jurisdiction over Haefner until the restitution order and any supplemental restitution orders arising from future medical expenses, including Schuyler's restorative dental work, were paid in full.

C. Notice of Appeal filed to Superior Court of the State of Delaware for New Castle County and the Supreme Court of the State of Delaware

On January 18, 2000, the Superior Court of the State of Delaware for New Castle County denied Haefner's motion to proceed in fonna pauperis. On February 28, 2000, the Supreme Court of the State of Delaware dismissed Haefner's Petition for Allowance of Appeal from an interlocutory order of the Superior Court, stating that "under the Delaware Constitution, only a final judgment may be reviewed by this Court in a criminal case." Haefner v. State of Delaware, 748 A.2d 407 (2000) (emphasis in original). On March 27, 2000, the Superior Court dismissed Haefner's appeal for lack of jurisdiction, because, under the Delaware Constitution, only cases in which the sentence exceeds one month of imprisonment, or a fine exceeding one hundred dollars are directly appealable to the Superior Court. See Del. Const. Art. IV § 28.

D. Complaint filed in United States District Court for the District of Delaware

In his complaint, Haefner alleges six causes of action against Schuyler that all relate to his allegations that, in contrast to the determination of the Court of Common Pleas, she attacked and beat him. First, Haefner alleges a claim for assault, arguing any contact that he initiated with Schuyler was in self-defense. Second, Haefner alleges a claim for battery, arguing that Schuyler physically attacked him, causing him physical impartment and pain. Third, Haefner alleges a claim for intentional infliction of emotional distress. Fourth, Haefner alleges a claim for negligent infliction of emotional distress. Both of these claims are based on allegations of emotional distress that arose from Schuyler's alleged attack on him. Fifth, Haefner alleges a claim for damage to property, asserting that Schuyler damaged his vehicle. Last, Haefner alleges a claim for fraud and abuse of process, arguing that during the restitution proceeding against him Schuyler failed to disclose that she had a preexisting dental condition prior to the January 6, 1998, incident.

II. DISCUSSION

A. Motion to Dismiss

Schuyler has moved to dismiss all of Haefner's claims. She claims that each of Haefner's claims is barred by the doctrine of collateral estoppel, arguing that Haefner's criminal conviction should bar the retrial of issues in this civil case that were actually litigated and decided in Haefner's criminal trial.

Collateral estoppel, also known as issue preclusion, bars the "relitigation of a matter that has been litigated and decided" in a previous case. Lomax v. Nationwide Mut. Ins. Co., 776 F. Supp. 870, 874 (D. Del 1991), rev'd on other grounds, 964 F.2d 1343 (3d Cir. 1992). As the Supreme Court explained in Parklane Hosiery Co. v. Shore, 439 U.S. 322, 326, 58 L. Ed. 2d 552, 99 S. Ct. 645 (1979), "collateral estoppel . . . has the dual purpose of protecting litigants from the burden of relitigating an identical issue with the same party . . . and of promoting judicial economy by preventing needless litigation."

In determining the collateral estoppel effect of a state proceeding, a federal court must apply the law of the state where the criminal proceeding took place and must also ascertain whether the party against whom the estoppel is asserted had a full and fair opportunity to litigate the issue decided in the state court. Anela v. City of Wildwood, 790 F.2d 1063, 1068 (3d Cir.), cert. denied, 479 U.S. 949, 93 L. Ed. 2d 384, 107 S. Ct. 434 (1986). Under Delaware law, there are four requirements that must be satisfied for a finding of collateral estoppel: (1) the issue in the present case must be identical to the issue in the previous case; (2) the issue must have been fully litigated in the previous case; (3) the issue must have been "material and relevant" to the disposition of the previous case; and (4) the determination of the issue in the previous case must have been "necessary and essential" to the judgement in the previous case. Lomax, 776 F. Supp. at 874-75; cf. Tyndall v. Tyndall, 238 A.2d 343, 346 (Del .1968). In this case, Schuyler seeks to use collateral estoppel defensively; Schuyler, as defendant, seeks to bar Haefner from relitigating an issue that he previously litigated and lost.

See Parklane, 439 U.S. at 329.

1. Does collateral estoppel bar the litigation of Haefner's claims for battery, assault, intentional infliction of emotional distress, negligent infliction of emotional distress, and property damage?

With respect to Haefner's claims for battery, assault, negligent and intentional infliction of emotional distress, and property damage, the court finds that each of the requirements for applying collateral estoppel has been met. Haefner raised and litigated each of these five claims in the Court of Common Pleas. The Court of Common Pleas criminal conviction of Haefner precludes him from relitigating the disputed facts underlying his conviction.

Haefner bases his claims for battery, assault, intentional and negligent infliction of emotional distress, and property damage on Schuyler's allegedly unprovoked attack on him. After reviewing the factual record and hearing testimony pertaining to Schuyler's alleged conduct, the alleged damages she caused to Haefner's vehicle, and his alleged resulting distress and depression, the Court of Common Pleas definitively concluded that each of his allegations were without merit. Moreover, that court expressly determined that Haefner was the one who attacked Schuyler and that he had not acted in self-defense. At trial, the Court of Common Pleas stated:

The Court also finds that there was an intentional act on your part Mr. Haefner and that your explanation on the stand was not believable at all by the Court. Nor is your argument of self-defense accepted by the Court as trier of fact. Self-defense requires some credible evidence and I found no credible evidence whatsoever of your defense.

State of Delaware v. Haefner, CM No. 98-01-1788-1789, Hr'g Tr. at 163 (May 27, 1998).

Haefner apparently does not contest that the issues that underlie his current tort claims were raised and adjudicated by the Court of Common Pleas or that they were material and necessary to the Court of Common Pleas judgment. Rather, Haefner argues that collateral estoppel does not apply in this case because he did not have a full and fair opportunity to litigate the issues in the state criminal proceeding. In support of his argument, Haefner relies on Looney v. City of Wilmington Delaware, 723 F. Supp. 1025, 1033 (D. Del. 1989). Haefner claims that certain language in Looney invoked the general sentiment of the Restatement (Second) of Judgements, § 28 (1982), which suggests an exception to the general rule of collateral estoppel when the party against whom preclusion is sought could not, as a matter of law, obtain review of the judgment in the initial action. See id.; Restatement (Second) of Judgments, § 28(1) (1982).

Haefner's reliance on Looney is misplaced. In Looney, the plaintiff had been convicted in the Municipal Court of the City of Wilmington of the criminal charge of menacing. Plaintiff then brought a federal civil rights action, pursuant to 42 U.S.C. § 1983, against the City of Wilmington and two police officers in their individual and official capacities alleging that the defendant's violated his rights under the Fourth and Fourteenth Amendments to the United States Constitution to be free from unreasonable search and seizure. Plaintiff also alleged a state law claim of battery against the defendants. The defendants moved for summary judgment on a variety of grounds and sought to use the collateral estoppel effect of the plaintiff's menacing conviction to preclude the plaintiff from relitigating a particular issue relating to the battery claim. In discussing the issue of collateral estoppel, the Looney court ruled that while it was correct that plaintiff was unable to appeal his menacing conviction because the $ 100 fine was below the amount in controversy requirement that Delaware law requires for a direct appeal, see Del. Const. Art. IV § 28, plaintiff nonetheless could have sought a writ of certiorari to the Superior Court, but failed to do so. The court in Looney found that, even though the scope of review afforded pursuant to a writ of certiorari was more limited than that of a direct appeal, the use of collateral estoppel should not be barred because Looney failed to seek any review. Looney, 723 F. Supp. at 1033.

In this case, as in Looney, the court finds that collateral estoppel should not be barred where "review is available, but is not sought." Restatement (Second) of Judgments § 21(1) cmt. a (1982). Haefner had a full and fair opportunity to litigate the very issues that he raises before this court in the Court of Common Pleas. Moreover, Haefner had the incentive to litigate issues relating to his fault fully, because of the threat of fines and incarceration in the criminal proceeding before the Court of Common Pleas. He litigated the issues of his fault and lost. After his conviction in the Court of Common Pleas, Haefner failed to file a writ of certiorari. The only petition that Haefner filed in the Supreme Court of Delaware is a "Petition for Allowance of Appeal," in which he prematurely sought review from the Superior Court's denial of plaintiff's motion to proceed in forma pauperis. Haefner's own failure to file a writ of certiorari cannot rob the Court of Common Pleas' findings of their preclusive effect.

In sum, Haefner's allegations of wrongful conduct on the part of Schuyler involve the very issues that were fully addressed and ruled upon in the previous criminal action against Haefner. The Court of Common Pleas determined that Haefner was guilty of assault against Schuyler based on the standard of beyond a reasonable doubt, a standard that is more stringent than the preponderance of the evidence standard that would be applicable in Haefner's civil action before this court. In making its determination, the Court of Common Pleas decided that Haefner committed criminally wrongful acts against Schuyler during the January 6, 1998 incident. Haefner is now attempting to relitigate in this court the issue of his fault by arguing that Schuyler was the wrongdoer. He cannot do so. Because Schuyler has established all of the required elements of collateral estoppel, Haefner is barred from raising his first five claims in this court.

2. Should Haefner's fraud and abuse of process claim be dismissed?

Haefner also raises a claim for fraud and abuse of process, alleging that Schuyler "used a legal process against [him] primarily to accomplish a purpose for which it is not designed. . . ." and that Schuyler "engaged and continues to engage in an effort to harass [him] and to cause him financial and emotional injury." Pl. Compl. at P 42. As a preliminary matter, the court notes that the restitution proceeding was initiated pursuant to an order of the Court of Common Pleas and not by the defendant in this case.

Haefner is correct that his fraud and abuse of process claim is not subject to collateral estoppel because it has not yet been fully litigated. Nonetheless, this is both the improper time and improper place for Haefner to raise this claim. Haefner's own papers demonstrate that the matter is still open in the courts of the State of Delaware. The Court of Common Pleas has retained jurisdiction over the restitution proceedings to consider medical expenses that were estimated, but not yet incurred, such as expenses relating to Schuyler's dental reconstruction. Therefore, as a matter of comity, this federal court will abstain from asserting jurisdiction over Haefner's restitution-based claim. See Younger v. Harris, 401 U.S. 37, 27 L. Ed. 2d 669, 91 S. Ct. 746 (1971) (federal courts should not interfere with ongoing state proceedings). Moreover, even if the restitution matter were fully adjudicated by the state court, this court's subject matter jurisdiction over the claim would be precluded by the Rooker-Feldman doctrine, which provides that "a party losing in state court is barred from seeking what in substance would be appellate review of the state judgment in a United States District Court based on the losing party's claim that the state judgment itself violates the loser's rights . . . .", Johnson v. DeGrandy, 512 U.S. 997, 1005-1006, 114 S. Ct. 2647, 129 L. Ed. 2d 775 (1994). Because the relief that Haefner seeks would require this court to review the state court's restitution decision, this court would not assert subject matter jurisdiction over Haefner's restitution-based claim. See Rooker v. Fidelity Trust, 263 U.S. 413, 68 L. Ed. 362, 44 S. Ct. 149 (1923); District of Columbia Ct. of Appeals v. Feldman, 460 U.S. 462, 75 L. Ed. 2d 206, 103 S. Ct. 1303 (1983); 28 U.S.C. § 1257.

B. Motion for Sanctions

Schuyler has also moved for the court to impose sanctions against Haefner, pursuant to Federal Rule of Civil Procedure Rule 11 and Local Rule 1.3(a), on the grounds that his complaint was without merit and was filed for an improper and harassing purpose. Therefore, in addition to seeking a dismissal, she requests that the court award her court costs, reasonable attorney fees, and any additional fines and penalties that the court deems appropriate.

Dr. Haefner should be aware that his filing in this case borders on frivolous and that his intent to harass Ms. Schuyler is clear. He should be on notice that future filings by him regarding this matter, in this court or other courts, that are patently frivolous or brought expressly for the purpose of harassment will not be tolerated. Neither this court nor any other court will hesitate to impose appropriate sanctions based on the record in this case.

Further, while the court declines to impose sanctions at this time, to the extent that Ms. Schuyler wants to pursue the imposition of sanctions, the court invites her to re-file a motion for sanctions within thirty days that sets forth the specific relief she seeks from this court and provides a factual record of the costs and attorney fees she has incurred in this matter, and any other such relief she seeks.

III. CONCLUSION

In sum, Haefner is barred from recovery under the doctrines of collateral estoppel and judicial abstention. The court will enter an order in accordance with this memorandum opinion.

MARGO HUDSON, Plaintiff-Appellant,

v.

BRYAN COLEMAN;
ERIC RODGERS, Defendants-Appellees,
CITY OF FLINT, Garnishee-Appellee.

No. 01-1653

UNITED STATES COURT OF APPEALS
FOR THE SIXTH CIRCUIT

347 F.3d 138

December 12, 2002, Argued
October 14, 2003, Decided
October 14, 2003, Filed

BATCHELDER and MOORE, Circuit Judges; FORESTER, Chief District Judge. FORESTER, D. J., delivered the opinion of the court, in which BATCHELDER, J., joined. MOORE, J. (pp. 15-21), delivered a separate dissenting opinion.

OPINION

Plaintiff appeals the district court's order granting the City of Flint's ("City") motion to quash Plaintiff's garnishment action against the City. For the following reasons, we AFFIRM the judgment of the district court.

I. FACTUAL AND PROCEDURAL BACKGROUND

Plaintiff filed an action in state court asserting state and federal causes of action against Officers Bryan Coleman, Eric Rodgers, and the City of Flint arising from the Officers' theft of Hudson's **Cocker spaniel**, "Brandy." The City removed the action to the Eastern District of Michigan based on Plaintiff's 42 U.S.C. §§ 1983 and 1985 claims.

The facts giving rise to this dispute are undisputed and merit only a brief discussion before turning to the determinative legal issue of subject matter jurisdiction. Hudson reported that her car had been stolen with her dog inside the car. Officers Coleman and Rodgers responded to a radio call to investigate Hudson's missing vehicle and dog. The Officers located the stolen vehicle and proceeded to take the dog from the car and ultimately to Officer Coleman's house. The Officers then lied by reporting that they did not find a dog inside the car. The truth concerning the theft of the would-be "$ 300,000 **Cocker spaniel**[1]" finally surfaced five months later during an internal police department investigation in which the Officers admitted to stealing the dog. The **Cocker spaniel** was returned to Hudson and the Officers faced discipline by the Police Department.

After the district court granted the City's motion for summary judgment dismissing it from the case, Hudson and the Officers entered into a consent judgment whereby Coleman would pay $ 200,000 and Rodgers would pay $ 100,000 in settlement of Hudson's claims. In an effort to collect upon the consent judgment against Coleman and Rodgers, Hudson filed writs of garnishment against the City. Hudson asserted that the City would be liable to pay the consent judgment because of an indemnity agreement between the City and the Police Officers Union.

The indemnification agreement under which Hudson attempts to collect the consent judgment from the City provides:

Whenever any claim is made or any civil action is commenced against an Employee for injuries to persons or property caused by negligence or other acts of the Employee while in the course of his employment, and while acting within the scope of his authority, the Employer will pay for or engage in or furnish the services of an Attorney to advise the Employee as to the claim and to appear for and represent the Employee in the action.

The Employer may compromise, settle and pay such claim before or after the commencement of any civil action. Whenever any judgment for damages, excluding punitive damages, is awarded against an Employee as the result of any civil action for personal injuries or property damage caused by the Employee while in the course of his employment, and while acting within the scope of his authority, the Employer will indemnify the employee or will pay, settle, or compromise the judgment. The Chief Legal Officer will make the selection of the attorney or attorneys to represent the Employee in any particular case, and allow the Employee to object to the selection if he has cause to do so.

---

[1] Officers Coleman and Rodgers agreed to pay $ 300,000 to settle Plaintiff's claims arising from the Officers' theft of the dog. As will be discussed, the legal issue presented is whether the federal courts have jurisdiction to determine whether the City is liable for this debt in Plaintiff's garnishment action against the City.

Pursuant to the above indemnity agreement, the City provided the Officers with legal counsel during the course of the proceedings. There is no evidence in the record indicating that the City's liability under the indemnification agreement has been established, or, more specifically, whether the Officers were acting within the scope of their employment and authority when they stole the dog. By the time Hudson instituted the garnishment proceeding against the City, the Officers each had paid $ 12,500 to Hudson in partial satisfaction of their debts.

The City filed a motion to quash the garnishment on the basis of several theories, including lack of subject matter jurisdiction. After the Magistrate Judge[2] filed a report and recommendation concluding that the court lacked jurisdiction, the district court adopted the report and recommendation and granted the City's motion to quash. Hudson timely filed a notice of appeal.

II. ANALYSIS

We review de novo a district court's determination of subject matter jurisdiction. See, e.g., Greater Detroit Resource Recovery Authority v. EPA, 916 F.2d 317, 319 (6th Cir. 1990). As an initial observation, it is well established that federal courts are courts of limited jurisdiction, possessing only that power authorized by the Constitution and statute, see Willy v. Coastal Corp., 503 U.S. 131, 117 L. Ed. 2d 280, 112 S. Ct. 1076 (1992); Bender v. Williamsport Area School Dist., 475 U.S. 534, 541, 89 L. Ed. 2d 501, 106 S. Ct. 1326 (1986), which is not to be expanded by judicial decree, American Fire & Casualty Co. v. Finn, 341 U.S. 6, 95 L. Ed. 702, 71 S. Ct. 534 (1951). Accordingly, "it is to be presumed that a cause lies outside this limited jurisdiction, and the burden of establishing the contrary rests upon the party asserting jurisdiction." Id (citing Turner v. Bank of N. Am., 4 U.S. (4 Dall.) 8, 11, 1 L. Ed. 718, 4 Dall. 8 (1799); McNutt v. General Motors Acceptance Corp., 298 U.S. 178, 182-183, 80 L. Ed. 1135, 56 S. Ct. 780 (1936)).

The district court found that it lacked jurisdiction over the garnishment, primarily because the action attempts to hold the City, a third party, liable for payment of a judgment on an independent legal theory, the indemnity agreement, which would require separate analysis and possible discovery concerning the City's defenses to liability. As set forth above, the City was dismissed from the action on September 30, 1998. The Officers then settled with the Plaintiff and a consent judgment was entered on February 29, 2000. It was not until June 30, 2000, that the Plaintiff served writs of

---

[2] We commend Magistrate Judge Paul J. Komives for a thorough and well-reasoned report and recommendation, much of which has been adopted in this opinion.

garnishment on the City relying upon Fed. R. Civ. P. 69.

The jurisdictional analysis in this garnishment action begins with a consideration of Peacock v. Thomas, 516 U.S. 349, 133 L. Ed. 2d 817, 116 S. Ct. 862 (1996), and its discussion of ancillary subject matter jurisdiction. As a starting point, it is necessary to understand that there are two situations in which a court may exercise ancillary jurisdiction over a claim otherwise not within the jurisdiction of the court: "'(1) to permit disposition by a single court of claims that are, in varying respects and degrees, factually interdependent; and (2) to enable a court to function successfully, that is, to manage its proceedings, vindicate its authority, and effectuate its decrees.'" Peacock, 516 U.S. at 354 (quoting Kokkonen v. Guardian Life Ins. Co., 511 U.S. 375, 379-80, 128 L. Ed. 2d 391, 114 S. Ct. 1673 (1994) (citations omitted)). The first category of ancillary jurisdiction identified above has largely been codified in the supplemental jurisdiction statute, 28 U.S.C. § 1367. The second category of ancillary jurisdiction is generally referred to as "ancillary enforcement jurisdiction."

In Peacock, the plaintiff obtained a federal court judgment against a corporation pursuant to the Employee Retirement Income Security Act of 1974 (ERISA), 88 Stat. 832, as amended, 29 U.S.C. § 1001 et seq. After efforts to collect on the judgment failed, the plaintiff filed a second suit seeking to hold Peacock, an officer and shareholder of the corporation, personally liable under a piercing of the corporate veil theory. The Supreme Court determined that it was without an independent jurisdictional basis for the suit because ERISA does not authorize a veil-piercing action. In addition, the Court rejected the plaintiff's argument that the federal courts had ancillary enforcement jurisdiction over the second suit.

The Court began its analysis by emphasizing that it has "reserved the use of ancillary jurisdiction in subsequent proceedings for the exercise of a federal court's inherent power to enforce its judgments." Peacock, 516 U.S. at 356. The Court further explained that, "in defining that power, we have approved the exercise of ancillary jurisdiction over a broad range of supplementary proceedings involving third parties to assist in the protection and enforcement of federal judgments-including attachment, mandamus, garnishment, and the prejudgment avoidance of fraudulent conveyances." Id. (citations omitted).

Nevertheless, Peacock concluded that it was without ancillary jurisdiction to entertain plaintiff's second suit. The Court cautioned that the recognition of ancillary supplementary proceedings has not extended beyond attempts to execute, or guarantee the eventual executability of a federal judgment. More specifically, the Court has "never authorized the exercise of ancillary jurisdiction in a subsequent lawsuit to impose an obligation to pay an existing federal judgment on a person not already liable for that judgment." Id. at 357. The Court further explained that 'in determining the reach of the federal courts' ancillary jurisdiction, we have cautioned against the exercise of jurisdiction over proceedings that are "'entirely new and original,'" or where "the relief [sought is] of a different kind or on a different principle" than that of the prior decree.

Id. at 358 (citations omitted).

Peacock concluded that the federal courts were without ancillary enforcement jurisdiction because plaintiff's action was "founded not only upon different facts than the ERISA suit, but also upon entirely new theories of liability." Id.

Here, it is undisputed that Plaintiff's indemnity claim does not raise a federal question and that the parties are not diverse. Accordingly, the Court is without independent subject matter jurisdiction over the "writs of garnishment." Peacock's analysis controls regarding exercise of the first category of ancillary jurisdiction, i.e., "ordinary" ancillary jurisdiction. According to Peacock:

The basis of the doctrine of ancillary jurisdiction is the practical need "to protect legal rights or effectively to resolve an entire, logically entwined lawsuit. Owen Equipment & Erection Co. v. Kroger, 437 U.S. 365, 377, 57 L. Ed. 2d 274, 98 S. Ct. 2396 (1978). But once judgment was entered in the original suit, the ability to resolve simultaneously factually intertwined issues vanished. As in Kroger, "neither the convenience of litigants nor considerations of judicial economy" can justify the extension of ancillary jurisdiction over [plaintiff's] claims in this subsequent proceeding.

Peacock, 516 U.S. at 355.[3]

Just as in Peacock, there is no rationale to support exercising ancillary jurisdiction over Plaintiff's state law indemnity claim against the City. The indemnity claim was not asserted until after the City was dismissed and the case against the individual defendants was settled. Accordingly, there are no factually intertwined issues to resolve and neither the convenience of the litigants nor considerations of judicial economy justify the exercise of ancillary jurisdiction over Plaintiff's state law indemnity claim.

---

[3] The Plaintiff attempts to distinguish Peacock on the basis that it involved a separate suit and the case at bar involves writs of garnishment against the non-party City proceeding under the same case number as the original suit. This distinction has no bearing on "ordinary" ancillary jurisdiction analysis, as such jurisdiction is discretionary with the Court and contemplates proceedings under the same case number in any event. See 28 U.S.C. § 1367. The "separate suit" issue and its bearing on ancillary enforcement jurisdiction is discussed infra at pp. 7-13.

Turning to the purported ancillary "enforcement" grounds for jurisdiction, we find that a proper reading of Peacock dictates that the federal courts are without jurisdiction to entertain this garnishment action. The precise issue presented by the Plaintiff in actuality is whether the fact that the garnishment action is proceeding under the same case number as the original action, rather than in a second lawsuit, sufficiently distinguishes the case from Peacock.

Peacock explained that ancillary jurisdiction is inappropriate in two distinct proceedings, only one of which involves a subsequent lawsuit. First, the Court indicated that ancillary jurisdiction is inappropriate in "proceedings that are entirely new and original." Peacock, 516 U.S. at 358 (internal quotation and citation omitted). Assuming without deciding that the garnishment action falls outside this first precept, the action is squarely prohibited by the second category identified in Peacock "where 'the relief [sought is] of a different kind or on a different principle' than that of the prior decree." Id. (quoting Dugas v. American Surety Co., 300 U.S 414, 428, 81 L. Ed. 720, 57 S. Ct. 515 (1937)) (alteration in original).

Plaintiff's garnishment claim seeks to impose liability on the City, a third party not a party to the consent judgment, on the basis of the indemnity agreement, a legal theory entirely independent from that in the original action. As stated above, there is no evidence in the record indicating that the City's liability under the indemnification agreement has been established, or, more specifically, whether the Officers were acting within the scope of their employment or authority when they stole the dog. In fact, the City was not served with the writs of garnishment until one year and nine months after being dismissed from the lawsuit. At this stage, there has simply been no interpretation of the indemnity clause in the labor agreement between the City and the Police Officer's union. The City has not been adjudged liable to indemnify the Officers' settlement with the Plaintiff, in that there remain substantial questions regarding the interpretation of the labor agreement, e.g., whether each Officer was acting "while in the course of his employment" and "within the scope of his authority." The interpretation of the indemnity provision presents unresolved issues such as whether each Officers' conduct giving rise to the suit constituted a frolic or a mere detour from duty.

In sum, the relief sought by the Plaintiff is based upon a vastly different principle than that of the prior consent decree. We find Hudson's reading of Peacock far too narrow and conclude that she has not carried her burden of demonstrating that this suit falls within either category of ancillary jurisdiction.

Hudson relies upon the statement in Peacock that "we have approved the exercise of ancillary jurisdiction over a broad range of supplementary proceedings involving third parties to assist in the protection and enforcement of federal judgments-including attachment, mandamus, garnishment, and the prejudgment avoidance of fraudulent conveyances." Peacock, 516 U.S. at 356 (emphasis added) (citations omitted). The Supreme Court's acknowledgment of the fact that garnishment sometimes falls within ancillary jurisdiction is obviously not imprimatur for all garnishment actions arising from previous factually similar underlying federal claims to proceed in federal court.[4] The type of garnishment proceeding referred to in Peacock does not contemplate making the garnishee personally liable on the judgment based on some independent legal theory as Hudson seeks to do in this case. Instead, the typical garnishment proceeding referenced in Peacock contemplates the garnishee's paying the judgment creditor/garnishing party directly for funds, such as a salary, owed by the garnishee to the defendant in the underlying action. Cf. Sandlin v. Corporate Interiors, Inc., 972 F.2d 1212, 1216-17 (10th Cir. 1992) (applying H.C. Cook Co. v. Beecher, 217 U.S. 497, 54 L. Ed. 855, 30 S. Ct. 601, 1910 Dec. Comm'r Pat. 511 (1910), a case with renewed vitality post-Peacock); Merrell v. Miller, 1998 U.S. Dist. LEXIS 23160, No. 91-493-A, 1998 WL 329264, at *2 (E.D. Va. January 8, 1998) (noting that Peacock prohibits "efforts, unsupported by an independent basis for federal jurisdiction, to establish a new defendant's personal liability for an existing judgment.").

Michigan law apparently acknowledges the above distinction in the forms of garnishment by labeling the typical form of garnishment as "periodic" and the type garnishment sought by Hudson as "non-periodic." To be sure, Hudson is not requesting that any wages owed by the City to the Officers be paid by the City to Hudson. Instead, Hudson seeks to hold the City individually liable under the indemnity clause for the full amount of the Officers' settlement. The state form used by Hudson is labeled "non-periodic" request and writ for garnishment and Hudson's attorney has mailed a letter to the City on July 10, 2000, indicating the belief that the City is responsible for payment of the entire judgment under the indemnity clause. As stated above, the type garnishment sought by Hudson contemplates making the third party City, a non-party to the consent judgment, personally liable on the consent judgment entered into by the Officers based on the independent legal theory of the indemnification

---

[4] Likewise, Fed. R. Civ. P. 69(a), providing supplementary proceedings in aid of executing a judgment, does not purport to confer ancillary subject matter jurisdiction for all garnishment proceedings arising out of a common nucleus of fact to the original federal proceeding. Instead, Peacock explains the limits of federal ancillary jurisdiction.

agreement. The City's liability under the newly presented indemnity principle is far from established; thus, the issues to be litigated under the indemnity agreement deprive the Court of ancillary jurisdiction. See Peacock, 516 U.S. at 358; see also, Travelers Indemnity Co. of Ill. v. Hash Management, Inc., 173 F.R.D. 150, 153 (M.D.N.C. 1997) ("However, if the proceedings are entirely new and original or seek relief different in kind, on a different principle, or to impose liability on persons not already bound by the previous action and judgment, the moving party must be able to assert an independent basis for federal jurisdiction over the controversy with the third party.").

Hudson also relies on Yang v. City of Chicago,[5] 137 F.3d 522 (7th Cir. 1998), permitting ancillary jurisdiction under Fed. R. Civ. P. 69 for an indemnification action against the City of Chicago after the City was dismissed from the original lawsuit. Yang involved police officer defendants who, after responding to a break-in at Yang's store, proceeded to continue the looting started by the original thieves. After Yang objected to the officers' looting, the officers drove for two blocks with Yang hanging on to the car door. One officer eventually pulled his gun and punched Yang before fleeing the scene.

The Yang district court entered judgment against the officers and dismissed the action against the City. Yang then sought indemnification from the City on the basis of Illinois' indemnification statute, 745 ILCS 10/9-102, providing in pertinent part that a local public entity must pay any tort judgment against an employee "while acting within the scope of his employment." The district court dismissed the indemnification petition on the basis of the Peacock decision.

The Seventh Circuit held that the federal courts had jurisdiction over the indemnification petition because the petition was not a separate lawsuit and involved the same core of operative facts as the original action. According to Yang, "a Rule 69 garnishment proceeding to collect a judgment from a

---

[5] Yang relies on the previous Seventh Circuit decision of Argento v. Village of Melrose Park, 838 F.2d 1483 (7th Cir. 1988). The Supreme Court in Peacock implied that Argento and its progeny were on the wrong side of a circuit split. See Peacock, 516 U.S. at 352 n.2; see also Yang, 137 F.3d at 526. Argento, predating Peacock, permits ancillary jurisdiction "when the plaintiff is proceeding in his original suit rather than by means of a new suit." Yang, 137 F.3d at 526 (citations omitted). This jurisdictional analysis based upon "original suit" versus "new suit" labeling is irreconcilable with Peacock's more substantive analysis prohibiting jurisdiction "where 'the relief [sought is] of a different kind or on a different principle' than that of the prior decree." Peacock, 516 U.S. at 358 (quoting Dugas v. American Surety Co., 300 U.S. 414, 428, 81 L. Ed. 720, 57 S. Ct. 515 (1937)) (alteration in original).

third person not party to the original suit is within a court's ancillary jurisdiction, providing the additional proceeding does not inject so many new issues that it is functionally a separate case." Yang, 137 F.3d at 526. (internal quotation omitted). Yang concluded that interpreting the scope of employment issue in order to resolve the indemnity question did not inject so many new issues into the action as to make it functionally a separate case. The Seventh Circuit then proceeded to resolve the scope of employment issue by concluding that under Illinois law the officer was acting within the scope of his employment when he pulled the gun on Yang. Id. at 525.

As an initial matter, Yang acknowledges that whether the garnishment arises by way of a separate action or under the same case number as the original action is far from determinative of ancillary jurisdiction. Instead, Yang focuses on whether the garnishment injects sufficient new issues as to make the garnishment functionally separate, thus destroying ancillary jurisdiction. Yang's "functionally separate" subjective framework is fact-specific and can be interpreted as facially consistent with the Supreme Court's pronouncement that ancillary jurisdiction is inappropriate in "proceedings that are entirely new and original" and in proceedings "where 'the relief [sought is] of a different kind or on a different principle' than that of the prior decree." Peacock, 516 U.S. at 358 (internal quotation omitted) (quoting Dugas v. American Surety Co., 300 U.S 414, 428, 81 L. Ed. 720, 57 S. Ct. 515 (1937)) (alteration in original).

We disagree with Yang's application of the "functionally separate" framework[6] in deciding the indemnification issue and hold that legitimate, unresolved disputes concerning whether conduct occurs within the scope of employment or authority deprives a federal court of ancillary jurisdiction in a garnishment action pursuant to Peacock. As stated, the City of Flint's liability under the newly presented indemnity principle is far from

---

[6] We acknowledge that the Peacock framework for denying ancillary jurisdiction "where 'the relief [sought is] of a different kind or on a different principle' than that of the prior decree" permits a certain degree of subjectivity in decision making. Perhaps Yang can be explained on this basis in that the litigation resulted in a more than six year saga due in part to delays by the City, including multiple reviews by the Seventh Circuit. Yang involved a remand with directions that the case be reassigned to a different district judge due to inordinate delays. See Yang, 137 F.3d at 527. In addition, the Court expressed, "Yang has waited long enough for this lawsuit to come to an end." Id. at 527. We regret the inconvenience and delay that may be associated with a separate state court garnishment proceeding; however, as stated earlier, it is well-established that we must presume that a cause of action lies outside the limited federal jurisdiction when presented with a subjective choice or close call concerning the existence of jurisdiction.

established; thus, the issues to be litigated under the indemnity agreement deprive the Court of ancillary jurisdiction. It is inappropriate for a Court to decide legitimate scope of employment and/or scope of authority questions without the benefit of fact-finding and briefing.

Our determination in this action overrules Childress v. Williams, 121 F. Supp. 2d 1094 (E.D. Mich. 2000). Childress attempts to distinguish the disputed application of the indemnity agreement from Peacock's ambit by stating:

If all the prerequisites of the indemnification agreement were met, the City would be liable for indemnification at the time the judgment was rendered against the defendant Williams . . . . Because Defendant Williams may have a right to collect from the City, so too may plaintiff.

Childress, 121 F. Supp. 2d at 1096 (emphasis added).

Instead, as we have set forth above, the very contingencies identified in Childress ("if," "would be," and "may") require sufficient fact-finding and legal analysis to distinguish the garnishment proceeding from the original action, rendering the federal courts without ancillary jurisdiction.

III. CONCLUSION

Based upon the above, we AFFIRM the district court's order granting the City of Flint's motion to quash Plaintiff Hudson's garnishment action.

DISSENT

KAREN NELSON MOORE, Circuit Judge, dissenting. I respectfully dissent from the majority's conclusion that the district court lacks subject matter jurisdiction over Plaintiff-Appellant, Margo Hudson's ("Hudson"), garnishment action against Defendant-Appellee, the City of Flint ("City"). Contrary to the majority, I conclude that Hudson's garnishment action is merely a post-judgment proceeding following her prior § 1983 action against Defendants-Appellees, Bryan Coleman and Eric Rodgers (collectively "police officers"), and that the garnishment action will not inject so many new issues as to become a functionally separate lawsuit. I further conclude that Hudson is merely seeking to collect her judgment, rather than to impose liability upon someone not otherwise liable for the judgment. Therefore, the doctrine of ancillary jurisdiction gives the district court subject matter jurisdiction over the garnishment action. For the following reasons, I would REVERSE the district court's order granting the

City's motion to quash Hudson's garnishment action and REMAND for further proceedings.

As discussed in the majority opinion, Hudson brought §§ 1983, 1985, and state law claims against the police officers arising from the police officers' theft of Hudson's dog[7]. On February 29, 2000, Hudson and the police officers entered into a consent judgment, whereby the police officers agreed to pay $ 300,000 in settlement of Hudson's claims. Then, on June 30, 2000, Hudson, seeking to collect the consent judgment, filed writs of garnishment on the City pursuant to Federal Rule of Civil Procedure 69(a) ("Rule 69(a)") and Mich. Comp. Laws § 600.4011(1).[8] The district court found that it lacked subject matter jurisdiction over the garnishment action because the garnishment action seeks "to hold the City, a third party, liable for payment of a judgment on an independent legal theory, the indemnity agreement, which would require separate analysis and possible discovery concerning the City's defenses to liability." Majority Op. at 5. The majority affirms the district court's order quashing Hudson's garnishment action based upon the same reasoning employed by the district court.

The Michigan garnishment statute allows a prevailing plaintiff to seek a writ of garnishment against an obligation owed to the defendant, if the obligor is subject to personal jurisdiction in Michigan. See Mich. Comp. Laws § 600.4011(1). Section 600.4011(1) provides:

The court has power by garnishment to apply the following property or obligation, or both, to the satisfaction of a claim evidenced by contract, judgment of this state, or foreign judgment, whether or not the state has jurisdiction over the person against whom the claim is asserted:

(a)Personal property belonging to the person against whom the claim is asserted but which is in the possession or control of a third person if the third person is subject to the judicial jurisdiction of the state and the personal property to be applied is within the boundaries of this state.

---

[7] 1 Hudson named the City as a defendant in her complaint, but the district court granted summary judgment in favor of the City on September 30, 1998.

[8] Rule 69 directs district courts to employ the procedures for executing judgments of the state in which the district court sits. See Fed. R. Civ. P. 69(a). Rule 69(a) provides: The procedure on execution, in proceedings supplementary to and in aid of a judgment, and in proceedings on and in aid of execution shall be in accordance with the practice and procedure of the state in which the district court is held, existing at the time the remedy is sought, except that any statute of the United States governs to the extent that it is applicable. Id.

(b)An obligation owed to the person against whom the claim is asserted if the obligor is subject to the judicial jurisdiction of the state.
Id.

Contrary to the majority, I would hold that the doctrine of ancillary jurisdiction gives the district court subject matter jurisdiction over the garnishment action. Unlike the majority, I conclude that the Supreme Court's holding in Peacock v. Thomas, 516 U.S. 349, 133 L. Ed. 2d 817, 116 S. Ct. 862 (1996), does not prohibit this use of ancillary jurisdiction. Instead, I conclude that the Seventh Circuit's reasoning in Yang v. City of Chicago, 137 F.3d 522 (7th Cir. 1998), cert. denied, 525 U.S. 1140, 143 L. Ed. 2d 40, 119 S. Ct. 1031 (1999), and the Eastern District of Michigan's reasoning in Childress v. Williams, 121 F. Supp. 2d 1094 (E.D. Mich. 2000), correctly analyze Peacock's effect on the doctrine of ancillary jurisdiction in Rule 69 proceedings.

In Peacock, Thomas had been awarded a judgment of $ 187,628.93 by the district court in his ERISA class action against Tru-Tech, his former employer. Peacock, 516 U.S. at 351. The district court had found that Tru-Tech breached its fiduciary duties in administering the corporation's pension benefits plan, but the district court had also explicitly ruled that Peacock, an officer and shareholder of Tru-Tech, was not a fiduciary. Id. Unable to obtain the money from Tru-Tech, Thomas sued Peacock in federal court alleging various theories, including a veil-piercing claim under ERISA. Id. at 352.

The Supreme Court held that ERISA does not authorize veil-piercing claims; therefore, ERISA did not provide a basis for federal jurisdiction over Thomas's veil-piercing claim. Id. at 353. The Court further held that the doctrine of ancillary jurisdiction did not apply to Thomas's veil-piercing claim, and as a result, the district court lacked subject matter jurisdiction over Thomas's action against Peacock. Id. at 355-59. In so holding, the Court stated that "a federal court may exercise ancillary jurisdiction '(1) to permit disposition by a single court of claims that are, in varying respects and degrees, factually interdependent; and (2) to enable a court to function successfully, that is, to manage its proceedings, vindicate its authority, and effectuate its decrees.'" Id. at 354 (quoting Kokkonen v. Guardian Life Ins. Co., 511 U.S. 375, 379-80, 128 L. Ed. 2d 391, 114 S. Ct. 1673 (1994)). The Court held that Thomas's veil-piercing claim did not involve the first accepted usage of ancillary jurisdiction, as Thomas brought his veil-piercing claim in a subsequent lawsuit, and thus "the ability to resolve simultaneously factually intertwined issues vanished." Id. at 355. The Court further held that Thomas's veil-piercing claim did not involve the second accepted usage of ancillary jurisdiction because, although ancillary jurisdiction may be used to enforce judgments, the Court has "never authorized the exercise of ancillary jurisdiction in a subsequent lawsuit to impose an obligation to pay an existing federal judgment on a person not already liable for that judgment." Id. at 357.

In Yang, a post-Peacock decision, the Seventh Circuit held that the doctrine of ancillary jurisdiction gave the district court subject matter jurisdiction over Yang's Rule 69 garnishment action. Yang, 137 F.3d at 526. Yang had been awarded a substantial monetary judgment in his §§ 1983 and 1985 actions against two police officers. Id. at 522-23. Approximately three months later, "Yang filed a petition for indemnification and writ of execution, seeking indemnification of [his judgments against the officers] from the City of Chicago pursuant to 745 ILCS 10/9-102. Section 9-102 directs a municipality to indemnify a tort judgment entered against an employee if the employee's misconduct was within the scope of his employment." Id. at 524. The court held that "a Rule 69 garnishment proceeding to collect a judgment from a third person not party to the original suit is within a court's ancillary jurisdiction, providing 'the additional proceeding does not inject so many new issues that it is functionally a separate case.'" Id. at 526 (quotations omitted).[9] The court concluded that Yang's garnishment action fell within the district court's ancillary jurisdiction because the only new issue raised in the action was whether the officers were acting within the scope of their employment when they violated Yang's constitutional rights. See id. The Yang court further distinguished Peacock by noting that the plaintiff in Yang was not trying to impose liability for a money judgment on a person not otherwise liable for the judgment, because if the officers were acting within the scope of their employment, the city would be liable for their judgment. Id. at 525 n.1. Similarly, in Childress, the Eastern District of Michigan held that the doctrine of ancillary jurisdiction gave it subject matter jurisdiction over Childress's Rule 69 garnishment proceeding because the only new issue raised in the proceeding was whether the officer was acting within the scope of his employment when he violated Childress's constitutional rights. Childress, 121 F. Supp. 2d at 1096.

The courts in both Yang and Childress reasoned that the Rule 69 garnishment actions were not separate lawsuits because they were post-judgment proceedings, and because the factual issues in the garnishment actions would overlap substantially with the factual issues in the underlying

---

[9] 3 This holding is not inconsistent with the Tenth Circuit's view in Sandlin v. Corporate Interiors, Inc., 972 F.2d 1212, 1217 (10th Cir. 1992), a pre-Peacock decision, in which the court held that the district court lacked subject matter jurisdiction over the plaintiff's subsequent veil-piercing claim because the claim involved new parties, new issues, and new theories of liability. The Tenth Circuit explicitly noted that the plaintiff was not bringing a traditional indemnity claim. Id.

claims. See Yang, 137 F.3d at 526; Childress, 121 F. Supp. 2d at 1096. Thus, the garnishment actions involved the first accepted use of ancillary jurisdiction--resolving factually interdependent claims in a single proceeding. The courts in both Yang and Childress also reasoned that the district court's exercise of ancillary jurisdiction over the Rule 69 garnishment proceeding was necessary to effectuate the district court's prior judgment. Yang, 137 F.3d at 526; Childress, 121 F. Supp. 2d at 1096-97. Thus, the garnishment actions involved the second accepted usage of ancillary jurisdiction--protecting judgments.[10] In fact, the courts in both Yang and Childress relied upon the following passage from Peacock to support their holdings: "we have approved the exercise of ancillary jurisdiction over a broad range of supplementary proceedings involving third parties to assist in the protection and enforcement of federal judgments -- including attachment, mandamus, garnishment, and the prejudgment avoidance of fraudulent conveyances." Peacock, 516 U.S. at 356 (cited in Yang, 137 F.3d at 525; Childress, 121 F. Supp. 2d at 1096).[11]

I find the reasoning of the courts in Yang and Childress both convincing and applicable to the present case. Here, Hudson entered into a consent judgment with the police officers for $ 300,000. Hudson then brought a garnishment proceeding against the City pursuant to Rule 69 seeking to collect from the City in accordance with City's indemnification agreement with the police officers. Hudson's Rule 69 proceeding was a post-judgment proceeding, not a separate lawsuit. The factual issues in the garnishment proceedings will overlap substantially with those in Hudson's underlying §§ 1983, 1985, and state-law claims; therefore, the Rule 69 proceeding will not inject so many new issues as to become a functionally separate lawsuit. Unlike the plaintiff in Peacock, Hudson is not seeking to impose liability on the City for post-judgment conduct; rather, the City's potential liability arose when the police officers committed the conduct underlying Hudson's initial § 1983 action.[12] The only new factual issue involved in the Rule 69 garnishment proceeding will be whether the police

---

[10] Federal courts have exercised ancillary jurisdiction in supplemental proceedings to effectuate judgments for over one hundred years. See Root v. Woolworth, 150 U.S. 401, 410-11, 37 L. Ed. 1123, 14 S. Ct. 136 (1893). Peacock did not strip federal courts of subject matter jurisdiction over proceedings to effectuate judgments. Peacock v. Thomas, 516 U.S. 349, 356, 133 L. Ed. 2d 817, 116 S. Ct. 862 (1996).

[11] Furthermore, in a footnote in Peacock, the Supreme Court explicitly stated that a Rule 69(a) proceeding was an effective mechanism for a district court to use in effectuating its judgment. Peacock, 516 U.S. at 359 n.7.

[12] For the same reason, the City cannot be considered a party that is not otherwise liable, because if the police officers were acting within the scope of their employment, the City would be liable for the police officers' conduct.

officers were acting within the scope of their employment.[13] This is the exact same factual issue that both the Seventh Circuit and the Eastern District of Michigan found insufficient to render the Rule 69 garnishment proceedings separate, subsequent lawsuits. Additionally, the Rule 69 garnishment proceeding is necessary to enable the district court to effectuate its prior judgment against the police officers. Requiring a separate state-court lawsuit to enforce a federal-court judgment would compromise the federal interests that were resolved in the initial federal-court proceedings and would impose an unnecessary burden on state courts. Childress, 121 F. Supp. 2d at 1097. I respectfully dissent.

Whenever any judgment for damages, excluding punitive damages, is awarded against an Employee as the result of any civil action for personal injuries or property damage caused by the Employee while in the course of his employment, and while acting within the scope of his authority, the Employer will indemnify the employee or will pay, settle, or compromise the judgment.

---

[13] The indemnification agreement between the City and the Flint Police Officers Association provides, in pertinent part:

MICHAEL MADRUGA, CHRISTINE MADRUGA, and KATHERINE MADRUGA, by and through her Guardian ad litem CHRISTINE MADRUGA, Plaintiffs,

vs.

COUNTY OF RIVERSIDE, RIVERSIDE COUNTY SHERIFF'S DEPARTMENT, LARRY SMITH, JOHN F. CLARK, and DAVID ELDEN SMITH,

Defendants.

NO. SACV 03-445-SGL

UNITED STATES DISTRICT COURT FOR THE CENTRAL DISTRICT OF CALIFORNIA

431 F. Supp. 2d 1049

November 22, 2005, Decided
November 22, 2005, Filed

For Michael Madruga, Christine Madruga, Katherine Madruga, by and through her Guardian ad Litem, Christine Madruga, Plaintiffs: Stephen E Miller, Steven K Beckett, Brunick McElhaney & Beckett, San Bernardino, CA.

For County of Riverside, -- Erroneously Sued As, Riverside County Sheriff's Department, Larry Smith, in his official and individual capacity, John F Clark, in his official and in his individual capacity, David Elden Smith, in his official and in his individual capacity, Defendants: Arthur K Cunningham, John M Porter, L Alexandra Fong, Lewis Brisbois Bisgaard &

Smith, San Bernardino, CA; Christopher D Lockwood, Arias Aaen, San Bernardino, CA.

STEPHEN G. LARSON, UNITED STATES MAGISTRATE JUDGE.

OPINION

ORDER GRANTING PLAINTIFFS' MOTION FOR SUMMARY JUDGMENT AND DENYING DEFENDANTS' MOTION FOR SUMMARY JUDGMENT

Before the Court are the parties' competing motions for summary judgment regarding the constitutional propriety of Riverside County Sheriff Deputy David Elden Smith's warrantless entry into the front courtyard of the plaintiffs' residence during the early morning hours of August 5, 2000. For the reasons set forth below, defendants' motion for summary judgment is DENIED, and plaintiffs' motion for summary judgment is GRANTED.

I. STANDARD FOR EVALUATING MOTIONS FOR SUMMARY JUDGMENT

Summary judgment is proper only where "the pleadings, depositions, answers to interrogatories, and admissions on file, together with the affidavits, if any, show that there is no genuine issue as to any material fact and that the moving party is entitled to judgment as a matter of law." FED. R. CIV. P. 56(c); see also Matsushita Elec. Indus. Co. v. Zenith Radio Corp., 475 U.S. 574, 106 S. Ct. 1348, 89 L. Ed. 2d 538 (1986). The moving party bears the initial burden of demonstrating the absence of a genuine issue of material fact. See Anderson v. Liberty Lobby, Inc., 477 U.S. 242, 256, 106 S. Ct. 2505, 91 L. Ed. 2d 202 (1986). Whether a fact is material is determined by looking to the governing substantive law; if the fact may affect the outcome, then it is material. Id. at 248. Moreover, in construing all the evidence in the record and the reasonable inferences that can be drawn therefrom, the Court must defer in favor of the non-moving party. See id. at 255; Brookside Assocs. v. Rifkin, 49 F.3d 490, 492-93 (9th Cir. 1995).

II. FACTS

Many of the facts in this case have been set forth earlier in this Court's April 20, 2005, Order, and are well-known to the parties. The Court will accordingly confine its discussion to those facts which provide a general overview of what precipitated Deputy Smith's presence at the Madruga residence on the night in question and those particular facts which provide an account of Deputy Smith's entry into the Madrugas' property.

Michael Madruga sideswiped a car driven by Buffy Paveloff as Madruga was driving the wrong way in a parking lot at 10 o'clock at night on August 4, 2000. A heated argument ensued between the two over Paveloff's request for Madruga to provide her with his "information." The dispute ended abruptly after Paveloff accused Madruga of being under the influence of alcohol and sent her husband to call the police. Madruga flung his checkbook at Paveloff and fled away from the scene on foot.

When Riverside County Sheriff's Deputy John F. Clark arrived at the scene of the accident, Paveloff informed him that Madruga refused to provide his "information" to her and that Madruga became argumentative with her after she made the request. Deputy Clark reviewed the information contained in the checkbook Madruga left behind and also determined that the car that was left behind in the parking lot was in fact registered to Madruga. Deputy Clark went to Madruga's house in La Quinta, California, just after midnight and spoke with Madruga's wife, Catherine. She informed him that her husband was still out. Deputy Clark informed Mrs. Madruga that her husband was involved in a hit-and-run collision, that her husband left the scene, and asked Mrs. Madruga to give him a call when her husband came home, "because I want[] to talk to him about the crash."

Shortly after one o'clock in the morning, Deputy Clark was advised that Madruga returned to his home. Deputy Clark asked Deputy Smith, who was on patrol in La Quinta at the time, to proceed to Madruga's residence and to detain Madruga until Deputy Clark was able to get to the scene. Deputy Clark later explained that by "detain" he simply meant he wanted Deputy Smith to "just stand by with him [Madruga], that I just wanted to talk to him," and "the reason for detaining him was to make sure he wasn't at home pounding down beers before I got there."

This purpose for his presence at the residence, however, was not relayed to Deputy Smith. Indeed, while en route to Madruga's residence, Deputy Smith sent a message on the mobile data terminal inside his patrol vehicle, asking Deputy Clark to "confirm detained as in handcuffed or just sit with him," but no reply was ever tendered in response. Deputy Smith later gave the following account during the criminal prosecution of Madruga of what he believed his purpose was when he arrived at the Madruga residence that night:

Q. When you got to that address and got out of your patrol car, what was your purpose for being there?

A. To contact and detain a subject reference [in] an earlier traffic collision that he left the scene of.

Q. And by "contact and detain," could you please tell the jury exactly what you mean by "contact and detain"?

A. My -- my goal was to go contact the subject that was described to me as Michael Madruga, who lived at that address. The deputy asked that I detain him for further questioning and possibly -- I believe he wanted to take photographs and fingerprints of him at the Palm Desert [sheriff's] station. So therefore I would go and detain him and hold him for the other officer so he would not flee the scene again.

. . .

Q. And by detaining him, you meant physically restrain him, is that right?

A. I could detain him by talking to him, placing him in the back of my unit. I could detain him by placing handcuffs on him. Whatever at the scene seemed necessary.

Deputy Smith further explained that it was his understanding that he was told to detain Madruga because Madruga committed a crime: "I was -- I was told that the crime had been committed, and under good faith I went to detain him," and "I was requested by Deputy Clark . . . to contact the suspect of a 2002 V.C. [Vehicle Code] . . . and detain him." [1]

When Deputy Smith arrived in front of the Madruga residence it was just a little bit past one in the morning. There were no street lights illuminating the area. Deputy Smith parked his patrol car across the street from the Madruga residence, stepped out of his cruiser, and retrieved a flashlight.

The entire residence -- a single story, 1397 square-foot home -- is enclosed by a five-foot, four-inches tall solid wall composed of cinder block and plastered with stucco, with intermittent stretches made of large wooden planks with narrow slats between the planks. The wall increases in height at the point where it runs parallel to the side yard to the home. Moreover, when it reaches the side-yard, the wall lies but a few feet away from the house proper. The part of the wall enclosing the front of the house had two, solid, wooden gates (also five-foot, four-inches tall), one for foot traffic and the other fronting the entire driveway. Upon the upper right corner of the wooden gate blocking access to the driveway was a large yellow sign with the word "WARNING" written in large letters against a

---

[1] The code section referenced by Deputy Smith requires a driver involved in an accident to provide, "upon request," a copy of "his-driver's license and vehicle registration" before leaving the scene of the accident. CAL. VEH. CODE § 20002 (a) (1).

red background, and beneath that word a picture of a Doberman pincher and a German shepherd with the words "Guard Dogs." The wooden gate fronting the driveway was only a few feet from the wooden gate foot traffic used. Moreover, the "WARNING Guard Dogs" sign was affixed on the portion of the driveway gate that was closest to the foot-traffic gate.

With respect to the front of the house, the block wall runs parallel with the house and is built seventeen feet in front of the house proper. "There are no sidewalks running along the exterior of the solid wall," save in front of the wooden gates; instead a planter bed with low-growing vegetation bordered the wall. Between the wall and the front of the house proper is a courtyard that is used for events such as family barbeques, gatherings, or to simply sit outside and read a book or newspaper. The nature of the wall, both in terms of its dimensions and the materials of which it is composed, is such as to completely shield from public view any activities taking place in the interior courtyard. (See Addendum to Opinion containing Pl's Exhibits 16 & 68 representing photographs of the front of the residence).

The gas and electric meters for the home are located in the courtyard. Utility servicemen stand on the outside of the block wall and extend a long pole over the top of the wall and read the meter with a mirror; they do not enter into the courtyard itself or climb the wall and peer over. The mailbox for the home is located across the street from the house near where Deputy Smith parked his patrol car that night.

"Both gates are always kept closed unless they have to be opened to walk or drive through," and were so closed on the night in question. The wooden gate for foot traffic had a door knob and a deadbolt, either of which could be locked independently of the other, but both of which were left unlocked on the night in question. Immediately next to the front wooden gate for foot traffic, the Madrugas normally kept a handbell either on top of the block wall or attached to the front doorhandle itself to allow visitors and others a means of announcing their presence and seeking permission to enter into the courtyard. On the door knob on the inside of the gate door the Madrugas kept a jingle bell which would sound as a person passed through the gate into the courtyard. On the night in question, however, the Madrugas are unsure whether the handbell was in its designated location or whether it fell into the planter bed beside the gate. They are, however, sure, and there is no contrary evidence, that the jingle bell was affixed to the interior door knob that evening.

When he arrived at Madruga's residence, Deputy Smith, who did not have a warrant, opened the unlocked wooden foot traffic gate, entered the courtyard, proceeded to the home's front door, opened the front exterior metal screen door, and knocked on the front interior wooden door with his flashlight. Deputy Smith asserts that he did not see the guard dog sign or hear or see a bell -- be it a handbell or a jingle bell -- when entering through the front gate into the courtyard. He did notice, however, that a porch light next to the front door to the home was illuminated.

Madruga came to the door and Deputy Smith asked him if he would come outside to talk with him. Madruga refused. Deputy Smith again asked if Madruga would come outside to talk. Madruga crossed his arms and in a loud voice refused Deputy Smith's request. At that point Deputy Smith later stated, "You could tell [Madruga] . . . didn't really want to talk." Notwithstanding his clear understanding that Madruga did not want to speak with him, Deputy Smith asked a third time whether Madruga would talk to him. When pressed why he continued to seek a tete-a-tete with Madruga even after his earlier refusals made clear his wish not to talk, Deputy Smith admitted it simply was a means on his part "to keep an eye on [Madruga] at all times." Madruga refused Deputy Smith's third request to talk, locked the front screen door, and walked away from the door and toward the kitchen area.

Mrs. Madruga was standing nearby. Deputy Smith asked her if he could come inside and she agreed, unlocking the screen door and opening it for him. The time from when he first knocked on the door until Mrs. Madruga admitted him inside the home was about a minute and a half. Not long after entering the home, Deputy Smith walked up to Madruga and grabbed his right hand. A melee quickly ensued, leading to Deputy Smith spraying Madruga (and perhaps, accidentally, Mrs. Madruga) with pepper spray and striking Madruga with his baton, and ending with Madruga in handcuffs and under arrest.

A few days later some sheriff's deputies paid a visit to the Madruga residence. Those deputies announced their arrival by calling out to those inside the home from the other side of the block wall, seeking their attention. Before receiving admittance they did not fling open the wooden gate, walk through the courtyard, or knock on the home's front door.

III. ANALYSIS

The only Fourth Amendment challenge at issue in the instant competing motions is Deputy Smith's entry into and continued presence in the front courtyard before being admitted inside the Madrugas' home. The Madrugas asserts that Deputy Smith's warrantless entry into the front courtyard through the front wooden gate on the perimeter of their home violated the Fourth Amendment, as the block wall/wooden gates demarked the boundaries of the curtilage to their home and, therefore, the area just inside the same -- the courtyard -- was cloaked in the same protections against unreasonable searches and seizures as are afforded to their home itself.

The Fourth Amendment protects the rights of "people to be secure in their persons, houses, papers, and effects" from unreasonable searches and seizures. U.S. CONST. amend. IV. "[T]he protective force of the fourth amendment [is no] more powerful than it is when the sanctity of the home is involved." Los Angeles Police Protective League v. Gates, 907 F.2d 879, 884 (9th Cir. 1990). That a person's home is the one place most resolutely protected under the Fourth Amendment arises from a view, as old as the common law, that "[t]he house of every one is to him as his castle and fortress, as well for his defence against injury and violence, as for his repose." Wilson v. Layne, 526 U.S. 603, 609-10, 119 S. Ct. 1692, 143 L. Ed. 2d 818 (1999)(quoting Semayne's Case, (1604) 77 Eng. Rep: 194, 195 (K.B.)); see also 4 WILLIAM BLACKSTONE, COMMENTARIES *223 ("the law of England has so particular and tender a regard to the immunity of a man's house, that it stiles it his castle, and will never suffer it to be violated with impunity"). A home stands as the one place, and perhaps the final place, to where a person can retreat and seclude themself from the rest of the world free from intrusion, interference or surveillance, by the government or by others. See Boyd v. United States, 116 U.S. 616, 630, 6 S. Ct. 524, 29 L. Ed. 746 (1886)(speaking of "the sanctity of a man's home and the privacies of life"); Silverman v. United States, 365 U.S. 505, 511, 81 S. Ct. 679, 5 L. Ed. 2d 734 (1961)("At the very core stands the right of a man to retreat into his own home and there be free from unreasonable governmental intrusion"); Katz v. United States, 389 U.S. 347, 361, 88 S. Ct. 507, 19 L. Ed. 2d 576 (1967)("a man's home is, for most purposes, a place where he expects privacy")(Harlan, J., concurring); Gates, 907 F.2d at 884 ("The sanctity of a person's home, perhaps our last real retreat in this technological age, lies at the very core of the rights which animate the amendment"); United States v. On Lee, 193 F.2d 306, 315-16 (2nd Cir. 1951)(Frank, J., dissenting)("A man can still control a small part of his environment, his house; he can retreat thence from outsiders, secure in the knowledge that they cannot get at him without disobeying the Constitution. . . . [s]ociety must provide some such oasis, some shelter from public scrutiny . . . some inviolate place -- which is a man's castle").

The protections the Fourth Amendment affords to a person's home do not stop at the home's walls, doors, and windows, but extend to the curtilage of the house as well. See Oliver v. United States, 466 U.S. 170, 104 S. Ct. 1735, 80 L. Ed. 2d 214 (1984). The curtilage was a concept devised under the common law to distinguish between petty and menacing trespass to a person's property. "In the common law of England the curtilage was the part of a person's property that a criminal had to break into in order to be guilty of burglary. Since burglary was a capital offense, there was a felt need to confine it to the most alarming forms of breaking and entering." United States v. Redmon, 138 F.3d 1109, 1130 (7th Cir. 1998)(Posner, C.J., dissenting).

The curtilage, as distinguished from "open fields," thus understood has since been invoked to describe the "area intimately linked to the home, both physically and psychologically," California v. Ciraolo, 476 U.S. 207, 212-13, 106 S. Ct. 1809, 90 L. Ed. 2d 210 (1986), and against which intrusion from governmental agents, much like the burglars of old, is sought to curb.

Aside from these abstractions concerning the evil against which the curtilage sought to protect against under the common law, the term was also given a more concrete definition. "The word curtilage is derived from the Latin cohors (a place enclosed around a yard) and the old French cortilliage or courtillage which today has been corrupted into courtyard. Originally it referred to the land and outbuildings immediately adjacent to a castle that were in turn surrounded by a high stone wall. Today its meaning has been expanded to include any land or building immediately adjacent to a dwelling. Usually it is enclosed some way by fence or shrubs." United States v. Romano, 388 F. Supp. 101, 105 n.4 (E.D. Pa. 1975). One noted jurist explained the meaning of a home's curtilage as follows:

[T]he constitutional boundaries of the home are somewhat larger than the walls of the house; they include the curtilage, that area to which extends the intimate activity associated with the sanctity of a man's home and the privacies of life. The concept arises out of the common law, which viewed a man's home as his castle of defence. The curtilage included not only the castle walls, but also those turrets, moats and baileys that adjoined the residence and whose breach the owner would regard as a violation of the security of the home. At the same time, no distant barn, warehouse, or the like, are under the same privileges. When we consider modern homes, we might include within the curtilage an adjoining garage, the yard within the white picket fence, or the gazebo where the kids keep their pool toys. The real question is whether the home owner might reasonably regard those structures as part and parcel of the home itself.

United States v. Johnson, 256 F.3d 895, 911 (9th Cir. 2001) (en banc)(Kozinski, J., concurring).

The initial question thus becomes whether the courtyard to the Madrugas' home was part of the home's curtilage. If not, then Deputy Smith's entry upon it does not run afoul of the Fourth Amendment. See Oliver, 466 U.S. at 180 ("only the curtilage, not the neighboring open fields, warrants the Fourth Amendment protections that attach to the home").

The Supreme Court in United States v. Dunn, 480 U.S. 294, 301, 107 S. Ct. 1134, 94 L. Ed. 2d 326 (1987), identified four factors for courts to consult in determining whether the homeowner may reasonably regard the area in question as "part and parcel of the home itself": (1) The proximity of the area to the home; (2) whether the area is included within an enclosure surrounding the home; (3) the nature of the uses to which the area is put; and (4) the steps taken by the resident to protect the area from observation by people passing by. These four considerations, however, are just that: Simple guideposts. They are not to be "mechanically applied," nor do they yield a definite answer, but are merely meant as "useful analytical tools" to consult in deciding "whether the area is so intimately connected to the home that it should fall under the umbrella of the Fourth Amendment's protections." Johnson, 256 F.3d at 901, 911.

Consulting these four factors, the Court finds that it cannot be seriously questioned that the front courtyard to the Madrugas' home fell within the home's curtilage. The courtyard was immediately adjacent to the home, it was completely surrounded by a five-foot, four-inches tall solid wall that shielded the courtyard from public view, there was a "WARNING guard dog" sign posted a few feet from the wooden foot traffic gate, the two solid wooden gates (themselves over five-feet tall) that provided access to the courtyard and driveway had two separate locks and were in fact closed (if not locked) at the time of the entry in question, and the courtyard itself was used for activities intimately associated with those that take place inside the house itself such as barbeques, parties, or as an area of quiet contemplation.

That the courtyard is part of the curtilage to the Madrugas' home and, hence, deserving of Fourth Amendment protection does not mean that limits on access to the home and the courtyard are co-extensive. Access to one's home is strictly forbidden absent a warrant or exigent circumstances. See Payton v. New York, 445 U.S. 573, 590, 100 S. Ct. 1371, 63 L. Ed. 2d 639 (1980). Encroachment upon the curtilage, however, is viewed more pragmatically than categorically. Much of this stems from the varying uses to which a home's curtilege can be put, as well as to the fact that, more often then not, such areas are located outdoors leaving the possibility that others can see what is going on and are regularly trodden upon by individuals other than the homeowner. These considerations tend to diminish the expectation of privacy and, accordingly, provide less of a Fourth Amendment impediment to entry than is true for one's home.

It is precisely this malleability that Deputy Smith seeks to exploit in this case, arguing that his crossing through the courtyard falls within the implied invitation exception to intrusions upon a home's curtilage as he was simply seeking to talk with Madruga. The exception he invokes basically seeks to exclude from Fourth Amendment protection those causeways, sidewalks, and other access routes postmen, visitors, and salespersons take to and from the home's entrances to speak to the home's occupants. If a homeowner allows visitors and other third parties to use those routes to speak to them, then there is no constitutional basis to place law enforcement officers who seek to use those same means of egress and ingress over the curtilage to speak to the home's occupants in a different position. See Redmon, 138 F.3d at 1130 (Posner, C.J., dissenting)("Most homeowners extend an implicit invitation to social and business invitees to walk up to the front door"). It is not the identity of the visitor that is determinative, but the homeowner's expectation of privacy. The likelihood of such entry over the curtilage negates any expectation of privacy the homeowner may have regardless of the identity of the person making the entry. With this understanding, law enforcement has developed an investigative technique known as the "knock and talk" to use when officers do not have a warrant on hand to enter a home. As one court explained the technique:

[T]he police approach a house or apartment in which they suspect [criminal activity] is occurring. They listen outside the door for a brief period of time, and then they knock on the door and attempt to persuade whoever answers to give them permission to enter. If consent is forthcoming, they enter and interview the occupants of the place; if it is not, they try to see from their vantage point at the door whether [any indicia of criminal activity] is in plain view. If it is, then they make a warrantless entry. As this description makes plain, the knock and talk' procedure typically does not involve the prior issuance of a warrant.

United States v. Johnson, 170 F.3d 708, 711 (7th Cir. 1999).

Simply stating post facto that an officer's entry was part of a "knock and talk" is insufficient to justify the intrusion. The knock and talk rule has limits. See id. at 720 ("the police themselves must recognize the inherent limits in this more informal way of proceeding"). Key to the legitimate invocation of the knock and talk technique are two factors that reasonable police officers are expected to recognize: The purpose for which the officers undertake such an intrusion into the curtilage; and whether the homeowner took any actions to express a higher expectation of privacy over the means of egress and ingress to his home than is ordinarily the case. Is the officer there to ask questions of or otherwise talk to the occupants as any ordinary citizen would, or does the officer's purpose for being there have a much more narrow law enforcement objective -- to search the curtilage or otherwise intrude upon it in order to arrest the occupant? If the latter, then the knock and talk exception does not apply. As the Ninth Circuit noted long ago:

Absent express orders from the person in possession against any possible trespass, there is no rule of private or public conduct which makes it illegal per se, or a condemned invasion of the person's right of privacy, for anyone openly and peaceably, at high noon, to walk up the steps and knock on the front door of any man's castle' with the honest intent of asking questions of the occupant thereof -- whether the questioner be a pollster, a salesman, or an officer of the law.

Davis v. United States, 327 F.2d 301, 303 (9th Cir. 1964)(emphasis added); see also Redmon, 138 F.3d at 1130 (Posner, C.J., dissenting)("in doing so the homeowner does not, as it were, waive curtilage.' The social and business invitee, including a police officer whether invited or uninvited, must confine himself to the prescribed route, rather than treating the invitation as one to roam the property at will, peering into the windows of the home").

Neither consideration supports Deputy Smith's reliance on the knock and talk technique in this case. First, unlike a salesperson or pollster, he did not enter the curtilage to the Madrugas' home with "the honest intent of asking questions," but rather to "detain" Madruga. Second, it is clear that the Madrugas did in fact take measures to keep sales representatives and other such social and business invitees from being able to walk up to their front door, knock, and attempt to talk to them unannounced. Given the measures the Madrugas took to ward off entry by such uninvited third parties, it should have similarly been clear to Deputy Smith that the generally understood implied invitation to walk up to the front of the home and talk to the home's occupants was revoked.

1. Intent

Here it is undisputed that, when Deputy Smith walked through the curtilage to the Madrugas' residence, he did so with the intent to detain Madruga, not for the purpose of conversing. Deputy Smith candidly admitted that his efforts to engage Madruga in conversation through the front screen door were nothing but a ruse on his part to keep Madruga pinned inside the home and unable "to flee" until Deputy Clark arrived. If his efforts at talking to Madruga did not avert Madruga from attempting to leave his home, Deputy Smith made it clear that he would have placed Madruga in handcuffs and/or put him in the back of his patrol car until Deputy Clark arrived. Such an intent to detain is altogether at odds with the rationale for the knock and talk exception -- allowing law enforcement the same visitation privileges homeowners extend to third parties who wish to engage in a bona fide conversation with them. Deputy Smith did not want to talk, he wanted to detain. The same cannot be said of other persons who use the same causeways to and from the home's front door, be they salespersons, trick-or-treaters, or deliverymen. In each instance, the intent of the third party is to briefly speak with the occupant in the hopes of making a sale, receiving candy, or handing over a package; it is not to keep the occupant from being able to leave his or her home.

Deputy Smith claims that the law is unsettled as to whether the knock and talk exception is inapplicable to situations where police officers use a home's ordinary causeways when they have no intent to talk but only an intent to detain or arrest a home's occupants. Not so. To begin, the court's announcement of the knock and talk exception in Davis -- over 40 years ago -- made clear that it applied only when the officer had "the honest intent of asking questions." 327 F.2d at 303. The message from the court's reference to "honest intent" is clear and unambiguous: The exception is limited to only those situations where a law enforcement official was genuinely seeking to do something that the homeowners allowed other third parties to do -- approach the home to talk to the occupants. Here, Deputy Smith had no such honest intent on his part. Rather, his expressions of seeking to talk to the Madrugas was a ruse designed to detain Mr. Madruga for however long it was necessary. This intent is borne out by Deputy Smith continuing to speak to Madruga even after it became apparent that Madruga did not wish to speak to him. Even the most persistent salesperson would not continue to make a sales pitch after a homeowner rebuked him three times, locked the door, and walked away from him.

Putting to rest any ambiguity on this point, two paragraphs after the sentence announcing the court's holding in Davis, the Ninth Circuit distinguished the circumstances giving rise to the knock and talk exception from those "wherein the intent of the several officers at the time of their entry on the premises without possessing a legal warrant for search or arrest, was actually either to arrest without warrant or search without warrant." Id. at 304 (emphasis added); see also United States v. Ochoa-Almanza, 623 F.2d 676, 677 (10th Cir. 1980)(making the same distinction that the implied invitation exception is inapplicable to situations where the officers possessed an intent to search or arrest the home occupants). Deputy Smith's actual intent in this case was plain and unambiguous -- to "hold" Madruga by whatever means necessary, be it by a feigned conversation, handcuffs, or placement in the back of the patrol car, "so he would not flee the scene again" until "the other officer" arrived. Deputy Smith's candor as to his actual purpose lays bare any assertion on his part that he believed the knock and talk exception somehow sanctioned his intrusion into the courtyard.

That Deputy Smith did not seek to arrest Madruga but rather sought to detain him is irrelevant, as in either instance the officer's entry upon the curtilage had a purpose that would normally require some showing -- be it probable cause for an arrest or reasonable suspicion for a detention -- to justify the officer's encroachment upon the curtilage, see United States v. Charley, 396 F.3d 1074, 1079 (9th Cir.2005)("not every detention by law enforcement officials amounts to arrest or custody under the Fourth Amendment. Arrests and detentions are both seizures' under the Fourth

Amendment, . . . the former requires a showing of probable cause, while the latter can be justified by reasonable suspicion of criminal activity"), something which is not needed if the officer is simply there to knock and talk. See United States v. Cormier, 220 F.3d 1103, 1109 (9th Cir. 2000)("no suspicion needed to be shown in order to justify the knock and talk'"). Moreover, it seems apparent to this Court that Deputy Smith's "detention" of Madruga was but a prelude to the arrival of Deputy Clark, who would formally arrest Madruga. Deputy Smith himself admitted that Deputy Clark wished to have Madruga "detained" so Deputy Clark could "fingerprint" him and "take him down to the police station." Fingerprinting and taking a suspect down to the stationhouse are reserved for instances when someone is under arrest, not simply stopped or detained. In any event, Deputy Smith's intent when he approached the Madrugas' home on the night in question ran far afield from that Davis contemplated in announcing the knock and talk rule.

Given that Deputy Smith did not have "an honest intent of asking questions," but instead the intent to detain Madruga by restraining his freedom of movement, the implied invitation exception does not apply in this case.

2. Enhanced Curtilage

The knock and talk rule is grounded on the understanding that the curtilage over which an officer is intruding to gain access to the home's front door is open to the public to use. See Redmon, 138 F.3d at 1130 (Posner, C.J., dissenting)("Most homeowners extend an implicit invitation to social and business invitees to walk up to the front door"). Davis, however, recognized that in some instances this assumption may prove untrue, specifically when a homeowner has taken additional measures to impede or otherwise block access to the front door by the viewing public. 327 F.2d at 303 (noting that knock and talk inappropriate when there exists "express orders from the person in possession against any possible trespass"). In those instances, Davis recognized that the privacy enhancement made to the curtilage by the homeowner would serve to apprise the officer, as it would any would-be salesperson, that access to the home's front door would require the homeowner's pre-approval. Id.

The measures taken by the Madrugas in enclosing and secreting from view the courtyard to their home were such as to express a clear intent to exclude uninvited visitors to keep away. The imposing edifice of the five-foot, four-inch high block wall, the corresponding closed and high solid wooden gates in front of the driveway and the courtyard proper, and the "WARNING Guard Dogs" sign all communicated quite explicitly to any would-be salesperson that it was not business as usual in attempting to approach the home's front door. By taking these measures the Madrugas could reasonably expect all such visits to cease when they have expressed their intent to exclude strangers by sealing the property around their home and posting a "WARNING Guard Dogs" sign. Indeed this clear sentiment was observed and readily understood by utility workers who did not enter into the couple's courtyard, but instead used a long pole with a mirror to read the utility meters located in the courtyard.

The block wall in this case is a far cry from the stereotypical white picket fence Hollywood movie studios have portrayed to the viewing public as surrounding the typical American suburban home. Here it stands nearly six-feet tall, necessitating individuals to climb up on or otherwise find some means to look into the courtyard as it is effectively shielded from human eyes. Such blockage of sight from a person walking along the street extends even to the home's driveway. The two gates similarly operate to obfuscate the courtyard from view. They are made out of solid wood with thin slats that are as tall as the block wall itself. Simply put, the curtilage to the Madrugas' home is more on a par with the moat and castle walls of old than the white picket fences of modern times. Compare with United States v. Baldwin, 691 F.2d 718, 722 (5th Cir. 1982)(terming "the dilapidated fence [the officers] had traversed was regarded as no more than a barrier designed to keep the hogs in, not to keep anyone out,' and hence could not be characterized as a privacy or exclusionary fence"). Such extensive measures to shield the area from view are not merely an attempt at landscape design or aesthetics, but clearly serve the practical purpose of conveying an obvious message to any who happen upon it: Keep away, this area is private, and it is not for you to look at, pry into, or, much less, walk through unannounced and uninvited.

If the size and scope of the wall surrounding the courtyard did not impress this message upon the viewer, the posting of the "WARNING guard dog" sign on the wooden driveway gate just a few feet away from the wooden foot traffic gate -- and within view of any reasonable person walking through the wooden foot traffic gate even at night (see Addendum Pl's Exhibit 68) -- would reasonably dispel any doubt. Other courts have found that the use of similar signs convey this message. See, e.g., People v. Mendoza, 122 Cal. App. 3d Supp. 12, 14, 176 Cal. Rptr. 293 (1981) (noting that where there is "a locked gate, a high solid fence blocking the front yard from view, a written notice to keep out or beware of dog, or perhaps a doorbell at the front gate," it would be understood by "anyone having reason to talk to the residents" that they could not simply "open the front gate" and proceed to the front door (emphasis added)); State v. Poulos, 149 Or.App. 351, 356-57, 942 P.2d 901 (1997)(placement of no trespassing sign and beware dog sign, even in the absence of a gate, fence or barrier, was enough to apprise "even the customary casual visitor [they] would [not] be welcome on defendant's property"). Defendants' attempt to cast doubt on the significance of this sign because it did not contain the words "No Trespassing" or "Keep Away" is divorced from reality and elevates form over substance: Common sense and common experiences teaches us that such "WARNING Guard Dog" signs are placed to dissuade people, be they intruders, sales representatives, delivery agents, or even police officers, from approaching the home. Such signs are meant as a warning to potential visitors that entry is dangerous, as they may be mauled by a dog if they approach unannounced.[2] Making threats to one's life and limb clearly illustrates a homeowner's effort to communicate to uninvited guests to stay away. Simply put, anyone seeing such a sign would understand that the homeowner seeks to exclude them from entering the area beyond the sign.[3]

In effect, the various measures taken by the Madrugas to seclude the courtyard from public attention effectively transformed the courtyard into the home's foyer or antechamber. That this message of exclusion and expression against entry into the courtyard was obvious to those who saw it, one need look no further than the actions of the sheriff deputies who arrived at the Madruga residence a few days after the incident in question. Those deputies did not contact the Madrugas by opening the wooden gate, walking through the courtyard, and knocking on the front door as Deputy Smith had done. Instead, those deputies called out to the Madrugas from the other side of the block wall, seeking their attention.

The Court finds that these circumstances are such an instance of an express command against unannounced entry into the home's curtilage to approach the front door for purposes of asking questions or making sales pitches. None of the cases cited by defendants alter the Court's conclusion.

The case of United States v. Hammett, 236 F.3d 1054 (9th Cir. 2001), pressed by defense counsel at the hearing herein, is readily distinguishable. There agents were surveilling the Hawaiian countryside by helicopter for marijuana plants growing amongst the lush flora and fauna when they spotted a home that had "a distinct green color beneath the translucent

---

[2] Defendants make much of the fact that the Madrugas did not, at the time, own any guard dogs in the true sense of the word, but instead only had a three-legged chihuahua and a **cocker spaniel**/poodle mix. Aside from the danger of underestimating any **cocker spaniel**, the breed of the dogs owned by the Madrugas is irrelevant to the issue in this case. What is relevant is that the Madrugas took steps to communicate to the public that they could not simply walk up to their front door unannounced, not whether they would have been able to carry through with the threat such a sign conveys to the viewer.

[3] To make sure that Spanish-only speaking visitors would also understand this message, the Madrugas posted a Guard Dog sign in Spanish on an interior fence located at the back of the driveway.

roof" of the home. Such markers raised suspicions of whether or not drug activity was afoot at the home. An unimproved dirt road leading to the front of the house, provided access to the only door to the home. At the entrance to the dirt road was a sign prohibiting trespassing, and two steel poles connected by a chain. Moreover, the property boundaries to the home were not marked or enclosed with a fence. The agents landed the helicopter in an open field approximately 150 yards from the side of the home, marched through the open field to the front of the home, and knocked on the door seeking to talk to the home's occupants. By taking this path the officers never crossed the dirt road, nor saw the no trespassing sign or the chained posts barring entry onto the dirt road leading to the home. When no one responded, the agents proceeded to circle to the rear of the house, knocking on the walls to the home as they did so in an effort to rouse anyone who may be inside. As they did so, one of the officers noticed a small crack in the side of the house and, from that vantage point, observed three marijuana plants growing inside the home. The homeowner later complained that the officers' approach to the home's front door was an unlawful encroachment upon the home's curtilage. 236 F.3d at 1056-57.

The Ninth Circuit disagreed, noting that officers may approach a home through its curtilage when it is done "for the purpose of asking questions of the occupants." Id. at 1059. As for the officers circling to the rear of the home, the court observed that "there is nothing unlawful or unreasonable about going to the back of the house to look for another door, all as part of a legitimate attempt to interview a person." Id. at 1060. With respect to the no trespassing sign, the court dismissed the significance of such signage by noting that the photographic evidence submitted clearly indicated that the officers would not have seen the sign from where they entered the property. Id. The court also dismissed the suggestion that the officers deliberately took a path in order to avoid seeing the sign as being similarly dispelled by the photographic evidence, which "clearly illustrate that the area where the officers set the helicopter down was the closest open area to [the] home and, as such, offered a logical landing site." Id.

Here, however, Deputy Smith did not enter into the home's curtilage for the purpose of asking questions, but to detain Mr. Madruga. Moreover, the efforts at excluding entry into the courtyard -- a large, solid block wall and accompanying large-sized solid wood gates -- were far removed -- even to the casual observer -- from the open fields surrounding the home in Hammett. Moreover, the photographic evidence submitted to the Court in this case, unlike in Hammett, also clearly depicts the "WARNING Guard Dog" sign as being prominently posted within a few feet of the wooden foot traffic door that Deputy Smith used to gain entry into the courtyard. His path, unlike the officers in Hammett, took him within viewing distance from the sign.

The other cases to which defendants cite are similarly distinguishable. They either did not involve a fence, be it solid or otherwise, obscuring from view the access route in question and/or did not have signs prominently displayed on the property evincing the homeowner's intent for others to keep away. See, e.g., United States v. Roberts, 747 F.2d 537, 540-42 (9th Cir. 1984)(upheld police entry upon road that had signs marked "Private Road Keep Out," "No Hunting," "No Trespassing" alongside the road; court noted that road in question was shared "with residents of five other houses" something which "is incongruent with the common law concept of curtilage," that "[t]he private road does not provide the setting for intimate activities of home life," and that "the road is easily accessible to utility companies," thereby negating any inference conveyed by the signs that the "private road [was] an area for protected intimate activities"); Palmieri v. Lynch, 392 F.3d 73, 75-76, 82 (2nd Cir. 2004)(entry into backyard of home was upheld even though there was "stockade fencing" that "completely encloses the side and rear [side] area of the property physically" and the gate allowing entry to the rear through the side yard had affixed to it a sign with the words "PRIVATE PROPERTY -- NO TRESPASSING" and another sign with the words "Beware of Dog"; court noted that, despite stockade fencing of the side to the property, the back of the property did not have similar fencing and was completely exposed to public view as it abutted a harbor where boatgoers could see unhindered what was going on in the backyard, and the fence itself was not high enough to block views of the backyard from neighbors' property, hence homeowner's privacy interest in backyard was "severely diminished"); United States v. Hatfield, 333 F.3d 1189, 1194 (10th Cir. 2003)(finding that officers parking their patrol car upon driveway and walking about on concrete parking pad was not violative of home's curtilage as "driveway was open to the public," a point which court termed "an important factor"; no indication of any signs posted in front of the driveway or that the driveway was enclosed or otherwise access to the same was blocked from the public); United States v. Bradshaw, 490 F.2d 1097 (4th Cir. 1974)(no mention of any enclosures or signs); United States v. Titemore, 335 F.Supp.2d 502, 504-06 (D. Vt. 2004)(curtilage enclosed by a "rail fence along . . . [r]oad that partially restricts access to [home's] porch," but is "essentially decorative"; porch "area was not enclosed or blocked from public view" despite fence and "[t]here were no signs restricting access to the porch in any way"); United States v. Gonzales-Barrera, 288 F.Supp.2d 1041 (D. Ariz. 2003)(no discussion of any signs excluding entrance or barriers (be it fences, gate, etc.,) to entry upon the causeways to the home's front door); United States v. Barrera-Martinez, 274 F.Supp.2d 950, 958-59 (N.D. Ill. 2003)(entry onto cement apron in front of an apartment's garage was upheld as "the apron . . . could easily be observed from the alley"; again no mention of signs or fences).

Indeed, in some of the cases cited by defendants the court made no mention of the knock and talk rule at all, but instead held the area intruded upon by the officers was part of the open fields surrounding the home -- an area not even protected by the Fourth Amendment -- and not part of the home's curtilage. See United States v. Baldwin, 691 F.2d 718, 720 (5th Cir. 1982)(upholding officer's viewing of a metal shed behind a house in the country as being part of the open fields to the home, not home's curtilage; the shed was surrounded by a "three feet high [fence] that was constructed of chicken wire and slatboard" and officer went to the edge of the fence and peered from that vantage point the activities inside the shed); United States v. Pace, 955 F.2d 270, 272-73 (5th Cir. 1992)(viewing the inside of a barn through a hole in the wall was upheld as barn was part of the 3 to 4 acres of open fields surrounding home, and not home's curtilage, even if the entire property was "surrounded by a fence . . . constructed of hog wire' topped with several strands of barbed wire . . . [and] approximately four feet high" and with a closed gate with a lock and chain and a "Beware of Dog" sign).

Finally, one of the cases cited by defendants actually buttresses the Court's conclusion that the measures taken by the Madrugas apprised the public of their desire to keep uninvited guests who wished to speak to them out of their courtyard. In Edens v. Kennedy, 112 Fed.Appx. 870 (4th Cir. 2004), an unpublished opinion by the Fourth Circuit, the home was surrounded on three sides by a fence and on the fourth side by dense vegetation. The gate to the fence was "kept locked, and the fencepost next to the gate [wa]s marked with a . . . No Trespassing' sign." Id. at 872. The fence, however, did not "obscure the view of the home from the road . . . because its rails are separated by wide gaps." Id. Moreover, there was "a gap approximately four feet wide between the fence and woods; this gap is near the road that runs in front of . . . home." Id. at 873. The officers walked through this gap unannounced in an effort to talk to the home's occupants. The Fourth Circuit held that, despite this gap in the enclosure, the officer's entry violated the Fourth Amendment as the homeowner's enclosing the curtilage with a fence, locking the gate to the fence, and posting of a No Trespassing sign communicated an intent to exclude uninvited strangers from approaching their front door. Id. at 875. "The effect for Fourth Amendment purposes [was] to extend the walls of the home to the edge of the curtilage. This is because the act of sealing the property creates an elevated expectation of privacy" on the par with being inside the home itself. Id. The same is true here.

3. Qualified Immunity

#***#

Accordingly, the Court finds that Deputy Smith's intrusion into the home's curtilage violated the Fourth Amendment. The defendants' motion for summary judgment is therefore DENIED and plaintiffs' motion for summary judgment is GRANTED insofar as it relates to Deputy Smith unlawful entry into the curtliage to the home.

IT IS SO ORDERED.

Date: November 22, 2005
STEPHEN G. LARSON
UNITED STATES MAGISTRATE JUDGE

MICHAELENE J. SCANNAVINO,

Plaintiff,

v.

FLORIDA DEPARTMENT OF CORRECTIONS, et al., Defendants,

CASE NO: 8:05-cv-684-T-23TBM

UNITED STATES DISTRICT COURT FOR THE MIDDLE DISTRICT OF FLORIDA, TAMPA DIVISION

242 F.R.D. 662

April 30, 2007, Decided
April 30, 2007, Filed

STEVEN D. MERRYDAY, UNITED STATES DISTRICT JUDGE.

OPINION

A February 1, 2007, order (Doc. 130) granted in part the defendants' motions (Doc. 109, 122) and required the plaintiff to submit, on or before March 1, 2007, to an independent medical examination (the "examination"). On February 20, 2007, the plaintiff submitted to an examination by Dr. Donald R. Taylor, Jr. ("Dr. Taylor"), who subsequently provided the court with a report summarizing the findings of his "Forensic Psychiatric Evaluation" of the plaintiff.[1] Because Dr. Taylor's findings (in addition to an array of circumstances described in the February 1, 2007, order) raised a substantial question as to the plaintiffs competency, an April 2, 2007, order (Doc. 136) noticed a full evidentiary hearing for April 25, 2007, to determine the plaintiffs competency. The evidence adduced at the hearing

---

[1] The court provided a copy of Dr. Taylor's report to the plaintiff's attorney on March 29, 2007 (during an informal chambers conference with the parties' counsel).

and the balance of the record establish that the plaintiff lacks the ability to adequately understand the meaning and effect of the litigation.

I.

No universally recognized measure determines a civil litigant's competency. Thomas v. Humfield, 916 F.2d 1032, 1034 (5th Cir. 1990). Although Rule 17(c) provides no standard for determining a party's competency, Rule 17(b) states that the capacity of a party to sue or be sued "shall be determined by the law of the party's domicile." Fed. R. Civ. P. 17(b); Thomas, 916 F.2d at 1035 ("[W]e interpret the term 'incompetent person' in Rule 17(c) to refer to a person without the capacity to litigate under the law of his state domicile and, hence, under Rule 17(b)."). The undisputed record evidence establishes that the plaintiff is a domiciliary of Florida residing at 5027 Bow Lane, New Port Richey, Florida.

Section 744.3215(3)(b), Florida Statutes, provides that the right "to sue and defend lawsuits . . . may be removed from a person by an order determining incapacity." Fla. Stat. § 744.3215(3)(b) (2006). Although Section 744.331, Florida Statutes, describes a lengthy administrative procedure for a determination of incapacity, the statute fails to define either "incapacity" or "incompetence." See Fla. Stat. § 744.331 (2006); McJunkin v. McJunkin, 896 So. 2d 962, 963 (Fla. 2d DCA 2005) ("Florida Statutes do not define 'capacity.'"). Section 744.102(10), Florida Statutes, defines an "incapacitated person" as "a person who has been judicially determined to lack the capacity to manage at least some of the property . . . of such person." Fla. Stat. § 744.102(10) (2006). Finally, Section 744.331(6), Florida Statutes, permits a court to determine a person's incapacity only by "clear and convincing evidence." Fla. Stat. § 744.331(6) (2006); Poteat v. Guardianship of Poteat, 771 So. 2d 569, 571 (Fla. 4th DCA 2000).

Although under Rule 17(b) a district court determining a party's capacity must use the law of that party's domicile, the court need not adopt any procedure required by state law but must only satisfy the requirements of due process. Cohen v. Office Depot, Inc., 184 F.3d 1292, 1296 (11th Cir. 1999) (explaining that "if the state law conflicts with a federal procedural rule, then the state law is procedural for Erie/Hanna purposes regardless of how it may be characterized for other purposes."); Thomas, 916 F.2d at 1035 ("[W]e reject the notion that in determining whether a person is competent to sue in federal court a federal judge must use the state's procedures for determining competency or capacity."). In the absence of a clear test for determining a party's incapacity or incompetence under Florida law, "a federal procedure better preserves the integrity and the interests of the federal courts." Id. at 1035.

"It is a well-understood tenant of law that all persons are presumed to be competent" and that the "burden of proof of incompetency rests with the party asserting it." Weeks v. Jones, 52 F.3d 1559, 1569 (11th Cir. 1995). Because "[a] person may be competent to make some decisions but not others," the test of a party's competency "varies from one context to another." United States v. Charters, 829 F.2d 479, 495 n.23 (4th Cir. 1987). In general, "to be considered competent an individual must be able to comprehend the nature of the particular conduct in question and to understand its quality and consequences." Id. (quoting B. Freedman, Competence, Marginal and Otherwise: Concepts and Ethics, 4 Int'l. J. of L. & Psychiatry 53, 56 (1981)). In the context of federal civil litigation, the relevant inquiry is whether the litigant is "mentally competent to understand the nature and effect of the litigation she has instituted." Bodnar v. Bodnar, 441 F.2d 1103, 1104 (5th Cir. 1971); Donnelly v. Parker, 158 U.S. App. D.C. 335, 486 F.2d 402, 407 (D.C. Cir. 1973) (stating that Rule 17(c) may require an inquiry into the plaintiff's "capacity to understand the meaning and effect of the litigation being prosecuted in her name").[2]

II.

The plaintiff has a long and well-documented history of mental illness. Both the complaint (Doc. 1) and the amended complaint (Doc. 52) describe the plaintiff as an emotionally fragile and psychologically disabled person. Indeed, the plaintiff's counsel argues for a tolling of the applicable statute of limitations in this action because of the plaintiffs long-term mental incapacity (Doc. 17 at 14-15; Doc. 33 at 15). Before commencing this action, on four separate occasions from March 26, 2001, through February 9, 2005, the plaintiff was involuntarily committed pursuant to Section 394.463, Florida Statutes ("the Baker Act").[3] Subsequent to commencing this action, the plaintiff was committed pursuant to the Baker Act in October, 2005, to a psychiatric hospital. See Doc. 37; Doc. 102 at 2 ("Ms. Scannavino is currently hospitalized and has had multiple hospitalizations [and] Baker Acts due to physical and mental disabilities."). Most recently, on

---

[2] Nothing in this order adjudicates the plaintiff's general competency. Eagan by Keith v. Jackson, 855 F. Supp 765, 775 (E.D. Pa. 1994) ("Rule 17(c) deals only with the protection of incompetents in their status as parties, and gives no general powers over their persons or property.").

[3] The Baker Act provides that if upon examining a person within the preceding forty-eight hours a mental health professional certifies that the person meets the criteria for involuntary examination, "a law enforcement officer shall take the person . . . into custody and deliver him or her to the nearest receiving facility for involuntary examination." Fla. Stat. § 394.463(2)(a) (2006).

October 8, 2006, the plaintiff was committed (again, pursuant to the Baker Act) to Harbor Behavioral Health after she was discovered "walking through parking lots, banging on things, and screaming irrationally," at which time the plaintiff admitted to failing to take her prescribed medication for the previous four months.

The plaintiffs mental incapacity has twice precluded mediation of this action. Peter Grilli, a seasoned and judicious mediator, twice attempted and twice failed to mediate the plaintiff's claims against the defendants. Following each attempted mediation, Mr. Grilli filed a mediation report stating that the mediation was cancelled pursuant to Rule 10.310(d), Florida Rules for Certified and Court-Appointed Mediators, which rule requires cancellation of a mediation if "for any reason a party is unable to freely exercise self-determination" (Doc. 56, 107).

During the April 25, 2007, competency hearing, the defendants called Dr. Donald R. Taylor, Jr. ("Dr. Taylor"), a board-certified forensic psychiatrist with eighteen years of experience. Dr. Taylor performed a psychiatric examination of the plaintiff on February 20, 2007, which examination yielded a thirty-four page report summarizing Dr. Taylor's findings. Dr. Taylor testified that the plaintiff suffers from schizo-affective bi-polar disorder, which is "characterized by persecutory and grandiose delusional beliefs that in my opinion have an adverse impact on her ability to understand things and to make rational decisions" (Doc. 153). Among Dr. Taylor's findings were that the plaintiff "has significant impairment of her ability to concentrate, retain information, behave appropriately, or make rational decisions" (Doc. 153). Dr. Taylor's report concludes, "It is my opinion that she does not have a rational and factual understanding of the proceedings and is unable to consult with her attorney with a reasonable degree of rational understanding. In summary, it is my opinion that the claimant is incompetent to understand the nature and effect of the litigation."

The plaintiffs counsel offered no expert testimony to rebut Dr. Taylor's findings but instead called only the plaintiff's alleged fiance, Fernando Gutierrez ("Gutierrez").[4] Gutierrez testified that he first met the plaintiff in 1995 during his delivery for Sears of an appliance to her home, shortly after which time Gutierrez quit his job and began living with the plaintiff. Pasco County Sheriff's Office records evince numerous domestic disputes between the plaintiff and Gutierrez, including reports of domestic violence

---

[4] Since 2000, Gutierrez has worked as the sole employee of the plaintiff's attorney in this case, John Shahan, Esq. At the hearing, Gutierrez admitted to working for Mr. Shahan on the instant action and assisting in the drafting of relevant pleadings and papers.

and battery by Gutierrez against the plaintiff (Doc. 109, Ex. E). Also, the plaintiffs medical records reveal that the plaintiff has reported to emergency room personnel and other medical staff that she fears Gutierrez because of his abusing her physically and mentally and stealing her money (Doc. 109, Ex. F).

On the issue of the plaintiffs competency, Gutierrez testified that the plaintiff (1) successfully attended (accompanied by Gutierrez) a real estate closing in 2002 to procure a second mortgage on her home, (2) once held a license as a real estate salesperson (although her license is presently inactive), (3) once designed a logo for her business, (4) "normally know[s] what season it is," (5) cleans her own house, (6) uses a computer, and (7) cares for her pet **cocker spaniel**. Even if believed, neither any nor all of this anecdotal "evidence" presented by a highly interested layperson (who benefits from living in a home paid for by the plaintiff) provides an adequate basis for the court to reject Dr. Taylor's informed and professional opinion that the plaintiff lacks the present ability "to understand the nature and effect of the litigation she has instituted." Bodnar, 441 F.2d at 1104.

The remainder of Gutierrez's testimony is either self-contradictory or contradicted elsewhere in the record. For example, Gutierrez testified that the plaintiff routinely pays her own bills, negotiates payment arrangements with her creditors, and attends to her medical and psychiatric appointments. However, Gutierrez also testified that he has intermittently held a power of attorney over the plaintiff since 1997 and that he has accompanied the plaintiff to "every single one" of her mental health appointments. Asked why the plaintiff needed a power of attorney, Gutierrez answered:

Because when she was having seizures she was in the hospitals, and sometimes you have to make payment arrangements on bills. If she couldn't do her bills because she was behind at a facility, then she needed somebody on the outside to help her administrate her home.

Gutierrez's answer confirms the obvious: an individual who has been involuntarily committed to a psychiatric hospital on at least six separate occasions during the past six years is incapable of handling her own affairs. In sum, the accumulated evidence establishes that the plaintiff does not routinely attend to her own affairs but rather is highly dependent on others to assist with some of her most basic needs.

After both parties rested, the plaintiff appeared as the court's witness. During her "testimony," the plaintiff appeared abnormally loquacious, emotionally fragile, and insufficiently lucid. She spontaneously claimed to have suffered at least eighteen grand mal seizures as a result of her "trying to get off Xanax." The plaintiff not only mistook the court-appointed mediator in this case, Mr. Grilli, for an attorney from her divorce proceeding, but she mistakenly "recognized" the court reporter as someone whom she knew. Responding to concise and direct questions from the court, the plaintiff rambled indiscriminately, her "answers" ranging from observations about the 1970's television show M*A*S*H to anecdotes about "Sonny" (the plaintiffs pet Yorkshire terrier), who reportedly died from ingesting a "poisonous bullfrog." Finally, the plaintiff was unable even to state her age despite her presumably successful memorization of her date of birth.

Measured against both Dr. Taylor's unrebutted expert testimony and the demeanor of the plaintiff during the hearing, Gutierrez's testimony lacks both credibility and weight. Dr. Taylor's examination, report, and testimony clearly and convincingly establish the plaintiff's incapacity for sustained and rational decision-making. Nothing in Gutierrez's testimony either undermines the correctness of Dr. Taylor's expert opinion or identifies any possible bias in Dr. Taylor's appraisal of the plaintiff's competency. "[W]here, as here, the expert testimony so clearly and overwhelmingly points to a conclusion of incompetency, the [court] cannot arbitrarily ignore the experts in favor of the observations of laymen." Strickland v. Francis, 738 F.2d 1542, 1552 (11th Cir. 1984); Brock v. United States, 387 F.2d 254, 257 (5th Cir. 1967) (holding that "some reason must be objectively present for ignoring expert opinion testimony which is sought to be rebutted only by the observations of laymen"). The defendants have established by clear and convincing evidence that the plaintiff is mentally incompetent "to understand the nature and effect of the litigation she has instituted." The evidence permits no other conclusion.

#****#

Pursuant to Rule 25(b), the Clerk is directed to substitute Ms. Reback (in only her capacity as guardian ad litem of the plaintiff, her ward, and not personally) as the named plaintiff in this action.

ORDERED in Tampa, Florida, on April 30, 2007.

STEVEN D. MERRYDAY
UNITED STATES DISTRICT JUDGE

MARYANNE L. COWART,
PATRICK COWART and SPENCER BARLOW,
a Minor by his mother and next friend,
MARYANNE L. COWART, Plaintiffs,

v.

CITY OF EAU CLAIRE,
CITY OF EAU CLAIRE POLICE
DEPARTMENT, CITY OF EAU CLAIRE
ADMINISTRATIVE REVIEW BOARD, JERRY
MATYSIK, TRAVIS QUELLA, BRADLEY VENAAS,
LISA ARLOSZYNSKI, NED DONNELLAN,
JENNIFER EBERT, JAMES FLORY, DAVID
OLSON, BRANDON BUCHANAN, STEPHEN
NICK, STEPHEN BOHRER and LUCIE MCGEE,
Defendants.

07-cv-410-bbc

UNITED STATES DISTRICT COURT
FOR THE WESTERN DISTRICT OF WISCONSIN

571 F. Supp. 2d 1005

July 16, 2008, Decided
July 16, 2008, Filed

BARBARA B. CRABB, District Judge.

OPINION

Plaintiffs Maryanne Cowart and Spencer Barlow (her son) assert that as a result of various ailments, it is necessary for Maryanne to have two service dogs available to assist her and for Spencer to have one dog available to assist him. Plaintiffs live in the City of Eau Claire, which has an ordinance prohibiting more than two dogs per household. Plaintiffs requested a variance from the city to allow them to keep all three dogs in their home. The city denied the request. In response, plaintiffs filed this lawsuit, in which they allege that the city's refusal to grant them a variance violates the Americans with Disabilities Act, 42 U.S.C. §§ 12101-12213, the Rehabilitation Act, 29 U.S.C. § 794, the Fair Housing Act, 42 U.S.C. §§ 3601-3631, the equal protection clause of the Fourteenth Amendment, their privacy rights under the Fourteenth Amendment and their rights to free speech and association under the First Amendment.

Now before the court are a host of motions. Because plaintiffs have failed to adduce evidence to support any of their claims, defendants' motion for summary judgment will be granted. Plaintiffs' motion to strike portions of defendants' answer to the amended complaint will be denied as untimely. Plaintiffs' motion for judgment on the pleadings will be denied, as will their motion for sanctions. Defendants' motion for sanctions and plaintiffs' motion to strike defendants' motion for sanctions will be denied as unnecessary. Because judgment will be entered for defendants and this case will not proceed to trial, plaintiffs' motion to "Expedite to Substitute Expert Witness" will be denied as well.

PLAINTIFFS' MOTIONS TO STRIKE PORTIONS OF DEFENDANTS' ANSWER, FOR JUDGMENT ON THE PLEADINGS AND FOR SANCTIONS

I turn first to plaintiffs' motions to strike portions of defendants' answer to the amended complaint, for judgment on the pleadings and for sanctions. Under Rule 12(f), a party may move to strike from any pleading statements that are "redundant, immaterial, impertinent, or scandalous" within 20 days after being served with the pleading if no response is required. Fed. R. Civ. P. 12(f)(2). Defendants filed their amended answer on January 7, 2008; plaintiffs filed the motion to strike on April 9, 2008. Therefore, it will be denied as untimely. (Plaintiffs make a last-ditch effort to argue that their timely filed motion to strike portions of defendants' original answer is still pending. This is a frivolous argument. Plaintiffs' amended complaint and defendants' amended answer are the operative pleadings in this case. The original complaint, answer and motion to strike portions of the answer became moot upon filing of the amended complaint.)

Plaintiffs' motion for judgment on the pleadings is difficult to follow. However, it is clear that it is contingent on success on their motion to strike portions of defendants' answer. Because I am denying the motion to strike, I must deny the motion for judgment on the pleadings as well. Finally, plaintiffs' motion for sanctions fails to conform to the requirements of Rule 11(c)(2). Even if it did, plaintiffs have not identified any misconduct by defendants that would merit sanctions and their motion will be denied.

MOTION FOR SUMMARY JUDGMENT

Before turning to the undisputed facts, a brief discussion about this court's summary judgment fact-finding procedures and their application to this case is in order. In short, plaintiffs' failure to follow the procedures was staggering in its scope and fatal in its effect. This court follows very specific rules regarding fact-finding at summary judgment. The parties are informed of these rules at the outset in an attachment to the pretrial conference order. All litigants in this court, whether they are represented or proceeding pro se, are expected to read, understand and comply with these rules. One of the most important rules is that parties opposing a motion for summary judgment must propose all facts necessary to defeat the motion. Procedures to be Followed on Motions for Summary Judgment, II.B, II.D.4.

Plaintiffs have ignored this requirement. In addition to responding to the facts proposed by defendants, they submitted a mere ten facts of their own, none of which have anything to do with plaintiffs' alleged disabilities, their dogs' training as service dogs or the sort of accommodation plaintiffs require. Instead, in their brief in opposition to defendants' motion, plaintiffs direct the court to review "the documents Plaintiffs have provided in support of their Response to Defendants' Motion for Summary Judgment." Plts.' Br. in Opp., dkt. # 96 at 37. Reviewing these documents is no small task. Among other things, they include Maryanne Cowart's Social Security Administration records, her medical records from several doctors for the years of 2004 through 2008 and Spencer Barlow's medical records, which also describe several years of treatment. This is precisely the sort of evidentiary quagmire that the court's procedures are intended to avoid. There is no efficient way for defendants to respond to the myriad allegations presented in plaintiffs' brief and supporting documents. It is unreasonable for plaintiffs to expect the court to sort through reams of filings to identify critical nuggets of evidence. United States v. Dunkel, 927 F.2d 955, 956 (7th Cir. 1991) ("Judges are not like pigs, hunting for truffles buried in" the record.). Accordingly, I have disregarded all facts not properly proposed and supported by admissible evidence. See, e.g., Chelios v. Heavener, 520 F.3d 678, 687 (7th Cir. 2008).

I find the following facts to be material and undisputed.

A. Undisputed Facts

1. Parties
Plaintiff Maryanne Cowart lives in Eau Claire, Wisconsin, with her husband, plaintiff Patrick Cowart, and her son, plaintiff Spencer Barlow.

Defendant Jerry Matysik is the chief of police for defendant Eau Claire Police Department. At times relevant to this case, defendants Travis Quella and Lisa Arloszynski worked for defendant Eau Claire Police Department; Quella was a sergeant and Arlozynski was an officer.

Defendant Eau Claire Administrative Review Board is an entity created by city ordinance to hear appeals from citizens who have been affected adversely by administrative decisions made by officials, agents and employees of the City of Eau Claire.

Defendant Stephen Nick is the Eau Claire city attorney. Defendants Stephen Bohrer and Lucie McGee are assistant city attorneys. McGee provides legal advice to the Administrative Review Board.

2. Legal matters regarding plaintiffs' dogs

In 2001, Maryanne Cowart was charged with Felony Mistreatment of an Animal, along with several other felonies. She entered into a plea agreement regarding two other felonies, and the charge of Felony Mistreatment of an Animal was "read-in" at sentencing.

Between March 2003 and May 2006, the police received and investigated four complaints regarding Maryanne's neglect or mistreatment of her dogs. When the police visited her home on March 23, 2003, they observed two unlicensed dogs and instructed plaintiff to get the dogs licensed.

On December 7, 2006, an Eau Claire police officer went to plaintiffs' home to investigate an anonymous, written complaint regarding animal neglect. When the officer arrived, she saw three adult **cocker spaniels**, one male and two females, as well as a litter of six puppies. The officer was concerned for the well-being of the dogs and recommended that an animal control officer conduct a follow-up investigation.

On December 13, 2006, defendant Arloszynski went to plaintiffs' house to investigate. She observed that none of the dogs were licensed and that the concrete floor of the dog pen was covered with organic material. (The parties dispute the nature of the organic material.) Defendant Arloszynski issued three citations as a result of this visit: (1) failure to license three adult dogs; (2) keeping more than two adult dogs at the residence; and (3) failure to promptly remove and dispose of animal excreta.

3. Variance request

In response to the citation for keeping more than two adult dogs at the residence, Maryanne Cowart requested a variance from the police department to allow her to keep more than two dogs. On January 11, 2007, she met with defendant Bohrer. At that meeting, she described the dogs as "service dogs."

On January 29, 2007, the police department denied Cowart's request for a variance. The stated reason for the denial was "the number of past (police) contacts at your residence regarding your dogs, neighbor concerns reference (sic) past care of animals, (and) a review of past ECPD reports which highlight past problems documented by officers." On January 30, 2007, defendant Arlozsynski and two other animal control officers surrounded Cowart when she visited City Hall.

On February 20, 2007, Cowart filed a discrimination complaint with the Equal Rights Division of the Wisconsin Department of Workforce Development. In the complaint, Cowart alleged that her dogs were service dogs. Ultimately, that complaint was dismissed.

On February 24, 2007, Cowart appealed the police department's denial of her variance request. In her appeal, she alleged that the dogs were service dogs. A hearing before the Administrative Review Board was scheduled initially for March 28, 2007. At that hearing, Cowart had the burden of proof to show that the police department's decision to deny her variance request should be reversed.

The hearing was rescheduled for April 25, 2007, because Cowart had recently hired an attorney. In support of her variance request, plaintiff submitted letters from physicians in support of her use of "psychiatric service dogs." The hearing was then postponed until May 16, after plaintiff's attorney asked that it be held in closed session. At the request of defendant Review Board, defendant McGee drafted a legal opinion regarding whether the board could legally hold the hearing in a closed session under Wisconsin's open meetings law. Defendant McGee concluded that it would not be lawful to hold a closed hearing.

On May 10, 2007, plaintiff's attorney wrote a letter to the city, in which he asked again that the hearing take place in closed session. That day, a notice was issued for the Review Board's hearing on May 16. In spite of defendant McGee's opinion, the notice indicated that Cowart's variance request was on the agenda for the hearing and that the hearing might go into closed session when her request was considered. The fact that the meeting might go into closed session was not communicated expressly to either Cowart or her lawyer.

On May 16, 2007, the Review Board held its hearing. Neither the plaintiffs nor their attorney attended. At the hearing, defendant Venaas presented the police department's case, including Cowart's history of animal cruelty, the history of dog-related complaints and her use of the dogs in a commercial breeding operation. The Review Board voted unanimously to deny plaintiff's appeal.

In June 2007, police officers responded twice to complaints regarding plaintiffs' dogs. On June 13, Cowart called the police department to report harassment by her neighbors and defendant Arlosynski. On July 20, 2007, two police officers delivered a letter from defendant Venaas to plaintiffs' home. In the letter, Venaas insisted that plaintiffs comply with the ordinance.

B. Opinion

As noted above, plaintiffs contend that defendants violated their statutory and constitutional rights in a myriad of ways. Because these claims are repetitive and fall into several broad categories, I will consider them as groups.

1. Disability-related claims

Plaintiffs Maryanne Cowart and Spencer Barlow contend that defendants violated their rights under the Americans with Disabilities Act and the Rehabilitation Act of 1973 in several ways. First, they contend that the Administrative Review Board's "refusal" to hold its hearing regarding Cowart's request for a variance in closed session constituted a failure to provide her (and plaintiff Spencer Barlow) a reasonable accommodation for their disabilities. Next, they contend that the City's refusal to grant their variance request to allow them to keep a third dog constituted a failure to accommodate their disabilities. Finally, they contend that the defendants retaliated against Cowart by threatening to enforce the licensing rules and by surveilling her home.

Both the Americans with Disabilities Act and the Rehabilitation Act prohibit discrimination against qualified persons with disabilities. Title II of the Americans with Disabilities Act is concerned with public entities, which are prohibited from excluding qualified persons with disabilities from participation in or receiving the benefits of the services, programs or activities offered by the entity and from discriminating against qualified disabled persons. 42 U.S.C. § 12132. The Rehabilitation Act prohibits organizations that receive federal funds from discriminating on the basis of disability. Community Services v. City of Milwaukee, 465 F.3d 737.

The protections of both the Americans with Disabilities Act and the Rehabilitation Act may be invoked only by a person who is a "qualified individual with a disability." In the context of these statutes, the term means an individual with a disability who, with or without reasonable modifications to rules, policies, or practices, the removal of architectural, communication, or transportation barriers, or the provision of auxiliary aids and services, meets the essential eligibility requirements for the receipt of services or the participation in programs or activities provided by a public entity.

42 U.S.C. § 12131. The Rehabilitation Act provides that the ADA standards are to be applied to determine whether the Rehabilitation Act has been violated. 29 U.S.C. § 794(d). Therefore, I will consider them together.

A person is disabled within the meaning of the Americans with

Disabilities Act if she suffers from a physical or mental impairment that substantially limits one or more major life activities. 42 U.S.C. § 12102(2). Major life activities include "functions such as caring for oneself, performing manual tasks, walking, seeing, hearing, speaking, breathing, learning and working." 29 C.F.R. § 1630.2(l) (1998). A major life activity is "substantially limited" when the person is unable to perform it or is significantly restricted in the manner, condition or duration in which she can perform it in comparison to the general population. Kampmier v. Emeritus Corp., 472 F.3d 930, 938 (7th Cir. 2007), citing 29 C.F.R. § 1630.2(j).

To avoid summary judgment, plaintiffs were required to "demonstrate that there is at least a genuine issue of material fact as to whether [they are] disabled." Squibb v. Memorial Medical Center, 497 F.3d 775, 780 (7th Cir. 2007); Contreras v. Suncast Corp., 237 F.3d 756, 763 (7th Cir. 2001) (stating that it is plaintiff's burden on summary judgment to demonstrate he can "come up with evidence to show he could meet his ultimate burden of showing [a] . . . recognized disability").

As discussed above, plaintiffs proposed no facts having anything to do with their alleged disabilities, either in support of their opposition or in response to defendants' proposed findings of fact. Because plaintiffs have failed to adduce any information to support their allegation regarding this crucial, threshold question, defendants' motion for summary judgment will be granted.

Even if plaintiffs could show that they were disabled and entitled to protection, there is no indication that defendants failed to provide them a reasonable accommodation. First, there is no evidence that plaintiffs' dogs were trained as service dogs. Moreover, Maryanne Cowart had a long record of complaints against her regarding her care of her animals (and she pleaded guilty to a crime involving animal cruelty). This was the only information before the board when it denied Cowarts' variance request. She was not present to present any information regarding her need for a variance, even after the board agreed to hold a closed session to avoid public disclosure of private information. It was not unreasonable for the board to deny plaintiff's request to keep more dogs than the ordinance allowed when it had before it information about her long history of questionable care of animals and no countervailing evidence regarding her need for a service dog.

Finally, plaintiffs appear to assert that their Americans with Disabilities Act and Rehabilitation Act claims are actionable under § 1983 as well as the statutes themselves. I need not consider that question in this case, because I have concluded that plaintiffs have failed to adduce any evidence that defendants violated either the Americans with Disabilities Act or the Rehabilitation Act.

2. Fair Housing Act

The Fair Housing Act makes it unlawful "to make unavailable or deny, a dwelling to any buyer or renter because of a handicap . . . ." 42 U.S.C. § 3604(f). Therefore, communities must make reasonable accommodation to zoning rules when necessary to afford a handicapped person the "equal opportunity" to obtain housing. Wisconsin Community Services v. City of Milwaukee, 465 F.3d 737, 746 (7th Cir. 2006). The Act applies only to accommodations that are "necessary," meaning that, without the accommodation the plaintiff will be denied the ability to obtain housing of her choice. Id. Plaintiffs' claim fails because they have not adduced evidence regarding their alleged handicaps. In addition, they have not shown that a variance to the city ordinance prohibiting a third dog denies them the ability to obtain housing.

3. Constitutional claims

In their complaint, plaintiffs identify a plethora of alleged constitutional violations stemming from their variance dispute with the city. Defendants moved for summary judgment with respect to all of plaintiffs' claims; plaintiffs responded with respect to some of these claims, but not all. Specifically, plaintiffs did not respond to the motion with respect to their claims that defendants violated their First Amendment rights to free speech and association. Plaintiffs' failure to offer any opposition to these arguments constitutes a waiver. Wojtas v. Capital Guardian Trust Co., 477 F.3d 924, 926 (7th Cir. 2007) (failure to oppose argument permits inference of acquiescence and "acquiescence operates as a waiver") (internal citations omitted).

Next, plaintiffs allege that the city violated their rights under the equal protection clause of the Fourteenth Amendment when it denied their variance request. In their complaint, plaintiffs contend that they were denied a variance as a result of discrimination based on race and disability (plaintiffs allege in their complaint that Patrick Cowart and Spencer Barlow are African-American and that plaintiffs Maryanne Cowart and Spencer Barlow suffer from numerous physical and psychological maladies).

The equal protection clause provides that "all persons similarly situated should be treated alike." City of Cleburne v. Cleburne Living Center, 473 U.S. 432, 439, 105 S. Ct. 3249, 87 L. Ed. 2d 313 (1985). Actions or rules that allegedly violate the equal protection clause are subject to varying levels of judicial scrutiny. The proper level of scrutiny for a claim that does not involve a fundamental right and involves no suspect class is the rational relationship test. Discovery House, Inc. v. Consolidated City of Indianapolis, 319 F.3d 277, 282 (7th Cir. 2003). Claims involving discrimination based on disability fall in this category; a governmental entity may treat the disabled and non-disabled differently so long as there is a rational relationship between the treatment and a legitimate governmental purpose. City of Cleburne, 473 U.S. at 446. Regulations that discriminate based on race must withstand strict scrutiny and will be sustained only if they are suitably tailored to serve a compelling state interest. E.g., Grutter v. Bollinger, 539 U.S. 306, 326-27, 123 S. Ct. 2325, 156 L. Ed. 2d 304 (2003). But whatever level of scrutiny applies here, no reasonable jury could conclude that either Patrick Cowart and Spencer Barlow's race, or Maryanne Cowart and Spencer Barlow's disabilities had anything to do with the City's denial of their request for a variance. Plaintiffs have adduced no evidence that defendants have granted variances to other residents who are of another race or who are not disabled. In contrast, there is ample evidence that the Board's primary concern when denying the variance were the repeated police calls regarding plaintiffs' care of their animals.

Finally, plaintiffs contend that their Fourteenth Amendment rights to privacy were violated because they would have had to discuss publicly their medical conditions in order to persuade the Administrative Review Board to grant them a variance. This is a frivolous argument. Plaintiffs' privacy rights cannot possibly have been violated by being forced to disclose private, medical matters in public because Maryanne refused to attend, much less speak at, the hearing at which her variance request was considered. Moreover, the city agreed to hold any sensitive portions of that hearing in closed session. It does not matter whether the city conveyed this information to plaintiffs or their attorney directly and individually; as required by Wisconsin law, the public notice for the meeting, which was released six days in advance of the meeting, stated that this portion of the hearing might go into closed session.

MOTION FOR SANCTIONS

Finally, defendants have moved for dismissal of plaintiffs' case as a sanction for alleged discovery misconduct, dkt. # 112. Rather than responding directly, plaintiffs filed a motion to strike the motion, dkt. # 133. Defendants' allegations are serious: they assert that plaintiffs encouraged and pressured third parties to sign affidavits that plaintiffs knew contained false information. However, because plaintiffs' case will be dismissed in its entirety on substantive grounds, I need not consider whether it could be dismissed as a sanction for discovery violations as well, or whether defendants' motion was presented properly. Therefore, defendants' motion for sanctions will be denied as unnecessary, as will plaintiffs' motion to strike defendants' motion for sanctions.

ORDER

IT IS ORDERED that

1. The motion for summary judgment of defendants City of Eau Claire, City of Eau Claire Police Department, City of Eau Claire Administrative Review Board, Jerry Matysik, Travis Quella, Bradley Venaas, Lisa Arlozynski, Ned Donnellan, Jennifer Ebert, James Flory, David Olson, Brandon Buchanan, Stephen Nick, Stephen Bohrer and Lucie McGee, dkt. # 31, is GRANTED.

2. The motion for judgment on the pleadings of plaintiffs Maryanne Cowart, Patrick Cowart and Spencer Barlow, dkt. # 48, is DENIED.

3. Plaintiffs' motion to strike portions of defendants' answer to the amended complaint, dkt. # 49, is DENIED.

4. Plaintiffs' motion for sanctions, dkt. # 50, is DENIED.

5. Defendants' motion for sanctions, dkt. # 112, and plaintiffs' motion for sanctions, dkt. # 133, are DENIED as unnecessary.

6. Plaintiffs' motion to "Expedite to Substitute Expert Witness," dkt. # 146, is DENIED.

7. The clerk of court is directed to enter judgment for defendants and close this case.

Entered this 16th day of July, 2008.
BY THE COURT:
/s/ BARBARA B. CRABB
District Judge

AMERICAN CANINE FOUNDATION; and FLORENCE VIANZON,

Plaintiffs,

v.

CITY OF AURORA, COLORADO,

Defendant.

Civil Action No. 06-cv-01510-WYD-BNB

UNITED STATES DISTRICT COURT
FOR THE DISTRICT OF COLORADO

618 F. Supp. 2d 1271

May 8, 2009, Decided
May 8, 2009, Filed

American Canine Foundation, Plaintiff, Pro se, Belfair, WA.

Florence Vianzon, Plaintiff, Pro se, Aurora, CO.

For Aurora, City of, Defendant: Julia A. Bannon, LEAD ATTORNEY, Dana R. Spade, Teresa Kinney, Aurora City Attorney's Office, Aurora, CO.

Glen L Bui, Defendant, Pro se, Belfair, WA.

Wiley Y. Daniel, Chief United States District Judge.

OPINION

FINDINGS OF FACT AND CONCLUSIONS OF LAW

THIS MATTER came before the Court on a bench trial held the week of November 17, 2008. The trial concluded on November 19, 2009. I found in favor of the Defendant and against Plaintiffs as discussed in the record on November 19, 2008. Defendant then submitted proposed findings of fact and conclusions of law.

After considering the testimony of the witnesses, the credibility of the witnesses, the exhibits submitted, the arguments of counsel, and Defendant's proposed findings of fact and conclusions of law, I now enter the following Findings of Fact and Conclusions of Law.

I. FINDINGS OF FACT

1. The City of Aurora, Colorado is a home rule city.

2. On October 24, 2005, the Aurora City Council adopted Aurora City Code Section 14-75, hereinafter referred to as the "ordinance", which forms the subject of this action. The ordinance went into effect on November 26, 2005.

3. The ordinance regulates the possession of specific breeds of dogs within the city limits of Aurora, Colorado. These breeds include pit bulls, american bulldogs (old country bulldogs), dogo argentino, canary dog (canary island dog, presa canario, perro de preso canario), presa mallorquin (pero de presa mallorquin, ca de bou), tosa inu (tosa fighting dog, Japanese fighting dog, Japanese mastiff), cane corso (cane di macellaio, Sicilian branchiero), fila brasileiro or any dog displaying the majority of physical traits of any one (1) or more of the above breeds. According to Cheryl Conway, public relations specialist for the City of Aurora animal control division, three of these breeds are breeds banned in most of the cities abutting Aurora's borders. The other breeds were breeds that the animal control officers in the field told management that they had concerns about and asked to be addressed in the ordinance.

4. Pursuant to the Aurora Colorado Charter, the City of Aurora has all powers which are necessary, requisite, or proper for the government and administration of its local and municipal matters, and all powers which are granted to home rule cities by the Constitution of the State of Colorado.

5. As testified by Cheryl Conway, pursuant to the Aurora City Charter, Section 3-9, the Aurora City Council has all legislative powers of the City and all other powers of home rule cities not specifically limited by the constitution of the State of Colorado and not specifically limited or conferred upon others by the Aurora charter. The Aurora City Council has, among other powers, the power to enact and provide for the enforcement of all ordinances necessary to protect life, health and property.

6. One of the plaintiffs in this matter is Florence Vianzon. Ms. Vianzon owns a dog which is a half Staffordshire terrier mix (half pit bull). Under the grandfather clause of the ordinance at issue in this case, Ms. Vianzon was able to maintain ownership of her dog by taking certain actions required by the ordinance.

7. The other plaintiff is the American Canine Foundation, which is an organization based out of the state of Washington. Mr. Glen Bui, a representative of the organization, attended the trial and testified on multiple occasions in this trial. Mr. Bui testified that American Canine Foundation is a non-profit, charitable corporation that advocates for responsible dog ownership.

8. At trial, Cheryl Conway testified that the Aurora City Council initially considered breed specific legislation in 2003. During that time frame, Aurora was the recipient of a number of dogs banned in other cities close to and/or bordering Aurora, and Aurora's animal control officers were voicing concern about the increasing numbers of these animals and their aggressiveness. Further, a concern was noted that breeding was a lucrative business in Aurora, and that these banned dogs were being bred increasingly for their aggressive tendencies. Finally, Aurora was receiving calls from constituents complaining that they were afraid of these dogs.

9. Rather than enact a breed-specific law at that time, the Aurora City Council opted instead to strengthen its dangerous and vicious animal ordinance. It did so by requiring certain animals to be spayed and neutered and increasing the penalties under that ordinance. The City also started a campaign to educate the public regarding these changes in the dangerous and vicious animal ordinance. Ms. Conway testified that this attempt to strengthen the dangerous and vicious animal ordinance fell short of its goal, as the number of reported bites continued to rise, the request for services from people related to dangerous and vicious animals increased, and the numbers of these dogs in shelters continued to increase.

10. In 2004 House Bill 1279 was enacted into a state law which prohibited cities from enacting breed specific legislation. The City and County of Denver, like the City of Aurora, is a home rule city. In 2005 Denver challenged that state law as it relates to home rule cities and prevailed in that litigation. The City of Aurora decided to await the outcome of that litigation before enacting the breed specific ordinance which is the subject matter of this case. While awaiting the outcome of that litigation, there was evidence at trial that incidents involving restricted breeds were continuing to occur inside and outside of Aurora.

11. After Denver prevailed in the litigation, the Aurora Code Committee held a number of policy meetings which were open to the public as well as a public hearing before the entire Aurora City Council on August 9, 2005 to consider whether restricted breed regulations would promote the health, safety and welfare of the citizens.

12. When contemplating enacting this ordinance, the Aurora City Council received input from Animal Care Officers, members of the American Canine Foundation, and members of the public who were both in favor of and opposed to the ordinance. Based on this input and data

provided to the City Council, the Aurora City Council found that it was necessary to ban the ownership of pit bulls and the other restricted breeds in order to protect the health, safety and welfare of the City's residents. Specifically, the ordinance at issue noted that pit bulls tend to be stronger than other dogs, often give no warning signals before attacking, and are less willing than other dogs to retreat from an attack and that pit bull attacks, more often than other types of dogs, result in multiple bites and attacks of greater severity. At trial the City of Aurora presented evidence that the Aurora City Council, when enacting the ordinance in question, had evidence that supported these findings as to pit bulls and the other restricted breeds.

13. In that regard, Ms. Conway was asked what information was provided to the Aurora City Council that supported these findings. She actually testified before the code enforcement meetings regarding the enactment of the ordinance, and responded to City Council's questions, requests and directives. Ms. Conway testified that Aurora animal control provided Aurora information that supported these findings, which came from officers in the field who deal with these animals. Animal care division staff advised the Council that these dogs are stronger than other dogs, as evidenced by the fact that when in the shelters they caused substantial damage to their kennels, as explained in the next paragraph. Further, concern was expressed from animal care division staff that there was a fighting propensity among pit bulls and that they were more aggressive than other dogs.

14. Ms. Conway also testified that information was provided by animal care division staff that the restricted breeds caused Aurora to incur costs with respect to impounding them that were different than the costs incurred with other breeds because of the damage they caused to their kennels. Aurora needed to put roofs over some of the kennels to keep dogs from these breeds from escaping, and had to replace a lot of gates. These breeds were destroying the sliding doors in the kennels, were known to take out the concrete cinder block walls, and destroyed their metal water buckets which needed to be replaced almost daily. Also as to the restricted breeds, Aurora was unable to divide a kennel in half to house two dogs instead of one as it did with other breeds because the restricted breeds were aggressive and there was a risk that they could destroy the sliding gate in the kennel and attack the dog on the other side of the kennel. In addition, during peak season, Aurora had to buy metal covers for the gates so that the restricted breeds could not see the kennel across the aisle from them. The dogs would destroy the gates if they could see a dog across from them, so that they could get to that other animal.

15. In addition, Ms. Conway testified that Aurora lost revenue from adoptions. At any given point in time, over a three year period, there was a

highly disproportionate number of restricted breeds in the kennels as compared to all other breeds of dogs combined. Because these breeds had to be housed until they went through the court process, Aurora had to move adoptable dogs out of the kennels. Further, because these breeds needed to be kept in the kennel for an extended period of time for them to go through the court process, Aurora's medical costs for those animals were increased.

16. Ms. Conway testified that the City Council also heard testimony at public hearings and from citizens at the code committee meetings and the full City Council meetings about the behavior of these dogs and that they are stronger than other dogs. The City Council watched a video at the code committee meeting which showed that pit bulls often do not give warning signals before an attack. The video showed restricted dogs attacking other dogs and showed a restricted dog attacking an animal control officer. Further, animal control staff provided information that the signals are different than other dogs. Most dogs will growl or bark as a warning, pit bulls do not. In fact, pit bulls can be wagging their tails and instantly go into an attack. Ms. Conway testified that a person appeared at a code committee meeting and advised City Council that his **cocker spaniel** was attacked by a pit bull that pulled the jaw completely off his dog. He presented photos of the injuries of his dog.

17. Further, Ms. Conway testified that information was provided to the City Council with respect to insurance companies. The requirements included in the grandfather clause of the ordinance were that people owning restricted breeds have $ 100,000 liability insurance. Counsel members heard from constituents that they were not able to obtain this liability insurance because insurance companies refused to ensure these dogs because of their dangerous and aggressive nature. Ms. Conway testified that City Council had tons of information coming from animal care, research that council members were doing on their own about these breeds, and information from constituents that supported their findings, including several bite incident reports.

18. Finally, Ms. Conway testified that the purpose of the passing of the ordinance at issue was for Aurora to take proactive action because the other ordinance with respect to dangerous and vicious dogs was not protecting the citizens of Aurora. She said that the City Council consistently tries to be proactive, especially where public safety is concerned.

19. Testimony of Ms. Grable, an Aurora animal care officer, supported the Aurora City Council's conclusions on several accounts. She testified that the number of bites from pit bulls started increasing significantly in 2000, and that bites from restricted breeds were more severe than other breeds. She also testified that she agreed with City Council's findings that pit bulls and other bully breeds (such as those included in the ordinance as

restricted) are stronger than other dogs, as shown by the fact that such breeds have chewed through chain metal links to get out in Aurora's kennels. Aurora has had to implement a number of remedial measures to keep these dogs safe. She testified that a pit bull also pulled another dog through the drain hole of the kennel and killed it, and she encountered a pit bull that had to be shot multiple times by officers in order to subdue it.

20. Further, Ms. Grable testified that pit bulls do not typically give warnings before they attack, unlike other breeds. In that regard, she testified about an incident where she was bitten on her leg from a pit bull after being invited into the owner's home. The pit bull did not give any indicators that he was going to bite her. She still has scarring from that bite. Her visit to that owner's home was made because the pit bull had been loose in the neighborhood earlier and had knocked down and scratched a child. Ms. Grable testified that when pit bulls or other bully breeds, including the cane corso (another restricted breed), are involved in an incident she is more cautious when responding than normal. Cane corsos are bred for bull baiting and if encountered in the field, Ms. Grable testified that animal control officers know that they will have to do battle with the dog.

21. Ms. Grable also testified about an incident involving two pit bulls named Smoky and Coal. Those two pit bulls were fighting when Aurora animal care officers responded to a call and impounded the dogs. The dogs were so strong that they were able to escape from the kennel's cages. Once they escaped, they fought in the middle of the kennel and it took several people to disengage the dogs and get them properly secured. These dogs were eventually euthanized.

22. Ms. Grable also testified about an incident in which two pit bulls had a family trapped in their home. After these pit bulls were killed, she examined them and found no evidence of scars indicative of fighting. Nonetheless, these dogs had apparently broken from chains as there was broken metal attached to the dogs. When Ms. Grable arrived at the home where the family was trapped by the pit bulls, one of the dogs leapt at her truck from a distance of approximately six (6) feet and violently threw itself against the driver's side window. In an attempt to corral the dogs in order to prevent them from terrorizing the neighborhood, Ms. Grable was forced to hit the dog with her truck. She estimated her speed at the time of impact to be at least 20 miles per hour. Even after being struck by the truck, the pit bull did not slow down or show any signs of injury. Eventually the police arrived and were forced to shoot and kill the pit bulls.

23. Ms. Merkle, field supervisor at the Aurora animal care division, also provided testimony that supported City Council's findings as to the ordinance. She testified that a pit bull can damage someone more than other breeds, as they have stronger bites and do not usually show when they are about to attack. The injuries caused by pit bulls are more significant

than other breeds. As examples, Ms. Merkle testified that a little boy lost his arm because he was attacked by a pit bull in his back yard, and that a two-year-old boy was disemboweled by a pit bull. She also testified from her experience that restricted breeds also will fight, will sometimes chew through their plastic pallets, and that they have chewed through the slider door in the kennels or jumped over the fences of the kennels to get to other dogs. Her experience is that animal control does not have the same problems with other breeds of dogs.

II. CONCLUSIONS OF LAW

1. The court has jurisdiction of the subject matter and the parties under 28 U.S.C. § 1343 because the case involves claims brought to enforce rights under the United States Constitution.

2. On May 28, 2008, I issued an Order ruling on Defendant's motion for summary judgment. The motion for summary judgment was granted as to the first claim (vagueness and overbreadth), second claim (commerce and freedom of contract), fourth claim (separation of powers) and the procedural due process claim in the fifth claim. The motion for summary judgment was denied as to the third claim (substantive due process and equal protection) and the takings claim contained in the fifth claim. The substantive due process, equal protection and takings claims all relate to Plaintiffs' argument that the ordinance at issue is not rationally related to a legitimate government purpose. Summary judgment was denied with respect to the aforementioned claims on the grounds that no evidence had been presented that the City of Aurora legitimately exercised its police power to curtail a menace to the public health and safety. Specifically, I found that no evidence had been presented that the classification of pit bulls or other breeds at issue in the ordinance had a rational basis in fact, i.e., that the breeds are dangerous animals and that the prohibition of their possession bears a rational relationship to the legitimate governmental objective of protecting the public's health, safety and welfare.

3. The question for the Court now is whether there is a rational basis for this breed ban. After listening to all of the evidence presented, I conclude that there is.

4. In Colorado, dogs are accorded qualified property status, Thiele v. City & County of Denver, 135 Colo. 442, 312 P.2d 786, 789 (1957), and are thus subject to the proper exercise of police power for the protection of the public's health, safety, and welfare. Colorado Dog Fanciers, Inc. v. City and County of Denver, 820 P.2d 644, 653 (Colo. 1991) (citing Stone v. Mississippi, 101 U.S. 814, 818, 25 L. Ed. 1079, 1 Ky. L. Rptr. 146 (1879)).

5. Ownership of a dog does not implicate any fundamental constitutional right. Colorado Dog Fanciers, 820 P.2d at 651. Thus, as

noted in the summary judgment Order, in order to withstand scrutiny under the Fifth and Fourteenth Amendments to the United States Constitution, the ordinance at issue must bear a rational relationship to a legitimate legislative goal or purpose. Exxon Corp. v. Governor of Maryland, 437 U.S. 117, 124, 98 S. Ct. 2207, 57 L. Ed. 2d 91 (1978); Colorado Dog Fanciers, 820 P.2d at 652. "In areas of social and economic policy, a statutory classification that neither proceeds along suspect lines nor infringes fundamental constitutional rights must be upheld . . . if there is any reasonably conceivable state of facts that could provide a rational basis for the classification." FCC v. Beach Communications, Inc., 508 U.S. 307, 313, 113 S. Ct. 2096, 124 L. Ed. 2d 211 (1993).

6. In this case, I found in the summary judgment Order and now affirm that it is undisputed that the City of Aurora stated a legitimate purpose in enacting the ordinance at issue--the protection of health and safety of the public. Thus, I must determine whether the ordinance bears a rational relationship to that purpose.

7. The Plaintiffs bear the burden of proof to show beyond a reasonable doubt that there is no rational basis to classify pit bulls or the other restricted breeds at issue and that the prohibition of their possession bears a rational relationship to the legitimate governmental objective of protecting the public's health. The ordinance comes to the Court "bearing a strong presumption of validity." Beach Communications, 508 U.S. at 315; see also Colorado Dog Fanciers, 820 P.2d at 647 (Colo. 1991). The Supreme Court noted in an equal protection case that "those attacking the rationality of the legislative classification have the burden 'to negative every conceivable basis which might support it.'" Id. (quotation omitted); see also Vance v. Bradley, 440 U.S. 93, 111, 99 S. Ct. 939, 59 L. Ed. 2d 171 (1979) ("those challenging the legislative judgment must convince the court that the legislative facts on which the classification is apparently based could not reasonably be conceived to be true by the governmental decisionmaker").

8. Moreover, the court does not require a legislature to articulate its reasons for enacting a statute, and "it is entirely irrelevant for constitutional purposes whether the conceived reason for the challenged distinction actually motivated the legislature." Id. Thus, equal protection "does not demand for purposes of rational-basis review that a legislature or governing decisionmaker actually articulate at any time the purpose or rationale supporting its classification." Nordlinger v. Hahn, 505 U.S. 1, 15, 112 S. Ct. 2326, 120 L. Ed. 2d 1 (1992). "In other words, a legislative choice is not subject to courtroom fact-finding and may be based on rational speculation unsupported by evidence or empirical data." Beach Communications, 508 U.S. at 315; see also Exxon Corp., 437 U.S. at 124 ("the Due Process Clause does not empower the judiciary 'to sit as a superlegislature to weigh the wisdom of the legislation. . . .'") (quotation and

295

internal quotation marks omitted). "'Only by faithful adherence to this guiding principle of judicial review of legislation is it possible to preserve to the legislative branch its rightful independence and its ability to function.'" Id. (quotations and internal quotation marks omitted).

9. In this case, I find that ample evidence exists to establish a rational relationship between the City's ordinance regulating the possession of pit bulls and other restricted breeds and the City's undisputed legitimate interest in protecting the health and safety of the City's residents. Specifically, evidence was presented to support Aurora's findings that pit bulls, as well as other restricted breeds, tend to be stronger than other dog breeds, that they often give no warning signals before attacking and are less willing than other dogs to retreat from an attack and that attacks from such breeds result in multiple bites and attacks of greater severity than other dogs. This evidence was primarily demonstrated through the testimony of Cheryl Conway, public relations specialist for the City of Aurora animal control division, as described in paragraphs 13 through 18 of the Findings of Fact. Her testimony about the evidence presented to the City Council from Aurora animal care and others supports Aurora's findings described above and also supports a finding that the restricted breeds are more aggressive than other animals. Evidence from Ms. Grable and Ms. Merkle as described in paragraphs 19 through 23 of the Findings of Fact also supports Aurora's findings.

10. In so finding, I note that I am not called upon to conduct factfinding regarding the wisdom of the ordinance. Instead, I find only from the above that Aurora had plausible reasons to support the ordinance, and there is no evidence that Aurora's City Council could not reasonably have conceived these reasons to be true. Plaintiffs did not meet their burden of showing that the ordinance is not rationally related to the legitimate purpose of protecting public safety and health.

11. Accordingly, I find that the ordinance is not an abuse of the City's police power. I further conclude that the classification of pit bulls and restricted breeds in Aurora's ordinance is rationally related to its undisputed legitimate interest in protecting the health and safety of its residents. Accordingly, there has been no deprivation of due process nor has there been a violation of the Equal Protection Clause.

12. I also find that Plaintiffs have not established a taking. As noted in Colorado Dog Fanciers, " [t]he United States Supreme Court has held that a state can deprive a citizen of property when such deprivation is justified as a legitimate exercise of police power." Id, 820 P.2d at 653. In this case, as noted above, I find that Aurora's ordinance which in some instances does grant the City the power to take a restricted breed from an owner is justified as a legitimate exercise of police power. In that regard, I find that the ordinance regarding restricted breeds had a rational basis in fact and bears

a rational relationship to the legitimate governmental objective of protecting the public's health, safety, and welfare.

13. Further, Colorado Dog Fanciers held that a city ordinance such as this one prohibiting the possession of a pit bull or other restricted breed does not result in a taking of private property if a dog owner may keep the dog by obtaining a license and complying with the minimum standards for keeping the dog in the city. Id. In this case, Plaintiff Vianzon owns a restricted breed but, according to her own testimony, is in compliance with Aurora's ordinance and has been allowed to keep her dog. Plaintiff American Canine Foundation does not own a restricted breed. Accordingly, no evidence of a taking of private property has been presented.

III. CONCLUSION

Based upon the foregoing, I find in favor of Defendant on the remaining claims in this case of substantive due process, equal protection and takings. Accordingly, it is

ORDERED that the Clerk of Court shall enter judgment in favor of Defendant and against the Plaintiffs on the claims of substantive due process, equal protection and takings.

Dated: May 8, 2009
BY THE COURT:
/s/ Wiley Y. Daniel
Wiley Y. Daniel
Chief United States District Judge

OVERLOOK MUTUAL HOMES, INC.,
Plaintiff,

vs.

VICKIE L. SPENCER, Defendant,
and JOEY SPENCER, Counterclaim-Plaintiff.

Case No. 3:07cv398

UNITED STATES DISTRICT COURT
FOR THE SOUTHERN DISTRICT OF OHIO,
WESTERN DIVISION

666 F. Supp. 2d 850

July 16, 2009, Decided
July 16, 2009, Filed

WALTER HERBERT RICE, UNITED STATES DISTRICT JUDGE.

OPINION

DECISION AND ENTRY OVERRULING PLAINTIFF'S MOTION FOR SUMMARY JUDGMENT (DOC. # 32)

This litigation arises out of the efforts of Vickie and Joey Spencer (collectively the "Spencers") to keep a dog in their dwelling at the residences managed by Plaintiff Overlook Mutual Homes, Inc. ("Overlook").[1] Overlook is a mutual housing corporation, which is operated by its members, all of whom are residents living at the property owned by Overlook. The members operate Overlook through an elected Board of Trustees ("Board"), which is authorized to adopt rules and regulations. One of those rules, the no pet rule, prohibits members/residents from having

---

[1] Overlook sued Vickie Spencer individually and in her capacity as parent and natural guardian of her daughter Lynsey Spencer ("Lynsey"). Joey Spencer became a party to this litigation as a Counterclaim-Plaintiff.

pets, except for service animals which are necessary to accommodate a resident's disability.

In April, 2007, after other residents had complained about the noise made by a barking dog in the Spencer's dwelling, Overlook provided written warning to them that they were with violating the no pet rule.[2] In response, Vickie Spencer submitted an affidavit, stating that the dog had been permanently removed. Subsequently, however, she visited the Miami Valley Fair Housing Center ("MVFHC"), which resulted in its President, Jim McCarthy ("McCarthy"), writing a letter to Overlook, under date of August 1, 2007. Therein, McCarthy requested a reasonable accommodation on behalf of the Spencers, to permit Lynsey to keep Scooby. McCarthy explained that Lynsey was currently receiving psychological counseling and that her psychologist had recommended that Lynsey have a companion/service dog to facilitate her treatment. McCarthy also enclosed a statement from Miriam Hoefflin ("Hoefflin"), Lynsey's treating psychologist, indicating that, as a result of her assessment and counseling of Lynsey, she had recommended that the child "have a service dog to facilitate treatment."

John Folkerth ("Folkerth"), an attorney representing Overlook in this litigation, responded to McCarthy's letter. In particular, Folkerth set forth therein his reasons for being skeptical of Vickie Spencer's assertion that her daughter needed to keep the dog as a service animal. He also indicated that, if Lynsey was disabled and in need of a service animal, Overlook would be willing to engage in a dialogue to determine whether a reasonable accommodation could be provided. In addition, Folkerth stated that Vickie Spencer would be required to fill out a form, seeking a waiver of the no pet rule and requested all manner of information concerning Lynsey's asserted disability and need for the dog as a service animal. He requested that the information be provided in two weeks and that, in the meantime, Overlook would refrain from initiating eviction proceedings against the Spencers. Thereafter, Vickie Spencer filled out an Overlook request for accommodation form, asserting that the dog was necessary to ameliorate her daughter's disability, which she described as anxiety disorder and neurological and emotional conditions. McCarthy also provided some additional information concerning Lynsey's disability and her need for the dog as a reasonable accommodation.

---

[2] The dog is a neutered, male Cockapoo named Scooby. A Cockapoo is a "designer dog" created by breeding an American or English **Cocker Spaniel** with a Poodle, usually of the miniature or toy variety.

On September 10, 2007, Folkerth wrote back to McCarthy, indicating that the information McCarthy had provided was not sufficient to permit Overlook's Trustees to determine whether Lynsey was disabled as defined by law and whether the accommodation requested was appropriate or necessary. Folkerth also included releases for Lynsey's medical and psychological records maintained by Hoefflin. In addition, he stated that, depending upon the content of the released records, additional information could be required and cautioned that if signed releases were not returned, the Trustees would file suit to obtain those records. On September 25, 2007, Michael Allen ("Allen"), the attorney representing the Spencers in this litigation, wrote to Folkerth in response, explaining that he had been retained by Vickie Spencer and the MVFHC in the matter of the request for a reasonable accommodation on behalf of Lynsey and that, while concerned about the failure of Overlook to grant same, he was most disturbed by the invasiveness of the inquiry into her medical records, which Folkerth had proposed. To bridge their differences, Allen suggested that he and Folkerth conduct a conference call with Hoefflin, during which Folkerth could ask the treating psychologist questions about why the dog was necessary to afford Lynsey the equal opportunity of enjoying the Spencers' unit at Overlook. Allen also indicated that Hoefflin would be on vacation and could not participate in a conference call until October 10, 2007, and that he would be available for such a conference call during the afternoons of October 10th, 11th and 12th. There is no evidence that the conference call proposed by Allen ever took place.[3] Overlook initiated this litigation on October 17, 2007.

In its Complaint against Vickie Spencer, Overlook requests that this Court enter relief, declaring the following, to wit: 1) that it must be provided with the medical and counseling records maintained by Hoefflin, in order to permit it to determine whether Lynsey is disabled within the meaning of the law; 2) that its request for records maintained by Hoefflin is not in violation of federal or state law prohibiting housing discrimination; 3) that, upon Vickie Spencer's failure to provide those records, it was not obligated to waive its no pet rule and could enforce same; and 4) that the dog, Scooby, is not a service animal as defined by law and does not qualify as a reasonable accommodation for purposes of waiving its no pet rule. Doc. # 1 at 7.

Vickie Spencer, joined by her husband Joey, responded to Overlook's Complaint, by, inter alia, asserting a Counterclaim. See Doc. # 3. In that

---

[3] Although Allen states in the Spencers' Memorandum in Opposition to Overlook's Motion for Summary Judgment that it did not (see Doc. # 33 at 5), statements of counsel in a memorandum are not evidence.

pleading, the Spencers have set forth the following claims for relief, to wit: 1) a claim that Overlook has violated the Fair Housing Act ("FHA"), 42 U.S.C. § 3601, et seq., by enforcing the no pet rule and failing to make a reasonable accommodation of that rule;[4] 2) a claim under Ohio's fair housing statute, § 4112.02(H) of the Ohio Revised Code, setting forth similar allegations against Overlook, and, in addition, alleging the making of impermissible inquiries on the basis of disability and coercing, intimidating and interfering with the Spencers because of their advocacy of disability rights; and 3) a claim of negligence under the common law of Ohio. Doc. # 3 at PP 46-56. The Spencers request injunctive relief; compensatory, statutory and punitive damages; and costs, including reasonable attorney's fees. Id. at 18.

This case is now before the Court on Overlook's Motion for Summary Judgment (Doc. # 32).[5] As a means of analysis, the Court will initially set forth the procedural standards it must apply whenever it rules on a motion for summary judgment, following which it will turn to the parties' arguments in support of and in opposition to the instant such motion.

Summary judgment must be entered "against a party who fails to make a showing sufficient to establish the existence of an element essential to that party's case, and on which that party will bear the burden of proof at trial." Celotex Corp. v. Catrett, 477 U.S. 317, 322, 106 S. Ct. 2548, 91 L. Ed. 2d 265 (1986). Of course, the moving party:

always bears the initial responsibility of informing the district court of the basis for its motion, and identifying those portions of "the pleadings, depositions, answers to interrogatories, and admissions on file, together with the affidavits, if any," which it believes demonstrate the absence of a genuine issue of material fact.

Id. at 323. See also Boretti v. Wiscomb, 930 F.2d 1150, 1156 (6th Cir. 1991) (The moving party has the "burden of showing that the pleadings,

---

[4] The FHA makes it unlawful to discriminate on the basis of handicap and defines discrimination to include "a refusal to make reasonable accommodations in rules, policies, practices, or services, when such accommodations may be necessary to afford such person equal opportunity to use and enjoy a dwelling." 42 U.S.C. § 3604(f)(3)(B).

[5] With that motion, Overlook has also requested that this Court preclude Lynsey's treating psychologist, Miriam Hoefflin, from testifying. This Court will rule upon that branch of Overlook's motion after it has conducted the hearing it discussed with counsel during the pretrial conference conducted by telephone on Friday, July 10, 2009.

depositions, answers to interrogatories, admissions and affidavits in the record, construed favorably to the nonmoving party, do not raise a genuine issue of material fact for trial.") (quoting Gutierrez v. Lynch, 826 F.2d 1534, 1536 (6th Cir. 1987)). The burden then shifts to the nonmoving party who "must set forth specific facts showing that there is a genuine issue for trial." Anderson v. Liberty Lobby, Inc., 477 U.S. 242, 250, 106 S. Ct. 2505, 91 L. Ed. 2d 202 (1986) (quoting Fed. R. Civ. P. 56(e)). Thus, "[o]nce the moving party has met its initial burden, the nonmoving party must present evidence that creates a genuine issue of material fact making it necessary to resolve the difference at trial." Talley v. Bravo Pitino Restaurant, Ltd., 61 F.3d 1241, 1245 (6th Cir. 1995). Read together, Liberty Lobby and Celotex stand for the proposition that a party may move for summary judgment by demonstrating that the opposing party will not be able to produce sufficient evidence at trial to withstand a directed verdict motion (now known as a motion for judgment as a matter of law. Fed.R.Civ.P. 50). Street v. J.C. Bradford & Co., 886 F.2d 1472, 1478 (6th Cir. 1989).

Once the burden of production has so shifted, the party opposing summary judgment cannot rest on its pleadings or merely reassert its previous allegations. It is not sufficient to "simply show that there is some metaphysical doubt as to the material facts." Matsushita Elec. Indus. Co. v. Zenith Radio Corp., 475 U.S. 574, 586, 106 S. Ct. 1348, 89 L. Ed. 2d 538(1986). See also Michigan Protection and Advocacy Service, Inc. v. Babin, 18 F.3d 337, 341 (6th Cir. 1994) ("The plaintiff must present more than a scintilla of evidence in support of his position; the evidence must be such that a jury could reasonably find for the plaintiff."). Rather, Rule 56(e) "requires the nonmoving party to go beyond the [unverified] pleadings" and present some type of evidentiary material in support of its position. Celotex Corp., 477 U.S. at 324. Summary judgment "shall be rendered forthwith if the pleadings, depositions, answers to interrogatories, and admissions on file, together with the affidavits, if any, show there is no genuine issue as to any material fact and that the moving party is entitled to judgment as a matter of law." Fed.R.Civ.P. 56(c). Summary judgment shall be denied "[i]f there are ... 'genuine factual issues that properly can be resolved only by a finder of fact because they may reasonably be resolved in favor of either party.'" Hancock v. Dodson, 958 F.2d 1367, 1374 (6th Cir. 1992) (citation omitted). Of course, in determining whether a genuine issue of material fact exists, a court must assume as true the evidence of the nonmoving party and draw all reasonable inferences in the favor of that party. Anderson, 477 U.S. at 255 (emphasis added). If the parties present conflicting evidence, a court may not decide which evidence to believe, by determining which parties' affiants are more credible; rather, credibility determinations must be left to the fact-finder. 10A Wright, Miller & Kane, Federal Practice and Procedure, § 2726. In ruling on a motion for summary judgment (in other words, in determining whether there is a genuine issue of material fact), "[a] district court is not ... obligated to wade through and search the entire record for some specific facts that might support the nonmoving party's claim." Interroyal Corp. v. Sponseller, 889 F.2d 108, 111 (6th Cir. 1989), cert. denied, 494 U.S. 1091, 110 S. Ct. 1839, 108 L. Ed. 2d 967 (1990). See also L.S. Heath & Son, Inc. v. AT&T Information Systems, Inc., 9 F.3d 561 (7th Cir. 1993); Skotak v. Tenneco Resins, Inc., 953 F.2d 909, 915 n. 7 (5th Cir.), cert. denied, 506 U.S. 832, 113 S. Ct. 98, 121 L. Ed. 2d 59 (1992) ("Rule 56 does not impose upon the district court a duty to sift through the record in search of evidence to support a party's opposition to summary judgment ...."). Thus, a court is entitled to rely, in determining whether a genuine issue of material fact exists on a particular issue, only upon those portions of the verified pleadings, depositions, answers to interrogatories and admissions on file, together with any affidavits submitted, specifically called to its attention by the parties.

With its motion, Overlook has set forth three arguments in support of its request for summary judgment, to wit: 1) that it is permitted to set pet policies for its tenants and to obtain the information necessary to evaluate the appropriateness of a tenant's request for a waiver of the no pet rule (Doc. # 32 at 10-12); 2) that an animal must have individual training to qualify as a "service animal" under the federal definition of that term (id. at 12-13); and 3) that it is entitled to summary judgment on the Spencers' negligence claim (id. at 13-15). As a means of analysis, the Court will address those three arguments in the above order.

A. Overlook Is Permitted to Set Pet Policies for its Tenants and to Obtain the Information Necessary to Evaluate the Appropriateness of a Tenant's Request for a Waiver of the No Pet Rule

As indicated, the Spencers allege that Overlook has violated 42 U.S.C. § 3604(f)(3), by failing allow them to keep Scooby.[6] "To prevail on a claim under 42 U.S.C. § 3604(f)(3), a plaintiff must prove all of the following elements: (1) that the plaintiff or his associate is handicapped within the meaning of 42 U.S.C. § 3602(h); (2) that the defendant knew or should

---

[6] The Spencers also claim that Overlook has violated § 4112.02(H) of the Ohio Revised Code by those actions. This Court does not discuss that claim separately, since the Sixth Circuit has noted, while not discussing the state claims separately, that such claims are equivalent to claims under the FHA. Groner v. Golden Gate Gardens Apartment, 250 F.3d 1039, 1043 (6th Cir. 2001). See also, Carter v. Russo Realtors, 2001 Ohio App. LEXIS 2273, 2001 WL 537019 (Ohio App. 2001) (noting that Ohio's fair housing legislation is to be interpreted in accordance with the FHA).

reasonably be expected to know of the handicap; (3) that accommodation of the handicap may be necessary to afford the handicapped person an equal opportunity to use and enjoy the dwelling; (4) that the accommodation is reasonable; and (5) that defendant refused to make the requested accommodation." DuBois v. Association of Apartment Owners of 2987 Kalakaua, 453 F.3d 1175, 1179 (9th Cir. 2006), cert. denied, 549 U.S. 1216, 127 S. Ct. 1267, 167 L. Ed. 2d 92 (2007). See also, Dinapoli v. DPA Wallace Ave II, LLC, 2009 U.S. Dist. LEXIS 23274, 2009 WL 755354, *5 (S.D.N.Y. 2009); Fialka-Feldman v. Oakland University Bd. of Trustees, 2009 U.S. Dist. LEXIS 60548, 2009 WL 275652, *6 (E.D.Mich. 2009); United States v. District of Columbia, 538 F. Supp.2d 211, 218 (D.D.C. 2008); Stassis v. Ocean Summit Ass'n, Inc., 2008 U.S. Dist. LEXIS 31856, 2008 WL 1776988, *2 (S.D.Fla. 2008); Means v. City of Dayton, 111 F. Supp. 2d 969, 978 (S.D.Ohio 2000); Schanz v. Village Apartments, 998 F. Supp. 784, 791 (E.D.Mich. 1998). The Sixth Circuit, however, has held that an accommodation must be necessary. See Howard v. City of Beavercreek, 276 F.3d 802, 806 (6th Cir. 2002) (noting that "'the concept of necessity requires at a minimum the showing that the desired accommodation will affirmatively enhance a disabled plaintiff's quality of life by ameliorating the effects of the disability'") (quoting Bronk v. Ineichen, 54 F.3d 425, 429 (7th Cir. 1995). Thus, the third above-quoted element has been effectively modified by the Sixth Circuit to replace the "may be" with "is".

Parenthetically, the Spencers claim under § 4112.02(H) includes allegations that Overlook violated that statute by making impermissible inquiries on the basis of disability and coercing, intimidating and interfering with the Spencers because of their advocacy of disability rights. Since those aspects of the Spencers' Ohio statutory claim have been omitted from the Final Pretrial Conference Order (see Doc. # 43 at 3), they have been waived.

Overlook contends that it is entitled to summary judgment, because it is permitted to set pet policies for its tenants and to obtain the information necessary to evaluate the appropriateness of a tenant's request for a waiver of the no pet rule. This Court will decline to enter summary judgment in favor of Overlook on this proposition. Initially, this Court cannot agree with Overlook that it is free to set pet policies for its tenants. On the contrary, such policies must comply with the FHA. Given that Overlook has failed to demonstrate that the evidence does not raise a genuine issue of material fact as to whether its no pet policy, as applied to the Spencers, violates the FHA, that question will be resolved by the jury after the presentation of the evidence.

For two reasons, the Court denies Overlook's request for summary judgment, on the basis that it was permitted to obtain information necessary to evaluate the appropriateness of a tenant's request for a waiver of the no pet rule. First, the Spencers have not alleged that Overlook violated the FHA by requesting information concerning Lynsey's disability and need for Scooby. Although they initially alleged that Overlook's request for such information violated § 4112.02(H), such a claim is not included in their claims that have been identified in the Final Pretrial Statement. See Doc. # 43 at 3. Therefore, that claim has been waived. Given that the Spencers are not alleging that Overlook violated either the federal or state statute by requesting such information, the Court questions whether Overlook's request for declaratory relief on that question presents an actual controversy. Until it is satisfied that Overlook's claim in that regard presents such a controversy, this Court will not proceed to trial on such a claim, let alone enter judgment in favor of Overlook on it.

Second, the Department of Housing and Urban Development ("HUD") and the Department of Justice ("DOJ") indicated in their Joint Statement on Reasonable Accommodations under the FHA that the provider of housing is entitled to obtain only that information necessary to determine whether the requested accommodation is necessary because of a disability. Construing the evidence most strongly in favor of the Spencers, the Court concludes that there is a genuine issue of material fact on the issue of whether the information sought by Overlook was necessary. Overlook initiated this litigation without taking advantage of the Spencers' offer to allow its counsel to participate in a conference call with their counsel and Hoefflin, Lynsey's treating psychologist. During that conference call, Overlook's counsel would have been permitted to question Hoefflin on Lynsey's disability and her need for Scooby. Consequently, there is a genuine issue of material fact as to whether Overlook was offered the opportunity to obtain the necessary information, an opportunity which it unilaterally chose to disregard.

Accordingly, the Court rejects Overlook's contention that it is entitled to summary judgment, because it is permitted to set pet policies for its tenants and to obtain the information necessary to evaluate the appropriateness of a tenant's request for a waiver of the no pet rule.

B. An Animal Must Have Individual Training to Qualify as a "Service Animal" under the Federal Definition of that Term

While this proposition is phrased somewhat abstractly, Overlook contends that it is entitled to summary judgment on the Spencer's claim under the FHA, because Scooby is not a "service animal." Although that term is not to be found in the FHA or in regulations interpreting that statue,[7] Overlook contends that this Court must apply that term and its definition found in regulations adopted to enforce a different statute, the Americans with Disabilities Act (ADA), 42 U.S.C. § 12101, et seq. In particular, "service animal" is defined in 28 CFR § 36.104, as:

any guide dog, signal dog, or other animal individually trained to do work or perform tasks for the benefit of an individual with a disability, including, but not limited to, guiding individuals with impaired vision, alerting individuals with impaired hearing to intruders or sounds, providing minimal protection or rescue work, pulling a wheelchair, or fetching dropped items.

(Emphasis added). The Spencers have not challenged Overlook's assertion that Scooby will qualify as a "service animal," under the ADA regulation, only if he was individually trained. Moreover, as Overlook argues, the uncontroverted evidence, Vickie Spencer's responses to its interrogatories, demonstrates that Scooby was not individually trained. Nevertheless, the Spencers argue that Overlook is not entitled to summary judgment on this point, because it is not necessary for Scooby to be a service animal, in order to qualify as a reasonable accommodation under the FHA. For reasons which follow, this Court agrees with the Spencers and, thus, rejects Overlook's argument that it is entitled to summary judgment on all claims under the FHA because Scooby was not individually trained, as is required of service animals under the regulations adopted to enforce a different statute, the ADA.

---

[7] A regulation adopted by HUD, a federal agency charged with enforcing the FHA, provides in relevant part:

(a) It shall be unlawful for any person to refuse to make reasonable accommodations in rules, policies, practices, or services, when such accommodations may be necessary to afford a handicapped person equal opportunity to use and enjoy a dwelling unit, including public and common use areas.

(b) The application of this section may be illustrated by the following examples:

Example (1): A blind applicant for rental housing wants live in a dwelling unit with a seeing eye dog. The building has a no pets policy. It is a violation of § 100.204 for the owner or manager of the apartment complex to refuse to permit the applicant to live in the apartment with a seeing eye dog because, without the seeing eye dog, the blind person will not have an equal opportunity to use and enjoy a dwelling.

24 CFR § 100.204.

In support of this premise, Overlook places primary reliance upon In re Kenna Homes Co-op. Corp., 210 W.Va. 380, 557 S.E.2d 787 (2001). Therein, the West Virginia Supreme Court addressed the issue of whether an animal had to qualify as a service animal under the regulations governing the ADA, in order to constitute a reasonable accommodation under the FHA. The West Virginia Supreme Court concluded that only a service animal could qualify as a reasonable accommodation under the FHA, writing:

> In sum, we hold that the Federal Fair Housing Act, 42 U.S.C. §§ 3601 to 3631, ... require[s] that a service animal be individually trained and work for the benefit of a disabled person in order to be considered a reasonable accommodation of that person's disability. A person claiming the need for an alleged service animal as a reasonable accommodation of his or her disability has the burden of proving these requirements. Further, under the Federal Fair Housing Act, 42 U.S.C. §§ 3601 to 3631 ..., a landlord or person similarly situated may require a disabled tenant who asserts the need to keep an alleged service animal to show that the animal is properly trained; to produce in writing the formal assertion of the trainer that the animal has been so trained; and to present a statement from a licensed physician specializing in the field of [the] subject disability which certifies that the alleged service animal is necessary to ameliorate the effects of the tenant's disability.

Id. at 392-93, 557 S.E.2d at 799-800. In Prindable v. Association of Apartment Owners of 2987 Kalakuna, 304 F. Supp. 2d 1245 (D.Hawaii 2003), affirmed on other grounds sub nom., DuBois v. Association of Apartment Owners of 2987 Kalakaua, 453 F.3d 1175 (9th Cir. 2006), cert. denied, 549 U.S. 1216, 127 S. Ct. 1267, 167 L. Ed. 2d 92 (2007), the District Court followed Kenna Homes and held that an animal did not constitute a reasonable accommodation under the FHA, unless it had been individually trained. 304 F. Supp.2d at 1256.[8]

---

[8] That case involved an owner of a condominium unit and his associate, who were in a dispute with the condominium owners association over the question of whether keeping a dog was a reasonable accommodation to the mental disability of one of the occupants. The District Court entered summary judgment in favor of the association, because the dog had not been individually trained. Upon appeal, the Ninth Circuit affirmed, noting that one of the elements of a claim under 42 U.S.C. § 3604(f)(3)(B) was that the defendant refuse to grant the plaintiff's request for a reasonable accommodation. Since the two had moved out of the unit and the association had not previously required that the dog leave, the Ninth Circuit concluded that the plaintiffs could not establish that essential element of their

In opposition, the Spencers contend that reasonable accommodations under the FHA are not limited to animals which qualify as service animals; rather, they contend that such animals include emotional support animals, the function which Scooby was fulfilling with Lynsey. The Spencers point out that the only place in the regulations adopted to enforce the ADA, in which service animals are discussed, other than the above quoted definition of that term, is 28 CFR § 36.302(c), which generally provides that a public accommodation "shall modify policies, practices, or procedures to permit the use of a service animal by an individual with a disability." The FHA, in contrast with the ADA, does not regulate disability discrimination by public accommodations and in places of public accommodation.[9] Rather, the FHA, inter alia, makes it illegal to discriminate against handicapped individuals in providing housing. 42 U.S.C. § 3604(f)(1). Simply stated, there is a difference between not requiring the owner of a movie theater to allow a customer to bring her emotional support dog, which is not a service animal, into the theater to watch a two-hour movie, an ADA-type issue, on one hand, and permitting the provider of housing to refuse to allow a renter to keep such an animal in her apartment in order to provide emotional support to her and to assist her to cope with her depression, an FHA-type issue, on the other.

Based upon the foregoing alone, this Court would conclude that accommodations under the FHA regarding animals are not limited to service animals. However, additional indicia demonstrate that the two

---

claim. In addition, the Ninth Circuit explicitly noted that it was not addressing the question of "whether the plaintiffs must prove that [the dog] is an individually trained service animal." 453 F.3d at 1179 n. 2.

[9] A public accommodation is defined by the regulations governing the ADA as "a private entity that owns, leases (or leases to), or operates a place of public accommodation." 28 CFR § 36.104. Places of public accommodation are defined by those regulations as "a facility, operated by a private entity, whose operations affect commerce and fall within at least one of [eleven] categories. The categories include places of lodging, such as motels and inns; establishments serving food and drink; places of entertainment or exhibition, such as movie theaters and stadia; establishments offering items for sale or rent, such as grocery stores and shopping centers; establishments providing services, such as banks, offices and hospitals; places of education; places of public display or collection, such as libraries and museums; places of recreation, such as zoos and amusement parks; terminals, depots, or other stations used for public transportation; and social service center establishments, such as day care centers, homeless shelters and food banks. Id.

federal agencies charged with enforcing that statute, HUD and the DOJ, take the opposite position from that advocated herein by Overlook. For instance, HUD recently revised its regulations concerning pet ownership by the elderly and persons with disabilities residing in HUD-assisted, public housing. See Pet Ownership for the Elderly and Persons with Disabilities, 73 F.R. 63834-38 (October 27, 2008). The revised regulation excludes from HUD's regulations prohibiting pet ownership in public housing "animals that are used to assist, support, or provide service to persons with disabilities." 24 CFR § 5.303. HUD has explained that the revised rule applies not just to service animals, as defined by the regulations implementing the ADA, but also to support and therapy animals. 73 F.R. 63834. Such animals are defined to include those "providing emotional support to persons who have a disability related need for such support." Id. As can be seen, HUD has declined to limit its regulation on keeping animals to those that have been individually trained, unlike the regulations implementing the ADA. HUD explained its reasons for doing so:

Finally, the Department believes that removing the animal training requirement ensures equal treatment of persons with disabilities who need animals in housing as a reasonable accommodation, for a wide variety of purposes. While many animals are trained to perform certain tasks for persons with disabilities, others do not need training to provide the needed assistance. For example, there are animals that have an innate ability to detect that a person with a seizure disorder is about to have a seizure and can let the individual know ahead of time so that the person can prepare. This ability is not the result of training, and a person with a seizure disorder might need such an animal as a reasonable accommodation to his/her disability. Moreover, emotional support animals do not need training to ameliorate the effects of a person's mental and emotional disabilities. Emotional support animals by their very nature, and without training, may relieve depression and anxiety, and/or help reduce stress-induced pain in persons with certain medical conditions affected by stress.

Comment: Proposed elimination of training component is inconsistent with the regulations implementing the Americans with Disabilities Act. Several commenters wrote that the applicable definition of the term "service animal" is contained in the Department of Justice regulations implementing the Americans with Disabilities Act (ADA) (42 U.S.C. 12101 et seq.). The commenters wrote that HUD regulations have never specifically defined the term "service animal." Under the ADA regulations at 28 CFR 36.104, a service animal is defined as an animal "individually trained" to do work or perform tasks for the benefit of an individual with a disability. The commenters wrote that this definition covers both ADA claims and claims under Section 504, which HUD is responsible for enforcing. Also according to the commenters, by eliminating the training requirement, the proposed rule contradicts the ADA definition.

HUD Response: The Department does not agree that the definition of the term "service animal" contained in the Department of Justice regulations implementing the ADA should be applied to the Fair Housing Act and Section 504. The ADA governs the use of animals by persons with disabilities primarily in the public arena. There are many areas where the ADA and the Fair Housing Act and Section 504 contain different requirements. For example, accessibility is defined differently under the ADA than under the Fair Housing Act and Section 504.

The Fair Housing Act and HUD's Section 504 regulations govern the use of animals needed as a reasonable accommodation in housing. HUD's regulations and policies pertaining to reasonable accommodation were constructed specifically to address housing and, furthermore, were enacted prior to the development and implementation of the ADA regulations. Thus, the requirements for assistance/service animals must be evaluated in the appropriate context of housing, and are independent of the ADA regulations that were formulated to meet the needs of persons with disabilities in a different context and were adopted subsequent to HUD's regulations.

There is a valid distinction between the functions animals provide to persons with disabilities in the public arena, i.e., performing tasks enabling individuals to use public services and public accommodations, as compared to how an assistance animal might be used in the home. For example, emotional support animals provide very private functions for persons with mental and emotional disabilities. Specifically, emotional support animals by their very nature, and without training, may relieve depression and anxiety, and help reduce stress-induced pain in persons with certain medical conditions affected by stress. Conversely, persons with disabilities who use emotional support animals may not need to take them into public spaces covered by the ADA.

Id. at 63836.[10] Although the revised rule applies only to HUD-assisted public housing, as opposed applying to housing generally, as does the FHA, the rationale in support thereof is equally applicable to all types of housing regulated by the FHA.

In addition, subsequent to the decision of the West Virginia Supreme Court in Kenna Homes, the DOJ, in conjunction with HUD, brought an

---

[10] Section 504 mentioned in the foregoing refers to § 504 of the Rehabilitation Act, 29 U.S.C. § 794.

action against that entity, alleging that it had violated the FHA by implementing a rule which limited the types of dogs residents could keep to dogs that were trained and certified for a particular disability, a rule which had the effect of denying a mentally impaired resident the ability to keep a dog which provided emotional support. United States v. Kenna Homes Cooperative Corp., Case No. 2:04-783 (S.D.W.Va.) at Doc. # 1. Kenna Homes and the Government subsequently entered into a consent decree, under which the former agreed to adopt an exception to any rule preventing residents from keeping pets, by permitting disabled residents to have service animals or emotional support animals. Id. at Doc. # 7. An emotional support animal was defined as an animal, "the presence of which ameliorates the effects of a mental or emotional disability." Id.

In sum, this Court concludes that the types of animals that can qualify as reasonable accommodations under the FHA include emotional support animals, which need not be individually trained. Accordingly, the Court rejects Overlook's assertion that it is entitled to summary judgment, because Scooby was not so trained.

C. Negligence

Overlook moves for summary judgment on the Spencers negligence claim, arguing that it is entitled to same because it has not taken action against the Spencers, pending disposition of Vickie Spencer's request for a waiver of the no pet rule. As a consequence, Overlook's argument continues, the Spencers have not suffered any harm. Based upon Vickie Spencer's declaration and other evidence before the Court, this Court concludes that the evidence raises a genuine issue of material fact as to whether the Spencers have suffered harm. Overlook, acting through its counsel, has raised the specter of evicting the Spencers for violating the no pet policy. In her declaration, Vickie Spencer states that she and her husband have lost sleep and suffered anxiety as a result of feeling that they will lose their home over the presence of Scooby.

Alternatively, Overlook argues that it is entitled to summary judgment on this claim, because it did not owe the Spencers a duty, a fundamental element of any claim of negligence. In particular, relying on Kenna Homes, Overlook contends that in determining whether a duty exists, its Board of Trustees was required to consider the interests of other tenants, who chose to live in a pet free environment, as well as the damage that can be caused by "[e]ven the most carefully controlled and well behaved pets." Doc. # 32 at 14. Simply stated, in the absence of Ohio authority to the contrary, this Court cannot conclude that the duty required in an Ohio negligence claim cannot be based on a violation of the FHA and Ohio's statutory counterpart, § 4112.02(H). This Court notes that Ohio courts have frequently recognized that a negligence claim can be based upon a violation of other anti-discrimination provisions of § 4112.02.

Accordingly, the Court rejects Overlook's request for summary judgment on the Spencers negligence claim.

Based upon the foregoing, the Court overrules Overlook's Motion for Summary Judgment (Doc. # 32).

July 16, 2009
/s/ Walter Herbert Rice WALTER HERBERT RICE, JUDGE
UNITED STATES DISTRICT COURT

PARLEY DREW HARDMAN, Petitioner,

v.

UNITED STATES OF AMERICA,

Respondent.

Case No. 3:09-0589,Crim. Case No. 3:02-00179

UNITED STATES DISTRICT COURT
FOR THE MIDDLE DISTRICT OF TENNESSEE,
NASHVILLE DIVISION

2010 U.S. Dist. LEXIS 43043

May 3, 2010, Filed

Parley Drew Hardman, Plaintiff, Pro se, HERLONG, CA.

For United States of America, Defendant: S. Carran Daughtrey, LEAD ATTORNEY, Jimmie Lynn Ramsaur, Office of the United States Attorney, Nashville, TN.

ROBERT L. ECHOLS, UNITED STATES DISTRICT JUDGE.

OPINION

MEMORANDUM

Pending before the Court is Petitioner Parley Drew Hardman's "Motion Under 28 U.S.C. § 2255 to Vacate, Set Aside, or Correct Sentence by a Person in Federal Custody" (Docket Entry No. 1). Petitioner has filed a Memorandum in support of his Motion (Docket Entry No. 6), the Government has filed a response in opposition to the Motion (Docket Entry No. 21), and Petitioner has filed a "Traverse" to the Government's response (Docket Entry No. 32).

I. FACTUAL BACKGROUND

After a jury trial, Petitioner was convicted of (1) solicitation to commit a federal crime of violence, that being the interstate stalking of his ex-wife,

Cherylynn Collins ("Collins"); (2) solicitation to commit Collins' murder; and (3) conspiracy to commit the interstate stalking of Collins. At trial, the evidence showed the following.

Petitioner met Collins in middle Tennessee in January 1999 when Collins was working at her second job as a dance instructor. In March 1999, Collins' father died and, two months later, she moved back to Michigan to live in her father's house on Pacific Street in Plymouth, Michigan.

While Collins was in Michigan, she and Petitioner continued to communicate and Petitioner visited Collins in Michigan, mostly on the weekends. From his visits, Petitioner knew the layout of the Pacific Avenue home, and knew that Collins had a **cocker spaniel** named Maggie.

In January 2000, Collins and Petitioner became engaged and they married in August 2000. Collins rented out the residence on Pacific Avenue and moved to Murfreesboro, Tennessee, to live with Petitioner with the understanding that, in the near future, they would return to live in Michigan.

Things did not go as planned because Petitioner did not want to move to Michigan. The couple separated in July 2001, and Collins testified that this was prompted by Petitioner physically assaulting her, telling her that he would not be moving to Michigan, and threatening her with "harm." Collins moved back to Plymouth, stayed for a couple of months in her mother's house and then moved into the home on Pacific Avenue.

After Collins returned to Michigan, Petitioner met Marvin Droznek ("Droznek"), a/k/a Marvin Drake, an admitted loan shark. Droznek was previously in the federal Witness Protection Program, having testified against the Mafia in Western Pennsylvania in the late 1980's. After being released from prison in 1990, Droznek moved to Nashville, Tennessee.

Petitioner learned about Droznek's loan sharking activities from Laura Tucker, one of Droznek's customers. Initially, Petitioner told Droznek he was interested in securing a loan, but, when Petitioner learned of Droznek's alleged mob connections, Petitioner's interest quickly evolved into having someone intimidated or hurt. Specifically, Petitioner told Droznek in May 2002, that Collins needed to be punished because she had "sullied" Petitioner's reputation, ruined him financially, and accused him of an inappropriate relationship with his underage daughter. When asked exactly what he wanted done, Petitioner told Droznek he wanted Collins legs' broken because she was a dancer, and her dog killed. Petitioner also stated that if Collins was killed in the process, "so be it."

Over the next couple of months, Petitioner repeatedly called Droznek and mentioned on numerous occasions that he wanted Collins killed. These conversations took place over the phone, or in person at the Waffle House or the Scoreboard sports bar on McGavock Pike in Nashville.

Droznek believed that Petitioner was serious about having Collins killed.

Droznek eventually told Petitioner that it would cost $ 20,000.00 to have Collins killed. Not having the means for that result, Petitioner "settled" on having Collins' legs broken and her dog killed. The parties agreed on $ 2,000 for such services, plus expenses. When Petitioner was asked whether he wanted Collins' legs broken in such a way that they could heal "nicely," Petitioner responded in the negative and maintained that he wanted Collins' legs ruined so that her dancing career would be over.

To carry out the task, Droznek enlisted the aid of Joe Roselli, a/k/a Joe Lucas, another former mobster who also had been placed in the government's Witness Protection Program after testifying against another arm of the mob in New York. In June or July 2002, Petitioner provided Droznek with a packet of information which contained Collins' home address, a sketch of the floor plan of the home, the address of her dance studio, her work schedule, and a list of her customary activities. The packet also included pictures of Collins, her dog, and a necklace that Petitioner wanted taken so that Collins would understand that Petitioner was responsible for the harm inflicted. Petitioner also wanted the necklace taken from Collins so he would know the attack actually happened.

Droznek gave Roselli the information packet and Roselli went on a "scouting trip" to Plymouth. Upon his return, Roselli told Droznek that the information provided by Petitioner was essentially accurate. Droznek then contacted Petitioner, told him about the scouting trip, and requested $ 700.00 for expenses which Petitioner provided. Petitioner expressed his pleasure that things were going forward.

Unbeknownst to both Petitioner and Droznek, Roselli contacted federal authorities after he had been offered the job. Federal agents, in turn, contacted Collins and told her of the plot. Agents staged a fake attack on Collins and provided Roselli with the necklace that Petitioner wanted as proof.

On August 8, 2002, Roselli reported to Droznek that he had completed the mission, but it was not as successful as expected. Roselli said he was only able to break one of Collins' legs because the attack occurred while Collins was walking her dog, and, during the attack, the dog created a "ruckus" causing someone in the home to turn on lights. Nevertheless, Roselli stated that the leg he broke was hit with such force by a 2 x 4 that it caused the wood to shatter.

Droznek called Petitioner to report the results and Petitioner said, "That's great." Droznek subsequently met with Petitioner and gave him the necklace which had been taken from Collins. Petitioner was so happy he became "bubbly," although he did express some dissatisfaction that both legs were not broken as requested.

A few days after the "attack," Collins received flowers from Petitioner with an enclosed note which read, "sorry about your unfortunate incident." Sometime shortly thereafter, Petitioner received an anonymous letter and a CD which contained the song "You're as Cold as Ice" repeated 22 times.

On September 20, 2002, Droznek was arrested in an unrelated reverse drug sting operation. He agreed to cooperate with the authorities, told them about the plot Petitioner had hatched to injure or kill Collins, and his role in the incident. He agreed to meet with Petitioner and to wear a wire to record the conversation.

That same day, Droznek met Petitioner at the Scorecard sports bar where Petitioner discussed the Collins matter and also discussed other possible jobs Droznek might be interested in, including killing country music singer Travis Tritt. During the meeting, the conversation between Droznek and Petitioner was recorded. Outside in the parking lot, Droznek gave Petitioner the information packet which had been provided to Roselli to aid in his contract job to injure or kill Collins in Michigan. Petitioner was then arrested by awaiting agents.

As indicated, Petitioner was convicted of the three charges contained in the Indictment. He was sentenced to a term of imprisonment of 180 months on each of the solicitation charges, and 60 months on the conspiracy charge, with all three sentences to be served concurrently. Those sentences were to be followed by a five-year term of supervised release.

Petitioner appealed both his conviction and his sentence. Petitioner's conviction was affirmed, but the sentence was remanded for reconsideration in light of United States v. Booker, 543 U.S. 220, 125 S. Ct. 738, 160 L. Ed. 2d 621 (2005). United States v. Hardman, Slip Op. No. 04-5249 (6th Cir., January 30, 2006). On remand, the Court imposed the same sentence and that sentence was affirmed on appeal. United States v. Hardman, Slip Op. No. 06-5798, 2008 U.S. App. LEXIS 28043 (6th Cir., March 24, 2008). His present § 2255 petition followed.

II. STANDARD OF REVIEW

To prevail on a § 2255 motion, the Petitioner must establish either an error of constitutional magnitude that had a substantial and injurious effect or influence on his criminal proceeding, see Brecht v. Abrahamson, 507 U.S. 619, 637-38, 113 S. Ct. 1710, 123 L. Ed. 2d 353 (1993), or the record must reflect a fundamental defect in the proceedings that inherently resulted in a complete miscarriage of justice or an omission inconsistent with the rudimentary demands of fair procedure. Reed v. Farley, 512 U.S. 339, 348, 114 S. Ct. 2291, 129 L. Ed. 2d 277 (1994); United States v. Todaro, 982 F.2d 1025, 1028 (6th Cir. 1993). Claims of error must be raised in the trial court and on direct appeal or such claims are procedurally defaulted. See Phillip v. United States, 229 F.3d 550, 552 (6th Cir. 2000).

Under Rule 8 of the Rules Governing Section 2255 Proceedings, the Court "must review the answer, any transcripts and records of prior proceedings, and any materials submitted under Rule 7 to determine whether an evidentiary hearing is warranted." Petitioner is not entitled to an evidentiary hearing if the § 2255 motion and the record of the case conclusively show that he is not entitled to relief. See Green v. United States, 65 F.3d 546, 548 (6th Cir. 1995). Finally, when the trial judge also hears the collateral proceedings, the judge may rely on his recollections of the prior proceedings in ruling on the collateral attack. Blanton v. United States, 94 F.3d 227, 235 (6th Cir. 1996).

III. ANALYSIS

In his Section 2255 Motion, Petitioner raises two grounds, both of which relate to the alleged ineffective assistance of his counsel. In ground one, Petitioner claims trial counsel, John Cauley ("Cauley"), was ineffective in failing to allow Petitioner to testify. In his second ground, Petitioner claims that appellate counsel, Matthew Robinson ("Robinson"), was ineffective because he did not raise on direct appeal Cauley's alleged ineffectiveness in relation to Petitioner not being allowed to testify at trial.

To establish ineffective assistance of counsel, Petitioner must show that his counsel's performance was deficient and that the deficiency prejudiced him. See Strickland v. Washington, 466 U.S. 668, 687, 104 S. Ct. 2052, 80 L. Ed. 2d 674 (1984); Evitts v. Lucey, 469 U.S. 387, 396, 105 S. Ct. 830, 83 L. Ed. 2d 821 (1985). Petitioner must show that counsel made errors so serious that he or she was not functioning as the counsel guaranteed by the Sixth Amendment, and that there is a reasonable probability that the lawyer's errors prejudiced the outcome of the proceedings against him. Strickland, 466 U.S. at 687; Arredondo v. United States, 178 F.3d 778, 782 (6th Cir. 1999).

A reasonable probability is one sufficient to undermine confidence in the outcome; it is a less demanding standard than "more likely than not." Strickland, 466 U.S. at 697. A court need not address both parts of the Strickland test if the Petitioner makes an insufficient showing on one. Id.

At trial, Petitioner was not called as a witness. He claims this was error and amounted to ineffectiveness of counsel for two interrelated reasons. First, Petitioner wanted to testify, but Cauley would not let him testify. Second, Cauley promised the jury that Petitioner would take the stand, but that promise went unfulfilled.

In response to the § 2255 Motion, the Government has filled an Affidavit from Cauley in which he states the following:

5. In preparation for the trial, I met with Mr. Hardman numerous times

317

and spoke with him by telephone. Among other things, we discussed the advantages and disadvantages of having Mr. Hardman testify at trial.

6. The trial began on March 25, 2003.

7. Initially I believed that Mr. Hardman would be exercising his constitutional right to testify at the trial, and I made reference to it in my opening statement. As the trial progressed, Mr. Hardman and I continued to discuss whether he should testify. As the case progressed, I believed that it was unnecessary for Mr. Hardman to testify and that, in fact, it might hurt our case for him to testify. I made my opinions known to Mr. Hardman but allowed him to make the final decision about his constitutional right to testify. He ultimately agreed with me and chose not to testify.

(Docket Entry No. 21-1 at 1-2, internal citation to Clerk's Resume of Trial omitted). In his "Traverse" to this filing, Petitioner writes that "[a]t no time did defense counsel discuss with hardman [sic] that he would not or should not take the stand." (Docket Entry No. 32 at 2).

At first blush, it would appear that the disputed versions about what actually occurred regarding Petitioner's failure to testify require a hearing. However, the Sixth Circuit "entertains a strong presumption that counsel adhered to the requirements of professional conduct and left the final decision about whether to testify with the client." Hodge v. Haeberlin, 579 F.3d 627, 639 (6th Cir. 2009). "To overcome this presumption, [Petitioner] would need to present record evidence that he somehow alerted the trial court to his desire to testify." Id. In this regard, the Sixth Circuit has stated:

A defendant who wants to testify can reject defense counsel's advice to the contrary by insisting on testifying, communicating with the trial court, or discharging counsel. At base, a defendant must alert the trial court that he desires to testify or that there is a disagreement with defense counsel regarding whether he should take the stand. When a defendant does not alert the trial court of a disagreement, waiver of the right to testify may be inferred from the defendant's conduct. Waiver is presumed from the defendant's failure to testify or notify the trial court of the desire to do so.

United States v. Webber, 208 F.3d 545, 551 (6th Cir. 2000)(internal citations and quotation marks omitted).

In this case, at no time during trial did Petitioner alert the Court that he wanted to testify or that he had a disagreement with counsel about whether he should take the stand. This is particularly significant since counsel first represented that Petitioner would take the stand, Petitioner did not take the stand, and, during closing, counsel indicated that the reason Petitioner did not take the stand was because "[i]t just simply wasn't necessary, but it was a decision that he and I made together[.]" (Tr. Trans. 574-575).

Notwithstanding the unequivocal representation by counsel that he and Petitioner reached a mutual agreement that Petitioner would not testify,[1] Petitioner never alerted the Court that he did, in fact, want to testify. He did not mention any alleged dissatisfaction with not being called as a witness in the three post-conviction letters to the Court where he complained about counsel and the government's actions. (Case No. 3:02-CR-00179, Docket Entry Nos. 48, 49 & 57). Instead, in hindsight, he now makes unsupported allegations to that effect. Petitioner's "present allegations that he wanted to testify and was prevented from doing so do not suffice to overcome the presumption that he assented to the tactical decision that he not testify." Hodge, 579 F.3d at 639.

Petitioner also claims trial counsel was ineffective because he failed to deliver on his promise that Petitioner would testify. In his opening statement, Cauley said:

You will hear from my client, Mr. Hardman, who will tell you what his involvement was in this. It is not what the government believes it to be. Mr. Hardman does not fault the FBI for what they did. They acted on information they received from criminals. They had no choice but to do that. But the criminals shouldn't be trusted to relay truthful information. Look to their motives to puff themselves up, and just be open minded. I ask you to listen to all witnesses carefully. This is not what it appears to be right now. Thank you.

(Tr. Trans. at 23-24). In his closing argument, Cauley addressed Petitioner's failure to take the stand and said:

The one thing that I did as an attorney, and it is one of those things that they teach you in a very basic litigation course, is you don't promise a jury something that you are not going to give them. I did that. I told you that you would hear from my client, and you didn't. That was a mistake that I made. You will be instructed not to hold that against him. It just simply wasn't necessary, but it was a decision that he and I made together.

(Id. at 574-75).

In support of his position that counsel was ineffective when he promised the jury that it would hear from Petitioner, Petitioner relies primarily upon McAleese v. Mazurkiewicz, 1 F.3d 159 (3rd Cir. 1993) and Hampton v. Leibach, 347 F.3d 219 (7th Cir. 2003). Those cases are

---

[1] Interestingly, Petitioner attaches to his § 2255 Motion pages from the trial transcript relating to counsel's opening and closing, but neglects to submit the page which indicated that both he and counsel agreed that Petitioner should not testify.

distinguishable, are not controlling, and do not stand for the proposition that the mere failure to keep a promise made in opening statements constitutes ineffective assistance of counsel.

McAleese dealt with a claim that counsel purportedly promised during opening statements that he would produce an alibi witness to testify on defendant's behalf. As Petitioner observes, the Third Circuit wrote that "[t]he failure of counsel to produce evidence which he promised the jury during his opening statements that he would produce is indeed a damaging failure sufficient of itself to support a claim of ineffectiveness of counsel." McAleese, 1 F.3d at 166. That broad language is clearly "dictum," United States v. Kemp, 362 F. Supp.2d 591, 594 (E.D. Pa. 2005), because the Third Circuit found that counsel in that case did not make any such promise. Moreover, that language conflicts with the Third Circuit's later observation that "even if we could imply into the opening a promise to" call the alibi witness, counsel's "later decision not to do so is not necessarily ineffective." McAleese, 1 F.3d at 167. Indeed, the Third Circuit ultimately reversed the district court's grant of habeas relief by concluding that counsel's mid-trial decision not to call the alibi witness was a "reasoned, strategic decision." Id. at 168.

Closer factually is Hampton. There, counsel promised in opening statements that defendant would testify and that there would be evidence showing defendant was not affiliated with a gang. Neither promise was kept, and counsel "reneged on his promises without explaining why he did so." Hampton, 347 F.3d at 257. While the Seventh Circuit found that counsel was ineffective, that finding was not based upon breach of the promises alone. Rather, the Seventh Circuit recognized that "turnabouts of this sort may be justified when 'unexpected developments . . . warrant . . . changes in previously announced trial strategies.'" Id. at 257 (quoting, Ouber v. Guarino, 293 F.3d 19, 29 (1st Cir. 2002)). Ultimately, the Seventh Circuit concluded counsel's "breach of the promises he made in the opening statement was not so prejudicial that it would support relief in and of itself, [but that] breach serve[d] to underscore the more important failure to investigate the exculpatory occurrence witnesses." Id. at 260.

Here, Petitioner's claim is based upon counsel's singular statement that Petitioner would take the stand,[2] but Petitioner did not testify. Counsel

---

[2] Petitioner also claims the Government "attempt[ed] to capitalize on Cauley's blunder," (Docket Entry No. 6 at 7), but that misconstrues the record. During closing, the prosecutor argued that the defense "promised that you would hear from the defendant about his involvement in this case," whereupon Cauley immediately objected. At a sidebar, Cauley argued that the statement was an improper reference to Petitioner's right to remain silent. In response, the Government explained that it was making no such comment, but instead was going to argue that Petitioner kept his word, and that the jury did in fact hear from the

explained during closing that he made a "mistake" and that the defense jointly (counsel and Petitioner) determined Petitioner's testimony was no longer necessary. Obviously, "once the trial was underway, defense counsel reconsidered," and even if the given "reasons now might seem insufficient," the court "'must indulge a strong presumption that counsel's conduct falls within the wide range of reasonable professional assistance of counsel because it is all too easy to conclude that a particular act or omission of counsel was unreasonable in the harsh light of hindsight.'" Williams v. Bowersox, 340 F.3d 667, 672 (8th Cir. 2003)(quoting, Bell v. Cone, 535 U.S. 685, 702, 122 S. Ct. 1843, 152 L. Ed. 2d 914 (2002)).

"The complex dynamics of trial engender numerous missteps, but only the most inexcusable will support a finding that counsel's performance was so substandard as to compromise a defendant's Sixth Amendment right to proficient legal representation." Ouber, 293 F.3d at 27. Counsel's admitted "mistake" in this case does not rise to that level.

In his supporting brief, Petitioner writes:

The facts here are indisputable, the government's star witnesses were career criminals. Joseph Roselli was involved with organized crime, as was Droznek. Hardman was without a criminal history, with testimony the jury needed to hear. Hardman could have told the jury that the alleged plot to harm his ex-wife was impossible based on their testimony. Hardman knew his ex-wifes [sic] habits, where she went and what she did. Hardman could have punched holes in their testimony mainly because of actual events.

(Docket Entry No. 6 at 9). Petitioner's contention that he could "punch holes" in Droznek's and Roselli's testimony and his contention that he could show the jury how the plot was "impossible" are conclusory and unsupported statements and, as such, are not sufficient to establish an ineffectiveness of counsel claim. See, Cross v. Stovall, 238 Fed. Appx. 32, 38 (6th Cir. 2007)("ineffective assistance of counsel claim is doomed by the fact [petitioner] makes nothing more than conclusory assertions").

As for the credibility of Droznek and Roselli, those issues were fully developed during argument and on direct and cross-examination of those witnesses. Both were shown to have extensive criminal histories, and both

---

Petitioner by way of the tape recorded conversation between him and Droznek. After the sidebar, the Government continued by arguing that the jury heard from the Petitioner in the taped conversation. Petitioner's argument on direct appeal that the Government improperly commented on his decision not to testify was found to lack any merit. Hardman, Slip. Op. No. 04-5246 at 3-4.

were shown to have motivation to slant their testimony in favor of the Government.

The theme of counsel's opening, and the subject on which he suggested Petitioner was going to testify, was that neither Droznek nor Roselli could be trusted because they were criminals and, therefore, their portrayal of the events leading up to the "attack" on Collins could not be believed. During trial, the jury learned that both Droznek and Roselli had been involved in the Witness Protection Program because both had testified against the Mafia in organized crime trials. They also learned that both operated under assumed names because of their past relationship with the Mafia.

With regard to Droznek, the jury heard that after testifying against the mob, he served time in prison. He admitted to being a loan shark by trade and that collection of loans sometimes involved the infliction of physical harm. The jury further heard that Droznek was willing to contract out a killing if the price was right. On cross-examination, Droznek admitted that he had just pled guilty to a host of crimes in this case and another which could lead to imprisonment of anywhere from twenty years to life, and that he was testifying for the prosecution in an effort to reduce his sentence. Droznek further admitted during cross-examination that he had considered having his ex-wife killed after his divorce had cost him $ 45,000.00.

The jury also learned from Roselli that he was a former member of John Gotti's crew who turned government witnesses. He admitted convictions for Hobbs Act violations, arson, loan sharking, conspiracy to commit burglaries, credit card fraud and "various other crimes." Through cross-examination, Roselli was made out to be the consummate criminal who had limited contact with Petitioner. Roselli wanted to ingratiate himself with Droznek whom he still believed to be a mobster, believing that if he was successful in entering into criminal activities with Droznek this would help Roselli get back into the Witness Protection Program. Roselli testified he was afraid that if he did not get back in the program he would be hurt or executed by his former mob associates. Cauley had Roselli explain his involvement with Droznek in loan-sharking operations, Roselli's belief that he could enter into a profitable cocaine trafficking relationship with Droznek, and Roselli's budding involvement with the Russian mob in the operation of a strip club.

Clearly, the jury was provided with more than sufficient evidence from which to determine the credibility of both Roselli and Droznek. Those witnesses were hardly left unscathed, notwithstanding the fact that Petitioner did not testify.

Moreover, to prevail on his ineffectiveness of counsel claim, Petitioner must show prejudice, meaning "that, but for counsel's alleged errors, the results of the proceedings would have been different." Strickland, 466 U.S. at 694. Prejudice does not exist where, even assuming some deficiency by counsel, the guilt of the defendant is overwhelming. See, Manley v. Ross Correctional Inst., 314 Fed. Appx. 776, 786 (6th Cir. 2008)(collecting cases).

Here, Droznek's testimony was particularly damning and, notwithstanding his checkered past, apparently believed by the jury. However, the jury did not just hear from Droznek and Roselli; they also heard from FBI agents involved in the case, and police officers who conducted surveillance on the Scoreboard sports bar when Droznek and Petitioner met. The jury also heard from a Plymouth police officer who testified that Petitioner did not seem surprised when the officer called to tell him they were investigating the "assault" on Collins.

Collins also testified about her stormy relationship with Petitioner and the receipt of flowers and the CD after the attack. Nancy Lee Ball told the jury she was an acquaintance of both Petitioner and Collins and that Petitioner had told her he was angry with Collins because she tried to ruin his business, had lied to him, was cheating on him, and that he wanted to kill Collins' dog.

Even Petitioner's own daughter testified that Collins "belittled" Petitioner, that Collins' placing her dog ahead of Petitioner "hurt" him, that Collins' relocation to Michigan was "traumatic" on Petitioner because he wanted to make things "work," and that he became "more and more upset" as the divorce proceedings went forward. Finally, the jury heard from Petitioner himself by way of the tape recorded conversation in which Petitioner acknowledged full involvement in the plot to harm Collins, telling Droznek that she deserved it because of what she had done to him, and expressing happiness that Collins had been harmed.

Petitioner makes no effort to show how his testimony could have overcome the evidence presented to the jury. He has not shown prejudice.

Thus far, the Court has discussed ineffectiveness of counsel in relation to trial counsel's performance. Petitioner also makes a general claim that Robinson, his counsel on appeal, was ineffective because he did not raise trial counsel's failure to present Petitioner as a witness, even though counsel told the jury in opening statements that Petitioner would be called as a witness.

This claim fails because the Court has already determined that trial counsel was not ineffective within the meaning of Strickland. Moreover, Petitioner cannot show prejudice because ineffective assistance of counsel claims are routinely rejected on direct appeal, United States v. Martinez, 430 F.3d 317, 338 (6th Cir. 2005), including claims that counsel was ineffective because he failed to deliver on a promise made during opening statements, United States v. Robinson, 2007 U.S. App. LEXIS 17952, 2007 WL 2112787 at *4 (6th Cir. 2007).

IV. CONCLUSION

For the foregoing reasons, Petitioner's "Motion Under 28 U.S.C. § 2255 to Vacate, Set Aside, or Correct Sentence by Person in Federal Custody" (Docket Entry No. 1) will be denied and this case will be dismissed with prejudice. No certificate of appealability will issue because Petitioner cannot demonstrate that reasonable jurists would find debatable or wrong this Court's conclusion that counsel was not ineffective either at trial on appeal, or that any alleged ineffectiveness prejudiced the Petitioner. See Slack v. McDaniel, 529 U.S. 473, 483-84, 120 S. Ct. 1595, 146 L. Ed. 2d 542 (2000).

An appropriate Order will be entered.

/s/ Robert L. Echols

ROBERT L. ECHOLS

UNITED STATES DISTRICT JUDGE

ORDER

For the reasons explained in the Memorandum issued contemporaneously herewith, Parley Drew Hardman's "Motion Under 28 U.S.C. § 2255 to Vacate, Set Aside, or Correct Sentence by Person in Federal Custody" (Docket Entry No. 1) is hereby DENIED. This case is hereby DISMISSED WITH PREJUDICE.

Further, because Petitioner cannot demonstrate that reasonable jurists would find the Court's assessment of Petitioner's ineffective assistance of counsel claims debatable or wrong, a Certificate of Appealability will not issue. See Slack v. McDaniel, 529 U.S. 473, 483-84, 120 S. Ct. 1595, 146 L. Ed. 2d 542 (2000).

It is so ORDERED.

/s/ Robert L. Echols

ROBERT L. ECHOLS

UNITED STATES DISTRICT JUDGE

JODY FABRIKANT & RUSSELL A. SCHINDLER, Plaintiffs,

-v-

CHRISTINE FRENCH; WILLIAM DERIDDER; HECTOR L. MEJIAS, JR.; JOHN SPINATO; CATHERINE PALMER-WEMP; WALTER SASSE; CHRISTINA KHULY; DAVID STARK; DIANE STARK; ULSTER COUNTY SOCIETY FOR THE PREVENTION OF CRUELTY TO ANIMALS; BRADLEY KNEE; AVERY SMITH; & LARAINE CALIRI, Defendants.

1:03-CV-1289-DNH-DRH

UNITED STATES DISTRICT COURT
FOR THE NORTHERN DISTRICT OF NEW YORK

722 F. Supp. 2d 249
July 13, 2010

David N. Hurd, United States District Judge.

OPINION

MEMORANDUM-DECISION and ORDER

I. INTRODUCTION

Plaintiffs Jody Fabrikant and Russell A. Schindler, Esq., pro se, filed their second amended complaint following the reinstatement of their claims pursuant to the mandate of the Second Circuit Court of Appeals, see Schindler v. French, 232 F. App'x 17, 19-20 (2d Cir. 2007). Fabrikant asserts, inter alia, that her federal constitutional rights were violated during the course of her criminal prosecution for animal cruelty, including her right to be free from malicious prosecution (Causes of Action Two and Four), her right to due process (Cause of Action Five), her right to a presumption of innocence (Cause of Action Six), her right to counsel (Cause of Action Eight), her right to free speech (Cause of Action Nine), and her right to be free from unreasonable searches and seizures (Cause of Action Ten). She also asserts pendent state law claims (Causes of Action One, Three, Eleven, Twelve, Thirteen, and Fourteen). Finally, Fabrikant and Schindler jointly assert a state law claim for libel (Cause of Action Seven).

Defendants Christine French, William DeRidder, Hector L. Mejias, Jr., John Spinato, Catherine Palmer-Wemp, Walter Sasse, Christina Khuly, David Stark, Diane Stark, Ulster County Society for the Prevention of Cruelty to Animals ("UCSPCA"), Bradley Knee, Avery Smith, and Larine Caliri (collectively "defendants") move for summary judgment of all claims pursuant to Federal Rule of Civil Procedure 56. Both plaintiffs oppose, but Fabrikant withdraws her claims for the alleged violation of her right to a presumption of innocence and legal counsel. (Pl. Fabrikant's Opp'n Mem. of Law, Dkt. No. 178, 25.) Accordingly, Causes of Action Six and Eight are not at issue and will be dismissed. Defendants' summary judgment motion was considered without oral argument.

II. BACKGROUND

This lawsuit arises from the investigation and subsequent criminal prosecution of Fabrikant (hereinafter "plaintiff") for alleged animal cruelty in violation of Section 353 of New York's Agriculture and Markets Law. In or around February 2002, plaintiff was in possession of fifteen animals, including one Rottweiler, two **Cocker spaniels**, one Chow, one Basenji mix, nine Basenji/Great Pyrenees puppies, and one cat. Complaints about the animals' treatment were made to law enforcement authorities and defendant UCSPCA after several people, including defendants Khuly, David Stark, and Diane Stark, visited plaintiff's home in response to an advertisement placing the puppies for adoption.

In their capacities as UCSPCA Investigators, defendants Spinato and Sasse visited plaintiff's home to assess the validity of the complaints of animal cruelty. Having received several reports and made their own personal observations of the animals at plaintiff's home, they applied for a search warrant to seize the animals. The warrant was issued on March 1, 2002 and authorized the seizure of the nine puppies, the Rottweiler, the Chow, and any other evidence of animal cruelty found within the residence. Defendants Spinato, Sasse, DeRidder, and Palmer-Wemp executed the search warrant on March 2, 2002. As UCSPCA's Operations Manager and Veterinary Technician, respectively, defendants DeRidder and Palmer-

Wemp were responsible for removing the animals from plaintiff's home and evaluating their overall health.

Defendant Spinato arrested plaintiff during the execution of the warrant while defendants DeRidder and Palmer-Wemp seized the nine puppies, the Chow, the Rottweiler, one of the **Cocker spaniels**, and the cat. Two of the remaining dogs were not seized because they appeared in adequate condition. After the house was secured, plaintiff was arraigned on animal cruelty charges, and the seized animals were taken to the UCSPCA for evaluation and medical treatment.

On March 6, 2002, a state court order was issued directing that the animals be allowed to remain at plaintiff's home during the pendency of the criminal charges. (See Ex. E to Pl. Fabrikant's Aff., Dkt. No. 179-6.) Notwithstanding the order, the seized animals remained in the care of the UCSPCA. During that time, UCSPCA's Executive Director, defendant French, sought foster homes for the nine puppies and the cat. She also ordered that the animals be spayed and neutered pursuant to UCSPCA's policy for animals leaving the shelter. While in foster care, one of the hind claws of one of the dogs was surgically removed due to an alleged infection.

Plaintiff was represented by her co-plaintiff, Mr. Schindler, during her criminal case. She appeared in court on March 6 and 13, 2002 for pre-trial proceedings related to the criminal accusatory instruments. On March 26, 2002, she moved to dismiss the charges against her based upon alleged prosecutorial misconduct and the violation of her right to due process. The motion to dismiss was denied on May 2, 2002. She next appeared in court on October 24, 2002, at which time the prosecution orally moved to dismiss the charge of animal cruelty related to the Rottweiler. The judge agreed to dismiss the charge in the interest of justice, but the four other animal cruelty charges remained. Plaintiff's trial on those charges began on October 24, 2002; however, a mistrial was ordered on October 29, 2002 following prejudicial statements made during Mr. Schindler's opening statement. (See Order of Mistrial, Ex. U to Adler Dec., Dkt. No. 169-32, 2.)

Following the mistrial, plaintiff moved to dismiss all charges in the interest of justice on April 10, 2003 based upon alleged misconduct by law enforcement and UCSPCA personnel. A hearing was held on May 13, 2003 before a new presiding judge, Rochester Town Justice Ronald W. Keillor, Jr. A separate hearing was later held on May 27, 2003 in connection with plaintiff's suppression motion. Although plaintiff's motions were denied, she was acquitted after a second jury trial conducted on October 10 and 11, 2003.

III. DISCUSSION

Summary judgment is warranted when the pleadings, depositions, answers to interrogatories, admissions, and affidavits reveal no genuine issue as to any material fact. FED. R. CIV. P. 56; Anderson v. Liberty Lobby, Inc., 477 U.S. 242, 247, 106 S. Ct. 2505, 2509-10, 91 L. Ed. 2d 202 (1986). All facts, inferences, and ambiguities must be viewed in a light most favorable to the non-moving party. Matsushita Elec. Indus. Co. v. Zenith Radio Corp., 475 U.S. 574, 587, 106 S. Ct. 1348, 1356, 89 L. Ed. 2d 538 (1986); Mandell v. County of Suffolk, 316 F.3d 368, 377 (2d Cir. 2003). Initially, the burden is on the moving party to demonstrate the absence of a genuine issue of material fact. Celotex Corp. v. Catrett, 477 U.S. 317, 323, 106 S. Ct. 2548, 91 L. Ed. 2d 265 (1986). After the moving party has satisfied its burden, the non-moving party must assert specific facts demonstrating there is a genuine issue to be decided at trial. FED. R. CIV. P. 56; Liberty Lobby, Inc., 477 U.S. at 250, 106 S. Ct. at 2511. The non-moving party "must do more than simply show that there is some metaphysical doubt as to the material facts." Matsushita Elec. Indus. Co., 475 U.S. at 586, 106 S. Ct. at 1356. There must be sufficient evidence upon which a reasonable fact finder could return a verdict for the non-moving party. Liberty Lobby, Inc., 477 U.S. at 248-49, 106 S. Ct. at 2510; Matsushita Elec. Indus. Co., 475 U.S. at 587, 106 S. Ct. at 1356.

A. Plaintiff's Federal Claims Pursuant to 42 U.S.C. § 1983

Plaintiff asserts one or more federal claims against each of the defendants pursuant to 42 U.S.C. § 1983 (" § 1983") (Causes of Action Two, Four, Five, Nine, and Ten). In order to establish a constitutional claim under § 1983, plaintiff must show that the defendants were acting under color of state law at the time of the alleged violation and that the action was a deprivation of a constitutional or federal right. Washington v. County of Rockland, 373 F.3d 310, 315 (2d Cir. 2004) (citing Hayut v. State Univ. of N.Y., 352 F.3d 733, 743-44 (2d Cir. 2003)). A defendant's "misuse of power, possessed by virtue of state law and made possible only because the wrongdoer is clothed with the authority of state law, is action taken 'under color of state law.'" United States v. Classic, 313 U.S. 299, 326, 61 S. Ct. 1031, 1043, 85 L. Ed. 1368 (1941) (citations omitted).

1. Malicious Prosecution Claims

Plaintiff asserts federal claims for malicious prosecution in Causes of Action Two and Four against defendants Spinato, Khuly, Sasse, Diane Stark, Caliri, Smith, and Knee. In order to demonstrate a violation of her right to be free from malicious prosecution, she must raise an issue of fact as to five separate elements:

(1) that the defendant initiated a prosecution against the plaintiff, (2) that the defendant lacked probable cause to believe the proceeding could succeed, (3) that the defendant acted with malice, [] (4) that the prosecution was terminated in the plaintiff's favor . . . [and] that there was (5) a sufficient post-arraignment liberty restraint to implicate the plaintiff's

Fourth Amendment rights.

Rohman v. New York City Transit Auth., 215 F.3d 208, 215 (2d Cir. 2000) (citations omitted).[1]

With respect to the first element, defendants Spinato and Sasse concede that they initiated a criminal prosecution against plaintiff due to their roles as authorized peace officers for defendant UCSPCA. In contrast, defendants Khuly, Diane Stark, Caliri, Smith, and Knee argue that there is no issue of fact as to whether they commenced the criminal prosecution against plaintiff because their involvement is undisputably limited to reporting their observations to law enforcement and UCSPCA personnel. Although civilians who provide law enforcement with information in good faith will generally not be considered to have commenced a criminal prosecution, see Weintraub v. Bd. of Educ. of City of New York, 423 F. Supp. 2d 38, 55 (E.D.N.Y. 2006); Du Chateau v. Metro-North Commuter R.R. Co., 253 A.D.2d 128, 131 688 N.Y.S.2d 12, 15 (N.Y. App. Div. 1st Dep't 1999), a citizen will nonetheless be deemed to have initiated criminal proceedings against a suspect if he or she instigated the arrest by being particularly insistent, or in some cases, providing false information to police. See Weintraub, 423 F. Supp. 2d at 55-56; Fowler v. Robinson, No. 94-CV-836, 1996 U.S. Dist. LEXIS 1710, 1996 WL 67994, at*6 (N.D.N.Y. Feb. 15, 1996) (McAvoy, C.J.).

Plaintiff disputes the veracity of the reports made by defendants and alleges that they instigated her arrest by providing false statements to law enforcement. By virtue of her co-habitation with the animals, plaintiff has personal knowledge of the conditions of the animals' treatment. Accordingly, she may rely upon her own statements to raise an issue of fact as to whether the defendants misled the police and the UCSPCA about her behavior. Whether defendants Khuly, Diane Stark, Caliri, Smith, and Knee in fact lied would require a factfinder to make several credibility determinations as between the defendants and plaintiff. Therefore, plaintiff has satisfied the first element of her malicious prosecution claims because she has raised an issue of fact which, if true, would tend to show that the defendants made false statements to law enforcement   and UCSPCA

---

[1] In New York, a state law claim for malicious prosecution will survive summary judgment so long as there is proof of the same first four elements as for a federal claim under § 1983; that is, the elements are the same under New York law but for the requirement for federal claims that a plaintiff suffered a post-arraignment liberty restraint. See Rohman, 215 F.3d at 215 (citing Posr v. Court Officer Shield # 207, 180 F.3d 409, 417 (2d Cir. 1999)).

personnel in an effort to encourage plaintiff's prosecution.

The second element of a malicious prosecution claim proves more difficult for plaintiff in light of the video recording and photographs taken of her home during the execution of the search warrant on March 2, 2002. (See Ex. K to Sasse Decl.; Ex. L to Sasse Decl.) The existence of probable cause will defeat a malicious prosecution claim. Dickerson v. Napolitano, 604 F.3d 732, 751 (2d Cir. 2010) (citing Jaegly v. Couch, 439 F.3d 149, 152 (2d Cir. 2006); Burns v. City of N.Y., 17 A.D.3d 305, 305, 791 N.Y.S.2d 851, 851 (2d Dep't 2005)). Probable cause exists when there is "'knowledge or reasonably trustworthy information of facts and circumstances that are sufficient to warrant a person of reasonable caution'" that a crime was committed. Dickerson, 604 F.3d at 751 (quoting Jaegly, 439 F.3d at 152). Section 353 of New York's Agricultural and Markets Law prohibits, in pertinent part, "any act of cruelty to any animal," including the deprivation of "necessary sustenance, food or drink" and other unjustifiable injury. N.Y. AGRIC. & MKTS. LAW § 353. The review of the video recording and photographs of plaintiff's home indicates that defendants had probable cause to believe that she had committed acts of cruelty based upon the condition of the animals' living quarters. In particular, the evidence shows that piles of feces and open garbage bags were left throughout the residence. Additionally, the animals were found locked in small crates, and at least two of the animals were locked together in a single crate making it difficult for either of them to move or lie down. At a minimum, the video recording and photographs indicated severely unhealthy living conditions for the animals. Taken together with the other accounts of abuse and plaintiff's own admission that she was having difficulty caring for the dogs, there was probable cause to believe she had committed animal cruelty. Therefore, defendant's motion as to Causes of Action Two and Four will be granted, and consideration of the remaining elements for plaintiff's malicious prosecution claims is unnecessary.

2. Due Process Claim

Plaintiff alleges defendants French, DeRidder, UCSPCA, Caliri, Knee, and Smith violated her right to due process when her animals were spayed, neutered, and/or amputated after being seized from her home (Cause of Action Five). As a preliminary matter, defendants contend they did not act under color of state law as required for a due process claim brought pursuant to § 1983.

A private entity such as the UCSPCA may be considered a state actor when:

(1) the entity acts pursuant to the "coercive power" of the state or is

"controlled" by the state ("the compulsion test"); (2) when the state provides "significant encouragement" to the entity, the entity is a "willful participant in joint activity with the state," or the entity's functions are "entwined" with state policies ("the joint action test" or "close nexus test"); or (3) when the entity "has been delegated a public function by the states," ("the public function test").

Sybalski v. Indep. Group Home Living Program, Inc., 546 F.3d 255, 257 (2d Cir. 2008) (alteration marks omitted) (quoting Brentwood Acad. v. Tenn. Secondary Sch. Ath. Ass'n, 531 U.S. 288, 296, 121 S. Ct. 924, 930, 148 L. Ed. 2d 807 (2001) (citations and internal quotation marks omitted)). In Sybalski, the Second Circuit considered whether the corporate owner of a group home for mentally disabled adults and five employees of the corporate entity were state actors under either the joint action or public function tests. 546 F.3d at 258-59. Ultimately, the court concluded the defendants were not state actors because the statutory regulations imposed upon the corporate entity did not circumvent the defendants' decision making authority, id. at 259, and there was insufficient evidence to conclude that care of the mentally disabled "was a function 'traditionally' and 'exclusively' reserved by the state." Id. at 260 (quoting Jackson v. Metro Edison Co., 419 U.S. 345, 352, 95 S. Ct. 449, 454, 42 L. Ed. 2d 477 (1974)).

Plaintiff contends that the UCSPCA and its employees were state actors because they were vested with authority under state law. Undisputably, several state statutes provided the UCSPCA and its two investigators, defendants Spinato and Sasse, with the power to apply for a search warrant, seize animals, and make an arrest. For example, New York's Criminal Procedure Law provides that "[o]fficers or agents of a duly incorporated society for the prevention of cruelty to animals" are among the groups of persons who shall have the powers of "peace officers." N.Y. CRIM. PROC. LAW § 2.10(7). Further, the state's Agriculture and Markets Law authorizes, inter alia, any agent or officer of a duly incorporated society for the prevention of cruelty to animals to issue appearance tickets, make an arrest, or interfere to prevent any act of cruelty upon any animal. N.Y. AGRIC. & MKTS. LAW § 371. Similarly, New York's Not-for-Profit Corporation Law bestows "[s]pecial powers" onto a society for the prevention of cruelty to animals, including the filing of a criminal complaint and assisting in the presentation of evidence to tribunals. N.Y. NOT-FOR-PROFIT CORP. LAW § 1403(b)(2).

Although such statutes are relevant to the state actor analysis for claims arising from the execution of the search warrant and the filing of criminal charges, plaintiff's due process claim is based upon only the spaying, neutering, and/or amputation of her animals. (See Pl. Fabrikant's Second Am. Compl., Dkt. No. 85, PP 154-57.) Plaintiff has not come forward with evidence suggesting that the medical attention administered by the UCSPCA and its employees, including the spaying, neutering, and/or amputation of plaintiff's animals from which Cause of Action Five arises, was authorized by state law. To the contrary, the defendants performed the medical procedures in furtherance of the UCSPCA's objectives and under the UCSPCA's control rather than under some statutory delegation of authority. Accordingly, the conduct alleged in plaintiff's due process claim brought under § 1983 was not carried out under color of law, and defendants' motion for summary judgment of Cause of Action Five will be granted.

3. First Amendment Claim

Plaintiff also asserts under § 1983 that defendants French, DeRidder, Mejias, Spinato, Sasse, and UCSPCA retaliated against her in violation of her First Amendment right to free speech (Cause of Action Nine). She alleges the defendants unlawfully seized her animals, performed an amputation, and prosecuted her for animal cruelty in retaliation for her speech related to the promotion of other animal rights groups, the defense of the criminal allegations against her, and her refusal to cooperate with the investigation of another animal owner. (See Pl. Fabrikant's Second Am. Compl., Dkt. No. 85, PP 175, 178.)

For the same reasons as with plaintiff's due process claim, plaintiff's allegations related to the spaying, neutering, and/or amputation performed on one or more of her animals does not give rise to a federal claim under § 1983 because none of those actions were under color of state law. Although defendants concede that the remaining allegations within Cause of Action Nine, i.e., the execution of the search warrant, the seizure of plaintiff's animals, and the filing of criminal charges, were state actions, the underlying motive for their conduct may not be called into question if there was probable cause to search plaintiff's home, arrest her, and prosecute her for animal cruelty. See Singer v. Fulton County Sheriff, 63 F.3d 110, 120 (2d Cir. 1995) (citing Mozzochi v. Borden, 959 F.2d 1174, 1179-80 (2d Cir. 1992)). Having denied plaintiff's suppression motion in state court, Judge Babcock already determined that the search warrant was supported by probable cause, and plaintiff is barred from relitigating this issue while prosecuting her federal constitutional claims under § 1983 in federal court. See Allen v. McCurry, 449 U.S. 90, 104, 101 S. Ct. 411, 420, 66 L. Ed. 2d 308 (1980) ("There is, in short, no reason to believe that Congress intended to provide a person claiming a federal right an unrestricted opportunity to relitigate an issue already decided in state court simply because the issue arose in a state proceeding in which he would rather not have been engaged at all."). Additionally, as already discussed in consideration of plaintiff's malicious prosecution claims, there was probable cause to arrest plaintiff in light of the animals' living conditions reflected by the video recording and photographs of her home on the day the search warrant was executed. Finally, plaintiff offers no opposition to defendants' argument with respect to her free speech claim despite being granted permission to submit a memorandum of law in excess of the traditional twenty-five pages afforded litigants under N.D.N.Y. Local Rule 7.1(c). (See Order, Dkt. No. 174.[2]) For all of these reasons, defendants' motion for summary judgment of plaintiff's free speech claim will be granted, and Cause of Action Nine will be dismissed.

4. Unreasonable Search and Seizure Claim

Plaintiff also asserts that defendants Nace, DeRidder, Spinato, Sasse, and Palmer-Wemp violated her Fourth Amendment right to be free from unreasonable searches and seizures when they executed the search warrant for her home and arrested her on March 2, 2002 (Cause of Action Ten). For the same reasons that plaintiff is estopped from relitigating the probable cause issue with respect to her First Amendment claim, she is also prevented from disturbing the state court's determination that the search warrant was supported by probable cause. See Allen, 449 U.S. at 104, 101 S. Ct. at 420. Additionally, the determination that defendants had probable cause to arrest her is fatal to her claim for false arrest. Therefore, defendants' motion for summary judgment of plaintiff's Fourth Amendment claim will be granted, and Cause of Action Ten will be dismissed.

B. The Remaining State Law Claims

In light of the decision to dismiss the federal causes of action, the exercise of supplemental jurisdiction over plaintiff's remaining state law claims (Causes of Action One, Three, Eleven, Twelve, Thirteen and Fourteen) and the state law libel claim filed by both plaintiff and Mr. Schindler (Cause of Action Seven) is declined.

IV. CONCLUSION

Summary judgment of plaintiff's federal claims is warranted for two

---

[2] Although plaintiff sought and was granted permission to file a fifty page memorandum of law, her brief totaled thirty-seven pages and failed to address defendants' arguments with respect to her ninth cause of action.

separate reasons. First, none of the conduct apart from the application for the search warrant, seizure of plaintiff's animals, and subsequent criminal prosecution occurred under color of state law. Although the UCSPCA and its employees are infused with some level of authority under New York law, the relevant statutes did not authorize the spaying, neutering, and/or amputation of any of plaintiff's animals. Instead, these actions occurred under the discretion of the UCSPCA and its employees, and therefore, cannot form the basis of plaintiff's § 1983 claims. Second, the existence of probable cause insulates the defendants from liability for their decisions to seize plaintiff's animals, arrest her, and commence criminal proceedings. Even though plaintiff raises an issue of fact as to whether some of the defendants made false statements to investigators, the video recording and photographs of her home demonstrate that the defendants had probable cause to believe she had violated New York's Agriculture and Markets Law.

Accordingly, it is
ORDERED that

(1) Defendants' motion for summary judgment of the federal claims asserted under Causes of Action Two, Four, Five, Six, Eight, Nine, and Ten is GRANTED and these claims are DISMISSED with prejudice;

(2) Defendants' motion for summary judgment of the state law claims asserted under Causes of Action One, Three, Seven, Eleven, Twelve, Thirteen, and Fourteen is GRANTED and these claims are DISMISSED without prejudice to allow plaintiffs to re-plead such claims in the appropriate state court; and

(3) The Clerk of the Court is directed to enter a judgment accordingly.

IT IS SO ORDERED.

/s/ David N. Hurd
United States District Judge
Dated: July 13, 2010
Utica, New York

7
METAPHORS OF THE COCKER SPANIEL

These three cases use the word cocker spaniel for no particular reason except to make an abstract point. All three are quotes: a juror's note to the Judge, a quote from Warren Buffet, and an argument about how to read the word "including".

United States v. Geffrard,
  87 F.3d 448 (1996)
Strougo v. Bea Assocs.,
  188 F. Supp. 2d 373, (2002)
Engle v. Liberty Mut. Fire Ins. Co.,
  402 F. Supp. 2d 1157 (2005)

UNITED STATES of America,

Plaintiff-Appellee,

v.

Yves GEFFRARD and Shannon Landry,

Defendants-Appellants.

No. 93-4339

UNITED STATES COURT OF APPEALS FOR THE ELEVENTH CIRCUIT

87 F.3d 448

July 5, 1996, Decided

Before HATCHETT and ANDERSON, Circuit Judges, and WOOD, * Senior Circuit Judge.

* Honorable Harlington Wood, Jr., Senior U.S. Circuit Judge for the Seventh Circuit, sitting by designation.

JUDGE HARLINGTON WOOD, JR.

OPINION

The two defendants, Geffrard and Landry, were found guilty on various counts of a five-count indictment charging cocaine, firearms and counterfeiting offenses except Landry was acquitted of Count III, the firearm count.[1] Two other defendants similarly charged were tried with

---

[1] Count I charged a conspiracy to possess cocaine with intent to distribute in violation of 21 U.S.C. §§ 841(a)(1), 846. Count II charged possession of cocaine with intent to distribute in violation of 21 U.S.C. §§ 841(a)(1), 846 and 18 U.S.C. § 2. Count III charged the using and carrying of identified firearms during and in relation to drug trafficking in violation of 21 U.S.C. § 846 and 18 U.S.C. §§924(C)2. Count IV charged an attempt to pass and utter counterfeit United States currency in violation of 18 U.S.C. §§ 472, 2. Count V charged possession of counterfeit United States currency in violation of 18 U.S.C. §§ 472, 2.

defendants, but acquitted on all counts. At sentencing, on the government's motion, the court departed upward.[2]

One issue relates to whether or not the district judge abused his discretion in excusing a juror for just cause after deliberations had begun and the jury had already acquitted the other two defendants on all charges. Thereafter Geffrard and Landry were found guilty by the remaining eleven person jury. Both defendants raise this juror issue, but only Landry questions his sentence. He objects specifically to enhancements for possession of a firearm and for obstruction of justice.

FACTUAL BACKGROUND

A special agent of the Bureau of Alcohol, Tobacco and Firearms received information from a confidential informant that Landry and Geffrard had a scheme to obtain cocaine from drug dealers by the use of counterfeit United States currency. The Drug Enforcement Agency and the Secret Service were then informed in order to conduct a joint investigation. Geffrard and Landry's plan was to flash the counterfeit bills to drug dealers in order to entice them to produce the cocaine, then Geffrard and Landry would kill the drug dealers, keep their counterfeit bills, and take the cocaine. There was also information that Geffrard and Landry had access to automatic weapons and a bulletproof vest.

During the joint investigation twelve telephone conversations between Landry, Geffrard, and a confidential informant were monitored and recorded. These conversations reveal that Geffrard and Landry wanted the confidential informant to arrange as part of their scheme for cocaine dealers to produce five to six kilograms of cocaine. Geffrard and Landry would have, they claimed, over $ 50,000 in counterfeit bills to flash. As it turned out, however, they had to make do with less. They had to pad the counterfeit money to make it look more impressive.

---

[2] The sentences imposed are as follows:

Geffrard was sentenced to 210 months imprisonment for Counts I and II to run concurrently, 180 months imprisonment for Counts IV and V to run concurrently with Counts I and II, 60 months imprisonment for Count III to run concurrently with Counts I, II, IV and V, five years supervised release for Counts I and II and three years supervised release for Counts IV and V, all to run concurrently (R3:97). Shannon Landry was sentenced to 235 months imprisonment for Counts I and II, eighteen months imprisonment for Counts IV and V to run concurrently with Counts I and II, five years supervised release for Counts I and II and three years supervised release for Counts IV and V, all to run concurrently.

Arrangements were made to follow up this plan with a meeting at a restaurant in Hollywood, Florida, on July 16, 1991, between Geffrard, Landry, the confidential informant, and the supposed drug dealers. Geffrard arrived by car with $ 6,770 in counterfeit money. He also had with him a loaded and cocked nine millimeter semiautomatic pistol available just behind his driver's seat. Landry arrived in his car, accompanied by the two co-conspirators (both later acquitted), with one in the front, one in the back, one of whom was armed. Then followed a conversation between Geffrard, the confidential informant, and the undercover agents posing as drug dealers with cocaine for sale. During the conversation Geffrard flashed the counterfeit bills he had with him in his car. Then it was all over. Geffrard and Landry were arrested along with the two co-defendants who had been riding with Landry. During the arrest one of the co-defendants tossed a loaded .38 caliber semiautomatic pistol under Landry's car; the gun was retrieved by the arresting agents.

THE JURY ISSUE

This unusual jury question constitutes the most substantial issue.

On the morning of Friday, January 29, 1993, the jury, after being charged and furnished copies of the instructions, retired to begin their deliberations. Later that day the jury submitted two questions, the first was whether the term "possession" applied to Count III, and the second asked for an explanation of "entrapment." Up until then entrapment had not been raised or mentioned in the trial and no instruction had been given on the subject. After conferring with counsel, but reaching no agreement, the district judge responded to the jury's first question by referring to a particular part of a given instruction. As to the second question the district judge responded that no explanation would be given about entrapment as entrapment was not an issue in the case. The jury was told it should apply the law given in all the instructions to the facts determined from the evidence. Then the jury was returned to court and dismissed until Monday morning. In a short colloquy between the district judge and the jury it was evident that all was not going well in the jury room. After the jurors were dismissed for the weekend the judge commented to counsel that the jurors were no longer "happy campers," and he was not sure what was going on in the jury room.

On Monday morning the jury reassembled and went back to its deliberations. A short time later the district judge announced he had received another jury note. That note informed the court that the jury now had a verdict for two of the defendants, but not for the other two. This caused differing opinions among counsel as to whether the verdicts on two of the defendants should be received and a mistrial declared as to the remaining two defendants, or whether deliberations should continue as to the remaining two. The district judge opted for the latter under Rule 31(b), Fed.R.Crim.P. which permits a partial verdict. The partial verdict was received and the two co-defendants found not guilty were discharged. The jury was then sent back to deliberate on the remaining two defendants, Geffrard and Landry. After the jury returned to its deliberations the district judge revealed the full extent of jury trouble that had come to his attention in the meantime.

The district judge advised counsel that earlier that morning he had received a letter from one of the jurors raising a new problem, one, as he understandably said, he could do without. After discussing the letter counsel were allowed to read it with the name of the juror excised. After counsel were given opportunity to consider the situation, but no agreement being reached among themselves, the district judge dismissed the letter-writing juror on his own motion. The district judge was convinced that that juror would not follow his instructions. The judge offered to give a curative instruction telling the remaining jurors not to speculate on the dismissal of the one juror. Defense counsel, however, declined the district judge's offer. Later that afternoon the eleven-person jury returned guilty verdicts on all counts for Geffrard and on all but one count for Landry. Both defendants moved for mistrials which were denied.

The juror's handwritten five-page letter[3] first identified herself as a person having religious beliefs based on the teachings of Emanuel Swedenborg.[4] A few excerpts from the letter of which the district judge took particular note and other passages from the letter will amply illustrate the problem. The letter opens with this explanation:

Because of my religious beliefs as a person who believes in Swedenborgianism which is a person who practices the teachings of Emanuel Swedenborg, which are mainly and above all: That real truth and yes logic comes from the heart and the soul first and then to the mind, I am afraid that my definition of truth may be different from your definition, and I don't mean to be unkind but to discuss the teachings of Emanuel

---

[3] A typewritten version of the complete letter is attached as an appendix to this opinion.

[4] Compton's Interactive Encyclopedia identifies Swedenborg as having been born in Sweden in 1688, dying in 1772. He was a scholar with many talents, but may be most noted for his unique interpretation of Christianity which rejected some of the basic teachings. He had a reputation throughout Europe. His followers founded the Church of the New Jerusalem. There is presently a Swedenborg Foundation in the United States which distributes Swedenborg's many writings and other related materials.

Swedenborg with the other jurors in relation to this case and how I interpret truth would be like discussing the theory of relativity with my **cocker spaniel** dog. Deep within my heart and soul I could not live with a verdict of guilty for any of the accused on any of the charges, as I believe deep within my heart and soul and mind that they were unjustly led into this so called transaction by a more intelligent and powerful figure for the soul [sic] purpose of greed. I do not know what you call this but I call this intrapment [sic] [original underlined three times] on the premise that these people were not tracked down on the charges they were accused of but were coheresed [sic] into it, as it was planned from the start by a paid government official and there would be no crime in question if this were not so.

* * * * * *

I do not know what your opinion of this case is, but mine is that something is horribly wrong with a society that seeks out its victim and finds its strength on preying off of the weakness of that victim.

* * * * * *

I am not an attorney or judge but neither am I a cheap entertainer who plays follow the bouncing ball. I am an artist and writer who prides her self [sic] on both seeking truth and writing truth through my particular art form which I express my ideals through and the argument against them.

* * * * * *

I will not be used as another pawn in a scheme to achieve an end that was immoral and dishonest to begin with, because then I [original underlined three times] will be the one who is guilty and my sentence will be eternal.

To get the full impact of this letter it should be read in its entirety. The district judge saw in the letter an inability of the juror to follow the court's instructions on the law. The juror could not, she writes, live with a verdict of guilty for any of the defendants on any of the charges because of her beliefs deep within her heart and soul. She labelled the factual circumstances to be entrapment by the government even though the jury had been instructed prior to the letter that entrapment was not an issue in the case. The defense did not raise the issue of entrapment. In addition the rest of the jury is referred to with intellectual contempt as being unable to understand the teachings of Swedenborg.

This unusual jury problem is obvious. It arose after jury deliberations had begun and two of the four defendants had already been acquitted. Since counsel could not agree on the best course for the court to follow the judge directed deliberations to continue with the eleven remaining jurors. Those deliberations resulted in guilty verdicts for both defendants except on one count for one defendant. The judge could have declared a mistrial, but double jeopardy possibilities were a factor. The eight-day trial was not long or complicated, so a new trial would not have been as great a burden as in some extended trials. The district judge might have used an alternate to replace the excused juror, if one had been available, but that is generally not a favored procedure after deliberations have begun. See United States v. Guevara, 823 F.2d 446, 448 (11th Cir.1987), and United States v. Kopituk, 690 F.2d 1289, 1309-11 (11th Cir.1982), cert. denied, 461 U.S. 928, 103 S. Ct. 2089, 77 L. Ed. 2d 300 (1983).

The district judge used the discretion permitted him under present Rule 23(b), Fed.R.Crim.P., which gives the judge discretion to excuse a juror for just cause and to then proceed to a valid verdict with the remaining eleven jurors. The discretion the rule permits covers this case. The juror, because of religious beliefs at odds with the factual situation and the law applicable to this case, made it plain she could not follow the court's instructions. To the contrary, she stated she had little regard for the other jurors, the judicial system, or a society which she saw as seeking out its victims. The juror did write that she would honor the court's decision as to what she should do about her disagreement with the rest of the jurors, but that has dubious meaning. It does not say that she would apply the judge's instructions to the facts as the jury might determine.

It is further argued that the district judge might have interviewed the juror, but the judge declined with good reason to get into a likely unproductive discussion with a juror about that juror's deeply held religious beliefs at odds with criminal procedure. That was not necessary and it appears from the strong statements in the letter that it would not have been useful. That discourse would surely have led to even more serious defense objections. The complete letter makes it a certainty that this particular juror could not reach a verdict following the judge's instructions as applied to the facts. That juror is fully entitled to her religious beliefs and may espouse them, but in this jury context, where the court's rules--not hers--apply, it cannot be said that the district judge abused his discretion.

No issue is made of the sufficiency of the evidence, and its sufficiency is apparent. The way this novel problem was handled by the district judge results in no miscarriage of justice.

SENTENCING ISSUES

The district court enhanced Landry's offense level under the Federal Sentencing Guidelines for possession of a firearm, U.S.S.G. § 2D1.1(b)(1), and by an additional two points for obstruction of justice. U.S.S.G. § 3C1.1.

#***#

Landry did not request any particular findings of specificity of perjury as found by the district judge. It is too late now to complain in this court.

The judgments as to both defendants are AFFIRMED.

APPENDIX

Dear Honorable Judge Rudker [sic],

Because of my religious beliefs as a person who believes in Swedenborgianism which is a person who practices the teachings of Emanuel Swedenborg, which are mainly and above all: That real truth and yes logic comes from the heart and the soul first and then to the mind, I am afraid that my definition of truth may be different from your definition, and I don't mean to be unkind but to discuss the teachings of Emanuel Swedenborg with the other jurors in relation to this case and how I interpret truth would be like discussing the theory of relativity with my **cocker spaniel** dog. Deep within my heart and soul I could not live with a verdict of guilty for any of the accused on any of the charges, as I believe deep within my heart and soul and mind that they were unjustly led into this so called transaction by a more intelligent and powerful figure for the soul [sic] purpose of greed. I do not know what you call this but I call this intrapment [sic] [original underlined three times] on the premise that these people were not tracked down on the charges they were accused of but were coheresed [sic] into it, as it was planned from the start by a paid government official and there would be no crime in question if this were not so. I am not an attorney or judge but neither am I a cheap entertainer who plays follow the bouncing ball. I am an artist and writer who prides her self [sic] on both seeking truth and writing truth through my particular art form which I express my ideals through and the argument against them.

I do not know what your opinion of this case is, but mine is that something is horribly wrong with a society that seeks out its victim and finds its strength on preying off of the weakness of that victim.

In conclusion under the premise of the questionable moral ethics of the intire [sic] Judicial system involved in this case and pertaining only to this case, I could not find any of the accused guilty on any of the charges, and further more, your Honor, I do not have any kind of personal vendetta toward any branch of government or person in government including yourself, on the contrary I think you are very nice and the prosecuting attorney is very talented with much style. But I am more interested in truth than government or style, because I know that as an artist and human being I can become everything I need to be through truth. But government falls under [original underlined twice] truth not truth under government.

I did not ask to be here but I was asked to come supposedly to express my opinion and that is what I am doing. When some one does not respect my opinion, they do not respect me.

I will not be used as another pawn in a scheme to achieve an end that was immoral and dishonest to begin with, because then I [original underlined three times] will be the one who is guilty and my sentence will be eternal.

I will honor your decision as to what I should do about my disagreement with the rest of the jurors. The ball is in your hands or may be more appropriately said in your court.

P.S. If you think that one who practices Swedenborgionism is not right in her mind perhaps you also think that Helen Keller, Ralf [sic] Waldo Emerson and William James were not in their right mind. For they also are Swedenborgians, but maybe there [sic] opinions would not be of value either in this court room.

ROBERT STROUGO,
Plaintiff,
- against -
BEA ASSOCIATES,
Defendant,
- and -
THE BRAZILIAN EQUITY FUND, INC.,
Nominal Defendant.

98 Civ. 3725 (RWS)

UNITED STATES DISTRICT COURT
FOR THE SOUTHERN DISTRICT OF NEW YORK

188 F. Supp. 2d 373

February 21, 2002, Decided
February 27, 2002, Filed

ROBERT W. SWEET, UNITED STATES DISTRICT JUDGE

OPINION

Defendant Credit Suisse Asset Management LLC ("CSAM"), formerly known as BEA Associates, the investment adviser for the Brazilian Equity Fund, Inc. (the "Fund"), has moved under Rule 56, Fed. R. Civ. P., to dismiss the Second Amended Complaint (the "Complaint") of plaintiff Robert Strougo ("Strougo"), a shareholder in the Fund, which alleged violations of Section 36(a) and 36(b) of the Investment Company Act of 1940 ("ICA"), as amended, 15 U.S.C. § 80a-35(a), (b). For the reasons set forth below, the motion is granted.

Strougo has been a determined litigant, attacking various practices of the Fund and related entities in an effort to remedy what he perceives as the "abysmal" performance of the Fund and its continued existence despite a market value consistently below its net asset value ("NAV"), sometimes referred to as its discount. These efforts have included, in addition to the instant action, a shareholder derivative claim against BEA Associates and the Fund's directors for alleged violations of the ICA in the Fund's 1996 rights offering, see Strougo v. Bassini, 112 F. Supp. 2d 355 (S.D.N.Y. 2000), and a similar action challenging a 1995 rights offering by the Brazil Fund, a separate closed-end fund, see Strougo v. Padegs, 27 F. Supp. 2d 442 (S.D.N.Y. 1998).

Despite a preliminary success in the Padegs action, see Strougo v. Padegs, 964 F. Supp. 783 (S.D.N.Y. 1997) (denying motion to dismiss fiduciary duty and ICA "control person" claims, except with regard to certain defendants), the decisions have not been favorable to the investor against whom the authorities are currently stacked. While the current revelations concerning the Enron Corporation challenge the validity of many of the precepts of corporate governance, the precedents remain in favor of the board of directors and the adviser.

#***#

The Facts

The facts are taken from CSAM's Statement of Undisputed Facts pursuant to Rule 56.1 of the Local Rules, Strougo's Statement of Disputed Issues, and the affidavits, depositions, and exhibits submitted by the parties. These facts are undisputed except as noted.

CSAM, then known as BEA Associates, established the Fund as a non-diversified, closed-end investment company, organized under the laws of the State of Maryland. It is a registered investment company under the Investment Company Act of 1940 ("ICA"), §§ 15 U.S.C. 80a-1 et seq., with an investment objective of long-term capital appreciation, and its investment mandate requires it to invest primarily in Brazilian securities. The Fund's shares trade on the New York Stock Exchange.

Although the Fund is "non-diversified," it is subject to Brazilian regulations limiting investments in any single issuer, and the Internal Revenue Code, which prohibits the Fund from investing, with respect to fifty percent of its assets, any more than five percent in any one issuer. Brazilian regulations require that the Fund retain a local administrator, and impose certain taxes on the Fund.

The Fund's performance has largely moved with the Brazilian stock market. During 1998, the main Brazilian exchange, the Sao Paulo Exchange, had its worst performance in over twenty-five years, with a loss of 33.5 percent. For the six months ending September 30, 1998, the Morgan Stanley Capital International Brazil Index fell 44.3 percent.

CSAM serves as the Fund's investment adviser under a contract between the Fund and CSAM known as the Investment Advisory Agreement (the "Agreement"). CSAM manages assets of over $ 300 billion and serves as adviser to fifty-four open-end and eight closed-end funds, including the Fund. Pursuant to the Agreement, CSAM, among other things, manages the Fund's assets in accordance with the Fund's investment mandate and all applicable laws and regulations, provides research, makes investment decisions, and exercises voting rights with respect to securities held by the Fund.

Previously, CSAM and Garantia Adminisdracao de Recursos ("Garantia"), the Fund's subadviser, were paid a fee equivalent to 1.35 percent of the first $ 100 million of the Fund's net assets. Garantia resigned as the Fund's subadviser in 1994, and CSAM assumed Garantia's responsibilities but declined to charge the portion of the fees that would have been otherwise payable to Garantia. The fee of one percent of the first one hundred million of Fund assets, which CSAM continued to receive under that structure, is within the median of fees received by managers of world equity funds.

As of 2000, under a new fee structure, CSAM's fee is based on the lesser of the Fund's average net assets or the market value of the Fund's shares. CSAM charges lower fees to institutional clients. These fees are negotiated at arm's length.

For the fiscal years ending March 31, 1997, 1998, 1999, 2000, and 2001, CSAM earned $ 914,200, $ 1,020,507, $ 420,08, $ 364,721, and $ 341,921, respectively, in fees. CSAM's profit margin for the years 1996, 1997, 1998, 1999 and 2000 was 18 percent, 57 percent, 11 percent, negative 102 percent, and negative 24 percent, respectively.

The Fund's operating expenses include expenses associated with investments in Brazil. The Fund's expense ratio is affected by the small size of the Fund and certain expenses associated with its closed-end structure, such as exchange listing fees and fees associated with the annual proxy solicitation, and the significant fees associated with the present litigation, as well as expenses related to Brazilian investment including higher custodian, accounting, and audit fees, the mandatory retention of a Brazilian administrator, and a Brazilian transaction fee of up to .38 percent. For the Fund's fiscal years 1996, 1997, 1998, 1999, 2000 and 2001, its expense ratios were 1.76%, 1.76%, 2.07%, 5.17%, 3.80% and 2.38%. Strougo's litigation has attributed 0.09%, 2.34%, 0.87% and 0.28% respectively to those amounts. CSAM also provides, at cost, administrative services to the Fund under an Administrative Services Agreement, including internal executive and administrative services, responds to shareholder inquiries, a closed-end fund website, and corporate secretarial services.

During the relevant time period, the Fund's board of directors was composed of eight directors. The six outside directors have been Dr.

Enrique Arzac ("Arzac"), James J. Cattano ("Cattano"), George W. Landau ("Landau"), Robert J. McGuire ("McGuire"), Martin M. Torino ("Torino") and Miklos A. Vasarhelyi ("Vasarhelyi"). None of the outside directors are disqualified from being a non-interested director under Section 2(a)(9)(B) of the ICA by virtue of family relationship, having an interest in any security issued by CSAM, acting as legal counsel to CSAM, or having been determined by the SEC to be an interested person.

Arzac is a professor of finance and economics at the Graduate School of Business of Columbia University. Landau is a senior adviser to the President of the Latin American Group of the Coca-Cola Corporation, and a former U.S. Ambassador to Venezuela, Chili and Paraguay. Torino is the chairman of the board of directors of Ingenio y Refineria San Martin Del Tabacal S.A., an Argentine sugar refinery, and an executive director of TAU S.A., an Argentine commodities trading firm. Cattano is the president of Primary Resources Inc., a trading firm that specializes in Latin American agricultural commodities. Cattano and Torino were formerly colleagues at Marc Rich & Co., along with Michael Pignataro, Chief Financial Officer and Secretary of the Fund, and Bassini, a former member of the board and current Chief Executive Officer of the Fund.

The Fund utilizes a staggered board divided into three classes, each class having a term of no more than three years. Except for the addition of McGuire and Vasarhelyi, who constituted the Litigation Committee, the membership has been constant.

Arzac, Landau, Cattano, and Torino currently serve as directors of eight, five, four, and three CSAM-affiliated funds, respectively. The board meetings as a rule take two to three hours and are held jointly with the other CSAM affiliated funds. There are over 100 agenda items, many of a routine nature.

The Fund's board of directors sets the compensation paid to directors for service on the Fund's board and the directors on the Fund's board receive $ 5,000 per year of service on the board, and $ 500 for each meeting attended by the director. Pursuant to a decision made by the Fund's board, as of May 8, 2000, the directors will receive 50 percent of their fees in the form of Fund shares. In the fiscal year ending March 31, 2001, the four outside directors who serve on other boards of fund companies advised by CSAM earned the following compensation for their services on all CSAM-advised fund boards: Arzac, $ 107,250, Cattano, $ 48,500, Landau, $ 55,000, and Torino, $ 40,500. According to Arzac, these fees amount to approximately 15% of his income and a de minimus percentage of his net worth. The other directors have made statements similar in import.

In 1998, a shareholder proposal to terminate the Agreement was submitted to the Fund's shareholders over an initial board opposition. The shareholders rejected that proposal. Also in 1998, the outside directors approved a share repurchase program and the Fund repurchased approximately $ 2 million worth of shares as of February 2000. In 2000, the outside directors, in their capacity as directors of other funds advised by CSAM, voted to merge the Latin American Investment Fund, Inc. into the Latin American Equity Fund, Inc. and the Emerging Markets Infrastructure Fund, Inc. into the Emerging Markets Telecommunications Fund, Inc. The mergers reduced the total compensation paid the directors by the Fund advised by CSAM.

In November of each year, the Fund's board meets to decide whether to renew the Agreement with CSAM. Within a week of each of these meetings, the directors receive a package of materials from CSAM. In particular, they receive information regarding, among other things, (i) a description of CSAM; (ii) an analysis of the profitability to CSAM for advising the Fund and the other closed-end funds that it advises; (iii) financial information relating to the Fund, including total return and market price data for the Fund's shares; (iv) data regarding fees paid by other CSAM clients; (v) a comparison of the advisory fee and expense ratio for the Fund with other similar funds prepared by Lipper, Inc., and (vi) a comparison of the performance of the Fund with that of other CSAM-managed funds and other registered and unregistered investment companies and the closest appropriate index. In every year since 1992, the board has renewed the Agreement with CSAM, and CSAM has continued as the Fund's adviser.

The outside directors have retained PaineWebber to make recommendations regarding the methods the Fund could implement to reduce its discount rate.

Discussion

I. Applicable Law

A. The Standard for Summary Judgment

On a motion for summary judgment, the movant has the burden of showing the absence of a genuine issue of material fact. Celotex Corp. v. Catrett, 477 U.S. 317, 322, 91 L. Ed. 2d 265, 106 S. Ct. 2548 (1986). A party seeking to fend off a summary judgment motion must respond by setting forth "specific facts showing that there is a genuine issue for trial." Fed. R. Civ. P. 56(e); Anderson v. Liberty Lobby, Inc., 477 U.S. 242, 248, 91 L. Ed. 2d 202, 106 S. Ct. 2505 (1986). Summary judgment should be granted where the moving party demonstrates that there is no genuine issue of material fact regarding the claims at issue and that it is entitled to judgment as a matter of law. Fed. R. Civ. P. 56(e); Matsushita Elec. Indus. Co. v. Zenith Radio Corp., 475 U.S. 574, 585-86, 89 L. Ed. 2d 538, 106 S. Ct. 1348

(1986).

B. The Investment Company Act

The ICA is a statute enacted by Congress in response to concerns that existing securities laws did not protect mutual fund shareholders from potential abuse by fund advisers, whose relationships with the funds they manage are "'fraught with potential   conflicts of interest.'" Burks v. Lasker, 441 U.S. 471, 481, 99 S. Ct. 1831, 60 L. Ed. 2d 404 (1979) (internal quotations omitted). With this in mind, Congress incorporated fiduciary duties into the ICA through Section 36(a), which allows actions against persons who have engaged in, or who are about to engage in "any act or practice constituting a breach of fiduciary duty involving personal misconduct in respect of any registered investment company . . . ." 15 U.S.C. § 80a-35(a).

Certain provisions of the ICA are relevant to the Section 36(a) claim brought in this action. Section 10(a) of the ICA, 15 U.S.C. § 80a-10(a), requires that at least 40% of the members of the board of directors of a mutual fund not be "interested persons." Section 15(c), 15 U.S.C. § 80a-15(c), requires that a majority of the disinterested directors approve agreements between a fund and a fund's investment adviser.

The ICA lays out several tests to determine whether a person is considered to be an "interested person" of an investment adviser. Under the first of these tests, the most applicable to the instant motion, an "interested person" is "any affiliated person" of an investment adviser or principal underwriter. 15 U.S.C. § 80a-2(a)(19)(B). An "affiliated person" is defined as "any person directly or indirectly controlling, controlled by, or under common control with such other person." Id. § 80a-2(a)(3)-(c). "Control," in turn, is defined as "the power to exercise a controlling influence over the management or policies of a company." Id. § 80a-2(a)(9). To defeat summary judgment on the Section 36(a) claim, Strougo must establish that CSAM is "controlling" the independent directors or raise a factual issue with respect to such control.

Section 36(b), a narrower provision of the ICA, imposes a fiduciary duty on the investment adviser not to charge excessive fees and creates a private right of action by a shareholder against the adviser for a breach of this duty. In pertinent part, Section 36(b) states:

The investment adviser of a registered investment company shall be deemed to have a fiduciary duty with respect to the receipt of compensation for services ... An action may be brought under this subsection by the Commission, or by a security holder of such registered investment company on behalf of such company, against such investment adviser ... for breach of fiduciary duty in respect of such compensation or payments paid by such registered investment company ... .

15 U.S.C. § 80a-35(b).

As this Court has held, Strougo must ultimately demonstrate that CSAM's fee "is so disproportionately large that it bears no reasonable relationship to the services rendered and could not have been the product of arm's length bargaining." Strougo v. BEA Assocs., 1999 U.S. Dist. LEXIS 3021, No. 98 Civ. 3725 (RWS), 1999 WL 147737, at *7-8 (S.D.N.Y. March 18, 1999) (quoting Gartenberg v. Merrill Lynch Asset Mgmt., Inc., 694 F.2d 923, 928 (2d Cir. 1982)).

II. Summary Judgment is Appropriate

A. Summary Judgment is Not Defeated on the Basis of Discovery Improprieties

#***#

B. Under the Controlling Authority the Directors Are Not Interested

In his Section 36(a) claim, Strougo asserts that CSAM has breached its fiduciary duty to the Fund because it accepted compensation under an invalid advisory agreement. He argues that the Agreement is invalid because the outside directors on the Fund's board are not independent of CSAM, thus running afoul of the ICA's requirement that advisory agreements be approved by independent directors. The circumstances that he alleges contribute to a lack of independence include: (i) service on Multiple CSAM-advised boards; (ii) failure to terminate CSAM, oppose CSAM, or lower CSAM's fees; (iii) insufficient attention to duty as a result of other, full-time occupations; (iv) insufficient information to monitor CSAM; and (v) dependency on CSAM for board positions as a result of staggered terms and re-election procedures. As mentioned before, to defeat summary judgment on his Section 36(a) claim, Strougo must establish that CSAM is "controlling" the independent directors or raise a factual issue with respect to such control.

The ICA specifically provides that "[a] natural person shall be presumed not to be a controlled person." Id. § 80a-2(a)(9). Courts have held that the burden to overcome this presumption is a heavy one. See, e.g., Olesh v. Dreyfus Corp., 1995 U.S. Dist. LEXIS 21421, 1995 WL 500491, at *16 (E.D.N.Y. Aug. 18, 1995); Rome v. Archer, 41 Del. Ch. 404, 197 A.2d 49, 54 (Del. 1964). See also In re Fundamental Investors Inc., ICA Release No. 3596 [1961-64 Transfer Binder]Fed. Sec. L. Rep. (CCH) P 76,887, 81,272 (Dec. 27, 1962) ("The burden of overturning the presumption against control of a natural person is not one that will be lightly assumed or easily carried to success.").

Nevertheless, there is some support for the position that the terms "control" and "controlling influence," as used in § 80a-2(a)(9) of the ICA, might extend beyond "actual" control.[1] The history behind the ICA indicates that the SEC has in the past found that controlling influence encompasses "influence" that is "less than absolute and complete domination," In re M.A. Hanna Co., ICA Rel. No. 265, 1941 WL 37412, at *5 (Nov. 26, 1941). The agency indicated that Section 2(a)(9) included "the latent power to exercise a controlling influence as well as the active exercise of such power." In re Transit Inv. Corp. & Broad St. Trust Co., ICA Rel. No. 927, 1946 WL 24141, at *8 (July 30, 1946). Accord The First Australia Fund, Inc., SEC No-Action Letter, [1987-1988 Transfer Binder]Fed. Sec. L. Rep. (CCH) P78,551, at 77,795 n.11 (Oct. 8, 1987); Moses v. Black, 1981 U.S. Dist. LEXIS 10870, No. 78 Civ. 1913, [1981 Transfer Binder]Fed. Sec. L. Rep. (CCH) P97,866, at 90,366 (S.D.N.Y. Feb. 3, 1981).

The SEC's report to Congress that served as the basis for the ICA emphasized that "control" or "influence" can assume many different forms, and often can be proven only by circumstantial evidence. See In re Chicago Corp., ICA Rel. No. 1203, 1948 WL 29459, at *3-4 n.7 (Aug. 24, 1948) (citing H. Doc. 246, 77th Cong., S.E.C. Reports on Investment Trusts and Investment Companies, Part Four, at 2). The SEC concluded that, in light of the legislative history and overall purposes of the ICA, "the statutory concept of control embraces within it those pressures and influences, at times admittedly delicate, by which an investment company can exercise a dominating persuasiveness in the affairs of the portfolio company." Chicago Corp., 1948 WL 29459, at *4.

More recently, in Verkouteren v. Blackrock Fin. Management, Inc., 37 F. Supp. 2d 256 (S.D.N.Y. 1999) ("Verkouteren I"), the Honorable Whitman Knapp, faced at the pleading stage the same issue presented to this Court, namely the degree of control, and the adequacy of mere "influence," sufficient to overcome the presumption of independence possessed by a natural person. He reiterated the factors set forth by the SEC in the First Australian Fund, Inc., Sec No-Action Letter, 1987 WL 108483 [1987-1988 Transfer Binder],Fed. Sec. L. Rep. (CCH) P78,551 (Oct. 8, 1987), as follows:

---

[1] 1 Both the courts and the SEC share concurrent jurisdiction to determine whether the presumption has been rebutted. See SEC v. S&P Nat'l Corp., 360 F.2d 741, 748-49 (2d Cir. 1966); Willheim v. Murchison, 342 F.2d 33, 42 n.6 (2d Cir. 1965).

(1) selection or nomination of the director by the controlling party; (2) existence of family ties; (3) social relations; (4) former business associations between the director and the controlling person; (5) the amount of time spent by directors at meetings; (6) respective ages; (7) participation in recommending, evaluating, and terminating policies; (8) independent knowledge of corporate affairs; (9) interlocking directors and officers, together with share ownerships; and (10) actual domination and operation.

Verkouteren I, 37 F. Supp. 2d at 261.

Certain of these factors appear to be implicated by the facts established above. At the outset, it is presumed that CSAM initially selected the directors who have remained in office, triggering factor (1). Factor (4) also appears to be implicated as there have been a number former business relationships among the leaders of CSAM and the Fund. Factor (5) appears to be triggered by the fact that board meetings consisting of agenda items from all of the various CSAM funds are routinely brief. There is evidence supporting doubt as to director participation and independent knowledge, factors (7) and (8), and the interlocking directorships, factor (9), have been discussed at length.

However, in Verkouteren I, Judge Knapp concluded that factors (1) and (5) were not dispositive, particularly in view of the importance he placed on factor (10), actual domination. After repleading, Judge Knapp again dismissed the amended complaint although additional indicia were set forth, some of which have been presented here. He concluded:

Unfortunately, those indicia could just as easily be rooted in other causes, such as ineffective performance by the directors of their duties or in attentiveness on the part of the shareholders of the funds in supervising the directors. Similarly, the alleged malignancies in the corporate by-laws clearly suggest that defendant could impose pressure on the outside directors to acquiesce to its wishes; they do not, however, suggest that defendant did impose that pressure.

Verkouteren v. Black Rock Fin. Management, Inc., 1999 U.S. Dist. LEXIS 10892, 1999 WL 511411 (S.D.N.Y. ("Verkouteren II"). This reasoning, emphasizing actual domination, was affirmed by the Court of Appeals in an unpublished opinion, 208 F.3d 204 (2d Cir. 2000), and has been used by other courts. See, e.g., Olesh, 1995 U.S. Dist. LEXIS 21421, 1995 WL 500491, at *16 (Proof of control "'demands a presentation of evidence establishing actual domination and operation. Mere influence would fall short of this level of proof.'") (quoting Acampora v. Birkland, 220 F. Supp. 527, 543 (D. Colo. 1963)).

Applying this reasoning to the instant action, the specific circumstances presented by Strougo are insufficient to establish "control." As the above authorities establish, service on multiple boards alone does not constitute control. With respect to the termination of CSAM and the continuation of its fees, Strougo has criticized the directors for contacting the SEC with respect to a proposed vote to terminate CSAM's advisory contract, but CSAM has advanced several good faith explanations for the board's actions. No additional information has been specified to demonstrate the directors' alleged ignorance, and no authority has held that full-time occupations and two-hour meetings sufficiently state a claim of inattention to duty. In view of their outside employment, the fees paid fail to overcome the presumption of independence. In the case of Arzac, who received the largest amount of fees, it cannot be said that a triable issue has been created. The remaining fees are within the range for directors' fees that have been acceptable under the applicable law. See, e.g., Migdal v. Rowe Price-Fleming Int'l Inc., 248 F.3d 321, 2001 WL 460752, at *5-6 (4th Cir. 2001) (dismissing claim alleging control where disinterested directors served on the boards of between twenty-two and thirty-eight other related funds and received $ 65,000 or $ 81,000 for their services); Krantz v. Prudential Inv. Fund Management LLC, 77 F. Supp. 2d 559, 563 (D.N.J. 1999) (dismissing claim that overlapping service on multiple boards of funds advised by the same adviser with an aggregate compensation of up to $ 135,000 rendered outside directors interested under the ICA); Olesh, 1995 U.S. Dist. LEXIS 21421, 1995 WL 500491, at *21 (compensation of over $ 50,000 did not render directors interested).

Strougo cites the director approval of the 1996 rights offering, in which the resulting dilution exceeded that originally forecast, as further evidence of control. However, this issue has been litigated and dismissed. See Strougo v. Bassini, 112 F. Supp. 2d at 358 (S.D.N.Y. 2000). Strougo did not mention these allegations in the Complaint, and the Court has found that the Fund's directors had a reasonable basis for their actions. See id. Strougo also cites a by-law change to give the board exclusive power to amend the by-laws, and an increase in the number of shares required to request a special shareholders' meeting as evidence of control by CSAM. CSAM has explained that these are issues of corporate governance resulting, in part, from changes in the Maryland law.

In the present climate surrounding corporate governance, some of the statements cited by Strougo may well reflect the realities of the marketplace. According to Warren Buffett, the legendary investor and chairman of the Berkshire Hathaway Group:

I think independent directors have been anything but independent. The Investment Company Act, in 1940, made these provisions for independent directors on the theory that they would be the watchdogs for all these people pooling their money. The behavior of independent directors in aggregate since 1940 has been to rubber stamp every deal that's come along from management -- whether management was good, bad, or indifferent. Not negotiate for fee reductions and so on. A long time ago, an attorney said that in selecting directors, the management companies were looking for **Cocker spaniels** and not Dobermans. I'd say they found a lot of **Cocker spaniels** out there.

Haywood Kelly, A Quick Q & A with Warren Buffett, Morningstar (May 6, 1998).

A realistic and common sense appraisal of the duties and performance of these directors might well raise a triable issue of influence approaching control, but given the alternative basis for the directors' act advanced by CSAM and set forth in the facts found above under Verkouteren I and Verkouteren II, summary judgment seems required.

C. Excessive Fees Have Not Been Established

#***#

Conclusion
For the foregoing reasons, the defendant's motion to dismiss the Second Amended Complaint is granted.

It is so ordered.
New York, NY
February 21, 2002

ROBERT W. SWEET
U.S.D.J.

TIARA ENGLE and PORTNER ORTHOPEDIC REHABILITATION, INCORPORATED, Plaintiffs,

vs.

LIBERTY MUTUAL FIRE INSURANCE COMPANY, et al., Defendants.

Civ. No. 04-00256 SOM/BMK

UNITED STATES DISTRICT COURT FOR THE DISTRICT OF HAWAII

402 F. Supp. 2d 1157
July 11, 2005, Decided

SUSAN OKI MOLLWAY, UNITED STATES DISTRICT JUDGE.

OPINION

ORDER GRANTING DEFENDANT LIBERTY MUTUAL FIRE INSURANCE COMPANY'S MOTION FOR PARTIAL JUDGMENT ON THE PLEADINGS; ORDER GRANTING LIBERTY MUTUAL'S MOTION FOR PARTIAL SUMMARY JUDGMENT

I. INTRODUCTION.

What does it mean to be included? Much of this insurance coverage dispute turns on how one dissects the unassuming word "including" as it is used in a Hawaii insurance statute. Plaintiffs, an insured and her treatment provider, say the word "including" introduces examples, so that a reference to an independent medical examination ("IME") as "including" a record review means that a record review is a kind of IME. Defendant Liberty Mutual Fire Insurance Company, by contrast, says that "including" introduces component parts, so that the record review is included in the IME, but is not itself an IME. This exercise in lexicography is the subject of a motion for partial summary judgment brought by Liberty Mutual and of a counter-motion brought by Plaintiffs Tiara Engle and Portner Orthopedic Rehabilitation, Incorporated. The court grants Liberty Mutual's motion for partial summary judgment and denies Plaintiffs' counter-motion.

Liberty Mutual also moves for judgment on the pleadings as to certain other claims. That motion is unopposed and is granted.

II. BACKGROUND.

On May 2, 2003, Engle was a passenger in a car that was involved in an accident. The car was insured by Liberty Mutual, and Engle sought benefits under the "Personal Injury Protection" provisions of Liberty Mutual's policy. Liberty Mutual paid Engle's bills for emergency room treatment on the day of the accident and for later massage and chiropractic treatment at Portner Orthopedic through August 2003.

On November 10, 2003, Liberty Mutual asked Dr. Clifford Lau, an orthopedist, to perform a "record review" of Engle's medical condition and to opine on, among other things, whether Engle required future treatment. In retaining Dr. Lau, Liberty Mutual cautioned Dr. Lau that his charges for completing the assignment could not exceed the fee limits for IMEs set forth in Haw. Rev. Stat. § 431:10C-308.5(b).

Based on his review of Engle's medical records, Dr. Lau opined that further treatment was not necessary. Liberty Mutual then issued a "Denial of Claim" letter to Engle, stating that Liberty Mutual would no longer pay for Engle's treatments. Engle continued to receive treatments, and Portner continued to bill Liberty Mutual for these treatments.

On March 8, 2004, Plaintiffs filed suit in the First Circuit Court of the State of Hawaii. Their Complaint alleged tortious breach of contract, as well as violations of Haw. Rev. Stat. §§ 431:13-103(a)(11), 431:10C-308.5(b), and Haw. Rev. Stat. Ch. 480. Plaintiffs sought general damages, special damages, "other economic and non-economic damages," punitive damages, treble damages, prejudgment interest, costs, and reasonable attorney's fees.

On April 21, 2004, Liberty Mutual removed that case to this court. In its Notice of Removal, Liberty Mutual stated that "the amount in controversy is greater than $ 75,000.00, exclusive of interest and costs."

III. STANDARD OF REVIEW.

Rule 12(c) of the Federal Rules of Civil Procedure states:

After the pleadings are closed but within such time as not to delay the trial, any party may move for judgment on the pleadings. If, on a motion for judgment on the pleadings, matters outside the pleadings are presented to and not excluded by the court, the motion shall be treated as one for summary judgment and disposed of as provided in Rule 56, and all parties shall be given reasonable opportunity to present all material made pertinent to such a motion by Rule 56.

The standard governing a Rule 12(c) motion for judgment on the pleadings is essentially the same as that governing a Rule 12(b)(6) motion. The motion will not be granted if, accepting as true all material allegations contained in the nonmoving party's pleadings, the moving party is entitled to judgment as a matter of law. Lake Tahoe Watercraft Recreation Ass'n v. Tahoe Reg'l Planning Agency, 24 F. Supp. 2d 1062, 1066 (E.D Cal. 1998). For a Rule 12(c) motion, the allegations of the nonmoving party must be accepted as true, while the allegations of the moving party that have been denied are assumed to be false. Hal Roach Studios, Inc. v. Richard Feiner & Co., Inc., 896 F.2d 1542, 1550 (9th Cir. 1989). Judgment on the pleadings is proper when the moving party clearly establishes on the face of the pleadings that no material issue of fact remains to be resolved and that it is entitled to judgment as a matter of law. Id. However, judgment on the pleadings is improper when the district court goes beyond the pleadings to resolve an issue; such a proceeding must properly be treated as a motion for summary judgment. Id.

Summary judgment shall be granted when

the pleadings, depositions, answers to interrogatories and admissions on file, together with the affidavits, if any, show that there is no genuine issue as to any material fact and that the moving party is entitled to a judgment as a matter of law.

Fed. R. Civ. P. 56(c); see also Addisu v. Fred Meyer, Inc., 198 F.3d 1130, 1134 (9th Cir. 2000). One of the principal purposes of summary judgment is to identify and dispose of factually unsupported claims and defenses. Celotex Corp. v. Catrett, 477 U.S. 317, 323-24, 106 S. Ct. 2548, 91 L. Ed. 2d 265 (1986).

Summary judgment must be granted against a party who fails to demonstrate facts to establish what will be an essential element at trial. Id. at 322. The burden initially lies with the moving party to identify for the court "the portions of the materials on file that it believes demonstrate the absence of any genuine issue of material fact. " T.W. Elec. Serv., Inc. v. Pac. Elec. Contractors Ass'n, 809 F.2d 626, 630 (9th Cir. 1987) (citing Celotex Corp., 477 U.S. at 323). "When the moving party has carried its burden under Rule 56(c), its opponent must do more than simply show that there is some metaphysical doubt as to the material facts." Matsushita Elec. Indus. Co., Ltd. v. Zenith Radio Corp., 475 U.S. 574, 586, 106 S. Ct. 1348, 89 L. Ed. 2d 538 (1986) (footnote omitted). The nonmoving party may not rely on the mere allegations in the pleadings and instead must set forth "specific facts showing that there is a genuine issue for trial." Id. At least some "'significant probative evidence tending to support the complaint'" must be produced. Summers v. A. Teichert & Son, Inc., 127 F.3d 1150, 1152 (9th Cir. 1997) (quoting Anderson v. Liberty Lobby, Inc., 477 U.S. 242, 252, 106 S. Ct. 2505, 91 L. Ed. 2d 202 (1986)). "If the factual context makes the non-moving party's claim implausible, that party must come forward with more persuasive evidence than would otherwise be necessary to show that there is a genuine issue for trial." Cal. Architectural Bldg. Prods., Inc. v. Franciscan Ceramics, Inc., 818 F.2d 1466, 1468 (9th Cir. 1987) (citing Matsushita, 475 U.S. at 587).

However, when "direct evidence" produced by the moving party conflicts with "direct evidence" produced by the party opposing summary judgment, "the judge must assume the truth of the evidence set forth by the nonmoving party with respect to that fact." T. W. Elec. Serv., 809 F.2d at 631. All evidence and inferences must be construed in the light most favorable to the nonmoving party. Id. Inferences may be drawn from underlying facts not in dispute, as well as from disputed facts that the judge is required to resolve in favor of the nonmoving party. Id.

IV. ANALYSIS.

A. This Court Has Jurisdiction In This Matter.

A district court has diversity jurisdiction over a case in which the plaintiff and defendant are not citizens of the same state and in which the amount in controversy exceeds $ 75,000, as measured at the time of removal. See Sparta Surgical Corp. v. Nat'l Ass'n of Sec. Dealers, Inc., 159 F.3d 1209, 1213 (9th Cir. 1998). When, as here, a defendant requests removal from state court and the complaint does not allege an amount in controversy, the removing defendant must prove the amount in controversy by a preponderance of the evidence. See Sanchez v. Monumental Life Ins. Co., 102 F.3d 398, 404 (9th Cir. 1996).

Although the Complaint did not state a specific damage amount, it clearly prayed for compensatory and punitive or treble damages, as well as attorney's fees. Liberty Mutual's Notice of Removal stated that "the amount in controversy is greater than $ 75,000.00." Plaintiffs do not present any evidence that, at the time of removal, a lesser amount was in controversy.[1] 1

---

[1] At the July 5, 2005, hearing on the present motions, Plaintiffs represented

Having examined the record, the court concludes, by a preponderance of the evidence, that the amount in controversy requirement is satisfied in this case.

B. Liberty Mutual's Motion for Partial Judgment on The Pleadings is Granted.

Plaintiffs have brought claims under Haw. Rev. Stat. § 431:13 and Haw. Rev. Stat. Chapter 480, and for tortious breach of contract. Under Fed. R. Civ. P. 12(c), Liberty Mutual moves for judgment on the pleadings on these claims, arguing that there is no private right of action under Haw. Rev. Stat. § 431:13, that Plaintiffs have no standing to bring a claim under chapter 480, and that the Hawaii Supreme Court has eliminated the cause of action for tortious breach of contract. Plaintiffs do not oppose Liberty Mutual's motion for partial judgment on the pleadings. Accordingly, Liberty Mutual's motion for judgment on the pleadings is granted with respect to these claims.

C. Liberty Mutual Was Not Required to Follow the IME Procedures Set Forth in Haw. Rev. Stat. § 431:10C-308.5(b) for Dr. Lau's Record Review.

1. This Court, Sitting In Diversity, Follows State Law.
Federal courts sitting in diversity must apply substantive state law. See Feldman v. Allstate Ins. Co., 322 F.3d 660, 666 (9th Cir. 2003). In this case, the court follows substantive Hawaii law. The court "must use its best judgment to predict how the Hawaii Supreme Court would decide the issue." Burlington Ins. Co. v. Oceanic Design & Const., Inc., 383 F.3d 940, 944 (9th Cir. 2004). A federal district court may look to state trial court decisions as persuasive authority, but those decisions are not binding on the federal court. See Spinner Corp. v. Princeville Dev. Corp., 849 F.2d 388, 390 (9th Cir. 1988); see also King v. Order of United Commercial Travelers of America, 333 U.S. 153, 161, 68 S. Ct. 488, 92 L. Ed. 608 (1948).

The court is aware that, on June 30, 2005, shortly before this court's hearing on July 5, 2005, Judge Bert I. Ayabe of the First Circuit Court of the State of Hawaii issued a minute order in Sakoda v. AIG Hawaii Ins. Co,

---

that, because many of the claims listed in the Complaint were not viable and were therefore the subject of a judgment on the pleadings, only a small damage claim and the possibility of punitive damages (plus interest, costs, and attorney's fees) remained in this case. The court, however, must measure the amount in controversy at the time of filing, not at the time of the hearing. Accordingly, Plaintiffs' statement does not affect this court's jurisdiction.

Inc., Civil No. 04-1-0436, interpreting the very provision at issue in this case. Judge Ayabe ruled that a record review was indeed an IME under state law. Under the rules articulated by the Ninth Circuit, Judge Ayabe's order is of persuasive value to this court, but is not binding authority.

2. A Record Review Is Not An Independent Medical Examination.

Having been informed of Judge Ayabe's ruling, this court, following the hearing on the present motions, restudied the IME issue. Notwithstanding the great respect this court has for Judge Ayabe, this court remains convinced that the Hawaii Supreme Court would not apply IME statutory requirements to a mere record review or to an opinion based only on a record review.

Section 431:10C-308.5(b) of the Hawaii Revised Statutes limits the charges that providers may receive for IMEs. The statute also imposes other requirements on IMEs and IME providers. The statute states, in relevant part:

The charges and frequency of treatment for services specified in section 431:10C-103.5(a) . . . shall not exceed the charges and frequency of treatment permissible under the workers' compensation supplemental medical fee schedule. Charges for independent medical examinations, including record reviews, physical examinations, history taking, and reports, to be conducted by a licensed Hawaii provider unless the insured consents to an out-of-state provider, shall not exceed the charges permissible under the appropriate codes in the workers' compensation supplemental medical fee schedule.

* * * *

The independent medical examiner shall be selected by mutual agreement between the insurer and claimant; provided that if no agreement is reached, the selection may be submitted to the commissioner, arbitration or circuit court. The independent medical examiner shall be of the same specialty as the provider whose treatment is being reviewed, unless otherwise agreed by the insurer and claimant.

Haw. Rev. Stat. § 431:10C-308.5(b).

Plaintiffs contend that, because Dr. Lau was not selected by mutual agreement and because he did not have the same specialty as the provider whose treatment was being reviewed, Liberty Mutual violated Haw. Rev. Stat. § 431:10C-308.5. Liberty Mutual, by contrast, argues that Haw. Rev. Stat. § 431:10C-308.5 does not apply to record reviews conducted in the absence of physical examinations. The court agrees with Liberty Mutual and concludes that the IME provisions in Haw. Rev. Stat. § 431:10C-308.5(b) do not apply to a record review performed in isolation, without other accompanying procedures necessary to complete an IME, particularly an in-person examination.

With respect to statutory interpretation, the Hawaii Supreme Court has stated:

When construing a statute, our foremost obligation is to ascertain and give effect to the intention of the legislature, which is to be obtained primarily from the language contained in the statute itself. And we must read statutory language in the context of the entire statute and construe it in a manner consistent with its purpose.

When there is doubt, doubleness of meaning, or indistinctiveness or uncertainty of an expression used in a statute, an ambiguity exists. . . .

In construing an ambiguous statute, the meaning of the ambiguous words may be sought by examining the context, with which the ambiguous words, phrases and sentences may be compared, in order to ascertain their true meaning. Moreover, the courts may resort to extrinsic aids in determining legislative intent. One avenue is the use of legislative history as an interpretive tool.

Gray v. Administrative Director of the Court, 84 Haw. 138, 147, 931 P.2d 580, 589 (1997) (internal citations omitted).

a. The Statute Does Not Equate Record Review With an IME.

This court's inquiry begins with the language of the statute. In construing the term "IME," the court gives the term its ordinary, natural meaning. See Leocal v. Ashcroft, 543 U.S. 1, 125 S. Ct. 377, 378, 160 L. Ed. 2d 271 (2004). Taken both in isolation and in the context of the statute, the term "IME" does not refer to a record review in the absence of an actual examination of the subject.

In its ordinary, natural meaning, the term "independent medical examination" refers to a procedure that includes an in-person examination. Numerous court orders, for example, use "IME" to refer to the "Physical and Mental Examination" procedures set forth in Haw. R. Civ. P. 35 and Fed. R. Civ. P. 35. See Sice v. Oldcastle Glass, Inc., 2005 U.S. Dist. LEXIS 550, No. Civ. A.03-BB-114, 2005 WL 82148 at *3 (D. Colo. Jan. 10, 2005) (holding that a motion for "IME" met Fed. R. Civ. P. 35(a) requirements); see also Liftee v. Boyer, 108 Haw. 89, 117 P.3d 821, No. 23760, 2004 WL 2943127 (Haw. App. Dec. 21, 2004) (describing a physical examination as a "Rule 35 IME"); Glover v. Grace Pacific Corp., 86 Haw. 154, 948 P.2d 575 (Haw. App. 1997) (motion for an "IME" involving an in-person examination could be filed pursuant to Haw. R. Civ. P. 35(a)). Physical and mental examinations performed pursuant to Haw. R. Civ. P. 35 and Fed. R. Civ. P. 35 necessarily involve in-person examinations. Both the Hawaii and the federal rules state that courts "may order the party to submit to a physical or mental examination . . . or to produce for examination the person" who is to be examined. Courts routinely use the term "IME" to describe procedures in which in-person examinations were conducted. Plaintiffs cite no instance in which any court or other entity has used the term "IME" to refer to a mere record review.

Rejecting this judicial use of the term "IME," Plaintiffs focus on the portion of section 431:10C-308.5(b) that states, "Charges for independent medical examinations, including record reviews, physical examinations, history taking, and reports, to be conducted by a licensed Hawaii provider unless the insured consents to an out-of-state provider, shall not exceed the charges permissible under the appropriate codes in the worker's compensation supplemental medical fee schedule." This sentence is not labeled as a "definition" provision and instead relates to billing issues. Indeed, the statute has the title "Limitation on Charges," although it does include several requirements not directly tied to fees.

Plaintiffs say that the word "including" in the statutory language indicates that reviews, physical examinations, history takings, and reports are types of IME. That is, Plaintiffs' position is that the word "including" introduces subsets of IMEs, in much the same way that one could refer to "dogs, including collies, **cocker spaniels**, and dachshunds." "Including," by Plaintiffs' reading, means "having as members," with each member being a full-fledged IME, just as a collie is, by itself, a dog.

Under Plaintiffs' reading, even a mere history taking is an IME. Thus, according to Plaintiffs, any "licensed Hawaii provider" performing a history has to be in the same field as the doctor whose work is being reviewed and has to be approved by "mutual agreement." Plaintiffs further say that an out-of-state provider may be used only with the insured's consent.

Nothing in the statute suggests that Hawaii's legislature intended to impose the exceptional burdens that flow from Plaintiffs' interpretation. Insurers would no longer be able to use in-house providers at all. An out-of-state insurer would have to retain licensed Hawaii providers absent insureds' consent. Plaintiffs' statutory interpretation would give insureds veto power even if a doctor were limiting herself to performing only a ministerial history taking, not rendering opinions.

Plaintiffs dismiss this possibility, explaining that the statute applies only to "medical" reviews, that is, reviews that result in the rendition of opinions by doctors. The statute, however, speaks of history taking and record review by licensed Hawaii providers. It is not limited to history taking and record review involving "medical" review or physician opinions. Plaintiffs are therefore adding language to the statute without any basis and going far beyond interpretation.

The more natural reading of the statute is to interpret "including" as meaning "having as parts." While the word "including" may certainly be used to introduce examples in various contexts, reading it as meaning "having as parts" requires fewer somersaults and interpolations in the context of the statute in issue. Indeed, Black's Law Dictionary lists "to contain as a part of something" as the definition of "include." Black's Law Dictionary 777 (8th ed. 2004). If "including" means "having as parts," then the statute is referring to an IME made up of several parts such as history taking and record review, with history taking and record review not being IMEs on their own. In that event, "including" would be used much as it is used in the statement "I prepared a brief, including doing the research, consulting with the client, drafting, and assembling exhibits." None of the items after "including" is itself a finished brief. A more homey example involves a parent's instruction to a child not to play video games until the child has finished his homework, including math, science, and social studies. The child could not then play video games upon solving math problems, because math was only a part of the required homework, not an example, complete in itself, of the homework referred to by the parent.

    b. The Legislative History Indicates that Record Reviews are Not IMEs.

    Like the statutory language, the legislative history of Haw. Rev. Stat. § 431:10C-308.5(b) establishes that mere record reviews are not IMEs. The language concerning charges for record reviews, physical examinations, history taking, and reports that are included in IMEs was added in a 1998 amendment. The added language is shown by the following underlining:

Charges for independent medical examinations, including record reviews, physical examinations, history taking, and reports, to be conducted by a licensed Hawaii provider unless the insured consents to an out-of-state provider, shall not exceed the charges permissible under the workers' compensation schedules for consultation for a complex medical problem.

1997 Haw. Sess. Laws 543.

    The Conference Committee Report for the amendment notes that the changes to the statute closed a perceived loophole in the statute that allowed doctors to charge insurers separately for in-person examinations and record reviews:

The bill incorporates measures designed to eliminate abuses and excessive charges associated with independent medical examinations (IMEs). The bill clarifies that the workers' compensation fee schedule charge allowable for IMEs may not be exceeded by submitting a separate charge for the report or other ancillary procedures incident to the conducting of an IME.

Conf. Com. Rep. No. 117 on H.B. 2823 (Haw. 1998).

The purpose of the 1998 amendments was to require that charges for an IME include charges for all parts of the IME, not just for the physical examination portion. Thus, the statutory restrictions on IME charges extended to any record review, history taking, or report that was part of the IME. The legislative history does not indicate that the amendment was intended to subject record reviews that are not part of IMEs to IME regulations. To the contrary, the Committee Report distinguishes between IMEs and parts of IMEs such as "the report or other ancillary procedures incident to the conducting of an IME."

Plaintiffs contend that the purpose of the statute was to regulate the IME process and to provide for fairness in an insurer's decisions. Because a record reviewer's recommendation that an insurer deny benefits has the same result as a doctor's decision to deny benefits following an IME, Plaintiffs argue that the same regulations should govern both procedures. A policy of achieving such fairness by regulating mere record reviews is not, however, suggested by the legislative history. Just as Plaintiffs' interpretation of the statutory language forced them to interpolate words, their policy analysis forces them to assume legislative intent that is nowhere evident in the legislative history.

The legislature's differentiation between an IME and a mere record review is logical. An insured has an interest in having a voice in which doctor will perform an IME because an in-person examination is a necessary part of an IME. An insured may be uncomfortable being examined by a doctor the insured knows is regularly retained by insurers and so may be biased against the insured. It is also conceivable that an insured whose medical problem involves, for example, sexual dysfunction may want to be examined by a doctor of the same sex. Such concerns are substantially diminished when no in-person examination occurs. Creating differing requirements for IMEs, which require in-person examinations, and nonintrusive procedures like record reviews balances the competing needs of insureds and insurers.

Plaintiffs express concern that allowing doctors to conduct record reviews free of the restrictions imposed by Haw. Rev. Stat. § 431:10C-308.5(b) will encourage insurers to eschew in-person examinations, leading to less well-informed coverage decisions. Again, Plaintiffs are seeking to reach a laudable goal without any evidence that the legislature shared that goal.

The legislature did not require an insurer to have any particular level of information before making a coverage determination. As Plaintiffs conceded at the hearing, an insurer may deny benefits for medical treatment without a doctor's review of any kind. See Weigel v. Liberty Mutual Fire Ins. Co., No. ATX-2002-134-P (D.C.C.A. Dec. 21, 2004). Such a decision may be based on a nurse's opinion, or on a review by an insurance administrator with no medical training. An IME certainly provides the insurer with more information on which to base an insurance decision, but the legislature nowhere required an IME or even a record review. If an insurer elects to deny coverage based on a procedure less complete than an IME, the insurer's record on any challenge to its denial may be more vulnerable than it would have been with an IME. An appeal of an insurer's denial of benefits may then be successful, but that is a risk the legislature left the insurer free to take. Nothing in the legislative history indicates otherwise.

#***#

V. CONCLUSION.

Liberty Mutual's motions for judgment on the pleadings as to certain claims and partial summary judgment are granted. Plaintiffs' counter-motion is denied.

This order leaves for future adjudication portions of Engle's breach of contract claim, and the bad faith claim insofar as it relates to those remaining portions of the contract claim.

IT IS SO ORDERED.
DATED: Honolulu, Hawaii, July 11, 2005.
SUSAN OKI MOLLWAY
UNITED STATES DISTRICT JUDGE

CONCLUSION

This book has been a collection of the 35 opinions of US Federal Courts that include the phrase "cocker spaniel". It is hoped that reading these cases presents a somewhat interesting snapshot of the meaning of the phrase and character of the animal in cultural and legal thought. The legal record presents a sort of mirror for cultural ideas and in these cases we see "cocker spaniel" appearing both literally and figuratively as a character in American law.

INDEX

ABOUT THE EDITOR

Joshua Warren is an artist, educator, scientist, practicing attorney, and doctoral student with an interest in politics, language and creativity.

This book is part of a series is entitled Law of the Horse.
The series is study on character creatures in
the opinions of U.S. Federal Courts.

The upcoming book "Zombie in the Federal Courts"
was funded through a Kickstarter project .
Visit the ZombieLaw blog at zombielaw.wordpress.com

Similar work on "Ninja in the Federal Courts"
is also available at ninjalaw.wordpress.com

<u>also available:</u>
Werewolf in the Federal Courts
Red Herring in the Supreme Court
Mad Scientist in the Federal Courts
more coming soon...

Other artwork by Joshua Warren can be found at:
www.warrbo.com

www.ingramcontent.com/pod-product-compliance
Lightning Source LLC
Chambersburg PA
CBHW030002190526
45157CB00014B/93